Tillers of a Myth

THE UNIVERSITY OF WISCONSIN PRESS

Tillers of a Myth

SOUTHERN AGRARIANS

AS SOCIAL AND LITERARY CRITICS

ALEXANDER KARANIKAS

MADISON · MILWAUKEE · LONDON   1966

To Helen

Preface

THE PURPOSE OF THIS STUDY IS TO OUTLINE AND EVALUATE THE SECOND phase in the development of a group of gifted Southern writers who were, in turn, Fugitive poets, Southern Agrarians, and New Critics. Each of their three phases has earned a permanent place in our literary history; combined, they form a powerful if not the dominant aesthetic of our century. Much insight into their poetry and criticism can be acquired through an understanding of their collective ideology, and this they expressed most clearly in their Agrarian period, roughly from 1929 to 1937. As creative writers and critics, these men have received considerable attention; but they have been relatively neglected as Agrarians, that is, as champions of a specific social ideal in sharp conflict with the modern industrial world.

They emerged on the national scene as Agrarians late in 1930. In a collection of essays entitled *I'll Take My Stand*, they made a frontal attack on the alleged evils of industrial society and proposed their own alternative. To the amazement of many readers, this attack came from the South, an area which Henry L. Mencken only a decade earlier had derided as a cultural desert. Most of the contributors to the Agrarian manifesto were associated with Vanderbilt University, either as teachers or former students. The Agrarians wrote in their Statement of Principles that they all tended "to support a Southern way of life against what may be called the American or prevailing way; and all as much as agree that the best terms in which to represent the distinction are contained in the phrase, Agrarian *versus* Industrial."

The economic crisis which began with the stock market crash of October, 1929, was only a year old when *I'll Take My Stand* appeared. Although it was not originally intended as such, the strong demand made in the book for the restoration of an agrarian economy wherever possible seemed to be another panacea offered to soothe the nation's perilous distress. Early critics were both attracted and often misled by the term "Agrarianism." Because the authors of the twelve essays in *I'll Take My Stand* equated Agrarianism with the Old South and asked that the Old South's general features be restored, they were scoffed at as young Confederates. In ridiculing the more untenable aspects of Agrarian doctrine—those that overly praised the Confederate ethic—most critics distorted the public image of the movement and made it seem more frivolous than it was. However, more cautious critics saw behind its quixotic economics a new and valid criticism of American industrial culture.

The true ideal of the Agrarians was the Middle Ages. The spiritual unity and aesthetic greatness that was absent from their halfway station, the Old South, the Agrarians found fully developed in the age of Dante. In most other respects their own regional tradition, as they interpreted it, sufficed. Their love of the Old South and their demands for the restoration of a traditional agrarian society helped to hide the fact that Agrarianism was actually a hard-headed conservative ideology that could hold its own in debate with liberalism, rationalism, democracy, or any other offshoot of the idea of progress. So broadly conceived was their disaffection from the national or American culture that only such inclusive terms as "the reactionary view" or "ultraconservative" can adequately frame their range of interest; some commentators went so far as to call them fascists. Regardless of label, they were one of the more aggressive segments of American conservatism.

In my opinion, the three phases of their development are more organically related than is generally conceded. During the time that they were known as Fugitives, they were already in the process of becoming Agrarians; later on, they carried into the New Criticism the basic ideas of Agrarianism, with the social militancy abandoned in favor of an emphasis on formal aesthetics. As New Critics they succeeded in doing what they had failed to do as Agrarians: to denigrate the democratic content in American literature, to smother its traditional note of social protest, and to elevate in its stead new literary gods and canons more acceptable to the rightist tradition.

In their role as New Critics, they and their followers dominated literary criticism in the 1940's and 1950's. Thus it is important that their basic assumptions be clearly understood. To conservative readers, the Agrarians will appear as heroes for having set a relatively early precedent for reaction. Liberals will regard them as villains with a nasty talent for writing persuasively. Some past estimates of the Agrarians suffer from being either too favorable or too hostile. The Agrarians are adequately self-revealing when allowed to speak for themselves. The chapters ahead will present a unified body of ideas, their ideology, which significantly flavors the formalism still governing much of today's literary criticism.

I am indebted to the following people for guidance and help: Miss Margaret Carpenter of Deering Library, Northwestern University, for arranging the loan of several doctoral dissertations; Professor Harrison Hayford, who guided me through many problems; Professors Wallace Douglas and Carl Condit, who volunteered references and gave me valuable insights; Professor Philip Denenfeld, Western Michigan University, who suggested improvements in my writing style; Professor Frederic E. Faverty, who was gracious and helpful on every occasion; Professor Meyer Weinberg, Wright Junior College, who discussed with me the pertinent economic history; Professor Robert Gorham Davis, Columbia University, who read and evaluated one of the early drafts of my manuscript; President David Dodds Henry and the Board of Trustees, University of Illinois, for granting me a sabbatical leave to continue my research; Mrs. Barbara Harvey, of the University of Wisconsin Press, for her brilliant editing; my wife, Helen, who encouraged me throughout the long process of research and writing; and the memory of F. O. Matthiessen, who long ago at Harvard inspired me to enter the field of American literature.

ALEXANDER KARANIKAS

June, 1965
Chicago, Illinois

Contents

Tillers of a Myth

Chapter I   The Agrarian Movement

THE GROUP OF SOUTHERN WRITERS, POETS, AND CRITICS REMEMBERED AS Agrarians chose to make their presence known through the publication of a symposium, *I'll Take My Stand,* twelve essays prefaced by a Statement of Principles, which appeared late in 1930. Symposia have always been popular with devotees of embattled doctrines who wish to explain their goals and influence public opinion. An impressive array of writers is usually gathered to add authority to the position taken. *I'll Take My Stand* was no exception. The volume had impressive authorship, it wished to influence public opinion, and its doctrines were embattled from the start. The Agrarian movement that it helped to launch contributed heavily to the Southern renaissance in literature which has astonished and enriched our century.

The publication of the symposium immediately added a new expression to the nation's vocabulary: Southern Agrarianism. The basic assumptions embraced by those two words touched off a controversy which has continued for over three decades. Since 1930 *I'll Take My Stand* has been a convenient guide for identifying one's attitude toward the South. Liberals invariably regard it as a naïve attempt to recapture the past or, worse, to stem the tides of progress. Conservatives usually praise its defense of tradition and the Southern "way of life." Furthermore, it is to *I'll Take My Stand* that scholars first refer when they discuss Agrarianism as a trend in American literature, even though the Agrarians subsequently wrote much more that qualifies as vital doctrine. Ranging widely in its comment, the book has engaged the interest of theologians, sociologists, economists, political scientists, historians, and literary critics. Regional studies of the South cannot avoid mentioning it; anthologies wishing to document the American heritage and the American "mind" have printed excerpts from it.

The writers who jointly challenged the values of industrial society in the symposium were John Crowe Ransom, Donald Davidson, Frank Lawrence Owsley, John Gould Fletcher, Lyle H. Lanier, Allen Tate, Herman Clarence Nixon, Andrew Nelson Lytle, Robert Penn Warren, John Donald Wade, Henry Blue Kline, and Stark Young. Most of the twelve had taught or studied at Vanderbilt University in Nashville, Tennessee. Several had been students there of John Crowe Ransom, an English professor. Ransom, Tate, Davidson, and Warren had already won a modest national reputation as poets through their publication of a literary magazine, *The Fugitive,* in the mid-twenties. According to Tate, the idea of "doing something about the South" had originated about 1926 and soon afterward the writers involved began to organize their energies toward isolation and regional defiance. In their Statement of Principles in *I'll Take My Stand* they encouraged all Southerners to oppose industrial inroads upon their inherited culture; the intrusion of false progress and prosperity emanating from the old enemy, the North, threatened to completely destroy the South's traditional society.

I'll Take My Stand quickly elicited both praise and scorn. Southern liberals have scoffed at the Agrarians as "neo-Confederates." Despite their detractors, the Agrarians have also been compared favorably with the New England Transcendentalists:

Each renaissance had its richest development through the friendship, by no means always serene, of the various members of the group within it. Each had a particular town as its locale. Each found its impulse in a single high-minded man. Each was furthered by the establishment of a magazine that had an important influence on the group itself and on a small but active band of readers outside the group. And the group identified with each movement made itself not the spokesman of the majority opinion in the country but instead an unusually significant minority voice.[1]

The Concord of the Agrarians was Nashville. Their Emerson was John Crowe Ransom. Their *Dial* was *The Fugitive.* They were staunch regionalists whose views had a great deal of universality. They had no utopia as concrete as Brook Farm, yet their ideal agrarian community was more utopian than not. And although they were not solely responsible for the Southern literary renaissance, as a group they were its major phalanx.

The Agrarians have been so often mentioned as a movement or school that it may be fruitful at the outset to discuss the major factors resulting in their cohesion. Perhaps the most obvious was their Southern birth and residence. The regional heritage into which they were born, and about which they became acutely aware, naturally influenced their emotional and mental development. The recurrence of "Southern" themes, characters, and settings in their creative work clearly indicates that they never forgot the land on which they had walked barefoot in their youth.

Another crucial factor was their collective experience in writing and editing *The Fugitive*. The Nashville and Vanderbilt University environment alone cannot account for this stage of their association. Other young poets practiced their art on that campus, but they did not qualify as Fugitives; Ransom taught many other English majors, but they did not become Tates and Warrens. Perhaps the most that can be said is that at a particular time in the early twenties a group of potential writers happened to meet, become friends, and eventually exchange poems. Led by Ransom and encouraged by interested citizens of Nashville, these talented poets managed to put out nineteen issues of their journal from 1922 to 1925. *The Fugitive* ranks as one of the finest of the little magazines that enriched the literary twenties. Its success in launching several important careers is already well known. Some authorities also credit it with having initiated the entire Southern literary renaissance. The latest, most complete, and most gossipy account of this period is Louise Cowan's *The Fugitive Group* (1959). She concludes her well-detailed reminiscence of the group with their final action as Fugitives: the publication in 1928 of their anthology. Perhaps even more than the magazine itself, the Fugitive anthology drew national attention to the Nashville writers. In his review of it, Edmund Wilson speculated that the South now seemed ripe for a literary renaissance comparable to the one in Ireland. "By reason of its very leisure," he wrote, "its detachment from the industrial world and its strong local tradition, the South at present enjoys unique advantages for the cultivation of literature; and it is not impossible to image its playing . . . a role similar in some respects to that which eighteenth-century Ireland has played in respect to modern London."[2]

The Fugitive experience did more than launch the individual careers of its participants; it also taught them the valuable habit of collaboration. They met frequently to discuss poetry, criticism, and philosophy and to help each other revise. The choice of the name "Fugitive," as they explained it, meant they were fleeing from the stultifying Brahminism of the Southern cultural tradition—from its maudlin romanticism, its parochialism, its superficiality, its sentimentalism. They wanted to write a hard intellectual poetry, not particularly local or regional, that escaped the appalling mediocrity of what had been passing as Southern verse. At this time of separation from one aspect of their heritage, they would have approved Howard Mumford Jones's ridicule of Southern romanticism.

A thousand stories have created the legend that is the South. Way down upon the Suwanee river the sun shines bright on my old Kentucky home where, bound for Louisiana, Little Eva has a banjo on her knee, and Old Black Joe, Uncle Remus and Miss Sally's little boy listen to the mocking-bird and watch a sweet chariot swing low one frosty morning! The gallant Pelham and his comrades bend forever over the hands of adorable girls in crinoline; under the duelling oaks Colonel Carter of Cartersville and Marse Chan blaze away at each other with pistols by the light of the silvery moon on Mobile Bay. It matters little now, Lorena, the past is in the eternal past, for I saw thee once, once only, it was on a July midnight and the full-orbed moon looked down where a despot's heel is on thy shore, Maryland, my Maryland.[3]

The Fugitives' rejection of the overly romantic in favor of the classical and intellectual, however, comprised only a narrow basis for disaffiliation from the Southern tradition. Indeed, for a number of reasons, the Fugitives soon developed a very militant loyalty to their region's culture. This process went hand in hand with a wider ideological unity as they found themselves in rebellion against the majority, or non-Southern portion, of American culture. Another important aspect of their cohesion, therefore, is their identity as a Southern manifestation of post–World War I disillusionment. Although the Fugitive-Agrarians never renounced their American citizenship or entertained serious thoughts of expatriation, *I'll Take My Stand* did signify a spiritual secession from the nation as a whole. Some critics deemed it a social and cultural revolution; others called it simply another example of personal alienation. No doubt it had elements of both.

The twenties were rife with instances of such alienation. Hardly any writer of the time accepted at its face value the arrogant commercialism which touted itself as the new civilization. Writers fled from the monstrous money power in every geographical and spiritual direction. Never before had art been in such peril of becoming merely a commodity in a community of Babbitts. Many writers, therefore, sought ways in which to rebel and still create without any loss of integrity. Among other observers, Solomon Fishman has written about how this splintering of the American cultural tradition affected the artist. Fishman includes the Southern Agrarians among those he talks about in *The Disinherited of Art*. Of them and other disaffiliates he says:

The key to this cycle of American literature is the term "alienation." It includes a whole constellation of attitudes associated with the literary twenties: isolation, individualism, bohemianism, dissidence, rejection, rebellion, disillusion, pessimism, defeat, decadence, disintegration, escape, exile. Alienation, in brief, implies a centrifugal impulse, the detachment of the particle from the mass.[4]

Some of these attitudes apply to the Agrarians; others do not. In regard to "escape" and "exile," the Nashville writers refused to join the exciting exodus to Paris, resisting the bohemian lures and intellectual pleasures so movingly recounted by Malcolm Cowley in *Exile's Return* (1934). Not that Ransom and Tate loved art any less than did the genuine expatriates. They might have made Nashville into a remote mountain outpost of dadaism, for instance, but they did not for a number of explainable reasons. They and some of their associates had been to Europe to soldier, to study, or to write; but the Europe of Ransom and Tate was not the animated bohemia of Malcolm Cowley. Nowhere in Agrarian literature can we find praise for such a rootless, cosmopolitan, and "modern" life. Even had the Agrarians been able to dwell for long in the Paris cafés, it is doubtful that their latent traditionalism would have permitted any deep dissociation from home, their "region of memory." Indeed, as happened with certain other expatriates like Thomas Wolfe, self-exile abroad might have had the effect of attaching them even more strongly to their native land.

However, "rejection" and "disillusion" were certainly two attributes of the Agrarian rebellion. They rejected industrialism, the prevailing "American way"; certain critics have accused the Agrarians of also rejecting everything which contributed to the dissolution of the medieval world. They were disillusioned with democracy because of the rise of an industrial society and the defeat of the South in the Civil War. They referred to democracy in the North as a "plutocracy" which travestied the ideals of the founding fathers. They said that the North had defeated the South only because it had more industries producing more and better arms. Thus, industrialism, along with science and technology, had long been an enemy of the traditional South.

In addition to the general postwar disillusionment, another source of Agrarian cohesion was the discovery of T. S. Eliot's teachings about the value to literature of a social tradition. *The Sacred Wood* had appeared in 1920. In it Eliot included his epochal essay, "Tradition and the Individual Talent." Two years later he wrote *The Waste Land*. Of the Fugitives it was Tate who "found" Eliot and soon began, as he affirmed, "an impertinent campaign in Eliot's behalf in the South."[5] We may assume the campaign engaged, first of all, his Fugitive friends. Perhaps Ransom's subsequent violent condemnation of *The Waste Land* had some remote connection with Tate's increasing addiction to Eliot's literary theories, to his drifting away from neo-classicism.[6] Be that as it may, Eliot's well-known argument runs as follows. Since the modern world is spiritually splintered—without a control in faith, often with no faith at all—the writer of sensibility needs a *tradition* to validate his views, to nourish his art, to formalize his life, and to find and recognize his God. It must be a concrete and usable tradition, unlike that of the Neo-Humanists which was too abstract; it must be anchored in a place and a time. For Eliot the time of Dante seemed best to fulfill these requirements. In an organic, enduring, traditional society the great artist, having no need to invent his subject matter, can concentrate his creative energies on brilliant, formal, aesthetic realization.

Learning from Eliot the literary value of a tradition, the Agrarians —so the argument goes—searched their own backgrounds and found in the Old South the necessary tradition. The Old South had an aristocracy, a kind of serfdom, a ritualized religion, a code; in short, it was a stable, organic, and spiritually unified society like the Middle Ages. It was also merely a legend, one might be quick to say; but as an inspiration for literature, need a legend be scientifically verifiable?

So much, at the moment, for the argument that Eliot's theories were a possible cause of Agrarian coalescence. That other causes were also at work almost goes without saying. Any literary history of the 1920's has to reflect the multiple alienations among its writers and that most of these alienations converged upon an anti-industrial, anti-machine, anti-capitalist bias. The Southern Agrarians, no doubt influenced by the general spirit of dissent, emerged as one of the trends most critical of civilization in the United States. It was the particularity of the Agrarians, their special kind of revolt, their basic assumptions, and the unusual conditions they made for accepting nationalism which set them apart.

Because they were more or less the products of their times, the Agrarians reacted similarly to three major influences: the varied sources of regional discord, the challenge posed by the "New South," and their own role in the Southern literary renaissance. Certain events in each of these categories further strengthened their personal ties, clarified and deepened their common ideology, and hardened their will to attack the revealed enemy. As for regional discord and the challenge of the New South, the Scopes trial and the labor violence at Gastonia were only two major events symbolizing the danger to the Southern tradition; even more insidious were the thousand-and-one signs that the money-hungry New Southerners were increasing their power everywhere.

Strong forces were at work undermining the Southern tradition and many of them formed part of the aftermath of World War I: new wealth for the middle classes (much of it from military camps), new war-born industries, a confident commercial spirit, wider opportunities for the returned veterans both Negro and white, a stronger nationalism dimming further the memory of the Civil War, a vast uneasiness among the Negro people, and the beginnings of a critical literature. Other forces included the spread of modernism in the Southern churches, the growth of liberal curricula in education, a wider acceptance of science, and a more enlightened and aggressive press.

Every move forward, however, produced a countermove on the part of those who feared change. Professor Edwin Mims, head of the English department at Vanderbilt, under whom Ransom and other Agrarians taught or studied, saw this process in 1926 when he wrote in *The Advancing South:*

The reactionary forces, stung to renewed action by evidences of the growth of the progressive spirit, are more outspoken, more belligerent, more apparently victorious, but their citadels are gradually being undermined by the rising tide of liberalism. The South, once so potent in the life of the nation, is passing through not only a remarkable industrial development, but an even more important and significant intellectual renascence. (p. vii)

By the end of the twenties the Agrarians had taken their stand with those "reactionary forces" that Mims spoke about. The epithet "Young Confederates" might have received added point from their going to the refrain of the Confederate marching song "Dixie" for their title, *I'll Take My Stand.* On the other hand, advocates of the New South like Mims welcomed progress, liberalism, and industrialism. Indeed, in more ways than one, *I'll Take My Stand* was written as an answer to *The Advancing South.*

The simple dichotomy between progress and reaction which Mims used, however, had deeper and more complex implications which must be briefly examined here. Contrary to what the Agrarians were to believe, the backward Southern hinterland did not always reject every influence coming from the North; and not all of these influences, by any standard, could qualify as liberal or progressive. For example, ugly race riots in Chicago and elsewhere in the North influenced the revival of the Ku Klux Klan, with its new headquarters in Atlanta. Various hysterias of national origin found regional sustenance in the South. The great steel strike in 1919, led by socialists like William Z. Foster, proved to many that Bolshevism was possible in America; in the view of A. Mitchell Palmer, the Attorney-General, it had to be crushed both above and below the Mason-Dixon line, by the use of midnight raids, jailings, and deportations. The traditional xenophobia that had often deprived Southern industry of the skills of immigrants now increased in magnitude, as the whole nation prepared laws to limit further immigration. The widely used epithet "radical alien" had a Southern definition, often meaning a "damned Yankee" or anyone interfering with the caste system under which the Negro lived. Full-page horror stories in Northern tabloids depicting scenes of a coming "red terror" or "yellow peril" had their Southern counterparts in neurotic fears expressed about the Negro, the Jew, and the Catholic. There were "liberal" books written that accuse the fundamentalists of conspiring to set up a theocracy, a union of church and state in which science and reason would have to surrender to the Bible as the revealed word of God. Conversely, many a fundamentalist preacher blared forth the warning that godless scientists and teachers were trying to impose atheism on the youth, to "destroy" Jesus Christ, under the pretense of advancing progress and truth.

In the midst of these many tensions—some critics say because of them—the South in the twenties experienced an upsurge in literary creation. Louise Cowan loses no time in assigning the credit; her Introduction begins, "The Nashville poets who published the little magazine *The Fugitive* during the early half of the 1920's have the distinction of being the inaugurators of the Southern literary renaissance."[7] The relatively recent compilation of *Southern Renascence* (1953), together with so much else since the twenties, testifies to the rich fulfillment of what was then more a welcomed promise than a fact.[8] For several decades no Southerner has needed to feel embarassed by the literary output of his region. However, in the days when Mencken derided the South as the "Sahara of the Bozart" and when the Ku Klux Klan and the "monkey trial" were powerful regional symbols, it was a novel idea indeed to expect great literature from the land of lynch mobs and boll weevils. Some writers doubted that what was happening should be dignified with the title "renaissance." Others completely overlooked the latent literary impulse and sought to rationalize its apparent dearth. Thus, the novelist Corra Harris, writing with unmistakable charm, explained: "We are less intellectual than Northern people because we have more natural sense and do not feel, as they do, an artificial craving for culture to make up for a native deficiency."[9] Miss Harris, it should be understood, was not trying to be funny.

During the mid-twenties and after, the reference by Edwin Mims to a "renascence" found many echoes both North and South. In commentaries of the late twenties, various reasons were given for the literary awakening. First was the active sense of tragedy and evil possessed by Southerners as being the only Americans ever to have suffered military defeat—indeed, to have known the violent despoilment of their homes. From its knowledge of death and grief the South had a deeper and more profound source for its art than did other regions. In William Faulkner, the South had a prime example of a writer who plumbed the most fearful reaches of this source. Secondly, the Southerner felt the sense of having lost a "precious object" because of the gradual demise of the Southern tradition and the "backward glance" of the bereaved Southern writer after World War I. According to at least one important Agrarian, Allen Tate, it was this look toward the past which more than anything else inspired the literary renaissance. It certainly inspired Tate's great "Ode to the Confederate Dead" and his novel *The Fathers*. A third causative factor for the upsurge in regional writing was thought to be the passive nature of Southern society, its rural backwardness, its lack of nervous hurry-and-go. Edmund Wilson commented in 1928, "It is perhaps the only section of the country where the educated classes possess at once enough cultivation, existences sufficiently unhurried and an intimate enough share in the life of their communities to produce intellectual work of real richness and depth."[10] A fourth cause was alleged to be the influence of the industrial and social revolution loosely labeled the "New South," with its worship of mass education, science, modernism, commerce, and progress. To the liberal, this revolution was bound to be the reason for anything good, including literature, that was produced in his region.

Even those observers who welcomed the signs of progress—in terms of what today is called the gross national product—sensed something different in the South, a residue of emotions unlike any to be found elsewhere. E. C. Lindeman touched upon this facet of the South when he wrote: "And there is something about the people—something deep and frightening at times, something which has grown out of suffering, something indigenous which might, if it were creatively released, provide the most potent stimulus for cultural advance since New England civilization disintegrated."[11] Still another source sensitive to incipient trends, the *Saturday Review of Literature,* commented that if that malaise of "the restless mind which results in literature is stirring anywhere in the United States it should be in the new South. The South is a box of fireworks awaiting a spark." This condition resulted mainly from the "racial and regional characteristics" diametrically opposed to the "leveling influence of prosperous mechanization."[12]

In 1927 Herschel Brickell wrote, "The dreary desert [the South] has become an oasis, at the moment the center of literary interest in this country."[13] He found it no "exaggeration to speak of a renaissance of literature in the South." He praised Faulkner as "delightfully cosmopolitan" and credited him with knowing as much about writing "the prose to which we give the convenient tag 'modern' as any habitué of the corner made by the crossing of the Boulevards Montparnasse and Raspoil in Paris. . . ." Among the newer poets Brickell singled out Tate, Ransom, and Fletcher as three who showed that "the Renaissance does not lack its singers."

Howard Mumford Jones, an important witness of the South's cultural scene, found not only a social awakening but also bewilderment. Writing in 1929 about the Southern legend, Jones said that nobody in the North knew what was going on in the cultural life of the South and, for that matter, not many Southerners knew either. "The intellectual quickening which has accompanied its industrial development has resulted in a series of bewildering shifts of values. It is a Georgia newspaper, the Columbus *Enquirer Sun,* which first effectively shattered the silence of the Ku Klux Klan."[14] He snapped back at those who attacked the South while overlooking serious problems in their own back yard. "It might be interesting," he wrote, "to weigh the stupidities of the Dayton trial in a little Tennessee town against the cruelties of the Sacco-Vanzetti case in cultivated Massachusetts, just as it would be possible to balance the power of travelling evangelists to sway illiterate whites against the morbid hold of tabloid newspapers over the emotions of half-baked clerks and silly stenographers."[15] Lest the enthusiasts overpraise the new Southern literature, Jones soon asked the question: Is there a Southern renaissance? No, was his answer, at least not yet. He praised the book reviews of Donald Davidson and others, but he disliked Ransom's and Tate's nostalgia for the civilization of the slave system. Jones maintained, finally, that there would be no great literature, "merely regional studies and topical books," until the South again stood for a significant idea.

Today, literary historians no longer doubt the reality of the renaissance or the vital role played in it by the Fugitive-Agrarians. Their part in the awakening helps to identify them as a distinct school; what they did is usually discussed as a collective effort. All the group's cohesive factors were reflected in the writing of *I'll Take My Stand*. Its importance as a generative and unifying force cannot be exaggerated; its articles of belief created a common intellectual ground for the participants. The "Twelve Southerners" were busy with research and writing projects of their own; yet they joined to initiate the new social and cultural movement and assumed responsibility for its success or failure.

From within the movement itself Donald Davidson has given the best account of what transpired during the year or so when the symposium was being readied.[16] Some of the pertinent correspondence was used by Louise Cowan in *The Fugitive Group* although her main interest ended with the publication in 1928 of the Fugitive anthology. If other Agrarians besides Fletcher and Young write autobiographies, they will no doubt provide added knowledge about the birth of Agrarianism. A brief glance at the twelve contributors just prior to *I'll Take My Stand* will indicate the wide range of talent the Agrarian principles were able to muster.

The year 1930 found John Crowe Ransom a busy professor of English at Vanderbilt. Besides teaching, he published *God Without Thunder,* which included a running attack on modernism and science. Derided as "theological home-brew" and praised as "the profoundest book" of Agrarianism, *God Without Thunder* became a religious and aesthetic companion piece to *I'll Take My Stand.* For the Agrarian symposium, Ransom acted with characteristic energy and insight; not only did he write the first draft of the Statement of Principles, but also the lead essay, "Reconstructed But Unregenerate." His double contribution, in the two books, signalized a period in Ransom's life when social and economic matters obsessed him fully as much as did literary affairs.

By 1930 Allen Tate—full name, John Orley Allen Tate—had established himself as a biographer, reviewer, essayist, and poet. He had published a book of poems, *Mr. Pope and Other Poems* (1928), and two biographies, *Stonewall Jackson: The Good Soldier* (1928) and *Jefferson Davis: His Rise and Fall* (1929). These three works, not to mention his other writings, testify to a considerable amount of industry; the biographics also indicate a deepening interest in his region's historic tradition. In growing recognition of his ability Tate received Guggenheim fellowships in both 1928 and 1929. The stipends enabled him to spend some time in France; before *I'll Take My Stand* was published, he had returned and settled near Nashville. For the symposium he wrote "Remarks on the Southern Religion," in which he made the famous statement that only "by violence" could the Southerner "take hold" of his tradition.

Donald Davidson, who had begun teaching English at Vanderbilt in 1920, writes of himself in relation to *I'll Take My Stand:* "I was attempting to edit a book page and to follow the various tergiversations that modernism produced among the rising Southern writers."[17] The term "modernism" in an Agrarian context usually meant any liberal departures from fundamentalism in religion. In another personal reminiscence, Davidson wrote:

From 1924 to 1930 (while teaching and writing poetry) I was literary editor of the Nashville *Tennesseean.* The book page which I edited was also published for a while in the Knoxville *Journal;* but the enterprise, which had grown to ambitious critical proportions, collapsed with the failure of Caldwell & Co., which dragged down the publisher-sponsor, Colonel Luke Lea.[18]

The poetry Davidson mentioned included two books, *An Outland Piper* in 1924 and *The Tall Men* in 1927, collections that represented the best of his Fugitive output. As Ransom had done in an essay entitled "The South—Old or New?", Davidson in "First Fruits of Dayton" strongly expressed views which anticipated their Agrarian stand.[19] Davidson's contribution to the symposium, "A Mirror for Artists," bitterly and often wittily delineated the alleged corruption of the arts under industrialism. Unless current trends were reversed, the South would be inundated by Babbittry, advertising, boosterism, and cheap art, the only kind permitted by finance capitalism.

For Robert Penn Warren, the fourth and last major Agrarian, the year 1930 was memorable in a number of ways. That was the year he received a B. Litt. degree from Oxford University where he had studied as a Rhodes scholar. In 1929 Warren had published his first book, a lengthy critical biography of John Brown, the abolitionist. Warren was only twenty-five when he wrote "The Briar Patch" for *I'll Take My Stand.* In it he discussed the Agrarian attitude toward the Negro in tones somewhat milder than those later to prevail. Although he advised the Negro to "sit beneath his own vine and fig tree," he also wrote, "The chief problem for all alike is the restoration of society at large to a balance and security which the industrial regime is far from promising to achieve."[20]

Of the remaining eight whom *I'll Take My Stand* attracted as co-authors, Frank Lawrence Owsley and John Gould Fletcher contributed most to Agrarian ideology. Owsley, a history professor at Vanderbilt, had written *State Rights in the Confederacy* (1925), in which he detailed how too much state sovereignty seriously impeded the Confederate war effort. At the time of the Agrarian symposium he was engaged in the research and writing that led to *King Cotton Diplomacy* (1931), an excellent study of the South's relations with foreign powers. In *I'll Take My Stand* Owsley defined "The Irrepressible Conflict" that led to war as fundamentally a struggle between an agrarian and an industrial civilization, and not one between slavery and freedom. In later essays, and notably in "The Pillars of Agrarianism,"[21] he made more specific the economic proposals which the symposium had left rather vague. Fletcher was best known before 1930 as an Imagist poet, but from then on his basic traditionalism and regionalism emerged strongly in many articles, reviews, and books. A major example of his growing interest in sociology was *The Two Frontiers: A Study in National Psychology* (1930). The book, a far cry from Imagism, contrasted the social dynamics of the United States and the Soviet Union. In his long essay written for the symposium, "Education, Past and Present," Fletcher stressed the alleged superiority of the old Southern school system over the Northern because it sought to create the superior individual, the gentleman.

John Donald Wade, another original contributor, had joined Ransom on the English staff at Vanderbilt in 1928. Besides teaching, he was working on a biography of John Wesley, the founder of Methodism, while the editing of *I'll Take My Stand* progressed. In his essay "The Life and Death of Cousin Lucius," he wrote a swiftly paced account of how one Southerner built a meaningful life for himself in a land whose established society had been smashed by military defeat. Andrew Nelson Lytle, another Vanderbilt graduate, had been in the East writing plays and acting. In a long essay, "The Hind Tit," he traced the various inroads of commercialism on the Southern yeoman farmer. He took a hypothetical farmer and considered the life of his household before and after he made an effort to industrialize it. Having fallen for the lure of money, the farmer became the "runt pig in the sow's litter" who was forced to nourish himself from "the little hind tit," usually quite dry. Lyle H. Lanier, who had been teaching at New York University, added to the Agrarian ideology by writing "A Critque of the Philosophy of Progress." He took time out from research on the psychology of race to decry the kind of "progress," supported by John Dewey and others that had permitted industrialism to dislocate the economy and corrupt our culture.

After the symposium the three remaining contributors wrote relatively little to develop further the common ideology. In fact, Herman Clarence Nixon later in the decade recanted somewhat his association with Agrarianism, having found its economics too narrow for his own convictions. Just prior to the publication of *I'll Take My Stand* Nixon had been studying the Populist movement and the problem of the tenant farmer. In his essay "Whither Southern Economy?" he sketched the growth of Southern industry and warned that agriculture, now seriously threatened, had created an agrarian civilization which must not be allowed to perish. Henry Blue Kline, a graduate student in English at Vanderbilt who had just earned his M. A., contributed a character study entitled "William Remington: A Study in Individualism." The protagonist finds himself alienated from Northern society because there are no real values to which he can become attached; yet when Remington goes to the South, a more traditional society, he happily finds a place where he "belongs." The final contributor to the symposium, Stark Young, was already a well-known and respected theater critic who wrote regularly for Northern periodicals. "Not in Memoriam, But in Defense" suggested the correct attitude that a Southerner in 1930 should have toward his regional tradition.

These, then, were the "Twelve Southerners" who initiated the Agrarian movement. Part of the movement's character, of course, came from its internal leadership. In this respect, scholars generally agree that the three pre-eminent thinkers were Ransom, Tate, and Davidson. They do not always receive this order of priority. Of the original Fugitives, only Tate, Ransom, and Warren went on to become both Southern Agrarians and New Critics. Davidson did not develop as a New Critic to the same degree as Ransom, Tate, and Warren, but his basic Agrarian convictions stayed relatively undimmed. He wrote a brilliant two-volume study of the Tennessee River in the "Rivers of America" series; and his regional loyalty persisted to the point that in 1957 he entitled a book *Still Rebels, Still Yankees.* Fletcher's later works, like *The Epic of Arkansas* (1936) and *Burning Mountain* (1946), also evidenced a powerful use of Agrarian themes. After the symposium, Andrew Nelson Lytle not only practiced subsistence farming but also wrote historical novels such as *Bedford Forrest and His Critter Company* (1931) and *The Long Night* (1936), inspired by Tate's biographies of the Confederate heroes Jackson and Davis. Stark Young wrote the popular romantic novel *So Red the Rose* (1934); set during the Civil War, it clearly reflected the idea that a noble agrarian way of life was being despoiled by an aggressive and inhumane industrialism.

Several other Southern writers besides these twelve had been invited to participate in the symposium, but for one reason or another they refused. Donald Davidson reports that among them was Stringfellow Barr, editor of the *Virginia Quarterly Review*. Instead of joining, Barr made an oblique attack on the budding Agrarian program by writing an article supporting industrialization of the South for the October, 1930, issue of the *Review*. He was promptly answered in a public letter signed by Ransom, Tate, and Davidson, who stated that any form of industrialism was bad and that any government control of it, which Barr had suggested, would inevitably lead to state collectivism such as was practiced in Soviet Russia. Directly contradicting Barr, whose views were strongly liberal and "New South," the letter maintained the position that the "effort to protect the traditional agrarian economy of the South was the best way to preserve the Southern way of life."[22]

The tiff with Stringfellow Barr had these immediate consequences. "On October 18, 1930 [six weeks before *I'll Take My Stand* appeared], George Fort Milton, the editor of the Chattanooga *News,* suggested in an editorial that the Nashville group hold a public debate with the young men of Richmond who agreed with Barr. The idea was taken up by the Richmond *Times-Dispatch,* and a debate was arranged between Barr and Ransom."[23] Having checked the newspaper reports, John L. Stewart found that the debate, held on November 14, 1930, attracted an overflow crowd of nearly 3500 people. Sherwood Anderson, presiding as chairman, "stole Ransom's best point in a little speech of introduction in which he stated his belief that controlled industry led straight to Communism." Some critics feel that Southern Agrarianism was indeed one of our earliest, organized, anti-Communist movements among intellectuals. Tate, Warren, and Lytle had even argued that the title for their manifesto should have been *A Tract Against Communism*. In the Richmond debate Barr's best point was his stress on the fact that "industrialism was already in the South and any attempts such as the Agrarians were making to ignore it simply weakened labor's attempts to protect itself and what remained of the old Southern ways."[24] Other debates were held in other Southern centers in the years that followed. By then, through their writings, the Agrarians had won a national audience for their views. It was the debate in Richmond, however, that brought the Agrarians out of the academic bower and placed them in the public arena; in a limited sense they became men of action as well as men of thought.

Another of their early clashes was with the Neo-Humanists led by Paul

Elmer More and Irving Babbitt. Allen Tate established the enmity in 1929 through an essay called "The Fallacy of Humanism." However, the most important Southern group to rival the Agrarians consisted of the liberal writers and thinkers centered in Chapel Hill, at the University of North Carolina. Howard Mumford Jones, writing in 1944, lamented the fact that New England had no comparable regional movements to clarify its heritage in relation to its cultural present. In his opinion the South had been more fortunate; a "fructifying influence" had poured forth from the two opposing centers, Chapel Hill and Nashville.

At the University of North Carolina . . . a group of men arose determined not merely that the Southern way of life should be improved, but also that it should be preserved. A second group arose at Vanderbilt. In the one university, men like Howard W. Odum, Frederick H. Koch, Rupert B. Vance, Paul Green, Edgar W. Knight, E. C. Branson, L. R. Wilson, and others decided to focus the best brains they could assemble upon the problem of Southern values. The result was not only a rich historical and sociological literature; their activities also had important repercussions in imaginative writing from the Carolina folk plays to the novels of Thomas Wolfe.

In the other university a group of young poets, weary of Southern sentimentalism, determined that the South was entitled to an intelligent literature. They were presently forced by the logic of their philosophy to consider the question of Southern values, and the result was the Agrarian pronouncement, *I'll Take My Stand*. One may debate endlessly the question whether the Tarheels or the Tennesseeans advanced the right solution, but the point is that a solution was looked for. And that solution focuses upon the assumption that the Southern way of life is both valuable and defensible.[25]

Thus, on the eve of *I'll Take My Stand*, the Agrarians were already embattled, first of all with fellow Southerners who had taken another kind of stand—for more industry, more liberalism, more science, and more progress. In opposition to the optimism of Southerners like Barr and Mims, *I'll Take My Stand* challenged all those who felt that the industrial revolution would ameliorate the region's social condition. What liberals found in this condition to be an evil—the stagnation and backwardness—the Agrarians found to be a positive good. They looked toward a more simple and gracious time in the past. With their odd perspective they could frequently cast a devastating light on the idiocies of modern life. In fact, their hostile criticism of the entire industrial culture has often been praised as the soundest of their strictly sociological contributions.

Chapter II   From Southern To Agrarian

EXCEPT FOR DEMAGOGUES LIKE SENATOR THEODORE BILBO, NO ONE IN THE thirties showed a greater attachment to the South than did the Agrarians. In the main, they were uncritical champions who found the South's traditional "way of life" superior to that of any other region. During the early and middle twenties, however, before they grew fully aware of their natural affinities, several of the future Agrarians found serious fault with their regional heritage.

A prime instance of disaffection occurred in the first issue of *The Fugitive* (April, 1922). In the Foreword, the authors disclaimed any affiliation with the Southern aristocratic past by writing that "THE FUGITIVE flees from nothing faster than from the high caste Brahmin of the Old South." Perhaps the fullest expression of anti-South sentiment, however, occurs in certain mid-decade writings of Allen Tate. At one time, for example, Tate's friends feared he was becoming anti-Southern because of his views on his region's cultural flaws. It should be said in his defense that Tate was merely putting into practice the Fugitive demand that a more self-critical literature replace lingering sentimentalism. His attitude at this time included criticism of nearly every one of the future Agrarian principles.

For example, in an essay in 1925, Tate chided the South for its intellectual stagnation. He wrote: "It [Southern self-expression] is certain to be an elegy on the perished amenities of the Old South, done much after the manner in which T. S. Eliot a few years ago lamented the decay of all modern culture. It is a scattering tradition, and its last living authority will scarcely survive the present decade." Tate said that the South of tradition was determined on "being a One-hoss Shay forever. Mastered by its one idea and so master of none, it fought four years in a fashion which a contemporaneous Cervantes . . . might have owned to be his proper milieu—to preserve this single, all-embracing idea."[1] By 1930 the Agrarians were to regard this conformity as further evidence that the South was a truly unified society.

Although Tate later rejected all aspects of liberalism, he now also chided the Old South for its lack of liberalism. He wrote that the essence of Southern culture consisted of eighteenth-century manners and the sterilized backwash of liberal thought from that period. While Agrarianism was to support the revival of aristocratic values, Tate now claimed that the Old South, to its great disadvantage, was strictly a political and economic aristocracy. Anxious to preserve its outmoded society, the South lost its chance for self-criticism, the "initial moral attitude which must preface the exacting business of beautiful letters."

Nor could Tate find anything noble in the religious quality of the Southern tradition. "The South, before the Civil War," he maintained, "probably had little more than an incidental commerce with the name of Deity." With respect to religion as an element in the general culture, Tate praised New England to the detriment of the South —a most insurgent act, had it taken place after 1930. While Tate here praised the old Puritan religion for having a system of ideas, the Agrarians would soon show a decided preference for religion as ritual. In his praise of New England Tate wrote:

While New England has preserved to some extent a culture of ideas in spite of its thorough absorption of industrialism—it articulated in the beginning a system of ideas of which the special notion was a God—it is significant that the South became, equally with the Middle West, rich soil for the secular and vulgar and moralistic churches.

In the essays and reviews written before he became an Agrarian, Tate often praised the New England cultural tradition; such praise revealed his persistent concern about the cultural poverty of his own region, the South. He said, "The Old South has degenerated into and survives only as a sentiment susceptible of no precise definition." The second generation after the Civil War "has no tradition of ideas, no consciousness of moral and spiritual values, as an inheritance; it has simply lost a prerogative based on property." With little mercy, Tate is here stripping the celebrated Southern tradition to its hard center of economic privilege derived from slavery. It is true, of course, that Tate always deplored the loss of the ancient "amenities" which flourished in the Old South, but so did many others. Even advanced liberals like Edmund Wilson considered that something extremely pleasant—the "gracious habits" of the South—vanished along with Negro slavery. Tate did think it a tragedy, however, that his people "were not so intelligent as they were gracious, that they never saw their cultural limitations critically enough to be creatively aware of their imperfections and to produce their Henry James."

Tate seemed to be systematically demolishing what would soon become the basic assumptions of Agrarianism, including even the proposition that aesthetic quality may be attributed to a certain locality. Evaluating a book by Edwin Mims, *The South in the Rebuilding of the Nation*, Tate wrote that Mims had succumbed to the sentimental, local-color fallacy, the "ingenuous opinion that a particular setting is intrinsically more 'poetic' than another."[2] During his Fugitive days, Ransom also was opposed to attributing any special value to locality; he said that the mind of the aristocratic thinker "is the most delivered from all sources of local excitement, and is the most independent of environment."[3] Tate advocated a cosmopolitan culture for his own region; again he did so against a background of veneration for New England. "The modern Southerner does not inherit," he wrote, "nor is he likely to have, a native culture compounded of the strength and subtlety of his New England contemporaries." Tate continued, "But he may be capable, through an empiricism which is his only alternative to intellectual suicide, of a cosmopolitan culture to which his contemporary in the East is emotionally barred. . . ."[4] A short time later, the Agrarians would maintain that "cosmopolitanism" implied a social and artistic degeneration and was completely hostile to their concept of regionalism.

One final example of pro-New England sentiment in the early Tate should further prove that he joined his friends in the Agrarian venture with reservations that had to be severely modified. Even as plans were underway for the publication of *I'll Take My Stand*, he said in a review of the Southern poet Chivers and his work:

The New England renascence was coming on as he reached manhood, and he found the rich mercantile society of the East more hospitable to writers, less disposed to think of them as useless and queer, than the planting aristocracy, which occupied itself mainly with politics (being on the political defensive), with gaming and fighting, with extreme Protestantism and with the novels of Sir Walter Scott.[5]

Perhaps Tate's boldest stroke was his praise of Mencken, the avowed enemy of Southern culture, because Mencken was bringing in a much needed critical spirit from the outside. These signs of doubts and hesitations do not imply that Tate was anti-Southern in general as some of his critics maintained; yet the scope of his disenchantment does indicate that he came to his own Agrarian stand with initially infirm convictions. One could say, of course, that he was honestly practicing what he preached; he was self-critical for the good of the South, unwilling like so many others to be both blind and benign.

Another future Agrarian, Donald Davidson, also found grave faults with the Southern tradition. After mentioning that Tate in *The Nation* had been the only writer so far to consider the Southern artist in relation to his environment, Davidson wrote: "And the most important question of all remains to be asked: that is, what does it mean to be a Southerner and yet be a writer; what is the Southern character, if such exists, and is it communicating itself to literature in any recognizable and valuable way?"[6]

Tate, as we have seen, had bowed to the cultural superiority of traditional New England; now Davidson bowed to that of modern New England. He believed that no Southern writer was so profound in his regionalism as to be universal as well. He commented, "Heyward's church-towers are Charleston towers and Charleston towers only. Robert Frost's birches and ax-halves and pasture-lots and rock walls, though they may incidentally be New England, are more definitely the phenomena of the universe as it is familiar to all men."[7] Davidson agreed with Tate that the Old South had left no culture of ideas that the Southern writer could use. He contrasted the South's literary treatment of its natural heroes with that of the North—especially of the two most important, Lincoln and Lee.

From Lowell and Whitman down to Robinson, Lindsay, and Sandburg, we have a creditable array of poems which have celebrated Abraham Lincoln as a national hero, and have done so with the dignity and seriousness that suited his heroic dimensions. What Southerner has performed a like service for Lee?[8]

Davidson's query reveals a regional concern, but it does not yet indicate the hostility toward the very idea of national heroes or the hostility toward the national concept of Lincoln as a man of dignity and worth which the Agrarians later displayed.

Although Davidson later penned many bitter words against commercialism, he now wrote that the businessman held the key to the right kind of progress for the South. He continued, "Under their touch art takes courage and independent opinion thrives." He might have had in mind *The Fugitive* itself, for every account of its origin and success mentions the financial support it received from retail merchants in Nashville. Davidson suggested that a progress appropriate to the South implied having an industrial system that would not be wholly utilitarian, a clergy that was liberal but possessed of fire and earnestness, and writers in touch with the new but "without ever allowing their own native character, idiom, consciousness of place to be obscured in their interpretations of the South. . . ."⁹

Other future Agrarians severely criticized the Old South. Frank L. Owsley wrote in *State Rights in the Confederacy* that the Confederacy "failed from internal political causes, mainly state rights."¹⁰ To speak of this failure without putting the blame on the evil machinations and power of Lincoln's North would have amounted to betrayal of the sectional cause a few years later. Owsley in his book did not hesitate to take up certain political facts which he said could be called the "seamy side" of Confederate history. Owsley castigated the doctrine of states' rights as the "seeds of death" sown at the birth of the Confederacy. Stubbornly adhering to their individual sovereignty, the Southern states weakened their own union and federalism by each insisting on maintaining its own troops of war and often managing those troops in a manner detrimental to the winning of the war.

Insisting thus upon the theoretical rights of their states, they sowed dissension among the people and destroyed all spirit of cooperation, finally, between the states and the Confederate government, and, at times, arrayed local against central government as if each had been an unfriendly foreign power.¹¹

Owsley's powerful indictment of state rights as a cause of internal dissension conflicts sharply with the Agrarian picture of the Old South, even in crisis, as a stable organic community.

These waverings in regional loyalty indicate the differences which had to be subsumed in the general ideology of Agrarianism. Before the Scopes trial (July, 1925) none of the future Agrarians had in any way distinguished themselves as champions of their region. It might seem odd that the Agrarians went from criticizing to praising their region in so short a time. However, the attacks on the South during and after the Scopes trial were frequent and severe, and the Fugitive-Agrarians responded by closing their ideological ranks. They henceforth minimized their disagreements and sought out a common set of assumptions.

Their gropings for a stable regional philosophy were quite natural for a group deeply interested in the rebirth of Southern literature. It was not yet clear what kind of social or aesthetic dynamic could best bring this phenomenon about. After gaining some recognition as Fugitive poets, they felt more confident about their personal contribution to that rebirth. From being simply poetic voices in Nashville they became spokesmen for their region, whether their region knew it or not. Although the initial hesitations outlined above did exist, of much

more importance to their future were the growing signs of coalescence
and unity—first on a Southern basis and then, by the end of the decade, on an Agrarian basis as well. No one can determine exactly when
a literary group or school begins to cohere and acquire a distinct identity—not even its own members. The more the future Agrarians understood the social and aesthetic value of the South, the more they protested, in articles and poems, against the main or modern direction in
which the South seemed to be heading. Eventually, they realized that
what they were in fact defending was the inheritable, backward, traditional, *agrarian* character of the South. Anyone could be merely a
Southerner who loved his native region, was born or lived there, and
had enough local patriotism to defend himself against his sectional
foes. However, to be both a Southerner and an Agrarian meant having
an entire set of integrated attitudes, a special ideology based on a
moral feeling about the land, about nature. To go from the simpler to
the more complex phase involved accepting a greater commitment, a
more active challenge.

In examining this developing viewpoint it is interesting to see the
extent to which the South as a region and later Agrarian ideas entered
into the Fugitives' poetry. Many of Ransom's poems had Agrarian
themes, without being Southern in setting. They inveighed against the
modern mania for abstraction, against the supposed dissociation of
sensibility (the split between feeling and idea), against an excess of rationalism, and against the smothering of natural instincts like love
and wonder. Other poems, like the often quoted "Antique Harvest-
ers," breathe the very spirit of the Old South. Perhaps the most famous poem written by a Fugitive during the mid-twenties was Tate's
"Ode to the Confederate Dead," in which Tate declaimed against
man's loss of moral significance because man had abandoned his traditional myths for the partial truths of science.[12] Man enjoyed a moral
identity when he had a stable society with values he could understand
and inherit; such a society was the Old South before the Civil War,
the one for which Confederate soldiers died. In the unstable society
created by science and technology, which demands constant renewal,
man finds himself whirled about helplessly in a chaos of abstraction.

Of all the future Agrarians, Davidson was the most romantic and
emotional about the Southern legend. In the following verse from
"The Tall Men" he snarls at America and democracy; his is clearly a
call of distress at the substitution of national vulgarity for Southern
purity.

> The Union is saved. Lee had surrendered forever.
> Today, Lorena, it is forbidden to be
> A Southerner. One is an American now;
> Propounds the pig's conception of the state—
> The constitution of, by, for the pig—
> Meanwhile pushing his trotters well in
> the trough.[13]

Robert Penn Warren, only seventeen when *The Fugitive* first appeared, arrived so late in its tenure that he hardly rates the title of "Fugitive" except for his very close subsequent relationship with the others. Even in his first experimental poems he showed signs of his later obsession with the problems of evil and moral decay. Stewart believes that the controlling concept in Warren's poetry is that in a world of lost innocence like our own man is inevitably permeated by evil, an evil equal to "knowledge" in the Garden of Eden. To the degree that man loses his original innocence by acquiring scientific knowledge, to that degree does he compound the guilt of his original sin. Warren made no poetic use of Southern materials until the Fugitive period was over: after 1928 he worked on a cycle of poems eventually gathered under the title "Kentucky Mountain Farm" and published in his first book of poetry, *Thirty-Six Poems* (1935). Regarding Warren's progress in the twenties toward the ideology of *I'll Take My Stand*, Stewart wrote: "When he combined his interest in the South with his interest in the relation of man with his homestead, he became an Agrarian."[14]

Some students of Southern Agrarianism consider the year 1926 a turning point for the Fugitives; in that year Allen Tate and John Crowe Ransom exchanged simultaneous letters—in a kind of mystical meeting of minds from afar—which expressed a will to action. Tate has written: "And then one day—I cannot be sure of the year, I think 1926—I wrote John Ransom a new kind of letter. I told him we must do something about Southern history and the culture of the South. John had written on the same day, the same message to me."[15] After quoting this passage in *The Fugitives,* Bradbury explains that Tate was seeking, and perhaps to some extent creating, a "common historical myth" to sustain his poetic vision. Tate's enthusiasm for Hulme and Eliot demanded a spiritual anchorage in a solid tradition; in his search Tate "rediscovers the Southern heritage which he had repudiated as a 'strictly political and economic aristocracy.' "[16]

Another student of the Agrarians, Louis D. Rubin, also mentions the Tate-Ransom exchange of letters in 1926, and says that it led to plans for *I'll Take My Stand,* "in which Tate, Ransom, and ten other Southerners set forth Agrarian counsels for what they felt was an increasingly industrialized, increasingly misled South."[17]

For both Bradbury and John L. Stewart, however, it was primarily the Scopes trial that galvanized the Fugitives into action on behalf of their embattled region. They were forced by the issues raised during the trial to choose between the Old South and the New. Not everyone becomes a reactionary simply because he listens to the pros and cons of a law that prohibits the teaching of evolution in the public schools of Tennessee. Liberal-minded educators could react by saying, as did Chancellor Kirkland of Vanderbilt University: "The answer to the episode at Dayton is the building of new laboratories on the Vanderbilt campus for the teaching of science."[18] And Nell Battle Lewis, a Southern critic of the South, wrote in words as caustic as those of Mencken: "This attempted union of Church and State by the Fundamentalists, this attempted dictation of legislation by a wing of the Protestant Church has nothing to redeem it. It is wholly to be condemned."[19]

Donald Davidson, on the other hand, chose to defend fundamentalism and attack modern industrial culture. He has continued to attack this culture throughout his career. In "First Fruits of Dayton" he argued that fundamentalism was salutary—despite its "wild extravagances"; it was "at least morally serious in a day when morals are treated with levity."[20] Davidson took note of the divided loyalties in his region, writing, "The South is asked to remold itself! In whose image, then, and after what heart's desire?" With deep-felt pessimism Davidson foresaw more industrialism arriving and asked, "What problems are to be visited upon the South, what strikes, agitations, nervous retchings of society, wage slavery, graft, mountebankery, idiocies of merchant princes?"[21] Ransom's response to the issues raised by the trial at Dayton was even more reactionary than that of Davidson: he began *God Without Thunder,* in which he defended not only fundamentalism but all forms of rigid religious orthodoxy.

Another factor leading to the development of the Agrarian philosophy was the liberal viewpoint being expounded by Edwin Mims, chairman of the English department at Vanderbilt. His book, *The Advancing South,* appeared in 1926, and it is quite possible that both Tate and Ransom had this publication in mind when they wrote each other that they should do something about the Southern situation. Its subtitle, *Stories of Progress and Reaction,* clearly indicated the general lines of Southern cleavage. Any future "stand" of social consequence had to be taken within the limits of the dichotomy which Mims described. Bradbury in his work states the following with regard to the Scopes controversy: "This answer of science to Fundamentalism [more laboratories for Vanderbilt] well may be credited with setting off the chain reaction which resulted in the movement of the Fugitive group out of its literary preoccupations into its social and religious concerns of the late twenties and the early thirties."[22] Bradbury then continues: "But the basis for those concerns . . . long had been laid, and their development undoubtedly had been accelerated by Dr. Mims." He claims rightly that the Agrarians never publicly gave Mims enough credit for helping them develop their views, but they were surely aware of him "as a symbolic nether pole in their accomplishments." One of the few instances of Agrarian praise for Mims was the inclusion of his name by Davidson in a list of "resident spiritual forces" working in behalf of further Southern enlightenment.

Several critics, among them Bradbury, have suggested that the city of Nashville itself influenced the formation of Agrarian attitudes by being visibly engaged in the social tug-of-war between the Old and the New South. Its success in having lured a sizable amount of industry by the twenties appeared, among other signs, in the constant smoke from the busy chimneys of factories. Fundamentalist ideas still dominated the rural hinterland, but the city of Nashville, as stigmatized by William Jennings Bryan, was "the center of modernism in the South." In this context modernism meant the near-atheistic rejection of Genesis as the sole explanation for the origin of mankind. Mims made essentially the same point with regard to the gulf between urban and rural areas when he wrote, "Many of the special reporters of the recent Dayton trial never learned the difference between Dayton and Nashville."[23] In Nashville, of course, was Vanderbilt University, the spiritual haven of the Fugitives and already a battleground of conflicting attitudes. Vanderbilt was the "Oxford at home" of those who had been to England as Rhodes scholars, like Ransom and Warren—except that their home had been infiltrated and betrayed. When England had her industrial revolution a century or so earlier, Thomas Carlyle saw the same factory smoke soiling the heavens and, contemplating the "modern disunities" of his time, he wrote *Past and Present* (1843). The Agrarians, who had been relatively placid Fugitive poets, gazed angrily at the factory smoke of the New South and composed *I'll Take My Stand*. Like Carlyle, they had found a past to romanticize, a legend to cherish.

Other writers and groups supported one or another of the ideas associated with the Agrarians. Many of these writers were Northern, some lived in big cities, others came from midwestern farms, and still others were immigrant arrivals. They wrote novels that celebrated the moral virtue of the soil and plays that condemned the evil machine. That other regions besides the South also had their "agrarians" is a point that needs no special stress; for example, as Maxwell Geismar says of Willa Cather:

For the whole range of Cather's values, standards, tastes, and prejudices, her tone, is that of an inherent aristocrat in an equalitarian order, of an agrarian writer in an industrial order, of a defender of spiritual graces in the midst of an increasingly materialistic culture.[24]

The leading Southern Agrarian, John Crowe Ransom, could not have been more aptly characterized.

Toward the end of the twenties, when the Fugitives were becoming "professional Southerners" and gradually turning into Agrarians, a number of books appeared which fed their ideology, so to speak, and greatly influenced its character and growth. Vernon L. Parrington's *Main Currents in American Thought* (1927) treated the South as a cultural entity whose insistence upon sectional particularity was justified by geography, history, and economic determinism. Although the book disdained Southern departures from Jeffersonian democracy, its recognition of the South as one of America's three major regions offered the Agrarians an argument for their viewpoint which could be refuted only by the theory that nationalism could countermand the "will of a region." Parrington also stressed the great importance of local cultures in the American heritage; his views strengthened the Agrarians' regional confidence and sanctioned their sectional bias.

In the same year, Christopher Hollis published *The American Heresy,* in which he claimed that the Civil War had destroyed the republican institutions of the Jeffersonian state. Without them, the state had become a pseudo-democracy through which the new plutocracy could dictate its will. The "heresy" of which Hollis spoke was that Jefferson's twin principles of human liberty and equality were not deduced from dogmatic religion. Instead, Jefferson built his political philosophy upon a denial of dogmatic religion. Hollis believed that liberty and equality without regulation by a religious authority could destroy a state. The agrarian ideal of Jefferson was the basis for Hollis's ideal society. Jefferson believed that to maintain freedom and equality a state had to be agricultural and allow for the ownership of property. "Only in an agricultural society," Hollis wrote echoing Jefferson, "could property be so distributed that all men might possess a little and therefore only in such a society could equality be preserved. An agricultural society also was the only free society."[25]

Hollis took a definitely racist attitude toward slavery and the Negro people. It is doubtful, however, that the Agrarians needed to be influenced on this particular point. Hollis stated that the abolitionists opposed slavery through their love of anarchy. They formed a "brainless and subversive" movement that was "but one part of a general programme, of which the other planks were free love, teetotalism, communism and extreme feminism" (p. 129). Nevertheless, Hollis felt that slavery could not be defended on any *moral* grounds, and it was a grave error on Calhoun's part to have called it a positive good. What vital social function did slavery perform? Hollis answered: "The old Southern slavery had been, at least, one of the institutions of a stable society. The new industrial slavery was to be mere brute force acting upon chaos" (p. 131). As for the Negroes living "free" in the era of brutal and chaotic industrial forces, he said, "There is very little reason to think that the negro race has at all benefited by the abolition of slavery" (p. 133).

In a bibliographical note, Allen Tate acknowledged Hollis's influence on his own *Jefferson Davis: His Rise and Fall* (1929) and said that *The American Heresy* was "the first effort to comprehend the supposedly mixed forces of American history under a single idea."[26] By mixed forces we may assume that Tate meant the South and the North, agriculture and industry, aristocracy and democracy, and slavery and freedom. In conformity with the Hollis viewpoint, Tate wrote in his book on Davis:

In a sense, all European history since the Reformation was concentrated in the war between the North and the South. For in the South the most conservative of the European orders had, with great power, come back to life, while the North, opposing the Southern feudalism, had grown to be a powerful industrial state which epitomized in spirit all those middle-class, urban impulses directed against the agrarian aristocracies of Europe after the Reformation.[27]

In terms of the defense in historic depth of the Southern tradition, these ideas were Agrarian pure and simple. Equally pure in the resurrected ideology was the following sequence of thought; again it defines the historic significance of the Agrarian position.

Southerners believed that they stood for "Christianity and Civilization" and, seen in the light of the main tradition of Europe, the assertion was literally true: theirs was the last stand, they were the forlorn hope, of conservative Fundamentalist Christianity and of civilization, based on agrarian, class rule, in the European sense. Europe was already being Americanized—which means

Northernized, industrialized—and the South by 1850 was more European than Europe.[28]

Tate seems to forget here that the industrial revolution came first to Europe, and especially to England, before it came to the North.

In 1925 Tate had severely criticized the economy of the slave empire, but by 1929 he had accepted the venerable opinion of John Calhoun that slavery was a positive good—with qualifications that he could easily allow to wither away. Slavery was a "necessary element in a stable society," he had written in his biography of Stonewall Jackson.[29] In another instance he praised the "astonishing, interwoven homogeneity of southern society," in which the Negroes were "treated neither like pet-lambs nor like beasts; their condition was not different from that of other laboring classes except that it bore the stigma hateful to the nineteenth century and that they were certain of care, often affectionate, to their graves. The overseer, usually the illiterate buffoon he is imagined to be, was sometimes, in the Lower South, a wandering Virginia gentleman whose gentility was not equal to the cotton scramble"[30] We may speculate on how this erstwhile gentleman might take out his frustrations on the slaves under his thumb.

Another powerful influence on the Agrarians was the work of T. E. Hulme, whose defense of a neofeudal Christian dogma fortified the prospect of a "homogeneous" community, such as the South could be. Hulme's book, *Speculations,* first appeared in 1924. Nearly every major idea of Hulme's regarding religion, philosophy, and literature is in accord with Agrarianism. The Agrarians had something more—a greater sense of economics. As a modern counterreformationist, Hulme attacked every thought and event which contributed to the historical fall of the Middle Ages. Hulme's image of man as a "wretched creature"—which determines his philosophy—developed directly from an extraordinary obsession with original sin. Nothing worse ever happened to the universe than the humanist heresy suggesting that man had some good in him apart from the grace which only God could bestow. Science and reason compounded the initial heresy by unsettling the traditional view of both God and man. Eventually, romanticism, beginning with Jean Jacques Rousseau, went to the unspeakable extreme of proclaiming man perfectible through the secular agency of his own mind. Hulme scorned most of the philosophers since the Renaissance because they contributed to Protestantism, science, and liberalism. They confused the human with the divine in such a fashion that the divine became ineffective if not unknowable. The positivist idea of continuity and correspondence between the two must, in

Hulme's opinion, be denied and replaced by the concept of a vast gap between the human and the divine. When this occurred, contingency and providence would be restored, church authority would be restored, and God would be restored. Only some kind of a rightist regime could make this restoration possible.

In the Middle Ages, according to Hulme, man was sensibly subjugated to certain absolute values: he was regarded as radically imperfect and suffused with sin. The breakdown of the Middle Ages culminated, through the impetus of romanticism, in the advent of the French Revolution. Hulme now predicted an opposite era in the making, the *classical*, by which he meant a social order in which the image of man is that of a finite, fixed, and evil being. "One may note here," Hulme said, "that the Church has always taken the classical view since the defeat of the Pelagian heresy and the adoption of the sane classical dogma of original sin."[31] This new era would also seem to require rightist politics. In the Introduction to *Further Speculations* (1955), Sam Hynes suggests that Hulme was a proto-Fascist and very close to the French anti-Semitic movement known as *L'Action Française*. T. S. Eliot's admiration for the ideas of Charles Maurras, a leader of *L'Action*, is also well known.

Almost at random we can mention other books published toward the close of the twenties which could be said to have nourished or at least reflected important aspects of Agrarian ideology. For example, *The Modern Temper* (1929) by Joseph Wood Krutch, used many of Hulme's ideas to make its own attack on modern science, materialism, and rationalism. The split or gap which Krutch demanded was that between what he termed the *natural* and the *human*. Whereas science purports to find a continuity between the two—a synthesis, an identity —what we need is a new division between them which would allow the following dichotomy. Naturalism would attend to a lower order of values—science, reason, and materialism. Humanism would encompass religion, love, and God. Such discontinuity would permit a new resurgence of faith in God despite the overpowering influence of materialism. Man could thus have it both ways as long as he recognized and accepted the split in his personality. Krutch praised, among others, Hulme and Eliot. Like them, he lamented the breakdown of medieval religious unity and blamed it on the invasion of science.

Thus, as the year of the Agrarian manifesto approached, other writers were helping the Agrarians to clarify and enlarge their thinking. It seems amply clear that the Agrarians were part of a larger ideological conflict involving the character and fate of American culture. Although *I'll Take My Stand* was addressed primarily to Southern youths who were in danger of being seduced by the industrial lures, we must bear in mind that Agrarianism was a comprehensive attack upon all of modern, progressive, capitalist America. Some of its later recruits, like Troy J. Cauley and Herbert Agar, wrote almost exclusively on social, economic, and other nonliterary matters. Since most of the early Agrarian leaders were creative writers, or critics, or both, the literary and aesthetic segment of their philosophy has received much elaboration. However, perhaps the very heart of Agrarianism is its economic thought, its stress on subsistence agriculture, and its celebration of the yeoman farmer and the social tradition which he allegedly represented.

Chapter III   Agrarian Economic Thought

AFTER THEY STATED THEIR ECONOMIC PROPOSALS, THE AGRARIANS WERE identified by many reviewers as proponents of a back-to-the-land movement based on subsistence agriculture. Their ideal was a self-sufficient farmer providing for all his family's needs away from the perils of the industrial system and a money economy. Examples of this Agrarian ideal still existed in the rural South as remnants of the ante-bellum establishment; but now the North threatened to complete the destruction of the South's traditional society by a new economic and cultural invasion. In defense, the Agrarians revived the once-revered idyll of "life close to the soil." However, for strategic reasons *I'll Take My Stand* avoided giving too detailed an economic blueprint; nor did the authors themselves set much of an example by going to the land. Speaking of unfriendly editors, and especially of the editor of the Nashville *Tennesseean,* Allen Tate said that "they need only to draw portraits of us plowing or clearing the spring to make hash of us before we get a hearing."[1] Unfortunately, agriculture in the United States, and especially in the South, was suffering a chronic depression. It had been depressed all during the twenties when business and industry enjoyed a boom. Also, the Agrarians acted after there had been several decades of "New South" activity to reform and modernize Southern agriculture with new scientific methods.

The authors of the symposium assumed that the reader understood the basic implications of the dichotomy, industrial versus agrarian. "Opposed to the industrial society is the agrarian," they wrote, "which does not stand in particular need of definition."[2] In line with this attitude they offered the following initial explanation of what they meant. More ample definitions were to follow.

An agrarian society is hardly one that has no use at all for industries, for professional vocations, for scholars and artists, and for the life of cities. Technically, perhaps, an agrarian society is one in which agriculture is the leading vocation, whether for wealth, for pleasure, or for prestige—a form of labor that is pursued with intelligence and leisure, and that becomes the model to which the other forms approach as well as they may. But an agrarian system will be secured readily enough where the superfluous industries are not allowed to rise against it. The theory of agrarianism is that the culture of the soil is the best and most sensitive of vocations, and that therefore it should have the economic preference and enlist the maximum number of workers. (pp. xviii–xix)

Much of the introduction to *I'll Take My Stand* was devoted to a many-sided attack on industrialism. Most of the time the Agrarians supported agrarianism only by implication. "These principles," they declared, " do not intend to be very specific in proposing any practical measures." Later the Agrarians were compelled by their critics to detail what could be done, right then and there, to advance the prospects of an agrarian society. The initial "stand" itself, however, disappointed those critics who wanted definite answers to such questions as: What exactly was meant by the "restoration of agrarian principles?" How could an agrarian economy survive alongside a powerful industrial economy? How should an Agrarian family live, conduct its daily affairs, and satisfy the normal demands of human existence? The answers to these and similar questions would determine the validity of the entire Agrarian challenge. Without a solid socioeconomic foundation, the whole ideology could be made to seem quixotic and untenable.

In his lead essay, "Reconstructed But Unregenerate," Ranson elaborated on some of the points first made in the Introduction. The agrarian society that he admired was primarily one in the English and Southern social tradition. He envied the "material establishment" of England and the "stable economic system by which Englishmen are content to take their livelihood from the physical environment." By "environment" Ransom meant the "soil." The early pioneers in Britain, presumably the Anglo-Saxons, "explored the soil, determined what concessions it might reasonably be expected to make them, housed themselves, developed all their necessary trades, and arrived by painful experiment at a thousand satisfactory recipes by which they might secure their material necessities." On these simple precepts the English built their establishment; they acquired a tradition which could be inherited, and along with it "a leisure, a security, and an intellectual freedom" which Ransom found possible now only in the remaining "self-sufficient, backward-looking, intensely provincial communities" (p. 5). It was not the England of the industrial revolution that interested Ransom—or the England of world commerce, or the England of the great empire on which the sun never set.

The fact that many provincial communities still existed in the American South encouraged Ransom to hope that some important check could be held against rampant modernism, industrialism, and progress. Like the England of tradition, the South of tradition "pioneered her way to a sufficiently comfortable and rural sort of establishment, considered that an establishment was something stable, and proceeded to enjoy the fruits thereof" (p. 12). He claimed for the Old South a proper balance between work and play; both were surrounded with "a leisure which permitted the activity of intelligence." The so-called aristocrats who led Southern society were not artificial and showy; they were "mostly home-made and countrified," and thus deserved to be called squires rather than aristocrats. The social orders, according to Ransom, were loosely defined, with interrelations that were personal and friendly. "It is my thesis," Ransom explained, "that all were committed to a form of leisure, and that their labor itself was leisurely" (p. 11). Nowhere in the essay was Ransom specific about the status of farm life in the actual contemporary South—the South that included Tobacco Road—with its problems of production, marketing, tenancy, sharecropping, the boll weevil, poverty, isolation, and the like. He composed a vague georgics whose main point was that the agrarian society provided man with the leisure necessary for his highest spiritual cultivation.

Nor was the historian Frank L. Owsley any more specific about defining agrarian economics in his symposium essay, "The Irrepressible Conflict," although in later writings both he and Ransom did seek to give a more solid economic basis to their concept of agrarianism. In his essay, Owsley outlined the historical importance of agrarianism to the South and to the Civil War and its aftermath. His emphasis on the economic causes of the conflict made it possible for him to minimize Negro slavery—the moral issue—as a mere red herring, even though earlier he wrote that the South was "ruined by the loss of nearly $2,000,000,000 invested in slaves," an item which seems to entangle morality with a lot of hard cash. He wrote:

Complex though the factors were which finally caused war, they all grew out of two fundamental differences which existed between the two sections: the North was commercial and industrial, and the South was agrarian. The fundamental and passionate ideal for which the South stood and fell was the ideal of an agrarian society. All else, good and bad, revolved around this ideal

—the old and accepted manner of life for which Egypt, Greece, Rome, England, and France had stood. History and literature, profane and sacred, twined their tendrils about the cottage and the villa, not the factory. (p. 69)

We might outline Owsley's idyll of the soil as follows. Blessed by climate and fertile land, the South from its earliest colonial days enjoyed the richness of an agrarian economy. Only a few of its settlers were of the gentry; most were yeomen from rural England with "centuries of country and farm lore and folk memory. Each word, name, sound, had grown from the soil and had behind it sweet memory, stirring adventure, and ofttimes stark tragedy. Thoughts, words, ideas, life itself, grew from the soil. The environment all pointed toward an endless enjoyment of the fruits of the soil." Owsley invoked Jefferson's dream of a free America as a "boundless Utopia of farms" requiring a thousand generations to fill. Speaking of the agrarian tradition, Owsley said the Southerner loved best of all the Romans of the early republic because they "were brave, sometimes crude, but open and without guile—unlike the Greeks. They reeked of the soil, of the plow and the spade; they had wrestled with virgin soil and forests; they could build log houses and were closer to many Southerners than even the English gentleman in his moss-covered stone house" (p. 70). Returning to the Old South, Owsley repeated Ransom's notion that it was "leisurely and unhurried" for the planter, the yeoman, or the landless tenant. Close to the soil, the system was a satisfying way of life and not a mere routine of planting and reaping for profit. Owsley wrote:

It might be organized about the plantation with its wide fields and its slaves and self-sufficiency, or it might center around a small farm, ranging from a fifty-acre to a five-hundred-acre tract, tilled by the owner, undriven by competition, supplied with corn by his own toil and with meat from his own pen or from the fields and forests. The amusements might be the fine balls and house parties of the planter or the three-day break-down dances which David Crockett loved, or horse races, foot races, cock and dog fights, boxing, wrestling, shooting, fighting, log-rolling, house raising, or corn-shucking. It might be crude or genteel, but it everywhere was fundamentally alike and natural. The houses were homes, where families lived sufficient and complete within themselves, working together and fighting together. And when death came, they were buried in their own lonely peaceful graveyards, to await doomsday together. (pp. 71–72)

Discussing the social and political issues of the "irrepressible conflict," Owsley focused on the basic economic antagonism between the agrarian South and the industrial North. The economics of the former was not again importantly reflected in *I'll Take My Stand* until the middle of the book, with Herman Clarence Nixon's article "Whither Southern Economy?" Nixon gave a relatively unemotional account, with supporting statistics, of the role that agriculture had played in Southern history. He seemed to be interested in agrarianism primarily as a balance against a "dollar-chasing industrialism" whose highest aim was commercial success. The spread of the "Southern worship of industrial gods" was deplorable, he wrote, "in view of the South's opportunity, as noted by Count Keyserling and Glenn Frank, to offer a hope of cultural escape from the evils of industrialism" (p. 177). From the outset Nixon conceded that Southern industry was here to stay, there being no point in a war with "destiny or the census returns." But he said the "industrial civilization under the capitalistic system does not offer a satisfying substitute in human values" for the traditional agrarian society that is now in grave peril (p. 199). Therefore, the South must check its industrial expansion, achieve the economic balance enjoyed by a country such as France, and try to prevent the United States from plunging into an imperialist industrial scramble which was bound to engender a major war.

The bulk of Nixon's essay recorded the rather familiar facts about the South's agricultural history, including the overriding importance of cotton. He blamed the Civil War for a number of specific evils, all of them related to the damage done to the evolving regional economy. Nixon believed that the war was not necessary, either for Southern industrial development or for the early end of slavery. He took the position, quite contrary to that held by Broadus Mitchell and D. A. Tompkins and other New South leaders, that the Civil War disrupted the South's natural evolution toward a balanced society. Whereas Tompkins wrote that *defeat* in the war eventually brought the South back to the balanced economy it was building prior to 1810, Nixon said: "The so-called old South, with its recruited aristocracy, was working toward a balanced industry, a reformed agriculture, and a free school system for the yeoman, when the war upset the orderly process of evolution" (p. 188). His outline of industrial progress within the agrarian South serves mainly as a warning to those who wish for too rapid and pervasive a growth of an alien, aggressive economy associated with the region's traditional enemies. Whither Southern economy? It should be toward a proper balance in which the agrarian values flourished as in the glorious past.

Ransom, of course, had indicated the same direction. He had asked, "Will the Southern establishment, the most substantial exhibit on this continent of a society of the European and historic order, be completely crumbled by the powerful acid of the Great Progressivist Principle?" (p. 17). He had appealed for a new kind of reconstruction and for new allies: the Western farmers and the "ancient New England townships," despite the fact that most of these townships had been abolitionist in the past. All rural life in America had to be defended so that society might return to "the quiet rural life of the early modern period," that is, to the Middle Ages. While other Agrarians compared the South's position in the United States with that of Ireland in respect to England (as Edmund Wilson had also done), Ransom preferred Scotland as his analogue and praised Scottish stubbornness as a trait for Southerners to emulate. A firm rejection of Americanism, which Ransom demanded, "would show decidedly a sense of what the Germans call *Realpolitik*. It could be nasty and it could be effective" (p. 17). Later on in *I'll Take My Stand*, Tate asked and answered an important question regarding strategy: "We are very near an answer to our question—How may the Southerner take hold of his tradition? The answer is: by violence" (p. 174).

The Agrarians disclaimed any attempt to exploit the difficulties besetting industrialism as a result of the depression; yet some of the most revealing aspects of their stand did emerge as solutions to the general crisis. As the decade advanced, the term "subsistence farming," as opposed to commercial farming entered more and more into their vocabulary. The term also signified the growth of a more specific economic program. In 1932, Ransom published an essay "Land!" with the subtitle "An Answer to the Unemployment Problem." In it he referred to the other important back-to-the-land movement of the day, the one sponsored by the industrialist Henry Ford. Ransom favored Ford's endeavor, but with one serious qualification. Whereas the Detroit magnate urged the farmer to operate a "money economy" on his farm during the warm months, and then work in a factory during the winter, Ransom urged him to remain on his land the year around on a subsistence basis. That is, the farmer as a true Agrarian had to be "his own carpenter, painter, roadmaker, forester, meat packer, woodcutter, gardener, landscape gardener, nurseryman, dairyman, poulterer, and handy man."[3] Thus, the farmer could do without the specialist in each of the categories and would not need to pay money for someone else's labor. Ransom wanted to see a kind of "Renaissance man" on the land who could be self-sufficient no matter how severe the social crisis outside his immediate holdings.

In another essay the following year, "Happy Farmers," Ransom detailed at some length the agrarian program supported by his group. So vital was this document considered that it was reprinted for wider distribution as a pamphlet. It appeared originally in a new journal, the *American Review*, whose pages were to remain open to Agrarian writers until its demise in 1937. By then its major policy was to give aid and comfort to the cause of General Franco in Spain. The magazine's editor, Seward Collins, wrote of Ransom's essay: "The longest discussion of Agrarianism has been Mr. Ransom's *Happy Farmers* (October)."[4] At about this time, 1932, Ransom was in England where he seems to have made a strenuous effort to learn more about economics. While there, he acquainted himself more fully with English Distributism, a doctrine defended especially by such Catholic writers as G. K. Chesterton and Hilaire Belloc. Distributism was not exclusively agrarian in tendency—indeed, it seemed more concerned with modern guildsmen and artisans than with dirt farmers—but it shared with Agrarianism a desire for small property ownership and a distaste for the giantism of finance capitalism. At any rate, Ransom in "Happy Farmers" again depicted the farmer as a Renaissance man with many types of skills. This jack-of-all-trades was expected

to raise the great bulk of the foods for the family, including vegetables, fruits, poultry, dairy products, meats; to can, preserve, and cure for the winter (this involves the smoke-house); to do plain carpentering to the extent at least of repairs; to paint and white-wash, to do amateur landscape gardening, in order that the home may be pleasant and decent; to work mainly with literal horse-power, mule-power, man-power; to feed all the animals, as well as the persons, from the land; to fertilize the land by the periodic use of grass crops. All these measures tend to cancel out heavily the farmer's need for money.[5]

To the massive statistics and other evidence of agricultural crisis the Agrarians had a stock reply based on their firm distinction between *subsistence* and *commercial* farming. Only commercial farming was doomed; the agricultural crisis developed when farmers tried to be rural capitalists and grew crops for money. "The only permanent rescue for commercial agriculture in this country," Ransom wrote, "would be by a desperate measure, the act of a Soviet or other tyranny" (p. 523). Like many other Southern spokesmen, he also blamed the protective tariff on manufactured goods for much of the regional poverty. The higher prices maintained for manufactured goods simply meant increased costs to the South for these goods without any compensatory return in terms of markets for Southern exports; in fact, many foreign markets were lost due to lessening American purchases from abroad. Another problem facing both commercial and subsistence farmers involved mortgages and taxation. Ransom wrote, "Not long ago the land received an exorbitant valuation, first from the bankers who lent money on it, and second from the public assessors who levied taxes" (p. 520). However, of the two basic kinds of farmer, the one practicing subsistence agriculture, according to Ransom, was in the better position to escape these ills.

To deliberately prevent the Agrarian farmer from wishing to be a rural capitalist, to keep him isolated from scientific methods, and to discourage his dependence on a profit crop, he should be forced to pay high taxes when buying commercial fertilizers, tractors, and other machinery. He should also be taxed for what Ransom called "fresh loans" in order to help him overcome a major cause of his past woes— his habit of borrowing. Local land taxes, on the other hand, should be reduced, and subsidies from the government should be relatively higher for the small householder. The prospective agricultural schools should teach the young how to operate a true subsistence economy and not merely how to make money on the land. Speaking of government and the New Deal, then in power in Washington, Ransom said, "It is the word Agrarian, or its equivalent, which we have been waiting to hear pronounced by this Democratic and pro-farmer administration" (p. 528).

The Agrarians were to wait in vain, even though the New Deal and President Roosevelt did show great interest in the economics of regionalism. At various times the Agrarians tried to influence the New Deal in their direction, but they met with little success because the administration was strongly oriented toward the liberals of "New South" persuasion, toward the social scientists represented by Howard W. Odum of North Carolina. Ransom praised the New Deal's recognition that the nation was composed of geographic regions, each with its own past development and special current problems; but this negative comment on President Roosevelt is more in keeping with the general Agrarian position.

He applauds the present movement from city to country, and will not see in it only one of those temporary distress migrations that occur in depressions when wretched labourers go anywhere to find work, but a movement that is good in itself and must not be reversed when prosperity returns to the city. With one hand he measures acreage out of production, and with the other hand waves city men to the farm. (p. 526)

Troy J. Cauley in *Agrarianism* echoed this thought of Ransom's when he wrote, "The New Deal is, of course, full of contradictions with respect to agriculture. At the same time that the government is hiring one group of farmers to destroy crops, it is lending money to another group to enable them to continue farming when they could not otherwise do so."[6]

Cauley had other complaints to make against the New Deal. He opposed the whole idea of the Agricultural Adjustment Administration because the "control of agricultural production is not within the powers of man" (p. 99). He considered the Subsistence Homestead Projects to be merely demonstrational in nature and not to be regarded as a means for the general restoration of agrarianism. Nor was the New Deal, in Cauley's opinion, a bulwark against possible unpleasant developments. He said, "Although the Roosevelt administration has not yet instituted any measures which can definitely be termed Communistic, it has launched upon a program which has some of the characteristics of what is usually called State Socialism" (p. 94). The basic criticism of the New Deal, however, was that it did not understand and promote a genuine agrarianism, but tried instead to help people earn money from working the land. In addition, it must be said that the self-styling of the Agrarians as "reactionaries" and "revolutionaries of the right" did not endear them to the agricultural leadership of the first Roosevelt administration. President Roosevelt, Secretary of Agriculture Henry A. Wallace, and other government leaders never regarded agriculture as a sacred "way of life." They surely never had a vision like that of John Crowe Ransom when he wrote:

It is tempting to write like a poet, philosopher, or humanist about the aesthetic and spiritual deliverance that will come when the industrial laborers with their specialized and routine jobs and the business men with their offices and abstract preoccupations become translated into people handling the soil with their fingers and coming into direct contact with nature.[7]

As the public debate engaging the Agrarians proceeded, the manner of acquiring and using land became of great importance. They had to answer the questions: How are the landless going to get the land they need on which to subsist? And what is the best way in which to use the available land? Herbert Agar in *Land of the Free* referred to Ransom in regard to the second question. The type of exploitation of the land depended on the two general and conflicting attitudes toward farming. Agar praised Ransom for having clearly distinguished between them. "For the purpose of fitting into our money-making economy," Ransom had written, "the abundance of our land is a national liability, and those who make a business of it are only infatuated. But for the purpose of home-making, for the breeding of citizens, for the attainment of personal happiness, it is the finest physical asset that we have, and enough to make us blessed among the nations."[8]

Agar found in another important Agrarian document, Owsley's "The Pillars of Agrarianism," a practical suggestion about how to offer available land to the landless. A realistic federal program would make possible "the restoration of the people to the land and the land to the people by the government purchasing lands held by loan companies, insurance companies, banks, absentee landlords, and planters whose estates are hopelessly encumbered with debt, and granting to the landless tenants, who are sufficiently able and responsible to own and conserve the land, a homestead of eighty acres with sufficient stock to cultivate the farm and cash enough to feed and clothe the family for a year."[9] Similar proposals were embodied in the Bankhead Bill aimed at establishing a Tenant Farms Corporation that would buy up to 15,000,000 acres owned by insurance companies, federal land banks, and indigent owners. Outright possession of the land would devolve to the farmer with annual payments of around $80 for some thirty years.

The most elaborate synthesis of Agrarian economic thought can be found in Troy J. Cauley's *Agrarianism: A Program for Farmers*. In reviewing the book for the first issue of the *Southern Review* Rupert Vance said that it marked "the transition from a literary movement to agricultural economics."[10] In the Preface, Cauley related his program to that already espoused by the Agrarians. "Many of the ideas expressed," he wrote, "are quite similar to those of the Nashville group of Agrarians as contained in their book *I'll Take My Stand* and in their other publications, notably the articles which have appeared in *The American Review*."[11] He agreed with the majority of their opinions and at the same time excused them from any responsibility for the defects to be found in his own. He wrote, "I have undertaken to work out something of a synthesis and to indicate briefly, and no doubt inadequately, a possible line of action." In the absence of Agrarian disavowals we can assume that the Cauley study was welcomed in the growing arsenal of documents. If *Agrarianism* did have certain serious defects, the others in the group seemed willing to overlook them.

The first six chapters present Cauley's analysis of the status of agriculture in the general economy of the time; the last five deal with the merits and the defects of agrarianism, the various causes for its decline and suggestions for its restoration. Of primary interest are Cauley's definitions, his attitudes toward social values, his criticisms of rival economies, and his concrete suggestions for the desired results—those "practical measures" which *I'll Take My Stand* declined to specify. Cauley's own broad definition of Agrarianism is very close to that of Ransom in the original Statement of Principles. He wrote:

Agrarianism may be roughly and tentatively defined as an economic and social system under which the chief method of making a living is that of tilling the soil, with a consequent rather wide dispersion of population and a relative meagerness of commercial intercourse. It is, probably, simply the antithesis of Industrial Capitalism. (p. 3)

Cauley also severely attacked both the capitalist and socialist veneration for industrial progress. He condemned science. He repeated Ransom's distinction between commercial and subsistence farming and based much of his argument on it. At the more abstract and philosophical level, he stressed the spread of individual freedom that he believed would accompany the successful growth of the Agrarian-Distributist program.

Cauley felt that, among other things, the modern South lacked a sufficiently widespread ownership of land, which was the key to a genuine agrarian economy. Each family, he wrote, should own enough land and equipment to afford it a decent and satisfying living with the use of reasonable effort and foresight. A farmer, self-sufficient on his land, was about "the most independent specimen" to be found in this country. He could be independent in politics, in ethics, in his general actions. Cauley said that private property, in the basic sense of the term, had disappeared in America, and its restoration was essential before the agrarian society could be reconstructed. Not as conscious as Ransom of the aesthetic values inherent in contact with the soil, Cauley was nonetheless aware of such values. He said, "There is something invigorating and inspiring in the struggle with the untoward forces of nature; there is nothing of the sort in the process of standing in line in front of an employment agency" (p. 109).

Cauley advanced a rather curious theory about the manner in which Agrarianism should deal with the problem of scarcity. The Agrarian economy need devote little effort to the increase of available goods. He said, "Chiefly it meets the problem by reducing the number and variety of material wants" (p. 137). People subsisting on the land will not feel poor if they can be convinced they have all they need. Cauley listed three ways by which the reduction of wants could be accomplished. First, by the natural isolation of rural life. "You don't want what other people have unless you see them or otherwise learn of their having it. Country people do not see each other in nearly so great numbers or nearly so often as do city people" (p. 113). Second, by insulation against the aggressive promotional practices of capitalist society. Genuine rural communities "are not afflicted by that most efficient creator of scarcity of all time, modern advertising." Cauley considered such salesmanship the essence of a highly organized exchange system; by the same token, it was utterly foreign to a self-sufficient Agrarian economy. Third, by the pursuit of other means of gaining prestige than by exhibiting lavish material goods. For instance, in country life the struggle for personal recognition could take the form of local contests such as log rolling and horseshoe pitching. He continues, "The Agrarian method of removing scarcity by reducing the amount of goods wanted has the further great merit that it offers leisure which is capable of being engaged—true leisure as distinct from mere enforced idleness. The essence of the beneficial use of leisure is complete relaxation from any nervous tension and the doing of things purely for the fun of doing them." (p. 117–18).

Cauley listed other major advantages of Agrarianism. There was greater hospitality and companionship in rural regions than in others. He said, "The point is that an agrarian community, together with the adjacent villages which are an integral part of agrarian economy, offers opportunities for contact with just a sufficient number of persons with the proper degree of leisure for the most satisfying human companionship" (p. 121). The farmer also had a satisfying relationship with nature, a point which Ransom developed quite fully when he discussed the merits of regionalism. People enjoyed better health in farm localities than in the big cities and suffered less from neuroses and insanity. Even the suicide rate was lower. Cauley cited the studies of Mencken and his associates on the *American Mercury*[12] to prove that "the rate of suicide in the near-agrarian Southern states is distinctly lower than in the industrial states of other sections of the country" (p. 122). Ruralism also fostered the growth of a number of other virtues: self-reliance, physical courage, moral integrity, and personal loyalty.

As for the defects of Agrarianism, Cauley justified some of them historically, pronounced others to be actual virtues in disguise, and then indicated how the remainder could be erased by a correct functioning of the Agrarian system. About the prevalence of poverty in the South, he said that it could not be denied "that in many localities the people as such are of inferior quality," but actually no more so in the South than elsewhere (p. 128). He admitted that laziness could be a special Southern trait—but for that one must blame the heat. Nature was also to blame for the paucity of farm animals. He said, "Perhaps the most frequent criticism made of Southern agriculture by experts is the lack of livestock on the farms; and one of the chief causes of this lack is the extreme prevalence of insect pests and parasites" not to mention the extremes of rain and drought (p. 133). Another weakness of Southern rural life was the Negro's apparent willingness to live in poverty. On the whole, they were "relatively well satisfied with extremely low standards of living" and on such a level of living they turned out products which sold "in competition with those of the white farmers" (p. 135). Cauley's point was that Negroes were able to undercut and undersell because they had less need for money. He did not indicate the sources regarding the alleged satisfaction of the Negro farmers.

Like the liberals, Cauley also considered the tenant system a blight on the Southern economy, but he felt its evils had been too often discussed to bear further rehashing in his book. One cause for its magnitude was the loss of Southern capital during the Civil War—capital which was never recovered. Another cause was the protective tariff. "The tenant farmer," Cauley wrote, "sells his bale of cotton in a world market at a world price, but the pair of shoes he buys for his barefooted wife was probably made in Lynn, Massachusetts, and the price which he pays for it includes a good increment made possible by a protective tariff" (p. 137).

Closely related to the low material standards of Southerners was a higher death rate and what Cauley called a higher "morbidity rate" than in most other parts of America. Southerners were often morbid in outlook and tended to brood over their fate. For this condition, too, the climate was mostly to blame. As for the primitive medical facilities, Cauley felt that this condition was more or less inevitable in an Agrarian mode of life. The farm folk had so much, they could not have everything. Besides, they had less need for medical care because they were healthier to begin with. Among the other defects of Agrarianism which Cauley mentioned and found means to rationalize were: isolation, religious intolerance, widespread ignorance, and excessive work for all including women and children. However, the new Agrarian society, according to Cauley, need have none of these admitted evils.

First of all, along with less desirable people there were already many people of good quality in rural areas, and a new Agrarianism would attract more of them, even from the cities. The relatively low standard of living in Agrarian communities (Ransom himself had stated this belief) actually constituted "one of their chief economic assets." Cauley explained this assertion by repeating the familiar argument that Agrarians should meet "the universal problem of scarcity by the simple expedient of reducing the amount of goods wanted" (p. 152). He advocated only a sufficient struggle with the untoward forces of nature to win from her an "honorable compromise" which would provide for reasonable human needs and leave much leisure for other pursuits.

Ignorance and intolerance, often attributed to Southern rural life, were by no means limited to this region of America. Seeming to follow an idea of T. S. Eliot, Cauley stated that "the people of any one culture are always prone to be intolerant of the ways of the people of another culture" (p. 157). On this basis Eliot had persuaded Christians that it was natural for them to feel animosity towards Jews. On the same basis, fundamentalists in the South might be somewhat bigoted, Cauley wrote, but on "aesthetic grounds" there was much to be said in favor of a "brush-arbor camp meeting in the hills of north Georgia." As for ignorance of the type derided by Mencken, it was at best a relative matter. As the Nashville Agrarians had indicated, successful farm living was richer and more complex than urban living. Once the alien commercial drive that had been imported into rural areas had vanished, farmers would have no particular trouble in supporting better schools. Besides, getting an education was really an individual problem; everyone could read books without attending a school at all. As for the final defect listed above—hard labor for women and children— such unhappy conditions applied to all of American agriculture, not only to the South; and they applied with more vengeance to commercial than to subsistence farming. The struggle to produce a cash crop was more urgent, more intense, while a "more diversified subsistence type of farming is not characterized by these sharp seasonal peaks in the demand for labor" (p. 168).

Toward the end of his book, Cauley examined the reasons for the decline of agrarianism. The major causes had been the growth of an urban industrial economy and an agriculture dominated by commercialism and the vagaries of a nonregional market. Other important causes for agrarian decline included the rapid advance in technology, the rise of science, the abundance of material resources in proportion to the population, and the breakdown of both tradition and revealed religion. To revive agrarianism on a large scale meant first to eliminate as many as possible of the causes of its decline. Cauley wrote, "If the farmer cannot make a great deal of money, relief is obviously to be found in reducing the amount of money which the farmer needs" (p. 187). The protective tariff, the tax system, and corporation laws had all increased the farmer's need for money without in any way enabling him to make more. As a result, he now needed cash for taxes, for interest on his mortgage and principle, and for manufactured goods and for what Cauley described as "exotic" foodstuffs.

The tax structure, he believed, should be revised downward in order to favor the farmer in his assessment. A satisfactory arrangement with respect to this matter would be to have all property of a single owner up to $5000 in value exempt from the general property tax entirely. For values above this figure the tax should be graduated. The extensive practice of Agrarianism would lower the cost of government because many of its present services could be curtailed or discontinued entirely; hence there need be no high taxes whatsoever. Cauley did favor a general sales tax, deeming it a sensible proposal because Agrarians with meager cash could not buy much anyway. On the serious problem of mortgages he suggested that the federal government furnish improved credit facilities to farmers in distress. To keep their restored economy stable, future Agrarians should not permit themselves to fall into any great debt. In order to lower the cost of necessary purchases, virtually all protective tariffs would have to be abolished.

Finally, every device known to the promotion experts had to be used to induce people to desire land. Cauley wrote, "People must come to desire the ownership of property as against the receipt of money income." The very heart of any realistic restoration of agrarianism was "the unencumbered ownership of the land by the tillers thereof" (p. 199). This idea became a refrain during the thirties among all the leading Agrarians. For example, Owsley wrote "Such property thus widely held must . . . in the very nature of things, be *personally controlled*, or it would cease to have much value as the basic instrumentation of the right to life, liberty, the pursuit of happiness, and self-government."[13] Thomas Jefferson had a similar concept of the relationship between liberty and property. Now, with the help of the government, society could realize this Jeffersonian ideal. To help destroy the non-Agrarian system of land ownership, Cauley advocated a particularly high rate of taxation on land held by absentee owners; in the past, an excess of land owned by townspeople had been responsible for the disastrous one-crop system of farming. The townsfolk were interested in the soil only for profit; they had no desire to make a living on the land itself. Cauley suggested that the tax on absentee landlords be made progressive on the basis of the degree to which they were "absent in a geographical sense." The farther away their holdings, the higher should be their tax. Other tax proposals were also meant to discourage commercial farming, by destroying the investment value of farm land and by helping families to settle new farms on a subsistence basis.

Cauley's views on government loans were equally radical and bold. He advised that loans be granted to farmers to the extent of 75 to 80 per cent of the combined value of their land and improvements thereon. As a transitional move leading to a system of individually-owned farms, the government should develop public inspection and regulation of existing landlord-tenant relationships. And for the ultimate achievement of these fundamental social changes, the United States needed a spiritual rebirth of the mass of the people. The obsolete idea that discontent is "divine" must disappear from the popular mind; instead, discontent must come to be regarded as the "generally undesirable thing" that it truly was.

Several months after the publication of *Agrarianism*, Cauley wrote an essay on the integration of Agrarian and exchange—that is, capitalist—economies for the *American Review*. He repeated some of the proposals he had made in his book as well as some that had been made previously by Owsley, the Agrarian, and by Hilaire Belloc, the English Distributist. He suggested, for example, that barter instead of money could provide for the exotic foodstuffs "such as sugar, spices, and tropical fruits."[14] Since man needed some medium or method of exchange, it was perhaps inevitable that barter should be proposed in view of the constant denigration of money. Another important idea in the essay originated from Owsley, who by this time (1935) had joined those who favored a system of regional governments as an effective means of fighting the economic and political leviathanism of modern society. The new tariff policy of America should be determined by treaty between these regional governments. Another novel proposal concerned the granting of government loans; it should be a condition of all loans made for the purchase of land that the borrower "pursue a programme of diversified farming, as against specialized one-crop farming, in a way approved by the County Agricultural Agent or some other qualified authority" (p. 593). As a further disciplinary measure, Cauley favored Owsley's plan that all land ownership should be on a "contingent" basis; a farmer could not keep the land unless he took all precautions to prevent its exhaustion through erosion and other causes. It was hoped that these measures would effect a system that could keep the farmers permanently divorced from addiction to money-making. The same result could eventually be achieved for those people who lived in towns; here, too, the Agrarian social ethic called for a general

AGRARIAN ECONOMIC THOUGHT | 49

distribution of property. "As Hilaire Belloc has pointed out," Cauley wrote, "the freehold miller can be a free man as well as the freehold farmer" (p. 591). This statement appropriately signifies the alliance which by mid-decade had taken place between the Agrarians and the Distributists.

The foregoing brings together all the vital *concrete* economic views which the Agrarians expressed in their writings. Their alliance with the Distributists had little or no effect on economic theory; that is, it required no alteration or compromise in principle. The fundamental advice for all Southerners remained: Return to the land, become a subsistence farmer, and remove yourself from reliance on money. As stated earlier, the Agrarians began issuing this advice at a time when agriculture everywhere was in a serious depression. The surprise and even ridicule that greeted *I'll Take My Stand* had some basis in the chronic rural crisis just mentioned. The American farmer had been in serious trouble since the catastrophic drop in market prices that occurred in 1921. The greatest drop had been in prices paid to the producers at the farm. This very real and desperate situation could not help but dampen the enthusiasm of those who might be followers of the Nashville regionalists. According to statistics cited by John D. Black in *Agricultural Reform in the United States,* the index of farm prices had skyrocketed during World War I to a peak of 210, with 100 (the level for 1915) forming the norm. In 1921, the index suddenly fell to almost 120, at a time when the factors causing overproduction had enormously increased. Black's charts illustrate that prices subsequently stabilized at too low a level to permit any significant economic recovery. Thus, agriculture in America went from the 1921 crash to the even worse crash of 1929 without having enjoyed an intermediate peak in prosperity.

Writing in 1929, Black states, "The outstanding fact in the agricultural situation at present is that financial improvement in agriculture has almost ceased since 1924. . . ."[15] This stagnation was reflected in the fact that from 1920 to 1928 the farm population declined by 3,820,000—from 31,614,000 to 27,794,000. One important reason was "the mechanization of agriculture which has taken a new spurt since 1915 with the wide adoption of the motor car and truck, the tractor, and the combine harvester for small grains."[16] The most vital reason of all, in Black's view, was the slackening of agricultural expansion into new areas. This cause of stagnation applied particularly to the South where agriculture had traditionally spread by the development of new lands. An added problem which ruined and otherwise impoverished countless farmers was the boll weevil, an insidious pest that destroyed crop after crop of cotton. There are numerous sources detailing the gravity of the agricultural crisis. Of course, not all farmers were indigent; but enough of them were to make their occupation financially unattractive. Even Cauley felt compelled to quote figures about the farmer's low income. As his authority he used Bernhard Ostrolenk who proved in *The Surplus Farmer* that "from 1919 to 1930 the average farmer received from his own labor and that of his family less than $700 annually. This is less than he paid his hired man for a whole year's work, and less by half than is paid to unskilled labor in American cities for a year's work."[17]

More pertinent to the present purpose are those sources that deal directly with the effects of the agricultural crisis in the South. To those familiar with the hard facts, the Agrarian praise for "life close to the soil"—their making a virtue of its very backwardness, stagnation, and poverty—seemed at best unrealistic and at worst a bit of humbug. The intent was misleading: to convince penniless farm people that their lot was actually a moral and spiritual boon, that they could enjoy a superior "way of life" without having to raise a money crop, that they could find satisfaction by reducing their wants, that they could be patriotic traditional Southerners, find God in nature, and rise above the evils of industrial society. The following, however, are some of the hard facts which liberal Southerners and other critics brought forth to refute the Agrarian position.

Rupert B. Vance, a social scientist associated with the liberal group at North Carolina, spoke of the "disastrous period 1920–1930" in regard to the great increase of *white* farm tenancy in the South, using this factor as an index of the chronic crisis in the agricultural system. He wrote, "Of the one and four-fifths million tenants found by the 1930 census in sixteen Southern states, over 60 *per cent* were white."[18] Tenancy had been looked upon as a modified form of serfdom attendant upon the destruction of Negro slavery, but, from 1880 to 1930 the trend was for its steady increase, not for its disappearance. Speaking of the earlier period, Vance said, "The first tenure census of 1880, showing over 25 *per cent* tenancy, brought dismay to those who believed that America would pass beyond the land tenure conditions of the Old World." In the fifty years that followed, the tenancy problem grew worse. Vance continued, "By 1930 about 53 *per cent* of the farmers operated leased land and 42 *per cent* rented all the land they tilled."[19] No doubt the Agrarians, if they searched, could find individual farmers happily subsisting here and there on their own land, but history testified against them. Most Southern farmers had been forced to become sharecroppers, metayers, renters.

Another liberal scholar, W. T. Couch, in *Culture in the South* (1935), outlined the evils prevalent in farm tenancy. The conditions existing in Southern rural life had become even worse than they had been before 1930. About the rural South which the Agrarians had ardently defended Couch had the following words to say:

> One finds 1,790,000 tenant farmers, white and black. One finds the last stronghold of child labor. One finds women who have to cook, sew, wash and iron, who have to work regularly in the fields planting, hoeing, and harvesting, and who are not protected by any laws or customs regulating their hours of labor. The system is so thoroughly bad that no laws can be devised which, so long as the system exists, can protect the women and children who are a part of it.[20]

Professor Couch admitted there were serious faults in the industrial culture of America, but he questioned the assertion that Agrarianism could provide a better life. Looking into the past, he could not find anything in the Southern tradition, insofar as the average person was concerned, that merited restoration. He concluded that the Agrarians had never known or imagined the long-drawn-out misery of overwork and undernourishment, of poverty and isolation, of ignorance, disease, and despair.

Despite these and other instances of agrarian crisis, the early depression years did in fact register a substantial movement from the big cities back to the land. Most observers attribute this not to the natural attractiveness of farming, whose conditions were bleak, but to the equally severe suffering of the urban jobless. The unfortunates forced to emigrate hardly needed the proddings of Henry Ford with his highly touted back-to-the-land crusade or the siren songs of the Agrarians urging them to exchange the debris of city slums for the dust of country roads. Statistics vary as to the extent of this social migration. William V. Owen in *Labor Problems* gave some interesting data: "In 1932 the movement back to the farm resulted in the rural areas showing a net gain from the cities of 266,000 persons. The tide shifted toward the cities with the recovery of the middle 1930's until in 1936 the cities had a net gain of 450,000 persons."[21]

Cauley in *Agrarianism* offered some figures on the actual number of people returning to the land without referring to the relative gain or loss mentioned by Owen. These figures apply to the entire nation and not just to the South: "More than 546,000 people moved from the cities to the farms throughout the country during the first three months of 1932, according to a statement issued by the federal department of agriculture. Still more impressive, as indicating the reversal of the trek from the farms to the cities during the decade from 1920 to 1930, is the report of the department that during 1931 656,000 city workers, mostly unemployed, went back to farm life, and 416,000 in 1930."[22] Cauley indicated that 86.7 per cent of the returnees had had previous farm experience; hence the best solution for the problem of 11,000,000 unemployed was to send them back to the farms from which they had originally come. "Especially in the South," Cauley wrote, "is this the wise course. Georgia's 50,000 abandoned farms offer a haven for those who are dispiritedly walking the streets of the cities looking for work that does not exist."[23]

Those who returned to the land, like most who had never left, were not Agrarians in the philosophical sense. They were simply people trying to make a living, trying to survive. Those who were most educated and literate had undoubtedly been reached to some extent by the dynamic message of such journals as the *Progressive Farmer*. Edited by Clarence H. Poe, a leader of the New South movement, the journal had 450,000 subscribers throughout the rural South. We get another glimpse of the depressed farm conditions in this comment about Poe made by Edwin Mims: "He compares the broken gates, gullied fields, neglected tools, shackly outhouses, unpainted and ill-kept residences of the South with the neatness and beauty of rural England. He saw more 'gullied, wasted, desolated, heart-sickening land' in fifteen minutes' time between Memphis and Birmingham than he saw in a thousand-mile trip of the Old World."[24]

With both the white yeoman farmer and the Negro cropper and tenant in chronic poverty, Poe saw that a great deal of rural reform had to take place to increase the profitability of the soil. His program fitted in with the forward-looking plans of the new agricultural colleges and the demonstration agents dispatched by the Department of Agriculture. Due to the prevalence of outdated farming methods, Poe found that the average Southern farmer made $500 a year less than the average Western farmer. The impoverished economy had its debilitating effect on all other Southern institutions. For this and other reasons Poe devoted himself to "teaching farmers the best methods of farming, the right use of farm implements, business management, the necessity of cooperative marketing, and all the other things that make for material success."[25] In the pages of the *Progressive Farmer* (which had been a Populist journal), he brought to his readers the world's best and latest agricultural experience. Like Walter Hines Page, Poe believed that the prosperity of all depended upon that of the average man, both white and Negro. He constantly attacked the "vampire delusions" which kept the South backward.

The success of the reforms which Poe proposed depended on the farmer's ability to educate himself in order to take advantage of the improved agricultural methods. He had to understand the new scientific facts as well as learn how to take part in cooperative marketing. To help the individual farmer, each locality needed a full-time demonstration agent schooled in the most advanced methods; each locality also needed a good superintendent of schools and a qualified health officer. Boys, girls, and adult women were advised to participate in discussion groups and what we today know as 4-H Clubs. Of great importance was Poe's call for the abolition of crop mortgages and time prices which forced farmers to pay up to 40 per cent interest on their accounts. Loans to landless farmers, health programs, old age pensions, a more equitable system of taxation—these and other measures administered by enlightened leaders would create a richer and finer rural civilization in the South. Mims adds a note of defiance at the conclusion of his summary of Poe's program: "If such ideas be called socialism, then make the most of it!"[26]

To these science-oriented plans for growth and progress both in the industrial town and in the rural areas, the Southern Agrarians in the 1930's offered strenuous resistance. They did so for nearly every conceivable reason. Perhaps their most potent argument was the degrading effect that industrialism allegedly had on morals, art, literature, religion, and indeed on life itself. Also, they knew to what extent their Agrarian ideal had already diminished in the South. In the half-century since 1880, their region had absorbed an enormous amount of industry. As the legend prospered in nostalgic literature of lost Southern grandeur, so prospered the new capitalist society that would make a return to the past impossible. The money-grubbing Hubbards in *The Little Foxes* represented a culture that had infiltrated the South to a high degree. Herman C. Nixon in "Whither Southern Economy?" complained that World War I had quickened the spread of Southern industry much as the Civil War had done for industry in the North. Even Nashville had rapidly expanding industrialism; the alien chimneys of thriving mills violated the landscape almost as if to taunt the Agrarians cloistered nearby at Vanderbilt. Herbert Agar, the leading Distributist ally of the Agrarians, lamented the results of Southern industrial development: "I know, of course, about the 'New South'—the industrial towns where the worst features of the North are copied while the good features are left out. But I do not think 'the New South' will flourish."[27]

Despite this prediction, however, the extent of that flourishing could not easily be denied, no matter how one deplored its bourgeois corruption of culture. One of the most complete studies favoring the change was Broadus Mitchell's *Industrial Revolution in the South* (1930). In the twenties and thirties many books and essays testified to the growing victory of the New South. These figures from an article by Oliver Carlson indicate the tempo of Southern industrialism in the fifty years before 1930.

In 1880 the value of all manufactured goods produced in the South amounted to $338,000,000. By 1900 this had risen to $1,184,000,000. Since the turn of the century the pace has become even more rapid, so that today the value of its manufactured goods amounts to nearly $10,000,000,000 and its wage earners number 1,588,000.[28]

Another dynamic set of figures given by Carlson shows the shift in the number of textile factory spindles in the South and New England. In 1880 there were 9,000,000 spindles in the United States with only 500,-000 of them in the South. In 1921, however, while New England had 18,388,000, the number in the South had risen to 15,709,000. During the twenties, New England *lost* 6,000,000 spindles while the South gained 3,000,000. By 1933 the relative positions were reversed. New England had only 7,228,000 spindles; the South had 16,858,000. A third type of record is that of relative increase in the number of industrial workers. Although the absolute number favored the North, the *rate of increase* from 1914 to 1930 strikingly favored the South. New England *lost* 3.6 per cent of its workers, the middle Atlantic states gained 8.7 per cent while the South gained a formidable 40 per cent. Nor could the Southern Agrarians reasonably argue that this progress meant only a deeper involvement of the region in the general crisis of capitalism. A depression had fallen upon Southern agriculture several years before the Wall Street market crash of 1929. The Agrarians sought to rationalize this fact by declaring that agriculture was indeed vulnerable to crisis when it emulated capitalism and existed only for the making of money. A system of true subsistence farming, they claimed, would have escaped the economic tragedy that visited the nation and much of the world. They minimized, for the sake of their ideology, the real depth of the Southerner's interest in being rich— money rich. For the same reason they overlooked the hard facts of Southern industrial and commercial progress; if Agrarianism were a positive good, industrialism had to be a positive bad.

Despite the factors which discouraged popular acceptance of their economic program, the Agrarians did gain some adherents. Among the most significant, because they too had an economic theory, were the

Distributists led by Agar. He and Allen Tate edited *Who Owns America?* in 1936. Similar to *I'll Take My Stand* in form, it lacked the novelty and the power of the earlier symposium. Five prominent Agrarians—Ransom, Tate, Davidson, Owsley, and Warren—contributed essays. For three years the Agrarians and the Distributists had been publishing jointly in the *American Review*. Successor to the *Bookman* and edited by the same person, Seward Collins, the *Review* was a conglomeration of ultra-rightist opinion. It was enthusiastic alike for Southern Agrarians, English Distributists, Neo-Humanists, T. S. Eliot Christians, and Fascists—with many articles by Fascists praising Moesly of England, Mussolini of Italy, and Franco of Spain. It was through the immediate influence of Agar, however, that the Agrarians and the Distributists effected their merger. It came none too soon, for Southern Agrarianism shortly afterward began to fall apart as an organized social force.

Students of Distributism have noted its reflection of the official views of the Roman Catholic Church on the ownership of small property. They recall, for the modern period, a number of papal encyclicals on the social question such as those composed by Pope Leo XIII. These historic statements of church policy were essentially anti-capitalist in nature. At the more secular level, the Distributists, like the Agrarians, admired the placid and integrated life of the Middle Ages. In this regard they emulated the famous Victorian medievalists Thomas Carlyle, John Ruskin, and William Morris. They would have concurred with the version of the Middle Ages depicted in Carlyle's *Past and Present.*They would have approved of Ruskin's proposed Guild of St. George, but deemed it inadequate in scope. They would have heartily endorsed the stress made by Morris on the importance of handicrafts, but they would have declared his flirtation with Fabian socialism out of character. As a matter of fact, W. P. Witcutt wrote an article entitled "William Morris: Distributist" in which he stated, "It remains to show that the logical position for William Morris to have taken up was not Socialism but what we now call Distributism." Witcutt went on to explain why he thought this was so:

The root problem is the problem of property. Restore the small man and you restore interest in the things made, rather than in the profits made. Restore that interest, and you are on the way to co-ordinating once more the brain and the hand, and bringing back beauty to the things made by man. So Morris's position follows logically from that of the Distributists. His place lies with us, and not with the Marxians, and so we claim him.[29]

A basic text of Distributism is *The Restoration of Property*, by Hilaire Belloc, a book which first appeared in several installments in the

American Review. Property, as defined by the author, meant the "control of the means of production by the family unit."[30] Such a limitation automatically ruled out as undesirable all the huge corporate aggregations which typify the modern industrial system. The two major methods of eliminating insecurity and want both did away with freedom: the first was the Servile State (finance capitalism in which a minority owned the means of production), and the second was Communism. Neither was acceptable because in neither could the individual be free. The best alternative was the Distributist or Proprietary State in which families owned the bulk of the productive means. Hence it was the ownership of small property that determined the nature of Distributism, just as it was the small farm that characterized Agrarianism. Society could fracture big holdings by establishing official machinery that fostered the propagation of small property holding; after all, such machinery existed to foster the destruction of small property by the large owners. The effort to restore property, Belloc wrote, would certainly fail if it were hampered by any "superstition" against the use of force as the handmaiden of justice.

The Agrarians had demanded a distribution of land among the landless farmers so they could subsist outside a money economy. Agreeing with the Agrarians generally but broadening the scope of his plan, Belloc demanded a deliberate "reversal of economic tendencies" in all of society. He wanted regulations that would perpetuate the division of property. A system of "well-divided property" had to be maintained by artificial means; if necessary, this meant the use of force as an instrument of policy. Here and in other writings Belloc used the medieval ideal as his point of departure. In regard to the fall of the Middle Ages, he said, "The first great blow was the destruction of the guilds, coupled with the seizure of collegiate property in all countries transformed by the Reformation, especially England."[31] Belloc regarded capitalism as a massive obstacle to the restoration of the medieval pattern. The problem of how to weaken and eventually destroy this giant was an immediate and a complex one; nor was Belloc's solution likely to strike terror in the centers of world capital. He wrote:

The process [of getting rid of capitalism] may be compared to the killing of a tree by one who must attack with instruments too feeble for cutting the tree down, let alone uprooting it, too feeble even for inflicting a serious wound upon its trunk, too feeble for cutting off main branches or perhaps even secondary branches, but *not too feeble for clipping leaves.*"[32]

Eventually the tree of capitalism would weaken and die, and then the sapling of Distributism would prosper.

Belloc went on to mention several of the steps required to weaken capitalism. A new series of taxes should be levied on all means of "large distribution"—a differentiated tax on chain stores, one on department stores based on "the number of categories with which it deals," and still another on the amount of turnover.[33] The reduction in the number of categories handled would benefit the small shopkeeper who specialized in one item, such as fish, tobacco, or dairy products. Whenever possible, society should substitute smaller units for the large units of production, industrial corporations and the like. For instance, the right to manufacture a new product should be assigned to a very small unit, preferably a family one. Otherwise, control should be exerted either to create well-distributed property in the shares thereof, or to manage the use of it as a communal concern. Lest the existing capitalists be alarmed that Distributism was another form of communism (albeit a primitive clerical type), Belloc declared that his effort to restore property did not aim at perfection or even at any large and universal upheaval of the present economic system. Rather, the aim was to preserve and to create anew the "middle class standard" as the factor of primary importance for the holding of property in the ideal state. In their *theoretical* attack on capitalism the Distributists could, of course, exploit other anti-capitalists such as Karl Marx and John Strachey. Herbert Agar explained that although Marxism had certain defects it could also be of service to Distributism because the "private ownership of the means of production" might well mean a system of Distributism. He wrote: "Marx thought he was writing a book to prove the necessity for either communism or catastrophe. His book can just as well be used as an argument for the Distributist State, for the historic American plan. There are moral arguments of a compelling nature in favour of such a state; it is well to recognize that the economic arguments are also strong."[34] By the "historic American plan" Agar means Jefferson's vision of an agrarian democracy with limited restraints on individual freedoms and with even these restraints emanating from remote sources of power.

Attitudes toward the land were naturally of dominant concern to the Southern Agrarians; the attitudes of the Distributists, although not so detailed, were complementary. In the Agrarian-Distributist axis, the *country* and *town* aspects of a common ideology were combined in a general synthesis of views. Discussing the nature of free men, Belloc wrote that they think of income as the product of property, and "the typical form of property, which is also the foundational form, is property in land."[35] Rural and urban land had to be regarded and treated differently; the former would serve to create and sustain a *yeoman,* while the latter would create and sustain a *craftsman.* Small owners in both town and country should cooperate in marketing their respective products, lowering production costs, and keeping intact their social status. They should all try to live within the means afforded by the income from their personal property whether it be a small farm or a small shop. And to keep this Agrarian-Distributist society in balance, "everything should be done by the artifice of the laws to make it easy for the smaller man to buy land from the richer man and difficult for the larger man to buy land from the smaller man."[36]

On such an amiable and possibly pious hope we can conclude this resumé of Agrarian economic thought. From 1930 to 1936—a busy period framed by the two symposia *I'll Take My Stand* and *Who Owns America?*—Agrarian economic thought had become more and more detailed and specific; this process of development was forced upon it both by its own inner dynamics and by external criticism. However, the strategy for establishing the desired system remained vague and inconclusive. Belloc—the Distributist—had suggested the ultimate use of violence; but his idea of revolution diminished to the rather futile gesture of "clipping leaves" from the tree of capitalism. Tate—the Agrarian—had also suggested "violence" as the means by which Southerners could "take hold" of their tradition; but here, too, the violence eventually petered out to become merely violent language.

Chapter IV   The Southern Tradition

FOR A TIME THE AGRARIANS PRE-EMPTED THE "SOUTHERN TRADITION";
like so many others in the twenties, the Nashville writers were searching for a usable past. However, the "tradition" is a multiple entity
subject to conflicts of opinion. One such conflict was posed by Davidson's question: "Whose ideal of progress for the South? After what
heart's desire?" Another conflict grew from the age-old argument
over Negro slavery—was it good or bad? The Agrarians determined
that at least it had been better than free labor under capitalism.
Still another conflict involved the varying images of the Old South
itself. Did it believe in science and industry? Did it love to accumulate money? Was its agriculture commercial or not? The basic conflict arose from the difference between the legendary and the actual
in Southern social history. These conflicts of opinion in the twenties and thirties divided the Old from the New, the conservatives
from the liberals.

Legends have played an important role in the formation of the
Southern tradition. Although useful subject matter for literature, they
tend to create difficulties for the historian. The more glamorous the
Old South, the more need there seemed to be to justify its use of slavery. When to its sublimation of guilt was added the melancholia of
the Lost Cause (or the "dynastic wound" as Frederick Hoffman calls
it), we have the South's fecund ingredients for massive legendry. Part
of the truth is this: Throughout the vast legendry, in all the nostalgic
novels and movies, the songs and jokes, in every mention of "Southern" lies the remembrance of how the South once fiercely fought for
the right to buy and sell human beings.

The major legend is built about the "good life" which this barter
made possible. It is for this "good life" that the Southern conservative
hungers when he laments the Lost Cause or vehemently defends his

"tradition." What differentiated the Agrarians from other traditional-ists was their disdain for the sentimental, overly romantic attitude which once helped to nurture this legend of the paradise which the evil North destroyed. However, their revolt against sentimentalism did not include revolt against the tradition itself.

The Agrarians settled upon a more defensible legend whose general outline went like this. The plantation system based on Negro slaves had created the best civilization yet devised—at least since the Middle Ages. From its close bond with nature, with the land, the Old South received a fine material bounty, a healthy moral fibre, a right relation with God, an innocent Eden-like leisure, and a high cultivation of art, beauty, and manners among a limited elite who alone could admire these qualities. Within the aristocracy developed the special individ-ual known as the Southern gentleman—the noblest type of man ever to preside over a culture. He cared more for his honor than his money; indeed, money was beneath his concern. Through his strict Code of Honor (usually spelled "Honour" because he admired the English) he knew how to walk the Path Perilous, the only road that gave life meaning. The Southern gentleman scorned riches for their own sake; he gathered them into his coffers mainly because they signified God's grace. He treated his Negro slaves kindly and often wept at their mo-ments of sorrow. With his beautiful lady at his side (a veritable Ma-donna of virtue), the Southern gentleman bore on his dignified shoulders the destiny of his state, his region, and his nation.

Under the gentleman the rest of society basked in peace and well-being. The organic culture of the Middle Ages had been reborn in the Cotton Kingdom. Both the aristocratic planter and the less cultured independent yeoman belonged to a natural order based on the land. The gentleman because of his education and higher intellect enter-tained himself with fox hunts, balls, lively conversation with his peers, etc. The simple yeoman amused himself with corn husking parties, log rolling contests, horseshoe pitching, square dances, and other robust games. However, the pursuits of each class were essentially *local, sim-ple, natural* ones which put the participants in a warm and satisfying relationship to their neighbors. The plantation then was no more than a larger, more communal, unit of society; the Negro slaves led the same good life as the free yeoman, except that by working in con-cert they produced a surplus that went to support the gentleman and his lady in their finer and more cultivated pursuits. Therefore, the slaves suffered not at all; indeed, they were often much better off than the yeoman because they were taken care of "from the cradle to the grave." The only one who suffered slightly was the gentleman who was deprived in part of the wholesome and beneficial closeness to the soil: but this was the cross he had to bear in return for the leisure which permitted him to create and maintain a superior culture.

Owsley in particular supported the thesis that the independent non-slaveholding class, the "yeomen," formed the backbone of the Old South. To make their legend consistent, the Agrarians had to play down various progressive trends which did appear within the Cotton Kingdom. These included a widespread interest in science, in modern technology, in factories, and in a thriving commerce. The task of sifting out the legendary from the real is vital to our understanding of what the authors of *I'll Take My Stand* said they wanted to restore, in principle at least, as an alternative to modern industrial America.

LEGEND: *Only the theory of Negro slavery was monstrous; its practice was usually humane. Not addicted to money and commerce, the Southern gentleman could afford to be just and kind to his slaves. It was tragic that his nobility should be replaced by bourgeois avarice and vulgarity.*

A brief glance at the history of Negro slavery in America may prove instructive at this point. Despite its greater magnitude, Southern slaveholding did not seem particularly onerous to the rest of the nation as long as Negroes, and sometimes Indians, were also enslaved in the North. Slavery became a sectional factor only after the Revolution when Southern states refused to pass laws of emancipation. The first state to pass such a law was Vermont, which freed its slaves in 1779; the last was New Jersey in 1804. The South, it is true, had a much greater investment in slaves than did any other region; its slaveholders had more to lose through emancipation. Therefore, despite the popularity of Jeffersonian democracy, despite Jefferson's own warnings on the issue, the South remained satisfied with the thought that gradual abolition of the African slave trade, state by state, would, in time, end slavery itself.

According to the Negro scholar W. E. B. DuBois, the most favorable time for the South to have freed its slaves was in that brief moment after the Revolution but before 1793, when Eli Whitney invented the cotton gin. Agriculture in the South did not then require widespread slavery for the mass production of cotton. A thriving Southern abolitionism, more active than that in the North, strongly pushed the moral argument against the continued used of slaves. This moment of least painful emancipation was allowed to pass without action. In 1790 the South produced only 8000 bales of cotton. For these relatively few bales, for the other products of slave labor, and for the capital invested in the slaves themselves, the Southern states decided to secede from the national economy—without even realizing the nature of their secession—and to prolong their peculair institution. Applied science in the form of the gin soon increased the value of slaves by greatly increasing their productivity. Thus the gin helped to make possible the social and economic miracle of the American "Cotton Kingdom." From 8000 bales in 1790, the number grew to 650,000 bales in 1820. This total, and all that it implied in economic growth, made the slave system so astonishingly profitable that by 1835 to speak against it on any grounds whatsoever was tantamount to regional treason.[1] In 1850, at about the time of the Dred Scott Decision, the plantations with their busy slave labor produced a spectacular 2,500,000 bales. Ten years later, on the eve of the Civil War, the total had gone even higher, to 4,000,000 bales—a number roughly equal to the nearly four million Negroes then living under slavery.[2] Broadus Mitchell writes that for the first forty years of the nineteenth century these growing mountains of cotton sold for over twenty-five cents a pound, a fabulous price to be maintained for so long a period.[3] Pressure for more slaves proved so insistent that South Carolina, one of the most prosperous of the so-called Black Belt states, reopened the African slave trade. In the short period from 1803 to 1807, South Carolina added 40,000 to her already dense Negro population.[4] Legal prohibition of the slave trade in other states inflated the market value of Negroes so much that smuggling became a lucrative business. In view of the profits, smuggling must have been widespread, although Clement Eaton, a liberal historian of the South, mildly disputes the estimate made by DuBois that 250,000 new slaves were smuggled into the South from 1808 to 1860.[5]

The Agrarian image of the planter as a benevolent feudal lord precluded his having anything on his mind so sordid and bourgeois as money. Lewis Cecil Gray's significant study of Southern agriculture, *Agriculture in the Southern United States to 1860*, supports the opposite view—that the plantation system was, above all else, *commercial*. It was an organic and stable "way of life" only because it did prove successful, for a limited time, in sustaining a small but powerful aristocracy. Even its "stability" can be questioned according to the findings of historian Herbert Aptheker on these two points: First, the South lived in perpetual dread of Negro insurrection because the slaves were machines of an intelligent nature that had to be "terrified and chained and beaten" for their owners to retain possession.[6] "The history of American slavery," Aptheker says, "is marked by at least two hundred and fifty *reported* Negro conspiracies and revolts."[7] Second, as a consequence of this unrest, the South became an armed camp in order to keep the Negro in bondage. The South's militarist tradition, nourished by its famous academies, surpassed that of any other region. Aptheker said: "The South itself was, so far as about one-third of its population was concerned, a huge fortress in which prisoners were held, at hard labor, for life. Like any other fortress it was exceedingly well guarded."[8] Additional evidence that slavery was a "chronic state of warfare" included the carrying of weapons by all Southern white men, the well-trained militia and volunteer military units, the omnipresent patrols, and armed overseers on all the plantations. Such an impressive use of power could force a society to seem organic, orderly, and stable.

Along with a kind of Spartan militarism, a one-sided economic growth, and an agrarian commercialism, the Old South developed a conformity in racism, religion, and politics. Southern religion intensified its defense of racism when the growing wealth derived from cotton culture needed extraordinary moral justification. Eaton records the fact that the "liberal phase of Southern religion began to fade in the decade of the 1830's."[9] Progressive religious leaders were silenced, especially in the colleges and seminaries. The churches permitted themselves to become a strong force in establishing the new and frightening conformity. As for the Negroes themselves, they were taught only a narrow sampling of religion lest they emulate their predecessors in human slavery and, like the early Christians, rebel against their modern Rome. Church trials with dreaded powers of excommunication kept the dissidents under control. According to Eaton's account, slaves could be excommunicated from their church—and thereby lose eternal salvation, the only kind that often seemed possible—for "stealing, running away from their masters, impudence to their mistresses, and having illigitimate children."[10] Religious leaders searched the Bible for scriptural refutation of Thomas Jefferson's doctrine of human equality. Since the Bible reflects a primitive, slave-holding culture, these leaders had little trouble in finding chapter and verse to suit their purposes.

Rationalizations for slavery were easy to find on many different grounds. In *Sociology for the South*, George Fitzhugh asserted bluntly: "A free negro! Why, the very term seems an absurdity. It is our daily boast, and experience verifies it, that the Anglo-Saxons of America are the only people in the world fitted for freedom."[11] This racist flattery of the Anglo-Saxon—usually in contrast to the Catholic Celt—prevailed throughout the British Empire at the time: and it existed in the South as well, most often among those aristocrats who considered themselves and their plantations to be an extension of the old English establishment. Fitzhugh believed that Negro slavery was only one of many instances of universal "unfreedom" needed to maintain social order. Anarchy would be the result if all classes could behave as they chose. Since society demanded the Negro's subjugation for its own stability, the abolitionist sought only anarchy when he demanded emancipation.

In their idealized picture of the Old South, the Agrarians never depicted the Negro people as objects of human exploitation. If forced to confess an evil in the plantation system, especially in regard to slavery, they often countered it by mentioning a Northern or capitalist evil, as did Fitzhugh and others before the Civil War. According to Tate, the Negro slave of the Cotton Kingdom was better off than the modern wage-earner because he could never join the ranks of the unemployed. Then there was Ransom's proposition that only the theory of slavery, and not its practice, was monstrous. This benevolent possibility might have been true here and there, just as an occasional overseer might have been, as Tate thought, a former Virginia gentleman who had fallen into misfortune. However, the evidence is overwhelming that stern economic necessity compelled the "gentleman" to squeeze as much profit as he could from the slave's labor. He even fed his prime hands better; the more they were able to work, the better they ate in order to sustain their rate of productivity. A Negro woman lost a good deal of her status if she proved to be barren and unable to conceive new slaves for her master.

As for the overseers, Lewis Cecil Gray does not agree with Allen Tate that likely as not they were Virginia gentlemen who could not make the social grade:

As a class, overseers were men of dense ignorance and narrow vision, with the obtuseness that resulted from long familiarity with slavery. Their agricultural knowledge consisted of the rule-of-thumb methods handed down for generations in the class of small farmers.[12]

Tate also claimed that the Negro slave—unlike the French peasant—was incapable of contributing to culture. Gray again puts a different emphasis on the matter by listing the official regulations that restricted education for the slaves. Teaching them to read and to write was prohibited by Georgia in 1755, Virginia in 1831, South Carolina in 1834, Alabama in 1832, and Louisiana in 1830; in Missouri, schools for Negroes were made illegal in 1847. Compulsory illiteracy made it easier for racist Southerners to regard the Negro as "naturally" inferior. No wonder the Negroes under slavery were unable to contribute much to what Tate considered to be white man's culture; the white man went to much trouble to prevent them from doing so.

As for the free Negroes living in the South, they were the segment whose happiness under freedom, had it been allowed to flourish, might have served by strong example to undermine the foundations of the Cotton Kingdom. In 1860 free Negroes numbered 250,787 throughout the South as compared with a total of 3,950,511 slaves. Southern society needed such a class, up to a point, to provide a sanctuary for those restless, brave, and intelligent Negroes who might otherwise turn into Denmark Veseys and Nat Turners if all exits from slavery were blocked. Also, whites who decided to free their slaves were thus permitted to practice their humanitarianism. However, the legal, economic, and social conditions under which free Negroes lived, as Gray records, remained wretched in the extreme. To keep them in bondage sometimes seemed more humanitarian than to set them adrift in a bigoted, hostile environment. Gray comments:

Without capital or the means of obtaining it; without education, from which they were frequently debarred by statute; without skill; subjected to numerous legal restrictions with respect to freedom of movement and economic activity; deprived of rights of citizenship; usually despised alike by whites and slaves; lacking all motive for exertion except the satisfaction of mere bodily needs;—such were the disabilities of free Negroes in the greater portion of the ante bellum South. (pp. 523–24)

LEGEND: *The Old South had a preponderance of subsistence agriculture. The small yeoman farmer knew how to subsist splendidly on his land. Being economically independent, he could be free in his politics and other beliefs. The subsistence farmer was and is the freest man in America.*

Subsistence agriculture did indeed exist in the Old South from the earliest colonial times, but it was precisely the type of life which the planters and gentlemen scorned. The farmers themselves sought every means of escape from their subsistence status. Southerners of those vigorous nation-building days were not satisfied merely to subsist. If subsistence were their only reward, it was usually from misfortune or incompetence, not from any conscious desire. Except when frontier conditions made subsistence an end in itself, or when land monopoly tended to freeze people in their "place," the poorer farmer had no greater wish than to make a lot of money, build himself a big white house, purchase slaves, and emulate the leisurely "good life" of the rich, cultivated gentleman.

In his impressive work, Gray documents the overwhelming monetary ambitions of the Old South. He equates the *progress* of Southern agriculture with its degree of commercialization, its ability to return a profit on investment. Gray could thus also reveal, without any loss of sentiment, that the plantation system was as subject to the vagaries of economics—prices, supply and demand, speculation, the market at home and abroad—as was the finance-capitalism of the Northeast. It is true, as the Agrarians often maintained, that the Southern gentleman had culture, had leisure, had manners; but he could not possibly have what he had unless he indulged in profitable, large-scale, commercial planting.

Next to Negro slavery, indentured servitude, or colonial impressment into the English navy, subsistence agriculture occupied the lowest economic and social level. It was regarded by the ambitious as merely a starting point for happier, better days. Curiously enough, Gray records instances of colonial aid to help establish families on the land which strikingly parallel the suggestions made by the Agrarians in the 1930's. Some of the Southern colonies, being sparsely populated, offered incentives to attract immigrants from other colonies.

In 1739 the council [of South Carolina] assigned each settler on the "Welch Tract," on the upper Pedee, tools, livestock, and food for one season, and exemption from surveyor's fees on fifty acres. The policy of the Georgia Trustees in promoting immigration was even more liberal. In addition to the provisions for transporting and outfitting European immigrants, the trustees advertised in other Colonies their arrangements for supplying immigrants with arms, tools, household furnishings, iron work, nails, a cow, calf, brood mare, and sow. (p. 89)

Owsley and other Agrarians in the 1930's made similar lists of what the federal government should grant prospective new farmers in order to settle them on the land. Yet the give-away plans cited by Gray were intended to solve a much less complicated problem existing on a frontier nearly two centuries ago. After this time, *subsistence* as opposed to *commercial* farming survived but developed outside the mainstream of Southern economy. Gray refers constantly to both types of farming and analyzes their status from period to period and region to region.

The two types of farming were well established long before the War of Independence. Even where self-sufficiency was the rule in wide and usually isolated areas, the farmers thus employed found it difficult to be content; this fact was even more apparent once the isolation vanished and commodities requiring hard labor to make at home could be bought at a store for a few dollars. Gray cites a situation which in effect shows the farmer's eagerness to take advantage of the general division of labor.

The self-sufficing farmer was not seeking profits, but a living. He incurred but little money expenses, invested little capital, and assumed no regular obligations. Yet, complete self-sufficiency was exceedingly irksome; it involved doing without many comforts or producing them at enormous cost of energy. Therefore, the self-sufficing farmer constantly sought a marketable product. He could afford to sacrifice much labor, as compared with the commercial planter, in the production and marketing of this salable product in order to enjoy some of the benefits of the world's division of labor. What if the production and hauling to market of hogsheads of tobacco did cost twice the labor incurred by commercial planters, provided the self-sufficient farmer could obtain a gun, ammunition, kettles, and medicines, which he could not produce at all or only by excessive labor and trouble. (p. 451)

One indication of the relative social status of this way of life can be found in Gray's comment that lands exhausted by tobacco or cotton were "abandoned" to subsistence farmers. Those "yeomen" who might have exemplified the Agrarian ideal within the Old South did not fare very well either socially or economically. They have been called "the most degraded race of human beings claiming an Anglo-Saxon origin that can be found on the face of the earth."[13] Governor James Hammond estimated that in 1850—actually the heyday of the Cotton Kingdom—there were no fewer than 50,000 persons in South Carolina with inadequate means of procuring a livelihood. *Tobacco Road* did not have to wait for the depression of the 1930's to find its characters; they belonged to the traditional South.

Gray states that the plantation was a strictly commercial enterprise. Its economic function was to produce valuable commodities that could be sold at a profit—the bigger the profit the better. Because of its extensive material resources, the plantation in its earlier stages of development was able to manufacture many goods of a non-agricultural nature. In its own blacksmith shop, for example, were made various tools and parts that did not have to be purchased in a hardware store. Yet this home manufacture did not mean that the planter hated industrialism. Rather, it reflected local necessity at a time when the world industrial revolution could not yet produce enough products at a low enough price. Gray says, "The increasing cheapness of factory products after 1815, and the expansion of commercial cotton planting reduced greatly the extent of household manufactures."[14] In the 1930's the Agrarians urged the farmer, in order to escape from debt, to become a jack-of-all-trades and make all he needed with his own hands—

from his clothing to his candles. They often referred to the Old South as a precedent for such great versatility on the part of the "yeoman" farmer. But in the only place where home manufacture was possible on a creditable scale, the large plantation (and here the artisan was usually an expert Negro slave), the trend of history favored a drop in such manufacture. Money earned by slave labor could easily buy the refined goods of Northern and European industry. However, the degree of their dependence eventually became a kind of economic bondage which Southerners deeply resented; it lay at the heart of the long and bitter tariff controversy. They sought to resolve the problem of economic imbalance—selling the raw materials cheap, buying the finished product dear—by political means. Dependence in some cases went to extremes. Gray comments that the tendency of the more favorably situated plantations to become increasingly commercial eventually led them to purchase even their food supplies. Hence self-sufficiency even in such a fundamental as food disappeared, or tended to, from the ideal economic unit of the Old South.

LEGEND: *The Old South disdained all forms of disruptive progress which threatened its organic tradition. Its leaders discouraged industry, science, and commerce.*

In reality, the leaders of the Old South were willing to utilize anything, whether backward labor or advanced machine, that would bring the greatest profit in the shortest time. Unlike the modern Agrarians, the ante-bellum planter was not *theoretically* opposed to new devices if they increased his wealth and improved his competitive position. Progress in technology was greatest on large, well-regulated plantations whose owners and managers read the latest agricultural literature or traveled widely. At the start of the nineteenth century clumsy wooden plows, crude harrows, sickles, scythes, and hoes, and occasionally a rude threshing machine made up the mechanical basis of husbandry. In the next sixty years—a period of great development in the industrial revolution—came numerous changes: the widespread substitution of the cradle for the scythe and sickle; the sporadic adoption of mechanical reapers; tremendous improvement in plows; the substitution of horse-drawn tillage implements such as cultivators, scrapers, sweeps, and skimmers for the hoe; the adoption of mechanical seeders, horse-rakes, and threshing machines; and improved machinery for cutting straw, grinding corn, and milling small grain. About 1855 a veteran farmer, looking back over a period of nearly eighty years, expressed the opinion that the amount of labor performed by a hand in Georgia had been nearly doubled.[15]

In fact, Professor Eaton speaks of an "agricultural revolution" that occurred first in the upper and then in the lower South from the 1830's on. As do other historians, Eaton mentions Edmund Ruffin of Virginia, the greatest agrarian reformer in the Old South, who founded a magazine known as the *Farmers' Register* to promote new methods of farming. Ruffin's journal complemented the more commercial and industrial-minded *Commercial Review of the South and Southwest* (or *DeBow's Review*). In regard to agrarian changes within the Old South, Eaton has written: "The experiments of Southern planters in growing new crops, in improving the breed of livestock, and in developing scientific methods of agriculture have never been properly appreciated."[16]

Perhaps one reason for this lack of appreciation has been the legend itself—the view that the gentleman planter was not mercenary, not concerned with the dull routine of running his own business, but was devoted only to living the good life of the gentle, urbane aristocrat. Another reason may be the liberal's emphasis on the stagnation of the entire slave economy. Broadus Mitchell writes in this vein:

As in India and China today, the cheapness of labor made ingenuity, enterprise and machinery unnecessary. Except in size and superficial appearance there was no change in the ante-bellum gin, gin-house and screw from 1820 to 1860. But after the War came a feeder, a condenser, a hand-press in the lint room, and cotton elevators.[17]

The Old South, it would seem, had more interest in "progress" than either ideological extreme was willing to admit. The liberals lamented the fact that the slave economy prevented the South's full participation in the industrial revolution; the Agrarians defended the South's alleged refusal to participate on grounds that it already had a superior way of life.

An exhaustive study of the extent to which the Old South utilized science for its own power and survival would again tend to discredit the legend. Such a survey was made in the 1930's by a Southerner, Thomas Cary Johnson, Jr., a professor of history at the University of Virginia. His work, *Scientific Interests in the Old South,* was "a study of the attitude of the planters, politicians, and professional men of the Cotton Kingdom and of their wives and daughters toward the natural sciences." Johnson found this interest to be genuine, eager, and universal. "If these opinions should be sustained by the evidence presented in this book," he wrote, "some of the most cherished ideas of American historians will have to be modified, for the possession of such an interest in science is incompatible with the traditional, and by the his-

torians generally accepted, account of the civilization that was destroyed by the Civil War."[18] In keeping with other traditionalists, the
Agrarians also held to the view which Johnson's study sought to correct. Had they understood their "tradition" in the light of its interest
in science—even though some of that interest might have been
superficial—they would have had to abandon a vital part of their ideology.

They would have had to do the same had they investigated more
thoroughly the extent to which the Old South was active in manufacturing and commerce, not only in practice—which was limited by the
profitablity of slavery—but also in planning for and theorizing about
the future. For example, the publicist DeBow, challenging the omnipotence of cotton, chose the slogan "Commerce is King" for his *Review*, the first issue of which appeared in 1846. Under other names and
in other cities besides New Orleans, the *Review* championed Southern
industrialization and commercial expansion until its demise in 1880,
when new and more powerful forces took up the same cause under
much more favorable conditions. DeBow frequently questioned the
basis for the currently dominant agrarian aristocracy. "The fashion of
the South," he wrote, "has been to consider the production of cotton,
and sugar, and rice, the only rational pursuits of gentlemen, except
the professions, and like the haughty Greek and Roman, to class the
trading and the manufacturing spirit as essentially servile."[19] DeBow
expresses here the wish of the commercial middle class to be regarded
as respectable by its snobbish social superiors, the old planters with
their refined manners and elaborate codes of honor. At first a nationalist and then a secessionist, DeBow detailed an advanced program of
economic growth that was to be championed again by the "New
South" movement in the eighties and later. Conceding that the South
would remain essentially agrarian, he nonetheless demanded more industry, more commerce, more railroads, more urbanization, along with
economics and business courses in colleges, Negro labor for factories,
and much else of a progressive nature. He also compiled a book on the
industrial resources of his region.[20]

In the heart of the Cotton Kingdom occurred the phenomenon of
Graniteville, the highly successful textile mill owned by the pioneer
industrialist William Gregg. Like other attempts at progress in the
South, however, this too was somewhat impeded by the traditional environment. In his biography of Gregg, Broadus Mitchell writes:
"Graniteville was like a feudal village, with the great stone factory
substituted for the turreted castle, and the wooden houses in place of

thatched huts; the Poor Whites came in for the protection of their overlord just as eagerly as did the peasants of centuries earlier. . . ."[21] In a society that tolerated dueling and held medieval tournaments in honor of nuptials with replicas of knights and ladies, with contests, judges, and prizes, it is not surprising that an industrial combine should also be suffused with the feudal spirit.[22] Despite the example of his own success, Gregg's call for a thorough-going industrial revolution in the South was ignored. He was one of several premature capitalists whose voices were lost in the clamor of profits from cotton. However we must repeat that enough industrialization occurred to create serious doubts about the integrity of the Old South legend as conceived by the Agrarians. For example, Eaton says, "By June, 1860, Virginia and North Carolina factories were producing 61 percent of all plug, smoking, and snuff tobacco manufactured in the United States."[23] The iron industry in Richmond and elsewhere had a venerable history; during the Civil War it served the Confederacy nobly in the production of armaments. While the production of cotton and tobacco still ruled in the region in 1860, the industrial revolution within the Cotton Kingdom had been growing despite all obstacles. After describing what he labels the "severe depression" of the 1840's in agriculture, Gray writes: "A rapid increase of cotton manufacturing occurred after 1845. Factories began to spring up along the fall line from Virginia to Alabama. By 1849, for instance, Columbus, Georgia, boasted twelve factories. The zeal for manufacturing extended to the lowlands, where the advantages of water power were lacking."[24] That some of the capital for these mills originated in the North does not detract from the fact that industrialism, within the general plantation system, was growing in power and value.

Inadvertently, the South was preparing the economic revenge it was ultimately to inflict upon New England by luring away so many of her textile factories. Even before the Civil War, and despite the relative lack of non-slave labor, the Southern manufacturer had certain important things in his favor: a differential of about a cent a pound in the cost of cotton transport, almost no taxation, lower wage rates, and less land rent for his business establishment. Both capital and available labor were scarce, and the quality of the labor was poor; but these and other obstacles served only to reveal the strength of the capitalist incentive which grew despite them. Gray writes, "In 1840 the capital invested in manufacturing in the South was nearly 20 per cent of the total for the United States. Between 1840 and 1850 Southern manufacturing capital increased nearly 76 per cent."[25] While the North began from a broader base and gained relatively more, the point to be made here is that the South, allegedly so agrarian was in reality so anxious to achieve a balanced economy.

Among the Southern Agrarians, Donald Davidson in particular deplored the "booster" spirit of the Southern Chambers of Commerce that had been set up to tout the wonders of the modern or "new" South. He feared that this spirit would infect the region further with Babbittry, money hunger, and other forms of Northern decadence. And yet something like this very spirit of boosterism had also manifested itself strongly within the ante-bellum South. The tense issue of abolition versus slavery, plus all the lesser issues that it bred, combined with an agricultural depression in the forties to make many of the best Southern thinkers dwell on the continuing stability of their social system. The sense of political alarm and economic unity "found expression in a series of notable commercial conventions, in which the broader economic, political, and social interests of the section were differentiated from the purely agricultural interests. . . ."[26] Even in agriculture, a field in which the South supposedly excelled, the contrast with agricultural progress in the North was often disquieting. Southern farm papers, critical of stagnant plantation methods, printed many articles comparing the exhausted soil, the low price of land, the general ruin and decay, and the inefficient methods of production in the South with the productive soils, high land values, and the thrift and prosperity of the neighboring Northern states. Professor Gray speaks of these commercial conventions as being motivated by a growing awareness of the economic supremacy of the North.

Resolutions were introduced in the conventions for the establishment of foundries, machine shops, and cotton factories; the levying of retaliatory direct taxes upon goods imported from the North; exemption of the products of Southern factories from sales taxes, and agreements boycotting Northern products. There were orations expounding the dignity of labor and movements to establish mechanics' institutes and trade schools.[27]

Despite the allegation that politicians eventually dominated these conventions, and though their over-all effect was often more rhetorical than practical, they expressed the nascent ideology of the New South as it existed within the Old. This expression occurred when apologetics for slavery, and the strict conformity of thought which they enforced, were at their peak. The later New South movement of the 1880's sponsored the ideology of the industrial revolution as it pertained concretely to the Southern regions. The name "New South" derived from an essay of that title written by Sidney Lanier in 1880; and also from a speech given by Henry Woodfin Grady before the New England Society of New York in 1886. Still later, in the 1930's, it was the continuing growth of this revolution that the Southern Agrarians wished first of all to stem; it was with the proponents of a "New South" that the Agrarians had their sharpest conflicts of opinion.

Historians often distinguish between two "New South" periods, the first in the 1880's and the second in the 1920's. Each period witnessed an intense effort to bring progressive changes in industry and agriculture, as opposed to the satisfied, backward-looking view typified by Agrarians. C. Vann Woodward in *Origins of the New South* speaks of the ambiguity of terms surrounding the notion of a "New South" and considers it more of a slogan than an achieved fact. Much did happen, of course, but the projected "Southern Ruhrs" did not materialize; neither did Southern counterparts of the Vanderbilts, the Morgans, and the Hills. Woodward states that from 1880 to 1900 despite the rise of cities, "the sum total of urbanization in the South was comparatively unimportant."[28]

Defeat in the Civil War opened the South not only to Northern attempts to democratize its tightly structured society, but also to Northern plunder. Indeed, much of the New South industrial and commercial progress constituted merely the Southern salient of the national conquest executed by the so-called Robber Barons. However, the degree of economic exploitation tended to be greater in the New South than elsewhere in the nation—just as it had been in the Old South under slavery. We need only recall the lures used to entice Northern capital southward: low or non-existent taxes (which meant an impoverished system of education); cheap labor, a high proportion of which consisted of children; cheap resources, which often came close to being mere giveaways; generous gifts of land from the public domain; a labor force hostile to unions and eager to side with the white boss against the Negro; investments "safe" from ruinous strikes; and so on. The wages paid workers were as low as the lure-of-capital literature claimed they were. As Woodward relates, the "wages of adult male workers of North Carolina in the nineties were 40 to 50 cents a day." He mentions the fact that mills often paid only 10 to 12 cents a day for children's labor and that "the work week averaged about seventy hours for men, women, and children."[29] Early in his career Broadus Mitchell, enthusiastic about the rise of cotton mills, justified at some length the rapid spread of child labor. He deemed it both natural and necessary at the time when it first appeared. From 1880 to 1890 the number of children employed in the mills was doubled; from 1890 to

1900 it trebled! Mitchell wrote, "The use of children was not avarice then, but philanthropy; not exploitation, but generosity and cooperation and social-mindedness."[30] Undoubtedly Mitchell gauged correctly the Southerner's readiness to accept child labor. It is exactly such ingrained backwardness that explains the pessimism of W. J. Cash in *The Mind of the South* when he writes about the failure of the "hillbilly" turned "millbilly" to shake himself loose from his stagnant past.

Some of these seamy aspects of the New South the Nashville Agrarians justly condemned. They failed to mention others, however, like the widespread use of convict labor in private enterprise, the forcing of the Negro into a peonage status under a new caste system—by 1900, 75.3 per cent of the Negroes were sharecroppers or tenants—and the often unabashed corruption and double-dealing in Southern politics.[31] Behind the bright visions of the New South's apostles often lay a grim and disturbing reality. Thus W. E. B. DuBois wrote bitterly that while his people were being steadily disenfranchised, "Henry Grady stood in Boston and told New England that the Negro was as free to vote in the South as the white laborer was in the North."[32] Woodward commented wryly that racism became a very useful instrument by which to stupefy and exploit the worker. He said, "It took a lot of ritual and Jim Crow to bolster the creed of white supremacy in the bosom of a white man working for a black man's wages."[33] In another reference to racism Woodward says, "A cult of racism disguised or submerged cleavages of opinion or conflicts of interest in the name of white solidarity, and the one-party system reduced political intolerance to a machine of repression."[34] The mass disquiet which found a temporary outlet in Southern Populism eventually came under control of a weird new phenomenon, the Southern demagogue. However, despite all, industrial progress did come to the region.

The Southern liberals who had absorbed the views of Lanier and Page seemed victorious by 1930, but, as Davidson wrote, "the economic crisis soon revealed the weakness of their position."[35] The social and economic miracles that Page had envisioned had not occurred. Davidson continued, "The money with which they [the liberals] could once persuade Southern Mummies to become Northern Babbitts has vanished."[36] In his critique of the New South, Davidson singled out Page for special derogation, although he also attacked Edwin A. Alderman, an educator; Governor Aycock, a politician; and two advocates of progressive farming, Clarence Poe and Seaman A. Knapp. In Virginius Dabney's *Liberalism in the South* (1932), Davidson found the fullest statement yet of the new liberal position, but he scoffed at Dabney for being unable to "contrive a definition" of liberalism that would fit all its historic manifestations.[37] Dabney could not furnish a test by which a genuine liberal could be recognized. Regarding contemporary reflections of the New South in literature, Davidson castigated writers like T. S. Stribling and Ellen Glasgow for "producing Southern versions of what New York thought was wrong with the South."[38] These writers, in other words, were engaged in a literary betrayal of the South.

Davidson's designation of Walter Hines Page as a primary Agrarian target was not accidental; Page, especially in his *The Rebuilding of Old Commonwealths* (1902), had written persuasively of the need for Southern awakening. More clearly than many other regional spokesmen and at an earlier date he realized that a thorough-going industrial revolution within the South implied many new demands upon the people. An entire new generation of skilled workers and professionals would be needed to replace the low quality of labor left as a legacy of the plantation system. Education would have to be reformed and expanded in a South at last able to face the future, facing facts instead of lamenting the dead Confederate past. Page felt that such a social and psychological change would eventually provide all Southern citizens with a highly rewarding culture; even the smallest localities would feel the beneficial effects.

Page wrote at the turn of the century when America as a whole stirred with imperial ambitions. For the first time since the Civil War, Northern and Southern men had worn a common uniform and fought a common enemy, Spain. Page gathered ample evidence to support his thesis that the industrial revolution in the South was proceeding apace, giving hope and new opportunity to hitherto backward, stagnant areas. Aware of the valuable untapped human resources that industrialism needed, he repeatedly stressed the importance of educating the "forgotten man," the average Southerner who in his ignorance was proud to be illiterate and reactionary. So indifferent to the fate of these people had been the post-Reconstruction social and political leaders, that in 1890 "there were living in other States 290,000 persons who were born in North Carolina."[39] By their self-imposed exile from the state of their birth they condemned the conditions from which they had escaped.

Seeming to reflect the ideas of William Morris on the virtues of a society, Page stated that the common people were the ones most to be considered in a civilized community. He continued, "A community is not rich because it contains a few rich men, it is not healthful because it contains a few strong men, it is not intelligent because it contains a few men of learning" (p. 3). Unfortunately, such communities led by the privileged few had been typical of the South before the Civil War. Such was still the situation at the turn of the century because of various powerful forces of retrogression—the archaic educational system, the organized church, the still too static economy, and corrupt politics. Page said:

The worst of it was that the stationary social condition indicated by generations of illiteracy had long been the general condition. The forgotten man was content to be forgotten. He became not only a dead weight, but a definite opponent of social progress. He faithfully heard the politician on the stump praise him for virtues that he did not have. (p. 22)

Like the politician, the preacher further deadened his ambitions by saying that God intended his poverty as a means of grace. In 1897 in a speech to female students at Greensboro, North Carolina, Page emphasized the tragic effect of religion on the average Southern woman. "If she be intensely religious," he said, "her religion is only an additional misfortune, for it teaches her, as she understands it, to be content with her lot and all its burdens, since they prepare her for the life to come" (p. 25). Here is a curious parallel to the idea of Marx that religion is the "opiate of the masses"; but whereas Marx deemed it an obstacle to the coming of communism, Page saw it as an obstruction to the development of capitalism in the South. Page felt that women had a far brighter future in helping to fashion the New South than they could ever have in staying with the ways of the Old South.

Page offered a full account of why the "old commonwealths" were unable to keep up with the rest of America. He noted that massive emigration had drained off many of the South's most aggressive and intelligent sons. He explained what he considered to be the major causes of stagnation.

Three influences have held the social structure stationary—first, slavery, which pickled Southern life and left it as it found it; then the politician and the preacher. One has proclaimed the present as the ideal condition; and, if any doubt this declaration, the other has bidden him to be content and make sure of the world to come. Thus gagged and bound this rural society has remained stationary longer than English-speaking people have remained stationary anywhere else in the world. It is a state of life that keeps permanently the qualities of the frontier civilization long after the frontier has receded and been forgotten. The feeling that you bring away with you after a visit to such a community is a feeling that something has intervened to hold these people back from their natural development. They have capacity that far outruns their achievement. They are citizens of an earlier time and of a narrower world who have not come to their own. And this is the cue to their character. (p. 121-22)

A more modern environment could reshape this character and develop its positive virtues. To bring this about was Page's major purpose in his demand for a New South. He recognized and encouraged two powerful regenerative forces: industry and public education. So great and benevolent would be their impact that a readjustment in race relations would make it possible for both Negro and white to contribute without friction to another and more lasting Reconstruction. The politicians could not build racial harmony because the Southern political machines which supported them were based on race differences; the greatest success in election after election had gone to the demagogue who cried loudest for white supremacy. With some passage of time, with adequate training, and with a sense of opportunity, the Negro could be counted on to take part in the process of renewal. As Page affirmed: "The white man has held the Negro back, the Negro has held the white man back; and dead men have ruled them both. Training to economic independence is the only true emancipation" (p. 126).

Page regarded as evil the once dominant idea that education "was a luxury for the rich, or a privilege of the well-born—if a necessity at all, a necessity for the ruling class. This class feeling in education was perceptible even within my recollection" (p. 6). In earlier times, when it was conceived to benefit only the aristocracy, education did not touch the masses of people. In North Carolina, for example, Page said there was no substantial progress in the broadening of educational opportunity "from the time of the colony till the beginning of the civil war" (p. 15). The Agrarians were later to challenge all such censure of education in the Old South. John Gould Fletcher and Allen Tate declared flatly that its education was superior to that in the rest of America. Page, on the other hand, blamed the South's class system for its failure to develop any top-notch colleges, famous scholars, and outstanding libraries. That the older traditions based on class snobbery and intellectual dry rot still stifled many college towns was cause for dismay. Speaking of one campus town where a professor, fearful of accusation as a "radical," kept copies of Matthew Arnold and Ernest Renan under lock and key, Page said: "It is in such a circle of the old

academic society and in the rural regions that you come upon the real
Southern problem—that unyielding stability of opinion which gives a
feeling of despair, the very antithesis of social growth and social mobility" (p. 131).

Despite the strong influence of tradition, Page believed that improved public education, together with industrialism, would in time
solve all major regional problems. The forgotten men, whose abilities
had hitherto been unused, would come into their own. Page was enthusiastic about the idea that "none can be well educated until all are
trained" (p. 146). He said in its praise, "This is native, and it is nothing different from Jefferson's creed and plan" (p. 141). Indeed, had
Jefferson's plan for education, training, and work been instituted earlier by Southerners, Page believed that a "stronger economic impetus
might have been given to diversified pursuits than cotton-culture gave
to slavery, and the whole course of our history might have been
changed" (p. 152).

In the realm of politics and government, education would show up
the essentially democratic nature of the Southern people. Up to the
present this nature had been smothered and thwarted by slavery and
the race question. The people's destiny, in Page's optimistic view, was
"a democratic order of society which will be an important contribution to the Republic that their ancestors took so large a part in establishing" (p. 153). Education in the abstract, however, could not bring
about this order of society. Only by the spread of industry could education be put into full and practical use in the destruction of lingering
reactionary hangovers. Industry had already transferred the crucial
power to a class of men who bring mobility to social life and opportunity to them that can take it. Like Sidney Lanier and other liberals,
Page did not favor a complete break with the earlier Southern tradition. Although the new factory system and its new industrial culture
would bring out the inherent democratic principles of the people, he
warned: "But no man who knows the gentleness and the dignity and
the leisure of the old Southern life would like to see these qualities
blunted by too rude a growth of sheer industrialism" (p. 141). Page
felt that a gradual but steady progress would not convulse society, yet
would end with towns having mills and shops and paved streets, electric lights, good libraries and schools, and an alert and cultured citi-
zenry. These were the essentials of Page's vision of a New South predicated on the people's ability to change and improve, to acquire skills
and demonstrate wisdom.

Many years later Edwin Mims gave optimistic facts about the extent to which this vision had been realized. He wrote that looms and furnaces, factories and stores, and railroads and water powers "have led to the prosperity of the few and the well-being of the many, and these in turn have been largely responsible for the symphony orchestra and the Parthenon of Nashville, the grand opera seasons of Atlanta and Chattanooga, the County Court House of Memphis, the Tennessee War Memorial Auditorium, and the increasing architectural beauty of colleges that stretch from Charlottesville to New Orleans."[40] Not that Mims was satisfied with the progress made; yet he genuinely believed the South was on its way forward.

Chapter V   Enormous Megatherions

In their struggle against the twentieth century, the agrarians often appeared to be rural Davids in arms against a potent urban Goliath. The giant had at his disposal countless agencies, both visible and invisible, engaged in destroying the remaining vestiges of a sound traditional society. Donald Davidson's metaphor for the magnitude of the modern enemy was "leviathan." *The Attack on Leviathan* (Chapel Hill, 1938) was the title he gave to his volume outlining various methods for coping with it. The industrial society nurtured by finance capitalism and its obedient genie the federal government constituted leviathan's form; but its spirit had a pernicious influence on morality, education, religion, and art as well.

In the Preface of *Land of the Free* Herbert Agar quoted Thomas Carlyle who had foreseen the problems now being confronted. Carlyle had written, "Enormous Megatherions, as ugly as were ever born of mud, loom huge and hideous out of the twilight Future on America; and she will have her own agony, and her own victory, but on other terms than she is yet quite aware of."[1] Carlyle's "Enormous Megatherions" fits as a metaphor for much that the Agrarians regarded as monstrous in modern society: big industry, big cities, and big government. Carlyle had made the comment in a long essay entitled "The Present Time" which was published in a book called *Latter-Day Pamphlets*. The essay includes a strong attack on democratic institutions in America. Carlyle scoffed at the idea that democracy could work and predicted that America would undergo great agonies before it realized that the wise will always have to govern the foolish masses. Hence the philosophy of medievalists both past and present proved to be an invaluable support for their stand.

Although they quarreled with the Neo-Humanists over the problem of giving tradition a "local habitation and a name," nevertheless the

Agrarians had a great deal in common with the conservatism of Babbitt, More, and Foerster. They were not Catholics, yet the Agrarians admired the Catholic church for its power to maintain social tradition, cultural stability, aristocratic government, and religious ritual. They were impressed and influenced by all that T. S. Eliot had to say on the above subjects; they agreed with Eliot that only a settled and well-ordered society could produce a Dante.

Through the works of T. E. Hulme, T. S. Eliot, and Charles Maurras, the Agrarians found support for their own views in those of the great French reactionaries, beginning with Joseph de Maistre, whose strenuous work it was to contain the cultural impact of the French Revolution. Perhaps the most immediate source of inspiration, however, was the Victorian precedent of feudalistic anti-industrialism expressed by Carlyle, Morris, and Ruskin. Morris was too much of a socialist to be a genuine Agrarian hero; and yet his love for the Middle Ages and his contempt for capitalism provided arguments for those who wished to condemn the new age.

Active support for the Agrarians came from some of the modern disciples of men like Ruskin; for example, from Arthur J. Penty, whose writings appeared both in English journals and in the *American Review* and had the distinction of impressing T. S. Eliot. "We have in the first place to take account of the fact," Penty wrote in the *Criterion*, "that in the Middle Ages the individual enjoyed a definite status, whether under the Church, the Guild or Feudal System; he had security, he was cared for during sickness, provided for in his old age and was rarely troubled with unemployment."[2] The Agrarians said exactly the same thing about Negro slaves when contrasting their status with the more precarious conditions of free laborers in the factory system. Penty felt that the economic tragedy of the Middle Ages was the failure of the guilds to establish themselves in rural areas after the break-up of feudal society. Had this occurred, "capitalism would never have got a foothold, and the whole subsequent economic and political history of Europe would have been different."[3] As it was now, a century and a half of industrialism had resulted in such great "social and economic confusion as to bring civilization to the verge of catastrophe."[4] Like the Agrarians, Penty also attacked progress, theories of social evolution, machines, science, and cosmopolitanism; he praised Ruskin and Carlyle. And in a passage which could have come directly from *I'll Take My Stand* he wrote:

It is only when a people live a local life, are rooted in local tradition, that they develop character; and, I may add it is only amid such local conditions of life and society that religion and art flourish, for it is only when the foundations of society are fixed, so to say, and where movement and flux are definitely limited, that the great traditions will take root.[5]

Penty's neo-Ruskinian essays appeared side by side with those of the Southern Agrarians during the thirties in the *American Review*. However, the Agrarians were aware of the Victorian medievalists as early as *I'll Take My Stand*. Citing the damage inflicted upon life and art by industrialism, Ransom had written, "Ruskin and Carlyle feared it nearly a hundred years ago, and now it may be said that their fears have been realized partly in England, and with almost fatal completeness in America."[6] When Ransom in *God Without Thunder* discussed the problem of American heroism, he posed the type of question (arising from the loss of a social tradition) which is associated with Carlyle. Modern life has been terribly disrupted; therefore, "We are not sure on what terms we may possess our heroes."[7] On another occasion Ransom proposed the revival of the Southern gentlemen as a solution; he alone had the honor, dignity, charm, wit, and urbanity which could make possible the contemporary hero. These qualities, inherent in the older agrarian society, were denied modern man by the new "slavery" of industrialism, which "fastens not only upon the poor, but upon the middle and better classes of society, too. To make this point it may be necessary to revive such an antiquity as the old Southern gentleman and his lady, and their scorn for the dollar-chasers."[8]

Other Agrarians seemed at times to lean on the medievalism of Carlyle and Ruskin even more heavily than Ransom. Speaking of Bertrand Russell, John Gould Fletcher said; "He is aware that Carlyle and Bismarck and even the Popes and Czars—the great reactionaries in short—were outwardly at least far more in accordance with the true facts of human nature, with all those local loyalties, familiar decencies, and human 'overbeliefs,' than were any of the Radicals."[9] The publication in 1935 of R. H. Wilenski's biography, *Ruskin*, afforded Fletcher another opportunity to record the Agrarian debt to him. Fletcher praised Wilenski for realizing that Ruskin, in his later years, became an important and forceful supporter of the "reformation and reclassification of society which the twentieth century is now attempting, halfheartedly and probably too late."[10] Fletcher felt that the Southern Agrarians had an important role among the many conservative movements making these attempts. He continued:

What Ruskin essentially foresaw, that no great art (as the past knew it) was possible so long as the industrial process was allowed to run hand in hand with unchecked competition, is now our dilemma; the attempt he made to bring society back to a frame of mind that would no longer be individual-istic, but co-operatively religious, must be resumed today under far less fa-vourable conditions.[11]

Pessimistic about the major trends in society, Ruskin predicted that industrialism would eventually wreck all "the local and particular loy-alties and patriotisms of mankind as well as the leading religious creeds," unless it were checked. For these and other views, Fletcher called Ruskin the greatest aesthetic and moral thinker that England produced in the entire nineteenth century.

Along with other thinkers of the past century, the Agrarians must have read Karl Marx even though they generally despised him; at least they made use of the Marxist idea, expressed in the *Communist Mani-festo*, that all art was degraded under capitalism by the "cash nexus," the profit motive that ruled supreme. Every art object was judged by the standard: Will it sell? How much money is it worth? There were, of course, other reasons why art and industrialism were incompatible, as the Agrarian Statement of Principles described.

Nor do the arts have a proper life under industrialism, with the general decay of sensibility which attends it. Art depends, in general, like religion, on a right attitude to nature; and in particular on a free and disinterested obser-vation of nature that occurs only in leisure. Neither the creation nor the un-derstanding of works of art is possible in an industrial age except by some local and unlikely suspension of the industrial drive.[12]

If a critic holds to such a theory, he is always tempted to reverse the argument to keep it in his favor and say: Whatever does get created in an industrial society cannot be art because art, as explained above, simply cannot exist under industrialism; that which is called art has to be something less worthy—a cheap imitation of the genuine.

In *I'll Take My Stand* the main job of condemning the effects of in-dustrialism on art fell to Donald Davidson. In his "A Mirror for Ar-tists" he tried to answer the important question: "What is the in-dustrial theory of the arts?" Following the example of Ruskin and Morris, Davidson attacked industrialism as a vicious process that both dirtied up the physical landscape and made man's life dull, mechani-cal, and mean. Conscious mainly of his own region, Davidson envis-aged the South pillaged by a horde of cultural reformers, missionaries of the industrial North, arriving to prepare the land for bathtubs and flush toilets. "Much as the Red Cross mobilizes against disease," he complained in a sardonic passage, "the guardians of public taste can mobilize against bad art or lack of art; one visualizes caravans of art, manned by regiments of lecturers, rushed hastily to future epidemic centers of barbarism, when some new Mencken discovers a Sahara of the Bozart."[13]

Even in the vital role of patron, industrialism tended to destroy the arts; the "industrial Maecenas" had not the intelligence or the sensibility to appreciate art. His attitude was strictly crass and commercial; he could work only on the principle, "We shall buy it, hire it, can it, or—most conclusively—manufacture it."[14] The primary trouble lay in the decadence of an economy which placed an exchange value on every object, including art. Davidson wrote bitterly that industrialism "will buy art, if any fool wants it. And industrialism is quite unconscious that the bargain (which the Middle Ages would have described as a devil's bargain, ending in the delivery of the soul to torment) involves the destruction of the thing bargained for." Reporting an imaginary dialogue between the industrial patron and the modern artist, Davidson had the former ask, "Incompetent wretch, is this sorry product what I bargained for?" And the poor artist replied in self-defense: "You do not understand the nature of genius. I do not expect to be appreciated in my lifetime anyway, and certainly not by vulgar persons unlearned in the modern theories of art. Art makes its own rules, which are not the rules of commerce."[15]

Furthermore, according to Davidson, the liberal's dream of mastering the machine for aesthetic purposes was futile. Neither the machine nor any object it created could ever be a proper subject matter for literature. Davidson wrote: "Wordsworth's hope that objects of science will become familiar as materials of art is still remote. Their role is mainly Satanic."[16] The only real hope for the arts lay in an Agrarian society; it was the only alternative to industrialism, for communism and capitalism were equally committed to the machine age. Only Agrarianism could end the current physical and spiritual despoilment of mankind. Man would not be forced to work so desperately nor would he work and play at cross purposes; his work and his play would merge in one joyful endeavor. Davidson believed that under industrialism even leisure was antagonistic to the creation of good art. People with spare time were conditioned to occupy themselves with mechanical gadgets. The arts therefore would "not easily survive" such an uncongenial environment. Everywhere they turned they would be rebuffed and frustrated.

Nor could the arts survive the natural extension into their province of the mass production principle, the tendency of the artist to think of a mass market; the facilities for mass distribution made matters worse when the art distributed so widely was bad art. Consequently, Davidson condemned such enterprises as book clubs for spreading a "gradual corruption of integrity and taste." He also pointed out that the arts under the capitalist system would be merely decorative since "poetry sells no bonds and music manages no factories."[17]

Davidson also criticized the museum in a manner reminiscent of William Morris's criticism of the separation of art and life. As Ransom had emphasized how the arts of the eighteenth century dominated every detail of the Old South society, so Davidson now repeated that art should be evidenced in all usable objects—in pots, pans, chairs, rugs, and so on. To collect art in specially consecrated "shrines" was to deny it any chance to permeate the total awareness of the people. "What is a picture for," Davidson asked, "if not to put on one's own walls?"[18]

Davidson declared that industry had made so much artificial progress in the wrong direction that a "remaking of life itself" was needed before the arts could resume their traditional role. Agrarianism, the counterforce, could bring about this remaking of life. Beginning with a solid base in the backward areas of the South, the artist must try to "restore and preserve a social economy that is in danger of being replaced altogether by an industrial economy hostile to his interests."[19] An Agrarian restoration could bestow enormous rewards on the artist; most important, he would be liberated from his enslavement to commerce. No longer would the arts be considered luxuries to be purchased, but would "belong as a matter of course" to the daily routines of life.

Another visible monstrosity of industrialism was the big city and its fraudulent, immoral, and artless culture known to the Agrarians as cosmopolitanism. From New York City and its lesser replicas emanated evil influences that increasingly menaced the former innocence of the hinterland. Cosmopolitanism was essentially the product of the modern industrial system. It was in cities that the "mentality" of industrialism blossomed, and this mentality was in no way beneficial to the arts. "Urban civilization," Davidson wrote, "produces an art without roots when it produces any art at all. Some of its artists tend to be dissociated from place, experimental, absolute, sophisticated; this is the art of the expatriates and cosmopolitans. Others are realists and propagandists; their art is the agent of the social conceptions out of which it grows."[20] It would seem that social conceptions aiding a literature growing out of a traditional agrarian culture was acceptable to Davidson, since the art thus produced was rooted in place and time.

Summing up the spiritual emptiness of the industrial society, Stark Young had declared:

It may be that the end of man's living is not mere raw Publicity, Success, Competition, Speed and Speedways, Progress, Donations, and Hot Water, all seen with a capital letter. There are also more fleeting and eternal things to be thought of; more grace, sweetness, and time; more security in our instincts, and chance to follow our inmost nature, as Jesus meant when he said he must be about his Father's business; more of that last fine light to shine on what we do. . . .[21]

The industrial society was also responsible for other doleful aspects of modern America. The youth enrolled in colleges, where in all innocence they inherited our culture, were already placed in a "false way of life" because they were thoroughly conditioned by commercial values; thus they could not make more than "an inconsequential acquaintance with the arts and humanities" or, if they did, "the understanding of these arts and humanities will but make them the more wretched in their own destitution."[22] To their credit, it seems to me, the Agrarians could see no value in a life based on bread, or money, alone. To again secure a worthy life, which implied a decent relationship to nature, religion, and their fellow man, the youth of college age had to reject all the pressing commercial lures of modern society. They could learn little from the Neo-Humanists because what Babbitt and More taught was too abstract, too removed from the soil, too distant from actualities. On the other hand, Southern humanism "was rooted in the Agrarian life of the older South and of other parts of the country that shared in such a tradition." Far from being merely theoretical, this humanism was founded on a life that was clearly defined "in its tables, chairs, portraits, festivals, laws, marriage customs." Asking for more hostility toward modern America than that shown by the leaders of Neo-Humanism, the Agrarians proclaimed: "We cannot recover our native humanism by adopting some standard of taste that is critical enough to question the contemporary arts but not critical enough to question the social and economic life [that is, industrialism] which is their ground."[23]

The Agrarians determined that higher education in the United States was untraditional, commercial, and hollow; under the industrial system, all institutions had to knuckle under to the necessity of "selling" their "commodities." Science and technology, prostituted to the same general end, had done much to undermine the status of the humanites. Hence teachers in the humanities created such tortured locutions as "biology of language," the "chemistry of drama," and "fossil forms of literature." Educators should reject all these evidences of industrial and scientific pressure. Instead, they should pursue the "general idea, held once in the old South and still in England, that education of the university sort, not professional or technical, is suited to a small number only."[24] Were this restrictive theory to prevail in practice, American colleges might become less "democratic, mobbed, and imitative." On several other occasions in Agrarian writings, the English teacher was specifically assigned the responsibility of preserving the humanities. To Davidson, for instance, he was "the latest defender of the humanistic culture that is threatened with destruction by the great invasion of scientific and utilitarian subjects."[25]

John Gould Fletcher, the well-known Imagist poet, began the discussion of Agrarian views on education in *I'll Take My Stand*. He blamed the great upheavals of the American Revolution and the Civil War for having disturbed what had been, in his opinion, a commendable educational system. From 1700, in a Southern populace which was mainly English, education was controlled by the Church of England. Because of this religious supervision, there was "probably actually more education of the poor in the South than in the North"—an opinion, it must be said, greatly at odds with that of Walter Hines Page and other supporters of the New South. Fletcher wrote that the demise of the Southern practice of hiring English tutors (a loss that occurred during the Revolution) was a serious blow to the traditional pattern of learning and "in a sense a victory for the North."[26] Using the Official Outline of Teaching in the Prussian High Schools to illustrate his points, Fletcher praised the Southern colonial academies for having the "profound philosophy inherent in all European schemes of learning" (p. 102). Training in these older academies was classical and humanist rather than scientific and technical and bridged the gap between what Fletcher called mere knowledge and the more vital power for independent work. After 1776, however, the agitation for free public schools in the South "was rapid and in the end disastrously complete"—another viewpoint with which Walter Hines Page was in absolute disagreement. Otherwise, Page's strong campaign for wider educational opportunities would have been unnecessary.

The main point in Fletcher's article was clearly the limitation of education to the aristocratic few. Its scope would undoubtedly include the new Agrarian elite, although its modern complexion was never adequately defined. Be that as it may, Fletcher maintained that Jefferson did not favor education for all, as some supposed, but only for "those persons whom nature has endowed with genius and virtue"

(p. 105). Natural differences in quality determined such an aristocratic education. Fletcher wrote, "The inferior, whether in life or in education, should exist only for the sake of the superior" (pp. 119–20). Fletcher asserted that we use our minds in order "to achieve character, to become the balanced personalities, the 'superior men' of Confucius' text, the 'gentlemen' of the old South." Education in modern America, then, must be directed toward the selection and training of those who can "form an intellectual elite—a thing we had from the Revolution down to the Civil War, and do not possess today" (p. 120). We have instead, because of industrial and democratic pressures, the "craze for simplifying, standardizing, and equalizing educational opportunities for all" (p. 110). The older Southern purpose of producing "good men" had given way to compulsory universal education, which meant slashing standards to fit the average if not the lowest rank of students. Fletcher said that educators who claimed Jefferson as a cobeliever in general education distorted his philosophy; consequently, the failure to follow his theory of natural selection had created a human product dangerously removed from the level of the gentleman and the elite. Today we have a mechanically trained individual capable of responding only to the materialistic attractions symbolized by New York City. Today youth are educated by the millions—in terms of quantity rather than quality. Fletcher said, "This fact has been seized upon by partisans of our present state of standardized mass production as a fresh proof that democratic America is culturally superior to 'feudal' Europe" (p. 116).

As might be expected, not much was said by any of the Southern Agrarians on the subject of educating Negroes. Fletcher considered futile the zeal of Northern and some Southern liberals to send Negroes to high school and college, since doing so "under the present social and economic conditions" would be a waste of everyone's time, including that of the Negro youth himself. Robert Penn Warren added in this regard that the "emphasis on vocational education for the negro is not, as has sometimes been thought and said, a piece of white man's snobbery."[27] To be properly absorbed, those Negroes who were in the professions needed "a separate negro community." By this was meant a kind of ghetto within a generally white community; the Agrarians emphatically did not propose, as did the communists for a while, an autonomous Negro republic within the borders of the United States. On the so-called "Negro question," the radicals of the left were miles apart from the radicals of the right. The views of the latter (which is what the Agrarians occasionally labeled themselves) indicated that while the humanities and other elite subjects should be stressed for the chosen few among the white people, only vocational training, if indeed that, should be given to Negroes.

The liberals, on the other hand, had created what the Agrarians derisively called the "New Negro." To enhance his prestige anthropologists and other social scientists had unearthed a "culture" in his African past. This debased, primitive, Negroid heritage was being foisted upon American civilization by the liberals. Another problem which especially troubled the Agrarians also had racist overtones—the big city's tolerance of Jews. The Agrarians imagined the alleged cultural influence of these two inferior peoples spreading to the South to the same degree as in New York City. The thought proved to be appalling.

Various unscientific theories about the influence of race on culture had existed long before *I'll Take My Stand*. What today qualifies as anti-Semitism can be seen in many examples of past literature; but it must not be assumed, however, that racism has applied only to Negroes and to Jews. The linguists in Victorian England opened a Pandora's box of racist theories when they tried to determine whether the Teutons or the Celts had most influenced the history of the English language. The long controversy branched out eventually into other fields—into politics, ethics, literature, and religion. Being a nation of "Celtic" origin, France was also brought into the debate. Essentially it became a racist argument which in time engaged such prominent persons as Matthew Arnold and Thomas Huxley.[28] In its course many reams of nonsense were published alleging that race determined character and culture. Richard Wagner, for example, expressed great alarm that German music was being corrupted by a mysterious quality he called "Jewishness."

Insofar as the Agrarians were concerned, the racism shown in white supremacy existed deeply in the Southern tradition which they admired and struggled to sustain. Allen Tate pointed out, however, that even under slavery the Negro had adversely affected the culture by his breaking of the bond between the gentleman and nature. He wrote, "The Negro slave was a barrier between the ruling class and the soil." As if he had a choice, we might add, but to work out in the hot sun while his master drank cool mint juleps on the white veranda. "If we look at aristocracies in Europe," Tate continued, "say in eighteenth-century England, we find at least genuine social classes, each carrying on a different level of the common culture. But in the Old South, and under the worst form of slavery [industrialism] that afflicts both races today, genuine social classes do not exist."[29] The Negro was not capable of contributing anything of value to white man's culture. Tate continued, "It was not that slavery was corrupt 'morally.' Societies can bear an amazing amount of corruption and still produce high culture. Black slavery could not nurture the white man in his own image." Tate did not specify what this nurturing would have involved had it been possible. He did explain that the Negro could not partake of a cultural maturation comparable to that which was achieved in France by the peasant class. "The high arts," Tate wrote, "have been grafted upon the peasant stock. We could graft no new life upon the Negro; he was too different, too alien."[30]

To the argument that the Negro was indeed engrafted with a new life (chattel slavery) and that he was not allowed to practice his own arts (which to an extent he did anyway), the Agrarians answered that the Negroes "came" to America, they were not brought in chains; furthermore, they rather enjoyed their status of oppression. Owsley wrote; "Negroes had come into the Southern colonies in such numbers that people feared for the integrity of the white race. For the negroes were cannibals and barbarians, and therefore dangerous."[31] Should we ask to what degree the effort was made to raise the Negro slaves culturally, the answer would be that they were racially too inferior to profit from any such effort; besides, as slaves they had a better life than did the free "slaves" of industrialism. Tate perhaps most frankly expressed the Agrarian feeling about Negroes.

I argue it this way: the white race seems determined to rule the Negro race in its midst; I belong to the white race; therefore I intend to support white rule. Lynching is a symptom of weak, inefficient rule; but you can't destroy lynching by *fiat* or social legislation; lynching will disappear when the white race is satisfied that its supremacy will not be questioned in social crises.[32]

Thus it is understandable why the Agrarians so strongly resented both Southern and Northern liberals, not to mention those on the extreme left, who sponsored just the kind of legislation which the Agrarians condemned. Ransom attacked the ideals of "progress" and "service" as forces of evil which helped industrialism win its vulgar triumphs. The idea of "service" seduced otherwise laggard men into fresh and disruptive struggles with nature. He obviously disparaged what had come to be known as a "social conscience," for he wrote of service:

It has special application to the apparently stagnant sections of mankind, it busies itself with the heathen Chinee, with the Roman Catholic Mexican, with the "lower classes" in our own society. Its motive is missionary. Its watchwords are such as Protestantism, Individualism, Democracy, and the point of its appeal is a discontent, generally labelled "divine."[33]

Ransom's scorn becomes even clearer if one inserts the "Southern Negro" in his list of the "apparently stagnant sections of mankind." Whether divine or not, discontent among the Negro is the last thing which the Southern white conservative wished to see.

Too many Americans, too many "aliens," from north of the Mason-Dixon line, had suddenly become too active in helping the Negro free himself from the Jim Crow system. Numerous delegations, mostly from Northern cities, came down to probe everything from the labor violence at Gastonia to the alleged facts in the celebrated Scottsboro Boys case. Even the fanciful communist proposal for an autonomous Negro republic in the South had the effect of bestowing dignity upon a supposedly "inferior" race that did not have enough intelligence to be self-reliant. The Agrarians also disliked the fact that the New Negro was appearing more and more as a positive character in literature. He was not a Noble Savage in the older sense, but a worthy person in his own right whose virtues had been overlooked because of racial prejudice. The concept of the New Negro, in the Agrarian view, had created a literary cult among Northern liberals which even included some Southerners, like T. S. Stribling. The Agrarians considered his depiction of Southern backwardness to be "hick-baiting." In an essay highly critical of Stribling, Robert Penn Warren wrote, "His method is to bring into collision a noble Negro, or rather a half-breed, and a white society considerable less noble."[34] In their own fiction the Agrarians seldom deviated from the inherited stereotype of the Negro as lazy, shifty, immoral, slow-witted, and potentially vicious.

They discussed at some length the influence of race on literature when they developed their theory of regionalism; however, the subject of race was also relevant to the cultural unity of their ideal community, in which respect they received valuable guidance from T. S. Eliot. His proper Christian community rejected the presence of Negroes and Jews because they divided the otherwise monolithic social unity. Their "racial memories" could not harmonize with those of the indigenous regional culture. In the Agrarian outlook, of course, the lack of assimilation was due strictly to alleged flaws in the Negro character, for which the ruling white majority was in no way to blame. After all, this majority already had a solution suitable to itself: the Negro must be content to *stay in his place*. It was bad enough for the Negro to have chosen to reside in the South; his very presence provided a ready excuse for Yankee radicals and assorted hotheads to invade the region on odious crusades to stop lynching, abolish poll taxes, and end all kinds of inherited discrimination. Should the monstrous industrial system expand without limit in the South, it would surely import violent class conflict and trade unions which might, in the end, admit Negroes and whites as equal members.[35]

Having ideologically betrayed their region, the Southern liberals were blind to these potential social dangers. Indeed, they often seemed perversely to welcome them. Writers like Stribling, who had been seduced by liberalism, slanted their work to please Northern publishers. Those writers wasted their talent in "getting out 'Yankee' novels about the virtues of the downtrodden black man and the vices of the depraved man in the south."[36] On the other hand, William Faulkner also depicted human depravity in his Southern stories; but his art did not incite desires to jettison the regional tradition. He searched deeply and genuinely into the Southern soul. Warren delcared that "the drama that engrosses Stribling is a drama of external circumstances, a conflict drawn in the purely practical world; the drama that engrosses Faulkner concerns a state of being, a conflict involving, to some degree at least, the spiritual integrity of a character."[37] That is to say that Stribling is superficial while Faulkner is profound.

Doubtless because Jews were less numerous than Negroes in the South, the Agrarians referred less to them than to the latter. However, enough evidence exists to indicate that a truly Agrarian society could not succeed if it had too many Jews. What "too many" meant was never specified. Sherwood Anderson raised the issue of race in his memoirs when he wrote about the Agrarians and about having met John Crowe Ransom one time in Colorado.

At Boulder, Ransom talked of a new attitude taken by many of the former agrarians. It seemed they had dropped agrarianism. There was a sort of fascist program, that seemed, as Ransom spoke of it, to involve continual subjugation of the Negro and hatred of the Jews. There was something about adopting the feeling of the community in which you lived. If hatred of the Jews, for example, was a characteristic of the community you did not oppose it. You gave yourself to it.[38]

In his comment Anderson implied that racism had been a constant factor in the Agrarian ideology and that it would continue even though the economics had been abandoned. The comment also implied that the Agrarians, like Eliot, believed in cultural relativism, at least in that aspect of it which justifies certain practices regardless of their being good or evil simply because they *exist* in an accepted social system.

In his University of Virginia lectures in 1933, during which he singled out Allen Tate in a favorable mention of the Agrarians, Eliot explained his theory of a homogeneous community. He stressed the need for a certain degree of racial purity, and he did so again in his book *The Idea of a Christian Society* (1939). Like the Agrarians, Eliot related the question of racial purity to that of a proper tradition; he cautioned that tradition should not be regarded too rigidly and without critical judgment. "What I mean by tradition," he said, "involves all those habitual actions, habits and customs, from the most significant religious rite to our conventional way of greeting a stranger, which represents the blood kinship 'of the same people living in the same place.'" When two or more cultures co-existed, they must be "fiercely self conscious or both become adulterate." On the matter of keeping an already pure community immaculate, as was presumably the case with the state of Virginia, Eliot advised: "What is still more important is unity of religious background; and reasons of race and religion combine to make any large number of free-thinking Jews undesirable." In his ideal Christian community, with its inherited structures and conformities, Eliot felt that a "spirit of excessive tolerance is to be deprecated."[39]

In many of his articles and books Eliot expounded views that were close to those of the Agrarians. For example, he favored "a small and mostly self-contained group attached to the soil and having its interests centred in a particular place, with a kind of unity which may be designed, but which also has to grow through generations."[40] These are the phrases and accents of Agrarianism; nor was Eliot in his general philosophy any less of a medievalist than the great Victorians who contributed to Agrarian thought. "One is to insist," Eliot wrote, "that the only salvation for society is to return to a simpler mode of life, scrapping all the constructions of the modern world that we can bring ourselves to dispense with. This is an extreme statement of the neo-Ruskinian view, which was put forward with much vigour by the late A. J. Penty."[41]

These and other related attitudes of T. S. Eliot toward the ideal community were thoroughly acceptable to Ransom, Tate, and their associates. This community, with its Agrarian and Distributist economic base, could save the world from rampant cosmopolitanism. In a sense it was to save the white Christian from his racial enemies. Of all the Agrarians, Davidson and Fletcher were most outspoken in what seemed to be anti-Semitic sentiments. Davidson condemned the effects of modern learning on the innocent youth lured away from his native habitat. He wrote:

The mountain boy could get a college education, but the system that built him a school also took out of his mouth the traditional ballad that was his ancient heritage, and instead of a ballad gave him a 'mammy song' devised in Tin Pan Alley by the urbanized descendent of a Russian Jew.[42]

Fletcher in reviewing a book on Alfred S. Stieglitz spoke, among other things, of his "Jewish" exclusiveness: "He was a moneyed man; and he possessed to the full the Jewish persuasiveness, and the Manhattan contempt for all that had emerged from the hinterland."[43] The distaste animating Fletcher's remark is self-evident. But it was probably Allen Tate who best substantiated Sherwood Anderson's passage on the Agrarian desire for continued subjugation of the Negro; it was Tate who made what might be considered the final statement on racial inequality. In a long critique of the liberal symposium *Culture in the South,* Tate asserted, "There will be no practical solution to the race question (as a problem it is inherently insoluble and ought to be, like all social problems in ultimate terms). . . ." As for those cosmopolitan liberals and do-gooders who wished to improve the South, Tate said that he had no "sympathy with reformers who are agitated about social equality, for there never has been social equality anywhere, there never will be, nor ought there to be. Every class and race should get what it earns by contributing to civilized life."[44]

The Agrarians often contrasted the values of aristocracy with the valueless average of modern society. Stark Young wrote of the Southern tradition: "The aristocratic implied with us a certain long responsibility for others; a habit of domination; a certain arbitrariness; certain ideals of personal honor. . . ."[45] Among the Nashville group it was Allen Tate who most openly defended the code of honor. "The price that aristocracy pays for power," Tate affirmed, "is a high standard of public and private conduct that the masses can respect, and the diffusion through society of the materials of civilized living in sufficient quantity to bind all classes together in a single culture."[46]

Tate depicts a duel in his only novel, *The Fathers.* In it he has one of his characters exclaim: "Men of honor and dignity! They did a great deal of injustice but they also knew where they stood because they thought more of their code than they did of themselves."[47] Tate blamed the incidence of Southern violence (presumably both of white against Negro and of white against white) on the "feudal spirit that the plantation system perpetuated in America." He continued, "This spirit to a large extent survives, but the code of honour that once gave it dignity, prescribing the kinds of grievances that justify killing and setting limits to the modes, has disappeared; we get plain murder in place of the duel." Tate went on to say, "The code of honour set little value upon mere human life; it tended to dignify life with a rigid conception of its ideal integrity, without which it is worthless."[48] During the postwar controversy over the awarding of the Bollingen prize to Ezra Pound (who had made wartime radio broadcasts from fascist Rome), Tate issued what was generally understood to be a challenge to a duel to William Barrett, editor of the *Partisan Review*. Barrett allegedly had declared that Tate and other Fellows of the Library of Congress were anti-Semitic. Describing Barrett as dishonorable and cowardly, Tate wrote the phrases which sounded like the invitation to a duel: "Courage and honor are not subjects of literary discussion, but occasions of action."[49] Whatever the intent, nobody seemed to have made a search for a boskage of dueling oaks under which the action could have taken place.

Anxious to secure allies for their cause, the Southern Agrarians at times praised someone for his conservative views but overlooked other aspects of his thought which might not have been compatible with their philosophy. For instance, Count Hermann Keyserling, the German philosopher, was acclaimed for his belief in an Agrarian aristocracy. Like Christopher Hollis and other European conservatives, Keyserling was greatly interested in the Southern tradition for he felt that the South could be the Achilles heel of American democracy. However, certain other aspects of Keyserling's thought tended to deny the Agrarians the hopeful role they had assumed in the restoration of aristocracy for he felt that the scholar and poet had little or no place in the new ruling class.

With Thomas Jefferson, the Agrarians had a more complex problem in attempting to use this powerful Southerner for their current Agrarian crusade. Those aspects of Jefferson's philosophy in accord with their modern "stand" were retained and savored; the rest were conveniently ignored.

On the positive side was the fact that he was a Southerner, a Virginian, an agrarian, a landed gentleman, and an aristocrat. His position on tradition was, according to Tate, that "the way of life and the livelihood of men must be the same."[50] At the beginning of his presidency if not throughout his life, Jefferson opposed a concentrated power in a federal government. This type of power structure was always condemned by the Agrarians, and most fully by Donald Davidson in *The Attack on Leviathan*. He said in respect to Jefferson, "In their fight against giant industrialism and its obverse, giant socialism, the Agrarians in effect were redefining the Jeffersonian principles that had set America off from Europe and had played an important part in forming American character."[51] In practice, as historians commonly agree, the Jeffersonian concept of democracy was confined to the rule of a selected class who acted *for the people* and were themselves governed by the popular consent; this was in contrast to the democracy of Andrew Jackson when government first became also *by the people*. Such a patrician rule would have been acceptable to the Southern Agrarians, provided that its conscious purpose was to maintain the Southern establishment intact, with its tradition, its formal religion, its white supremacy, and all the other ante-bellum values.

In utilizing Jefferson, the Agrarians had to overlook his untraditional belief in deism, his enormous devotion to science, and his prospect of an American republic in which Negroes were free. In theory at least, Jefferson was biased against the growing industrial and commercial power of the Northeast; yet the Embargo Acts of his second term greatly encouraged the tendency toward native American manufacture. Believing in a system of white supremacy, the Agrarians could not firmly support such ideas as: "We hold these truths to be self-evident, that all men are created equal, that they are endowed by their Creator with certain unalienable rights. . . ." Ransom had written that only the theory of slavery was monstrous, its practice was usually humane. Jefferson's view was more negative. He wrote: "There must, doubtless, be an unhappy influence on the manners of our people, produced by the existence of slavery among us. The whole commerce between master and slave is a perpetual exercise of the most boisterous passions, the most unremitting despotism on the one part, and degrading submissions on the other."[52]

From watching the daily treatment of slaves the young gentlemen of the Old South learned many valuable lessons in evil, in how to become effective tyrants.

Our children see this, and learn to imitate it; for man is an imitative animal. This quality is the germ of all education in him. From his cradle to his grave he is learning to do what he sees others do. If a parent could find no motive either in his philosophy or his self-love for restraining the intemperance of passion towards his slave, it should always be a sufficient one that his child is present. But generally it is not sufficient. The parent storms, the child looks on, catches the lineaments of wrath, puts on the same airs in the circle of smaller slaves, gives a loose to his worst of passions, and thus nursed, educated, and daily exercised in tyranny, cannot but be stamped by it with odious peculiarities.[53]

Had they lived in Jefferson's time the Agrarians undoubtedly would have joined the majority of other Southerners in rejecting Jefferson's philosophy. Nor could the Agrarians have agreed with Jefferson's estimate of the manners and morals of the Old South. "That man must be a prodigy," Jefferson declared, "who can retain his manners and morals undepraved by such circumstances. And with what execration should the statesman be loaded, who permitting one-half the citizens thus to trample on the rights of the other, transforms those into despots, and these into enemies, destroys the morals of the one part, and the amor patriae of the other."[54]

Jefferson's prophecy about statesmen loaded with execration has had ample fulfillment in the likes of Talmadge, Rankin, and Bilbo—demagogues of our century defending a modified form of slavery, the system of Jim Crow. In their behalf Davidson and the Agrarians solicited the nation's admiration. Undoubtedly aware of criticism of the Southern addiction to emotional and demagogic appeals, Davidson wrote, "Meanwhile it is worth noting with what uncalculating devotion he [the Southerner] follows the banners of Huey Long or Bilbo or Talmadge. Beware of using, too lightly, the word demagogue. Is it possible that these leaders win him because they are men of deeds, and not stuffed shirts?"[55] The view of some Southern liberals, on the other hand, was that the demagogue more often than not was in the secret pay of the very vested interests against which, in public, he loudly brayed. The humane anti-slavery views of Jefferson were smothered out in the Old South shortly after 1830. Thus the publication in 1930 of *I'll Take My Stand* could be seen in perspective as a kind of centennial for the death of Southern political liberalism. After 1830, neither Jefferson nor anyone else could with impunity speak about emancipation as he had done in 1784. In the famous passage in which he trembles for his country upon reflections on God's justice, he wrote:

I think a change already perceptible, since the origin of the present revolution. The spirit of the master is abating, that of the slave rising from the dust, his condition mollifying, the way I hope preparing, under the auspices of heaven, for a total emancipation, and that this is disposed, in the order of events, to be with the consent of the masters, rather than by their extirpation.[56]

Unfortunately, the order of events was quite other than Jefferson had desired; the totalitarian condition of the Old South, the intransigence that accompanied the outbreak of Civil War, was quite other than what Jefferson had foreseen.

Some emphasis has been given these Jeffersonian views because the Southern Agrarians used the great Virginian as a witness against the leviathanism of modern industrial and political power. All in all, however, he was a poor example of the kind of gentleman who created the "tradition" as understood and admired by the Nashville writers. Jefferson celebrated the Enlightenment, the Age of Reason, and the French Revolution. Had the Agrarians lived in the 1790's, they would have helped to hound Jefferson as a Jacobin, an agent of atheistic France, and they would have supported the Alien and Sedition Acts— for the Agrarians, as we shall see, heartily disliked foreigners and their alien ideas. Nor would they have easily forgiven Jefferson for joining men like Priestley and Paine in the creed of deism, a rational religion with a scientific and humanitarian God. Indeed, Jefferson was a bisected hero. Regardless of all else, the Agrarians praised him for his struggle with the growing capitalist power of the Northeast. "In this," Davidson said, "we followed Jefferson; but where the political role of the South was concerned we followed Calhoun."[57]

During the Civil War, of course, the South followed Jefferson Davis. For that period the Agrarians respectively used Davis and Lincoln as contrasting symbols of good and evil. All references to Lincoln were negative, while every reference to Davis, Lee, and other Confederate leaders, with few and very minor reservations, was laudatory. In reviewing William E. Dodd's *Lincoln or Lee,* Tate wrote, "Lincoln comes to Washington a well meaning, kindly, bewildered, inexperienced doctrinaire; he does not foresee the tendency of his party, which is to crush under a plutocracy the democracy that he loves; he is ignorant of the people and their history; he is hesitant; and the trouble begins."[58] Tate and his friends treated the Union President as a deluded, fumbling, yet well-intentioned leader who unwittingly served Northern capitalism in the crucial hour when this megatherion captured and enslaved the democratic process. Lincoln therefore helped to perpetrate the greatest crime in history: the crushing of the Confederate States of America and the subsequent creation of an almost omnipotent plutocracy based on industrialism. Davidson wrote, "By letting himself be used as an idealistic front for the material designs of the North, Lincoln not only ruined the South but quite conceivably ruined the North as well; and if Fascism or Communism ever arrives in America, Lincoln will have been a remote but efficient cause of its appearance."[59] Had not Lincoln failed to understand the nature of capitalism, Tate asserted, he would have joined Jefferson Davis instead of opposing him. Tate believed that historians were becoming increasingly aware that "the transitional period of early American politics, known as democracy" was not extended but was crushed out of existence by the Civil War.[60] Since then, by virtue of its bigness and its greed, finance-capitalism had despoiled everything it touched, be it democracy, the landscape, tradition, religion, love, education, art, or literature.

Chapter VI   The Aesthetic of Regionalism

DURING THE SUMMER OF 1930 A ROUND TABLE ON REGIONALISM WAS held at the Institute of Public Affairs, University of Virginia. Referring to this event in the *New Republic,* Allen Tate wrote that the words *regionalism* and *sectionalism* "appear in almost every essay on the relation of literature to American society that I have read in the last three years, and in most of the volumes of criticism."[1] Many critics had undoubtedly been reading the monumental works of Parrington. Whatever the reason, the interest in regionalism mounted during the coming decade. It may be said to have reached a climax in *American Regionalism* (New York, 1938), a huge volume prepared by Howard W. Odum and Harry E. Moore. They isolated and examined no less than twenty-eight different concepts of the "region." Their purpose, as they stated, was to organize "the extraordinary amount and variety of materials on regionalism to the end that clarification and unity of the great diversity of regional approaches might be attained."[2] Odum and Moore regarded the "New Regionalism" as a dynamic doctrine of national growth. As a force able to generate historic events it could be compared with the idea of class struggle developed by Karl Marx. However, regionalism had the advantage of being *above* class conflict. It also disdained all forms of "literary regionalism," including that of the Southern Agrarians. In fact, Odum and Moore could not proceed too far without conflicting with the Agrarians on the subject. In respect to Donald Davidson they wrote that he favored a kind of Federalism which would acknowledge the existence of sections and discover the means of adapting national polity to permit their healthy activity within this polity. Davidson also believed that the sections diminished the possibility of violent revolution and guaranteed that social changes must conform with democratic institutions. "What Davidson appears to overlook,"

Odum and Moore said, "is the fact that regionalism connotes unity in a total national composition, while sectionalism with its separatism is inherently different."[3] In general, they relegated the Agrarians to a minor role as literary regionalists primarily, and this type of regionalism was disparaged as "a sort of sentimental romanticism for the local area or for the historical period."

Minor or not, the Southern Agrarians did more than anyone else to develop the literary aspects of regionalism. They succeeded so well in exploiting the literary possibilities that most people, according to Odum and Moore, thought of regionalism as a literary movement. They complained in *American Regionalism,* "Thus the whole regionalist movement has often been described in terms of that regionalism discussed so effectively by the group commonly designated as agrarians."[4] It was the Southern Agrarians they had in mind. Another writer, Paul Beath, went so far as to credit the Agrarians with being its originators. They were not, of course, but his comment was flattering. He said, "The southern agrarian school led by Davidson, John Crowe Ransom, and Allen Tate initiated the current regional movement which has since spread to other sections, notably the Southwest and the Middle West."[5] Literary regionalism had older sources than *I'll Take My Stand* and other Agrarian documents. In one of its primitive forms it appeared in the school of "local color" writers, including Mark Twain and Bret Harte, who emerged after the Civil War. They exploited the specific locality for setting, action, character, and theme; for the first time in American literature, these writers tried to capture the authentic spoken dialect of the folk whom they depicted. In hitherto unexplored regions they found gold mines of material for their creative works.

If Beath had been mistaken in crediting the Agrarians with initiating the regional revival, Odum and Moore were equally mistaken in suggesting that the Agrarians were interested only in its more literary manifestations. Actually, they wrote a good deal about regionalism and sectionalism in respect to the South as a whole. In doing so they were acting within a school of thought that for several decades had been aware that regionalism, or something like regionalism, was one of the best means of apprehending the full significance of America. An important early figure in the growth of regional doctrine was Josiah Royce, professor of philosophy at Harvard University. Writing in 1908, he expressed seminal ideas which in transmuted form were to reappear in many Agrarian writings, and especially in Davidson's *The Attack on Leviathan.* Royce in his attack on the trend toward national conformity, however, wished to maintain the democratic power of the individual; the Agrarians in making the same kind of attack wished to promote a reactionary Southern "restoration," a society alienated from democratic American culture. That Royce was nevertheless largely in agreement with them may be seen from sentiments such as these.

And by the term "provincialism" I shall mean, first, the tendency of such a province to possess its own customs and ideals; secondly, the totality of these customs and ideals themselves; and thirdly, the love and pride which leads the inhabitants of a province to cherish as their own these traditions, beliefs, and aspirations. . . .[6]

Had they wanted to, the Agrarians could have said that in taking their stand they were putting into practice these ideas of Josiah Royce. Like many scholars who followed him, Royce also believed that regionalism should strive actively to withstand and negate the levelling forces at work in modern life. He wrote:

. . . because of the ease of communication amongst distant places, because of the spread of popular education, and because of the consolidation of industries and of social authorities, we tend all over the nation .. . . to read the same daily news, to share the same general ideas, to submit to the same overmastering social forces, to live in the same external fashions, to discourage individuality, and to approach a dead level of harassed mediocrity.[7]

Another important precursor of the "New Regionalists" was Frederick Jackson Turner whose studies of the western frontier had a vital influence on American historiography. However, his views proved only of limited value to the Southern Agrarians. In a review of Turner's *The United States* Owsley mentioned the author's stress on the democratic influence which the frontier allegedly spread eastward over the more settled regions. Although the Agrarians credited Turner with being among the first to foresee the need for regional interpretations, they disagreed with his central thesis that it was very beneficial for America to have the frontier act as a constant source of recurring democratic energy. Praise of the frontier as a perennial disturbance conflicted with the Agrarian desire for stable, traditional communities. What they could accept was Turner's emphasis on the "importance of the sections and regions in determining culture, social and political attitudes, and economic life."[8] This viewpoint further justified the Agrarians in defending the cultural particularity of the South. Besides ignoring Turner's egalitarian hopes, they found other elements in his thought which they felt needed to be rejected. They felt that Turner's main weakness as an historian was his blindness toward "sectional imperialism." It was considered a serious omission for him not to look upon the Civil War as *aggression* against the South by the other American regions.

Perhaps the most powerful source for the revival of regionalism was Vernon L. Parrington's *Main Currents in American Thought*. As a pronounced Jeffersonian, Parrington had a strong distaste for the aristocratic principles of the Old South; yet he could be valuable to the Agrarians because he tried to prove organic relationships between writers and the social environment which produced them and determined their character. These writers, therefore, were not nourished by that wicked abstraction, *America,* but by the real, localized, and definable *regions.* They and they alone could define the content of America; they alone were responsible for the actual culture of the nation. Thus the South, a most cohesive and traditional region, had the right to consider itself superior to the abstraction called America as the setting for genuine creative achievement. Parrington inadvertently lent support to the Agrarian demand for Southern cultural autonomy; in some instances, as clearly expressed in Davidson's *The Attack on Leviathan*, this cry for autonomy became political as well. The following analysis of regional divisions indicates how Parrington could be useful to the demand for Southern particularity.

The major interests of the three great regions of the country differentiated more and more sharply. The East was discovering its Utopia in an industrial capitalistic order. With the flocking of immigrants to the factories began the extraordinary expansion of the cities and the movement of centralization that was eventually to transform America from a rural to an urban society, supplanting the farmer by the business man and disintegrating the traditional psychology. The new manufacturing and the new finance were subjecting an agrarian people to the dislocations and readjustments implied in the industrial revolution, the outcome of which no man could foresee. The reaction of this new industrialism upon the South was immediate. With the improvements in textile manufacturing came greater demands upon the new southern staple, and an agriculture that had long been static with its traditional crops of indigo, rice, and tobacco, began to look forward confidently to a Utopia founded on cotton, and conceived an imperialistic dream of expanding fields of white bolls and black slaves, reaching into Mexico and embracing the West Indies.[9]

Thus Parrington, to the benefit of the Agrarians, recognized the basic division of America into historically determined regions. That he personally objected to the South's conservatism did not invalidate the South's right to be, culturally and politically, exactly what it wanted to be. All regions had their own internal dynamics, their own manifest destiny. If Parrington for his own purposes regarded the Old South as aggressive and imperialistic, what of it? The South had its own laws and customs to honor.

In addition to *Main Currents in American Thought,* other works published in the late twenties aided the revival of regionalism. Edmund Wilson's review in 1928 of the anthology of Fugitive poetry demonstrated his hope that the South, as a section with its own tragic heritage, could be to America, in literature, what Ireland had been to England. All other believers in a Southern literary renaissance also exhibited a regional consciousness. The writer who probably gave the movement its greatest impetus, however, was Benjamin Albert Botkin. In 1929 he published *Folk Say: A Regional Miscellany,* a collection of materials indigenous to various parts of the country which revealed the literary possibilites of the new approach.

Indeed, what acquired the label of regionalism was not restricted to the United States. French literature and state policy, for example, provided an excellent precedent for American literary regionalists. John Gould Fletcher touched upon this fact when he asserted, "The French regionalism of the last twenty years has been actively allied to the French royalist propaganda for provincial revolution. . . ."[10] These political overtones appealed to the Agrarians who in effect were inciting the South to rebel spiritually against the American leviathan, the federal government. Odum mentioned the "epics of the provinces" composed in the last century by Sand, Balzac, Stendhal, and Flaubert. "Seeing the extravagant interest displayed by foreigners [*le tourism*] in each traditional province," Odum wrote, the French "became conscious of the regions which had, heretofore, been an unconscious force in their cultural heritage. This awakening translated itself into modern French literature."[11] We are reminded here of Tate's remark that during the twenties many Southern intellectuals took a backward glance at their supposedly lost tradition, and the result was the astonishing "renaissance" in writing that surprised the nation. Lewis Mumford in *Technics and Civilization* broadened the scope of Odum's theory by saying that an interest in place and language—vital aspects of regional history—was a central characteristic of nineteenth-century culture. Mumford defined the progress of regionalism in the following significant passage.

This movement has gone through a similar set of stages in every country where it has taken place: in Denmark, in Norway, in Ireland, in Catalonia, in Brittany, in Wales, in Scotland, in Palestine, and similar signs are already visible in various regions in North America. There is, as M. Jourdanne has put it, at first a poetic cycle: this leads to the recovery of the language and literature of the folk, and the attempt to use it as a vehicle for contemporary expression on the basis of largely traditional forms. The second is the cycle of prose, in which the interest in the language leads to an interest in the totality of a community's life and history, and so brings the movement directly onto the contemporary stage. And finally, there is the cycle of action, in which regionalism forms for itself fresh objectives, political, economic, civic, cultural, on the basis, not of a servile restoration of the past, but of a growing integration of the new forces that have attached themselves to the main trunk of civilization.[12]

We may apply this theory of dynamics to the Fugitive-Agrarian movement even though the Agrarians were not themselves members of the Southern "folk." They were first-rate intellectuals with first-rate formal education. As declared regionalists, they defended the sanctity of the Southern "folk" and valued whatever literary works it inspired. Moreover, their concern with regionalism supported in many ways their special interest in the proposed Agrarian economy. Besides, as mentioned earlier, regionalism as a functional concept in literature was less vulnerable to hostile reaction than a grandiose Agrarian economic and social restoration, the initial call for which had drawn such scornful remarks as "A boy's Froissart of tales," "Canutes," and "Young Confederates." Paul Beath, for instance, could in the same breath praise the Agrarians for having begun the revival of regionalism and then say, "These critics have often been called, and I think rightly, unreconstructed rebels who are continuing the Civil War long after Appomattox."[13] Although the Agrarians were not "folk," their progress did bear out, superficially at least, the theoretical stages outlined by Mumford. They did have a rich poetic cycle in their experience as Fugitive poets. Their second or prose cycle may be said to have begun with *I'll Take My Stand*. It would be difficult, however, to separate the second from the third, or action, stage, because both seemed to have occurred simultaneously. During the thirties, the Agrarians did seek for themselves "fresh objectives, political, economic, civic, cultural." However, contrary to Mumford's description, the Agrarians did not seek a "growing integration" with the new forces of industrial society; they sought a rupture, regional autonomy, self-determination.

Both the Southwest and the Midwest, it should be noted, also had their groups of active regionalists exploiting native materials. Although no one to my knowledge has made a study of the subject, perhaps the splendid Guides to the various states and territories prepared by the Federal Writers' Projects will constitute the greatest monument inspired by the regional emphasis. To say that, however, confuses the *state* with the *region*, and reduces regionalism to simple geography, which it is not. However, taken as a whole, the Guides contain the results of the widest search for local tradition, resources, ethnic origins, folklore, and art yet produced in the United States. Regarding the active regionalists outside the South, Agar wrote, "In September, 1934, there began the publication of *The Midwest,* whose sponsors had the same attitude toward their region as the Southern Agrarians had toward theirs. Their alleged big enemy, too, was the cosmopolitan Northeast. One of its editorials said: 'We are tired of replenishing an arrogant Manhattan with live talent which it soon teaches to sneer at it own parents. . . .' "[14] During the depression, then, when necessity forced the country to welcome all ideas as possible solutions to this or that dilemma, regionalism occupied a central place of attraction.

Besides the major Agrarians, whose contributions to "literary" regional doctrine will form the bulk of this chapter, it was Howard W. Odum who did most to further the movement. In a long essay Davidson scoffed at liberals like Odum as sociologists in Eden.[15] Odum was identified with the rival group of liberal Southern scholars at Chapel Hill. In 1936 appeared his impressive study, *Southern Regions of the United States,* prepared as one of several studies conducted by various specialists for the Southern Regional Committee of the Social Science Research Council. The only Agrarian to serve on the Council was Herman C. Nixon. It had an ambitious program which motivated many social scientists to devote themselves to a serious examination of the South—a region of regions, actually, on the basis of the closest scrutiny. In *Southern Regions* Odum attempted to define the meaning of regionalism. The added fact that he summarized the several definitions in *American Regionalism* helps us to determine more exactly where the Southern Agrarians stood in the general movement.

Odum has a chapter in *Southern Regions* entitled "A New Regional Analysis: Southern Regions in the National Picture" in which he makes an interesting distinction between regionalism and sectionalism. He wrote, "In the first place, regionalism envisages the nation first, making the national culture and welfare the final arbiter. On the other hand, sectionalism sees the region first and the nation afterwards."[16] The difference in attitude could mean the success or failure of the national and regional planning programs instituted and supported by Washington to alleviate the economic crisis and effect basic reforms. As a liberal sympathetic to the New Deal, Odum wanted the South, "America's Economic Problem Number One," to receive maximum benefit from these programs. He regarded as very important the new "geographical and demographical" points of view in research and social analysis. He wrote:

These are all interlinked with the many practical aspects of current regionalism, such as regional mercantilism; industrial, political, administrative, and other phases of regional function and strategy; as well as the literary and artistic aspects of regionalism in America. As for the southern regions, the rest of the nation is tired of being told it must do missionary work in the South. The South is certainly no more enthusiastic. The middle ground of cooperative effort must be found through the regional way. (p. 253)

Odum warned, however, that revival of the older sectionalism, perhaps in the guise of the "new regionalism," could seriously damage the planning programs which could help the South. He said that sectionalism stresses political boundaries and state sovereignties, technical legislation, local loyalties, and groupings of states, all with common interests supposedly "menaced by federal action," whereas regionalism connotes "component and constituent parts of the larger national culture" (p. 255). According to Odum, sectionalism could be "likened unto cultural inbreeding, in which only home stocks and cultures are advocated, whereas regionalism is line-breeding, in which the regional cultures constitute the base but not the whole of new evolving cultures" (p. 257). Regionalism by the very nature of "its regional, interregional, and national cooperative processes implies more of the designed and planned society than sectionalism, which is the group correspondent to individualism" (p. 259). Sectionalism abounds in conflicts whereas regionalism subsumes all conflicts in joint regional-national planning. Lastly, sectionalism must have its inevitable counterpart in a strong coercive federalism, "which is contrary to the stated ideals of American democracy." Recalcitrant sections can provide excuses for "the theory and practice of dictatorship which ignores regional, cultural, and geographical differentials, and almost inevitably goes too far in coercion and regimentation" (p. 259). Regionalism, however, seeks harmony in the search for recovery and reconstruction. Odum listed a number of recent articles which indicated a substantial drift toward what he feared was a "new sectionalism." Among them were three written by the Agrarian leaders Donald Davidson, John Crowe Ransom, and John Gould Fletcher.

In the huge volume *American Regionalism*, Odum and Moore made a more extended and more theoretical study of the allegedly new approach to social meaning. They listed five basic types of regionalism within the six major regions of the United States. These types included (1) natural regions, such as mountain ranges, river valleys, and

great plains, (2) metropolitan areas, (3) sections or localities with identifiable loyalties, patriotism, and folkways, (4) regions for convenience
and administration, (5) group-of-state regions. The six major geographic regions were the Middle States and their "Middle West," the
Northeast and its New England, the Southeast and its "Old South,"
the Far West and its California, the Northwest and its Great Plains,
the Southwest and its Texas. The two authors wrote that "the real
theme of American regionalism is essentially that of a great nation in
whose continuity and unity of development, through a fine balance of
historical, cultural, and geographic factors, must be found the hope of
American democracy and, according to many observers, of Western
civilization."[17]

Whereas the Marxists and the left in general explained the depression as a crisis of capitalist economy, as an evidence of class struggle,
and as a motivation for socialism, Odum and Moore saw the depression as a result of imbalance and unevenness in regional development
and integration. To them the primary weakness of the more than one
hundred new political groupings and creeds, of the more than a thousand plans for "superimposition upon the American people, of the
dogmatizing of enthusiastic liberals and propagandists, lies in the essential artificiality of their proposals."[18] On grounds different from
those of the Agrarians, Odum and Moore also opposed the solutions
advanced by the Neo-Humanists. Babbitt and More stressed the reputed
breakdown of religious and moral sanctions, the lack of authentic formal bodies of knowledge, and the consequent confusion. Salvation for
modern man lay in the revitalization of religion and ethics, in the remaking of humanism, and in the rediscovery of values. Unlike the Neo-
Humanists, Odum, however, accepted the machine, accepted the idea of
progress, accepted the big city, accepted science. For him, the leading
non-Agrarian regionalist, it was the perfecting of regionalism—not the
restoration of religion, ethics, old values, or yeoman farming—that
would guarantee the economic and social security of the future.

The four major Agrarian writers, Ransom, Tate, Davidson, and
Warren, all wrote a good deal on regionalism and sectionalism. On
more sociological grounds, here was another justification of homogeneity, of social stability, of the backward community as envisaged by
them and by T. S. Eliot in their idea of Christian order. Thus the
Agrarians formulated their own definitions of regionalism and used
them in their literary theory. Allen Tate, for example, related regionalism to what he felt was a proper definition of tradition. Also, he
made the term *sectionalism* negative and the term *regionalism* positive

in his passing of judgment on contemporary Southern authors. Sectionalism was that face of a region that looked outward, possibly for conquest, certainly for active self-defense. Instead of accepting his region and its tradition, quite often the purely sectional writer—like T. S. Stribling and Paul Green—was obsessed with its alleged debasement and had the ulterior purpose of changing his region altogether. When confronting writers of Stribling's intention, Tate said, the reader "is forced to think that the social structure might be changed; he cannot look steadily at the section for thinking of the debased *mores* of society. . . ."[19] Genuine regionalism in a writer required acceptance of what the region had inherited.

Thus the regional writer must regard his locale traditionally, as something to be cherished for what it is. Again it must be noted that any large influx of foreign elements—Jews, liberals, labor leaders, Marxists, and so on—would disturb the region's homogeneity; from the Agrarian point of view, so would any great and sudden onrush of industry. Tate found that writers also had to guard against the "antiquarianism" which appeared in Josephine Pinckney and DuBose Heyward. Of their work Tate wrote that "as literature it was abnormal; it was too self-conscious; it was a mixture of sectionalism and regionalism, with folklore and antiquarianism stirred in by main force." What Tate demanded from his regionalist was an honest inner response to his inherited environment, a real fusion of past and present in his art, that it might possess the free and natural spirit of the region from which it grew. "By regionalism," he said, "I mean only the immediate, organic sense of life in which a fine artist works." Such an organic sense could not exist in modern industrial society; therefore, one may assume, this sense was predicated on the restoration of the traditional region. Tate never explained how this feat could be accomplished without the writer's being self-conscious about what he was doing; nor did he show how the writer could acquire his organic sense relative to a traditional region that had, in fact, nearly vanished from history. Tate did find some contemporary writers, however, who lived up to his stringent requirements.

In his opinion the best regional writer was Elizabeth Madox Roberts, for she was "both regional and traditional." Tate wrote that she and Stark Young, a fellow Agrarian, "approach their materials in a perfectly traditional manner. Both take the social order of which they write as final, or rather take the particular moment of society, with its unique balance of order and disintegration, as the inevitable moment for the characters of their choice." *Final* and *inevitable* imply the absence of that inorganic sense of life which seeks to overthrow traditions through social reform and even rebellion. Contrary to Tate's view, Kenneth Burke in *Counter-Statement* remarked that to take any social order as final is implicit propaganda for that society. Tate parried the criticism by saying, "This can be easily granted but the point has value only in the study of society."

The study of literature requires a subtle understanding of how tradition works in the writer's exploitation of his region. In pursuit of this understanding, Tate dwelled in some detail on the proper attitude of traditionalists toward regionalism.

More generally tradition is the knowledge of life that we have not had to learn for ourselves, but have absorbed out of the life around us. Its chief value, in literature as in living, is its economy; it releases the individual from the necessity to learn from the ground up all the mechanism of living, all the hard, trivial fundamentals; it gives us fixed procedures that we can rely on in the larger pursuit of the good life.

The creative use of a tradition demands naturalness. If the writer aspires to a regional content in his art, he must not set out deliberately to "express" a region, or to crudely search for "local color," or to try to reveal "one's past." For, as Tate proclaimed, "a self-conscious regionalism destroys tradition with its perpetual discovery of it; makes it clumsy and sterile." In various writings, Ransom, Warren, Eliot, and Davidson also rebuked the error of self-consciousness. In his work *The Attack on Leviathan* Davidson quoted Ransom who helped to define the problem.

First is the selfconscious regionalism which is the inevitable counter to a hard-driving cosmopolitanism. No matter what defects the critic may find in it [regionalism], it is, to use the words of John Crowe Ransom, "as reasonable as non-regionalism, whatever the latter may be called: cosmopolitanism, free trade, interregionalism, internationalism, eclecticism, liberal education, the federation of the world, or simple rootlessness; so far as the anti-regional philosophy is crystallized in such doctrines."[20]

Incidentally, the doctrines listed in Ransom's critical index represent an important array of *foreignisms* which the Agrarians rejected in their social and literary philosophy. A truly regional and Agrarian society would seek to expunge them as forces alien to the native culture. All such forces tended to dissipate and eventually destroy the region's integrity. Any attempt to reform the region violated its cultural chastity, so to speak, and resulted in spurious, illegitimate regionalism. Again a basic dilemma seems to arise, however, one which the Agrarians did not adequately try to resolve. How can the artist who aspires to be a regionalist escape from being also a reformist if he lives in a modern society—including most of the South by now—which has lost its "tradition" and must actively agitate for its return?

Tradition, even a local one, according to Tate, was "by nature private, and it should not be put up on a billboard or debauched in the conquest of the world."[21] Since tradition must operate unconsciously, a writer could not be constantly judging the moral value of human actions and emotions and at the same time see them objectively. He must take some kinds of conduct as inevitable in his framework of behavior; otherwise, he makes the mistake of inventing his conduct as he goes along. The normal literary attitude is, or should be, direct contemplation of character and emotion and not the social structure in itself. A conscious regional outlook, in becoming too social and abstract, may even undertake to defend the tradition, but in those circumstances it could never be really traditional in nature. "A real tradition is individual," Tate wrote, "it is a special organization of the individual sensibility that liberates the intelligence through the possession of habitual responses of life that are, moreover, relevant to the conduct of men." Applying this idea to the writer, he said, "To write traditionally is to approach the chosen matter with an instinct for the meaning, rather than with an abstract theory about it or with an air of contriving for oneself all the properties of the scene."[22] Modern society, it is easy to see, has little respect for habitual responses to life; from this observation one might conclude that Tate's theory has more validity for historical fiction than for that which is contemporary, rootless, without a past. Tate, looking back to a more settled time, again praised the Middle Ages when the polarities of medieval society were the barons and the priests: they were the men of action and the men of sensibility, the political leaders and the sturdy keepers of the tradition.

Ransom's long and significant essay, "The Aesthetic of Regionalism," appeared in the January, 1934, issue of the *American Review,* during the height of national interest in Southern Agrarianism. Although much of the discussion tended to be abstract, Ransom began with the remnant of the Pueblo Indians as a functioning example of real social and aesthetic regionalism. He proposed the idea that America was a land of "transplanted regionalisms," meaning that our social structure was somehow predetermined in the thought and purpose of the original settlers. He wrote, "New England they meant to be a Puritan England, Virginia an Elizabethan and royalist England."[23] In the process of transplantation, perhaps as a result of it, were involved various "importations" such as the Greek influence on the architecture and politics of the Old South and the French influence on Louisiana.

The Pueblo Indians, in the manner of their life, represented a perfect manifestation of regionalism. He continued:

It should be a comfort to us, however, that we scarcely know for certain of any regional culture that can be called, in strictness, "indigenous." A regional culture ordinarily represents an importation, or series of importations, that has been lived with and adapted for so long that finally it fits, and looks "natural." (p. 302)

In this passage is implied, though not stated as clearly as by Tate, the emphasis on the growth of a long tradition which could be enjoyed by the Agrarian hinterlands but was denied to the everchanging metropolis built by the power of industrialism. We can also see the implication that Negro slavery had been a series of importations, and that in the Old South it had been lived with so long that it seemed to "fit" and look "natural."

The occasion for Ransom's praise of the Indians of New Mexico was a train ride out of Albuquerque where he noticed some Pueblos, at threshing time, seemingly enjoying themselves. Unlike an anthropologist who might actually live among the Pueblos, Ransom merely watched them from the train window. Whereas Warren had mentioned the cult of Indian worship as being specious in literature, Ransom clearly contributed to such a cult in his enthusiastic praise for the Pueblo society. He called himself a "philosophical regionalist," saw the Indians working in the field, and wrote: "They laughed, and must have been pleased with their deities, because the harvest was a success, and bread was assured them for the winter. So this was regionalism; flourishing on the meanest of capital, surviving stubbornly, and brilliant" (p. 290). Though for the most part it went back unchanged to the Stone Age, their culture persisted, and they lived as they had always lived. Therefore, these Indians were a noble specimen. He continued, "Indians lead a life which has an ancient pattern, and has been perfected a long time, and is conscious of the weight of tradition behind it" (p. 290). From his window Ransom observed that their way of life was highly satisfying and that they preferred it above all others. He said that "they live where white men could scarcely live, they have sufficient means, and they are without that special insecurity which white men continually talk about" (p. 291). Again, had Ransom lived among the Pueblos, he might have heard samples of such talk. He felt that the Indians also enjoyed a subtler but scarcely less important benefit in that their life was pleasant; it felt right; and it had "aesthetic quality." Thus the animated scene of Pueblos working in the field appeared to Ransom as one much to be envied.

He then told a story about an Indian chief who refused a government subsidy of $20,000 "because it would be bad for the young men." Ransom felt that the chief knew "a culture will decline and fall when the people grow out of liking for their own native products. . . ." So the chief surrendered "an economic advantage which entailed an aesthetic disadvantage; probably assessing firmly the principle that the aesthetic values are as serious as the economic ones, and as governing" (p. 293). No statement is available from the Indian chieftain on the other reasons why he refused the money. They may be simpler reasons than those given by Ransom. Nevertheless, Ransom's views are indicative of one important aspect of his regional aesthetics—the need to avoid as many external disturbances as possible, even an abrupt influx of "wealth," because they may weaken the ancient social pattern.

When Ransom finished with his example of the Pueblo Indians, he proceeded to discuss more general aspects of regionalism and art. Rather than emphasize tradition, as Tate had done, he stressed how the regional economy naturally gave rise to aesthetic results. He continued, "A regional economy is good in the sense that it has always worked and never broken down. That is more than can be said for the modern, or the interregional and industrial economy" (p. 294). Another advantage of a regional system was the proximity to nature enjoyed by its industries. He wrote:

The industry is in sight of the natural resources of the region and its population. The farmers support themselves and support their cities; and the city merchants and manufacturers have their eyes on a local market and are not ambitious to build up trade with the distant regions. . . . (p. 294)

Of course, had the ante-bellum Cotton Kings followed this type of advice, they would not have sought a Northern and European market for their products, and the Old South as tradition knows it would have been an impossibility. Also, the acceptance of regional industries conflicted with the Agrarian distaste for industrialism, and accorded more, as has been indicated, with the New South movement. Ransom seemed to be much moved by the Pueblo Indians, but he neither mentioned nor deplored what both Northerners and Southerners had done in their past conquest of the continent, of the "wilderness," to destroy countless Indian cultures and "regionalisms" with as traditional and noble a past as that of the Pueblos. Nor did Ransom or any of his associates ever suggest that American Negroes also had a culture and a tradition which had been inherited from age to age.

Such an ennobling concept was prohibited by their belief in a militant white supremacy.

In theorizing about regionalism, Ransom wrote that its aesthetic "is less abstract, and harder to argue. Preferably it is a thing to try, and to feel, and that is what it is actually for some Europeans, and for the Indians of our Southwest" (p. 295). Nature herself was intensely localized; the writer, like Antaeus of old, needed contact with the soil to be truly creative. This contact was possible only in a rural area. To Ransom the relationship of regionalism to aesthetics meant the following:

As the community slowly adapts its life to the geography of the region, a thing happens which is almost miraculous . . . a work of grace perhaps, a tribute to the goodness of the human heart . . . an event of momentous consequence to what we call the genius of human "culture." (p. 296)

The miracle involved a qualitative change. "As the economic patterns become perfected and easy," Ransom continued, "they cease to be merely economic and become gradually aesthetic. They were meant for efficiency, but they survive for enjoyment, and men who were only prosperous become also happy" (p. 296).

When the initial struggle was over, and tradition had become established, men, "secure in their economic tenure, delight in this charm and begin to represent it lovingly in their arts." More accurately, their economic actions "become also their arts. It is the birth of natural piety . . . to the operation of transcendental spirit in nature, which is God" (p. 297). Out of God's grace, out of man's spontaneous joy about his condition, and from the natural goodness of his heart arise his aesthetic achievements. Ransom wrote:

The arts make their appearance in some ascending order, perhaps indicated like this: labour, craft, and business insist upon being transacted under patterns which permit the enjoyment of natural background; houses, tools, manufactured things do not seem good enough if they are only effective but must also be ornamental, which in a subtle sense means natural; and the fine arts arise, superficially pure or non-useful, yet faithful to the regional culture and to the moral patterns to which the community is committed. (p. 297)

Among these fine arts, in a manner reminiscent of William Morris, Ransom included cookery, architecture, interiors, clothing, social pastimes, pageants, speech, idiom, and literature. A good critic of the arts "must now know the region which produced them" (p. 299). The broad or eclectic view, in contrast with regionalism, now seemed too "fatuous." Ransom admitted that the regions needed capital cities even though they were "fortresses of eclecticism." Such a regional city could be useful, "and it is even creative in the way of aesthetic forms;

for example, the architecture of capitals and landscaping of parks, the drama, and the other fine arts; in all of which it had better condescend to try to catch the genius of the hinterland. If it invites the patterns from too many regions, in an excess of hospitality, and tries to compose its arts out of perfectly average materials, its aesthetic life will become a mere formality and perish of cold, and then it will be left with a function which is strictly economic and gross" (p. 299).

Ransom concluded his essay with an extended comment on the destructive effects of industrialism. He again stated how Negro slavery had contributed to the social solidity of Southern regionalism. "The peculiar institution of slavery," he wrote, "set this general area apart from the rest of the world, gave a spiritual continuity to its many regions, and strengthened them under the reinforcement of 'sectionalism,' which is regionalism on a somewhat extended scale" (p. 303). Although slavery was now gone, "The darkey is one of the bonds that make a South out of all the Southern regions" (p. 308). What Ransom affirmed here seems to contradict Allen Tate's belief that the Negro came between the Southern gentleman and his contact with nature, thus keeping him isolated from a creative relationship with the soil. Ransom continued by saying that industrialism had desecrated every region in the country. It did so first in New England and later in the South, which "was European, and mainly English, in origin, and it was to have a baleful effect upon the charming regionalisms of Europe" (p. 304). England was therefore author both of the traditional "establishment" admired by the Agrarians and of the industrial revolution which had done so much to destroy it during and after the Civil War. Ransom determined that industrialism had thrust itself upon the "perfected cultures" of Europe with the disruptive force of a barbarian conquest, turning the clock back, cancelling the gains of "many mellowing centuries," that is, centuries of feudalism and aristocracy. Tension was returned to man's labor. He said, "For under this economy the labourer is simply occupied with tending his abstract machine, and there is no opportunity for aesthetic attitudes" (p. 305). Throughout his essay Ransom is using the term *aesthetic* in a broad and rather loose philosophic sense, and not in the more limited sense implied by the question, "What is aesthetic about a poem?" He wrote that the products of the machine "may be used, but scarcely enjoyed, since they do not have much aesthetic character. Aesthetic character does not reside in an object's abstract design but in the sense of its natural and contingent materials, and the aesthetic attitude is piety" (p. 306).

Despite Ransom's limited praise for cities, he believed they "are without a history, and they are without a region, since the population is imported from any sources whatever; and therefore they are without a character." All in all, modern American life violated the basic principles of regionalism. In fact, the very "symbol of the aesthetic torpor and helplessness of the moderns lies in their money" (p. 306). A critic might say to this statement that during the depression Ransom was advising that the love of beauty could replace the need for bread. As for the free market under industrialism, that usually hungry devourer of machine-made goods, it had taken away all the real or private value of these goods. Ransom said, "To say that is simply to say that the age thinks it has discovered an aesthetic principle which is not regionalism." What man most needed was faith in his own region, in its literature and everything else. Even in Louisiana, the state Ransom called the most important for the South (it was governed by Huey Long at the time), regionalism was under duress. Ransom derived this judgment from the new buildings of the University of Louisiana at Baton Rouge. As for the new state capital, it was a "magnificent indiscretion," totally foreign to the regional architectural style.

Among the many other statements on regionalism made by the Southern Agrarians were two essays by Warren, "Some Don'ts for Literary Regionalists" and "Literature as a Symptom" (his contribution to *Who Owns America?*), and Davidson's previously mentioned volume *The Attack on Leviathan*. In it appeared, substantially unchanged, Davidson's "Regionalism and Nationalism in American Literature," which was published first in the *American Review* in 1935. Davidson used his opportunity to examine fully the regional attitudes of his friends Tate and Warren. Since Warren also became a New Critic, it is interesting to note that as late as 1936, two years before he and Cleanth Brooks, Jr., composed the significant text *Understanding Poetry*, Warren could thus stress with vigor the relevance of society to literature: "We exclaim at what now seems to be the beautiful organic relation of the work of such writers to the social matrix of their time and place, and remark: 'Ah, if we can only achieve a true regional spirit, then we'll have literature!' "[24]

Just as T. S. Eliot had cautioned in his Virginia lectures against a too rigid, crude, and mechanical approach to tradition, so Warren warned against a shallow and opportunistic approach to regionalism. Like Ransom and Tate, he regarded the regional impulse as an autonomous force hostile to the universal prevalence of nationalism. Like them he advised that regionalism be without self-consciousness, and he asked, "Did Hawthorne have to reason himself in his regionalism?" Above all, literary regionalism must not be a get-rich-quick fad, or what Warren termed "a facet of eclecticism." Early in 1936 Ransom had criticized Edith Wharton for being a "New York lady" who went out to a region to which she was unaccustomed, the "Massachusetts back country." As a result of her strange excursion, her writing revealed "the perturbation of an author wrestling with an unaccustomed undertaking, uneasy of conscience, and resorting to measures."[25] Hers was the unhappy fate of a cosmopolitan who tried, by force of will, to assume the practice of a regionalist. The product of such a false union was bound to be an aesthetic failure.

These, in paraphrased form, were the six primary injunctions that Warren issued in "Some Don'ts for Literary Regionalists."

1. Regionalism should not be quaintness, local color, or folklore; these factors were merely sentimental and snobbish "when separated from a functional idea." Presumably they were all right when wedded to an organic traditional culture.

2. Regionalism, when based on the literary exploitation of a race or society that had no cultural continuity with our own, tended always to be fake and precious. Warren said, "It is a touristic regionalism. The cult of Indian worship, as we often find it, is an example." Ransom's praise of the Pueblos, Warren could say, did not really add up to a "cult."

3. Regionalism should not necessarily imply an emphasis on the primitive or underprivileged character. Despite Warren's assertion, however, Solomon Fishman wrote many years later, "The strongest case for primitivism has been made by regionalists, particularly those of the West and Southwest, who advocate a 'hard' primitivism as distinguished from the 'soft' one of the Southern agrarians."[26]

4. Regionalism, according to Warren, should not demand of a writer that he relinquish any source of speculation or expression that he has managed to acquire.

5. Regionalism does not mean that literature is tied to its own region for appreciation. The Southern Agrarians, therefore, were free to seek as wide an audience as possible. They did not have to feel unpatriotic if they went North to sell their wares.

6. Even literary regionalism was more than simply a literary matter, and had a social purpose as an expression and defense of the region and its culture.

This sixth maxim seems to conflict rather sharply with what are generally considered to be the basic assumptions of the New Criticism, especially the aesthetic formalism. Warren also wrote that "only in so far as literature springs from some reality in experience is it valuable to us."[27] Perhaps we should not be surprised at such strongly sociological utterances from men who eventually became New Critics. Critics can alter their emphases if not entirely their minds . . . and even their minds when new revelations occur. Kenneth Burke arrived among the New Critics from the field of Marxism. And Austin Warren, surely a typical example, if any New Critic can be called "typical," once wrote in the *American Review* about the Southern Agrarians:

When these ironists and "metaphysicals" proved political economists also, as all good artists ought, we rejoiced that the "War between the States" had not disappeared—to the furtherance of our national monotony, but had, salutarily, been transmuted from bullets to tracts.[28]

Nor was Austin Warren being himself an ironist, as might be supposed, when he was writing this praise of the Nashville critics.

Robert Penn Warren's other major essay on literary regionalism, "Literature as a Symptom," made an extended contrast between the regional and the proletarian or Marxist theory of literature. During the thirties both approaches were popular with both writers and critics. Warren wrote:

The "regional movement" and the "proletarian movement" are the two rationalizations in greatest vogue at this moment. The regional movement may be defined, in brief and in part, as the attempt of a writer to reason himself into the appropriate relationship to the past; the proletarian movement, as the attempt to reason himself into the appropriate relation to the future.[29]

The regionalist also sought a relation to a special place, while the proletarian sought a relation to a class. Whereas the latter regarded property as a millstone about the neck (Maxim Gorky is quoted as witness for this assertion), the former connected property "with his idea of the relation of man to place, for ownership gives a man a stake in a place and helps to define his, for the writer, organic relation to society."[30] These facts helped to explain to us why the "hunger for land" became the theme for many regional novels. Modern writers who have drifted from the sense of a place were less happy than the old; they "may feel that something that once bound author and audience together, some common tie of values, some sustaining convention, is lost."[31] It seems ironic that later Warren himself, as a New Critic, was to help this drift away from place when he adopted a more formalist aesthetics. Now, however, he listed among the happier writers of the past Nathaniel Hawthorne, Herman Melville, Emily Dickinson, and Henry James.

Warren was applying to American literature the familiar theory of
T. S. Eliot that to create a Dante one had to have the kind of ordered
society which produced him. Warren amplified his application in an
omnibus critique of recent novels. This essay appeared in the *Southern Review* in 1936. He stated that Hawthorne and Melville didn't
need to hunt for a theme; the theme, the fundamental idea, the obsession, was already theirs, and it was theirs so easily, so naturally, so inherently, that they were relieved of any compulsion to deliberately
seek "ideas" with which to engage their talents. Warren went on to
explain:

What is valuable in the current "regional movement" is not new in so far as
it refers to the novel or, in final analysis, to poetry. The great classics of
American fiction, the best work of Hawthorne or of Mark Twain or of Melville, are something else before they are American. By inspiration, Hawthorne and Melville are, for instance, of New England; then, almost by political and geographical definition only, or by a mystical hocus-pocus of
definition, they are American. *Moby Dick* is, with very slight and mechanical
qualification, quite as "regional" as *The Scarlet Letter*. Its stage of action is
the deck of a whaler and not a New England village, but the whaler is only
New England afloat, New England with its edges whetted and its essence concentrated by the valiant rigors of that calling in which it discovered a special
congeniality. The premises of the story of Ahab and the White Whale afford
a more metaphysical approach to New England, and the tragedy of New England, than does the story of the lovers in *The Scarlet Letter*.[32]

Both the regional and proletarian movements, as might be expected,
were opposed to capitalism; they both "resent the indignity heaped by
that system of society upon the creative impulse, indignity which has
succeeded in estranging the artist from the proper exercise of his function as 'a man speaking to men.' "[33] Although both these movements
sought to heal the tragic rupture, the proletarian failed because it
dealt primarily with life as it existed under industrialism. It tended to
produce "politicalized literature" as a weapon for social change. It
dabbled in mere propaganda. Even the honest writer who had a theme
of social justice was often in serious danger for, as Warren said, "His
very sincerity, the very fact of the depth and mass of his concern, may
not do more than imperil his achievement unless his sensibility is so
attuned and his critical intelligence so developed that he can effect the
true marriage of his convictions, his ideas, that is, his theme, with the
concrete projection in experience, that is, his subject."[34] Coming from
one who became a first-rate novelist, this advice is valuable not only
for the Marxist but for the Agrarian as well. The regionalist could
more easily avoid these artistic pitfalls because he wrote about the
hinterland. He wrote without the violence of premeditated reform,

and he conformed to his established tradition, the very heart of his aesthetic endeavor.

It should be clear from the foregoing pages that the idea of regionalism produced a considerable amount of social and literary agitation during the 1930's. Journals such as the *Saturday Review of Literature,* as well as many others, gave it ample coverage. Both its devotees and its scoffers argued its merits and demerits; they did so realistically and otherwise, and in the process of debate many valuable insights accrued to the study of American literature. The debate was not without its touches of humor. James Gray expressed a rather delightful if caustic view when he wrote in "The Minnesota Muse," for the *Saturday Review:* "That militantly American doctrine called regionalism, which has tended in recent years to make of local prejudice something vaguely resembling a religion, would probably hold that the heavenly Muse does herself over, with protean variability, each time that she crosses a state line." Gray continued in the same mocking vein, "The costume assigned to the Minnesota Muse, in the regionalist's handbook, is a decent, though shabby, Mother Hubbard. She sings exclusively of ruined wheat harvests and she sings of them with a strong Swedish accent."[35] Discordant voices such as Gray's were quite rare. Instead, the new regionalism was almost universally regarded as valid; the conflicts it inspired centered around definitions and applications.

The final lengthy Agrarian discussion of regionalism and its meaning for literature appeared in Donald Davidson's *The Attack on Leviathan.* It was published in 1938, the same year in which Odum and Moore published their *American Regionalism.* Coming as it did when the Southern Agrarian movement had just about fallen apart, Davidson's book summarized the important attitudes which they had taken on the subject. He had previously agreed with Allen Tate that a good regional literature needed "the immediate, organic sense of life in which a fine artist works."[36] Regionalism, Davidson repeated, "may be described as a retreat from the artistic leviathanism of the machine age, symbolized by the dominance of New York during the nineteen-twenties."[37] Regionalism versus Leviathanism, Agrarianism versus Industrialism, Nature versus Cosmopolitanism—these dichotomies and others like them were constantly used by the Agrarians. One side of the struggle always tried to debase the other. Thus a special kind of odious regionalism (debased by the enemy) was the "dude" art written for "a tired metropolitan audience." It was a literature filled with stereotypes, according to Davidson, of the poor white, the Negro, and the mountaineer.

Tate had underscored the primacy of tradition in his concept of regionalism. Davidson, referring to Tate and Warren jointly, felt they were searching for a "usable past," as the Renaissance had found in the classic Greek tradition. The quest was arduous because science had brought such chaos into the world. Davidson wrote: "For five hundred years the peoples of the West have seen a series of advances and recessions in art, brought on by the continuous destruction of society under the auspices of scientific rationalism. . . ."[38] In many essays Tate had expounded in detail his anti-scientific doctrines echoed now by Davidson. As will be shown, Tate developed his thesis of the conflict, in poetry, between the *practical will* and the genuine *imagination*. Both he and Ransom also proposed the idea of *poetry as knowledge* in order to give it equal status with science, religion, philosophy, and other high disciplines of the human mind.

Davidson in his work also wrote of William Butler Yeats and T. S. Eliot: "Both have attacked cosmopolitanism at its weakest point—its failure of inner conviction." From the famous poem by Yeats, "The Second Coming," he quoted these significant lines:

> Things fall apart; the centre will not hold.
> Mere anarchy is loosed upon the world.[39]

Related to this idea of the spread of anarchy was Tate's comment about Theodore Dreiser, the leading naturalist, that he "has nothing to assume, because he does not know a kind of life where people assume anything."[40] A society inhabited by derelict artists such as Dreiser, unless they turned to genuine regionalism for their materials, could produce only empty abstract art.

This chapter has concentrated on the literary meanings of regionalism because it was this aspect which most intrigued and engaged the Agrarians. Yet they were interested also in other related fields, from the sectionalism of Calhoun to the modern need for political change to make the American system of government reflect more faithfully its regional base. William Y. Elliott, one of the original Fugitives who became neither an Agrarian nor a New Critic, proposed in *The Need for Constitutional Reform* (1935) that the states "should be supplanted, except as administrative areas or as convenient electoral districts, by geographically appropriate regions. As a suggestion I have termed these regions *commonwealths* and indicated an approximation of the present Federal Reserve districts, with perhaps one additional Western commonwealth, as a more rational basis for our federal structure."[41]

Davidson lavishly praised Elliott for the ideas in his book, but he saw dangers as well as benefits in the proposition. As one safeguard against Federalism (political leviathanism), Davidson wanted the regional commonwealths to have great power, "power for the South to preserve its bi-racial social system without the furtive evasion or raw violence to which it is now driven when sniped at with weapons of Federal legality. . . ." In other words, such a new Federalism, after being diluted by regional power, would be acceptable if it also recognized the propriety of white supremacy in the South. In return, Davidson was willing to grant "power for the Northeast to protect its union labor against Southern cheap labor."[42] He feared, however, that the former sectional imperialism against the South could still operate even under the new commonwealth arrangement advocated by Elliott. Davidson then issued a characteristic warning:

Yet the Northeast should do well to realize that there are people with a burning sense of wrong who wish retaliation, and would inflict it if the turn of events under the Old Federalism should permit—yes, and would cheerfully take the risk of any injurious recoil upon themselves.[43]

Therefore in their striving, out of modern disunity, for social and aesthetic unity, for association of sensibility, and for an honorable tradition, the Southern Agrarians looked to the promise of the New Regionalism and worked for its fulfillment with much zeal and perspicuity. They hoped to find "within the regional tradition the cultural assumptions often lacking in modern life."[44] Along with their special attitude on regionalism they brought a number of other important ideological doctrines—on nature, religion, myth, and science.

Chapter VII   Science, The False Messiah

"I'LL TAKE MY STAND" FAILED TO REFLECT THE SCOPE AND DEPTH OF Agrarian antagonism to science. No one attempted to chronicle for the symposium how science had helped the industrial society to destroy the Southern regional tradition, weaken spiritual values, and debase literature and art. John Crowe Ransom could have done so; he had just written *God Without Thunder*, a book suffused with anti-scientific argument. He had named one chapter "Satan as Science" and another "Christ as Science," and he clearly indicated that science served the aims of the former. In assuming the prerogatives respecting knowledge of the Deity, science became the "false Messiah," a phrase which Ransom seems to have appropriated from the title of a volume published in 1927 by Clarence Edwin Ayres. Allen Tate also could have written a major article condemning science. For three or four years prior to *I'll Take My Stand* he had repeatedly expressed anti-scientific views as a book reviewer for various New York journals. By 1930 he had developed a rather complete theory about the damage done to poetry by the rise of scientific rationalism.

The Introduction of the symposium, however, did indicate why the Agrarians were generally hostile to science, and to the applied sciences in particular. It stated, "The capitalization of the applied sciences has now become extravagant and uncritical; it has enslaved our human energies to a degree now clearly felt to be burdensome." The Agrarians said that industrialism means that a society has decided to invest its economic resources in technology. Apologists for the industrial system take refuge from criticism by saying they are devoted simply to science; but what they are really interested in is production and profit, and the more the applied sciences can increase both, the better. The Introduction continued, "Therefore, it is necessary to employ a certain skepticism even at the expense of the Cult of Science, and to say,

It is an Americanism, which looks innocent and disinterested, but really is not either."[1]

If science does have a contribution to make to labor it should appear in tools or processes that make work easier, leisure more possible, and happiness more secure. None of these benefits, the Agrarians believed, had accrued to the laborer under industrialism. "His labor is hard, its tempo is fierce, and his employment is insecure." Then shifting the basis of the argument, the introductory statement questioned the value of the labor-saving devices which the applied sciences allegedly had produced. It said that to assume that the saving of labor is pure gain is "to assume that labor is an evil, that only the end of labor or the material product is good."[2] On the contrary, the "act of labor" is one of the "happy functions of human life," and thus the scientists diminish human happiness when they invent new tools and set up improved processes.

Instead of an essay detailing the evils of science, a long essay attacking the "philosophy of progress" appeared in *I'll Take My Stand*. Written by Lyle H. Lanier, the essay declared at the start, "John Dewey believes that modern industrial technology provides us with a method for securing progress and for preserving our culture against decline; Oswald Spengler looks on industrialism and its concomitant manifestations as evidence of decay in the spirit of Western life."[3] In agreement with Spengler, Lanier devoted the bulk of his essay to attacking such manifestations of decay as naturalism, positivism, materialism, economic determinism, socialism, and communism—all of which had undermined traditional values in the name of progress. But he did not, for some reason, mention John Bagnell Bury's *The Idea of Progress* (1920), which defined the historic significance of "progress" and contributed much to the climate of opinion in the twenties. Many commentators on progress wrote with Bury's book in mind. In it he clearly showed the part that science and reason played in the breakdown of the Middle Ages and the rise of the modern world. It would seem advisable, therefore, to give a brief résumé of Bury's views as a further means of clarifying the Agrarian position on science as the "false Messiah."

In the basic dichotomy which Bury established, Progress stands opposed by Providence. Under the first are the categories of Free Will, Science, and This World; under the second, Fate, Faith, and After Life (heaven or hell). Speaking of the Idea of Progress, Bury said, "It was not till the sixteenth century that the obstacles to its appearance definitely begin to be transcended and a favourable atmosphere to be gradually prepared."[4] Writers who find higher values in Providence, like Hulme, Eliot, and the Agrarians, also date the collapse of medieval, Christian, and European unity at about this same time. Bury said that the rise of science seemed to be synonymous with the fall of medievalism, through Humanism, the Renaissance, and the Reformation. The idea of "Progress" then was widely accepted and became capable of governing values and moving men to action. It had not been so before. Friar Roger Bacon, for example, was an advocate of Progress, but he was immersed in a religious climate which, instead of giving man science, gave him inquisition, excommunication, and burnings at the stake—all for the sake of his soul. Bury said that a desperate hatred of Progress was the Vatican's inevitable reaction to its immense loss of temporal and spiritual power, not to mention its material holdings. In this regard Bury noted that Progress was regarded as an enemy in the *Syllabus* of errors issued by Pope Pius IX at the end of 1864, during the American Civil War. The eighteenth error encompassed Progress and Liberalism. "No wonder," Bury wrote, "seeing that Progress was invoked to justify every movement that stank in the nostrils of the Vatican—liberalism, toleration, democracy, and socialism. And the Roman Church well understood the intimate connection of the idea with the advance of rationalism."[5]

For their part, the Southern Agrarians militantly supported Providence against all the aspects of Progress; they did so most strenuously in respect to science. Indeed, anti-science is a leitmotiv which runs through all three phases of their career. There was no appreciable letup when the former Fugitives and Agrarians turned into New Critics. They believed that science, by having served industrialism and capitalism, had aided in the defeat of the Old South and its traditions. They believed that science, by unveiling the secrets of Nature, had stripped away her mystery and wonder. They believed that science had allied itself with urbanism and cosmopolitanism and thus was a foe of regionalism. They believed, also, that science had virtually destroyed religion and myth, thereby depriving the artist of his ancient moral and aesthetic values. They believed, finally, that science was incompatible with poetry and literature. The concept of *science as knowledge* was confronted by Tate and the Agrarians with their concept of *poetry as knowledge,* then by the broader idea of *literature as knowledge.*[6] In general, they meant that experience at the level of art had equal validity with experience at the level of fact. Critics favorable to the Agrarians on this point credited them with performing a service to poetry as noble as that performed by Matthew Arnold in maintaining and upgrading the status of poetry.

Of course, the Agrarians did not invent the idea of an animosity between science and poetry. Indicating the longevity of the conflict in an article entitled "Literature as Knowledge," Tate quoted from Coleridge a key definition of the supposed uniqueness of poetry.

A poem is that species of composition, which is opposed to works of science, by proposing for its immediate object pleasure, not truth; and from all other species—(having this object in common with it)—it is distinguished by proposing to itself such delight from the whole, as is compatible with a distinct gratification from each component part.[7]

Many others besides Coleridge have sought to define the differences between a prose and a poetic discourse. Some have tried to work out a means of co-existence between poetry and science; others, and this would seem to include the Agrarians, have felt the conflict to be a perpetual civil war with the issues so irreconcilable that one or the other must be destroyed. At any rate, literary history is filled with examples of discord between poetry and science. Robert Penn Warren, citing one of these examples, wrote that as far back as 1904 Paul Elmer More, the Neo-Humanist, remarked in an essay about Tolstoy on the "new antinomy of literature and science."[8] What interests us most at the moment is the manner in which the Southern Agrarians, from the twenties on, developed their own antagonism to science as a deadly enemy of poetry and literature.

Ransom, for instance, made an early attack on the scientific attitude in the *Literary Review,* an anthology edited by Christopher Morley and published in 1924. This was during Ransom's Fugitive period. Henceforth, his anger grew against abstractions, against the claims of scientific rationalism. The theme of contingency is to appear often in Ransom's religious thought. Man needed God to provide him with the spiritual means of coping with the precariousness of life. When science deprives man of God, as it always tended to do, it left man alone to face the harsh terms of his fate. Man had to surrender grace, salvation, virtue, humanity itself. He found himself in the spiritual "wasteland" which T. S. Eliot had dramatized so well in his poem.

After sweeping away the sacred mysteries surrounding nature, science then assumed the role of a new and false god, one whose benefits were illusory. At the same time the arts were reduced to an inferior position. In *God Without Thunder* Ransom offered the following reason for this eventuality: "Science is an order of experience in which we mutilate and prey upon nature; we seek our practical objective at any cost, and always at the cost of not appreciating the setting from which we have to take them." The falsity of science as the new Messiah affected the poet, in part, because "its knowledge is ruthless and exclusive, while aesthetic knowledge, aiming at the fullness of the object, is inclusive."[9] This is to say that science pierces reality like a dagger in search of fact and truth while art caresses reality looking for pleasure, grace, and beauty.

As for Allen Tate, his awareness of the scientific danger grew with his affinity for the South while he was reviewing books in New York in the twenties. As has been indicated, the Agrarians believed that scientific investigation—the demands for "proof," for instance—had smashed the great mythologies which had served poetry so well. Tate's disdain for scientific method appeared in a review which he wrote in 1926 on Edwin Muir's *Transition*.

The traditional mythology of European culture has been discredited by practitioners of the historical method, like Frazer and Rivers, and by the encroaching world of scientific hypothesis. . . . Our mythology is dead and we have not yet achieved a substitute for it out of the world-picture of modern science. For the precondition of all literature is the body of mythology to which the life-attitudes can respond freely as wholes. The traditional mythologies supported the spiritual equilibrium of man by rendering his origins sublime; but this is obviously no longer possible. The task of poets, then, in the present desperation, which became acute about the time of Ibsen and Baudelaire, is not the impossible resurrection of the myth but the construction of new myths which "idealize man's goal."[10]

In this early testing of his critical powers, Tate spoke of the abstraction to be found in science. No word in the aesthetic vocabulary of the Agrarians took more punishment than *abstraction*. Tate mentioned the "hopeless breach" between this aspect of science, however familiar it might become, and the "object itself, for which the abstraction stands and to which it is the business of the poet to return." Neither Tate nor Ransom ever saw in science the rich concreteness which alone makes a poem *good;* instead, they saw science as hypothesis, as theory, as principle, as Platonic abstraction—the "idea" of objects, not the objects themselves as concrete things to be seized by the poeticized senses. It must be conceded, of course, that anyone can limit his choices to those that best fit his ultimate purpose; and the ultimate purpose of the Agrarians was to blacken the name of science.

In Tate's opinion Muir made the mistake of wanting in some obscure fashion to submit science to a mystical change and thus to transfigure it into matter as suitable for poetry as the myths had been.

This was the very impossibility into which the Romantic poets had been trapped, Tate believed. The "defect" in their Romanticism was their rationality; they could possess only a limited faith. The scientific spirit, which the Romantics resisted, nevertheless was the very spirit into whose hands they played by failing to understand it. Matthew Arnold had also criticized the great Romantic poets for showing a certain lack of intelligence. Early in 1927 Tate had another opportunity to discuss the related problems of science, mythology, and poetry, this time in a review of I. A. Richards's *Science and Poetry* (1926). Although Tate seemed to be in agreement with most of the book's thesis, he found that Richards was a "victim himself of the modern dissociation."[11] He meant *dissociation of sensibility* which, along with *objective correlative* and other phrases used by Eliot, cropped up frequently in Tate's reviews. Writing about *Science and Poetry*, Tate again showed great concern for the modern demolition of the ancient myths. "What Mr. Richards calls the Magical View of the world, which with its vast systems of attitudes and beliefs forms the body of our traditional culture, had begun to totter, and poetry with it."[12] Tate then asked: Will poetry survive the downfall of the myths and beliefs upon which it had assumed to be radically based? An affirmative answer to Tate's question was doubtful because the entire economy seemed determined to serve the rationalism of science; our economy, and our society in general, was engaged with production at the level of the stomach and not with aesthetic creation at the level of the soul.

The Romantic poet, Shelley, who was later to be severely condemned by Ransom and Tate, now received high praise from Tate for having protested the destruction of the old mythologies. By this destruction, "The value, place, and future of poetry were rendered desperately infirm, and Shelley, facing the crisis, deepened and extended the significance of his art, clothed it with a reality and authority which had never been explicitly for it before."[13] Once again in 1927 Tate mentioned Shelley favorably, saying in a footnote to "Poetry and the Absolute" that "Shelley, in the *Defense of Poetry*, understood this principle [the primacy of the aesthetic purpose] when he said, concerning the relation of prophecy to poetry, that inferior poets make 'poetry an attribute of prophecy' rather than subordinate prophecy to an attribute of poetry."[14] Not often again was Tate to be so generous toward Shelley. By the time of Ransom's *God Without Thunder*, Shelley had become the despised "prophet of the God of science."

In this period Tate also reviewed the significant book entitled *Messages*, written by Ramon Fernandez, the French critic. On this occasion

Tate broadened his previous discussions of the role of science in damaging the total sensibility. Such a totality of aesthetic perception required a basic belief in original sin, the view that man's inherited nature was evil. "Scientific approaches," Tate asserted, "because each has its own partial conventions momentarily arrogating to themselves the authority of total explanation, must invariably fail to see all the experience latent in the work."[15] Poetry alone, or the equivalent of its essence in other forms of art, can give the total explanation. In writing on *The Theory of Poetry* (1926), by Lascelles Abercrombie, Tate had indicated that poetry had a special quality as *experience;* this idea was later joined to Tate's more comprehensive doctrine of poetry as knowledge. He said, "The preeminence of poetry as experience is unique, but to expect of it a metaphysical satisfaction is an effort to render it common."[16] The second part of this statement sounds like another blow struck against the abstractions that inhere in science.

Another major inroad of science, to the detriment of literature, was the use made of modern psychology in criticism. The name of I. A. Richards, of course, has to be highly regarded in this respect. In his *Principles of Literary Criticism* (1928) he has a chapter on a "psychological theory of art." Tate later ridiculed Richards for his charts of nerves and nerve-systems and his "hocus-pocus of impulses, stimuli, and responses."[17] It was on similar grounds that Tate condemned *Destinations,* a book by Gorham B. Munson. Munson was a Humanist and Behaviorist; thus he embodied two viewpoints which Tate abhorred. Rejecting the new discipline of psychology as a possibly fruitful means of analysis, Tate wrote that "from the viewpoint of literary criticism all scientific methods, good or bad, are in the end irrelevant; for when the method is taken out of the laboratory it becomes 'literary' and debased; its original standing as an exact science has no bearing on the new situation at all."[18] Poetry comprised a special type of knowledge; therefore, it needed techniques of criticism relevant to its special nature for correct aesthetic valuation.

Late in 1929 Tate reviewed Richards' *Practical Criticism* and again condemned scientific encroachments upon art. By now Tate's Agrarian ideas were well developed as was his loyalty to the South; *I'll Take My Stand* was in the planning stage. Again we find Tate concerned about the reasons why we were "losing our insight into poetry as a whole." He opposed the invasion of the mind by such "debased" scientific ideas as Behaviorism and Freudianism, "which vitiate our sense of the metaphor." The new Agrarian influence appeared in Tate's view that mechanized life under industrialism had had a "disastrous effect upon provincial communities, in which men developed a subtle art of humane communication." Both subtlety and humaneness were fading out. Radio and rapid transport had standardized character, and this fact was "peculiarly hostile to the immense individualization of emotion in poetry."[19] In praise of the Roman poet in "The Bi-Millennium of Virgil," Tate said that the ancients saw the objects of nature in all their individuality, their isolation, their three-dimensional unity, a power being lost by modern poets with divided sensibilities.[20] Of Dr. Samuel Johnson's poetry Tate wrote:

To write poetry so precise, lucid and pure, one must be what the Southern Negro calls a *settled* person; one must be mature; one must live in a world that offers the least evidence of ceaseless social change. One must not be distracted by too much speculation, or lost in the mutability of sensation. One's mind must be made up: such a poet will have taste.[21]

All the supposedly "settled" and static ages were regarded by the Agrarians with envy and veneration. Of the eighteenth century Tate said, "We are more ignorant than Theobald and Addison because we are ignorant of our own destiny when this is imagined apart from the immense physical organization of life which is industrialism."[22] Tate also quoted from Eliot's preface to *London* where appeared the affirmation: "I sometimes think that our own time, with its elaborate equipment of science and psychological analysis, is even less fitted than the Victorian age to appreciate poetry as poetry." Science not only debased poetry when it sought to be a method of valuation, but also debased itself as science. It lost its exactness, its own particularity as knowledge.

In any case, Tate's literary reviews from 1925 to 1930, and of course many later writings, bristled with hostility to science and its alleged effect on poetry, religion, and culture. All the views he expressed in his earlier works were incomplete when compared with the fuller explanations to be found in his first major book of criticism, *Reactionary Essays* (1936). His preliminary utterances are important because they indicated the anti-rational direction in which he was going. And although Tate became a New Critic after having been an Agrarian, his basic bias against science remained constant. The publication of *I'll Take My Stand* in 1930 made anti-science an official doctrine of the Southern Agrarians, whereas earlier it had merely been the opinion of this or that individual. Ransom had written the year before, relating science to art: "I will state my idea of the aesthetic essence rather flatly. Art has always been devoted to the representation of the particularity which real things possess, and therefore it has always been a witness against the claims and interests of science." Back of the art, Ransom had continued, was the "embittered artist," whose vision of the real was systematically impaired under the "intimidations" of scientific instruction, and who sought with "indignation as well as with joy" to recover it.[23]

The effect of science as *intimidation* of the poet recurred in the writings of Ransom, for example, in his excellent essay "Poetry: A Note on Ontology" written in 1934. Germinal ideas from this essay reappeared expanded and refined in "Wanted: An Ontological Critic" in Ransom's epochal work *The New Criticism* (1941). In the original essay Ransom discussed the time when, in his opinion, science first began to triumph over the poetic spirit.

What Bacon with his disparagement of poetry had begun, in the cause of science and protestantism, Hobbes completed. The name of Hobbes is critical in any history that would account for the chill which settled upon the poets at the very moment that English poetry was attaining magnificently to the fullness of its powers. The name stood for common sense and naturalness, and the monopoly of the scientific spirit over the mind. Hobbes was the adversary, the Satan, when the latter first intimidated the English poets. After Hobbes his name is legion.[24]

Tate soon followed Ransom in also believing that science had frightened the poets; this occurred, presumably, because of the new scientific insistence upon *truth*. The poets developed an inferiority complex when they had to confront the gigantic facts of science with their ancient myths, which were untruths at best. However, neither Tate nor Ransom investigated the extent to which John Donne, their favorite example of English poetry at its traditional best, actually used the new terms and structures of science in his metaphysical conceits. Regardless of that, Tate wrote in "Tension in Poetry" that "at a level of lower historical awareness than that exhibited by Mr. Edmund Wilson's later heroes of Axel's tradition, we find the kind of verse that I have been quoting, verse long ago intimidated by the pseudo-rationalism of the Social Sciences."[25]

The leading Agrarians did not always agree about the period when science made its initial inroads upon the hitherto sacred province of poetry. In the above-mentioned instance, Ransom seemed to date it with Bacon and Hobbes, that is, with the seventeenth century; yet in reviewing Edith Rickert's *New Methods for the Study of Literature,* Tate made a leap backwards to the ancient world. "But the purity and spontaneity of Graeco-Roman letters," he wrote, "had been suffocated in the descent—largely from within—of the barbarian; it was an age of cosmopolitanism and science."[26] Another critic writing in the twenties, J. W. N. Sullivan, agreed with Ransom that science consummated its triumph in the seventeenth century. This view, it must be said, distinguished neither Ransom nor Sullivan—except perhaps in the fact that Ransom, in blaming science for the despoilment of the metaphysical poetry of Donne's age, further rationalized the distress first voiced by T. S. Eliot over the alleged disruption of the English poetic tradition. The vitality of the following passage from Sullivan's essay lies in another direction, in its touching upon the doctrine of poetry as knowledge which came to mean a great deal to the aesthetics of Ransom and Tate.

With the disintegration of the three-centuries-old scientific outlook the way is clear for the construction of an adequate aesthetic criticism. It is true, as Mr. Richards insists, that the artist gives us a superior organization of experience. But this experience includes perceptions which, although there is no place for them in the scientific scheme, need none the less be perceptions of factors in reality. Therefore a work of art may communicate knowledge.[27]

On one occasion, William S. Knickerbocker, then editing the *Sewanee Review,* called the Agrarians "Southern Crocean critics."[28] Relevant to his identification was the opinion which Croce promulgated to the effect that art could be a form of knowledge separate from, but equal in importance to, other categories. Croce had written, "We have seen that intuition is knowledge, free from concepts and more simple than the so-called perception of the real. Therefore art is knowledge, form; it does not belong to the world of feeling, or to psychic matter."[29] In other words, art as *form* has objective reality, and this reality of form constitutes its knowledge; on this basis, art no longer has to depend for value on someone's subjective appreciation, on his mere feelings.

During the height of their reputation as Agrarians, Ransom, Tate, and Warren took part in a controversy with Aubrey Starke over the merits of Sidney Lanier as Southerner, Agrarian, poet, and critic. During this literary debate much was said that was related to science and aesthetics. Mention has already been made of the condemnation of Lanier as an anti-traditionalist, as a nationalist, and as a progressive for his desire to bring about a New South. In the argument with Starke, who had written a biography of Lanier in 1933, these indictments were repeated by the Agrarians. In addition, they examined the alleged effects of scientific rationalism on his poetic sensibility.

Tate and Warren initiated the debate in respective reviews of Starke's book. In them they used the new Agrarian arguments against Lanier. Starke came to the defense of the Southern poet in an essay entitled "The Agrarians Deny a Leader." In the same issue of the *American Review,* Ransom in turn defended the position taken by Tate and Warren. What especially angered Starke was criticism of Lanier such as this from Tate, that the " 'Psalm of the West' is praise of 'nationalism,' *argol* of Northern sectionalism, *argol* of industrialism."[30] What also disturbed Starke was the Agrarian view that Lanier was "the final product of all that was dangerous in Romanticism: his theory of personality, his delusions of prophecy, his uninformed admiration of science, his theory of progress."[31] These accusations sound like those leveled against Romanticism in general and Shelley in particular. Typical of the attitude in Tate's review, "A Southern Romantic," was the following:

For one thing, he shared with his age the delusion that the function of applied science is to make men at home in nature. The political direction of that scientific age was taking man out of nature in the religious sense, and enslaving him to a naturalistic order.

Having convinced himself, in an essay called "The New South," that the South would become, after the break-up of the plantations, a region of securely rooted small farmers, he was at liberty to misunderstand the social and economic significance of the Civil War, and to flatter the industrial capitalism of the North in a long poem, "Psalm of the West," a typical expression of Reconstruction imperialism.[32]

These are harsh words Tate uses to berate a fellow Southerner. In effect, Lanier was a regional traitor. The fact that he eventually left the South was also used against him. Ransom declared that Lanier "wrote admiringly of Georgia landscape and Georgia small farms, but the example he set was that of leaving Georgia."[33] This criticism later came back to haunt the Agrarians, for most of them also left the South in search of better opportunities in the North. They, too, wrote admiringly of the old tradition "down on the farm," but the example they set was to seek the benefits of the industrial society they condemned.

Among the many alleged sins of Sidney Lanier was that of urging the South to welcome science. Nor did he object to the factory system, said Ransom, "as one that subtracts the dignity from human labour and the aesthetic value from the product. In this respect he is behind Ruskin and Morris, his English analogues; behind them in his economic thought, behind them in his uneducated taste."[34] Warren claimed that Lanier was obsessed with an "evangelical concern" with science:

Science, along with the nature-metaphor, he regarded as an indication of the Love of Nature . . . the new *rapport* between Man and Nature. "We found," he said to his audience in Baltimore, "that science and poetry had been developing alongside each other ever since early in the seventeenth century; inquiring into the general effect of this long contact, we could only find that it was to make our general poetry greatly richer in substance and finer in form."[35]

That science enriches poetry not only in substance but also in its aesthetic form—this idea could only infuriate the Southern Agrarians. They had made a strenuous effort to prove that science and poetry were incompatible; Lanier made the mistake of confounding the one with the other, of feeling that science had actually improved poetry. Consequently, Lanier's social philosophy, which was permeated with scientific rationalism, compelled him to be a "doctrinaire" in aesthetics; that is, "he appreciated a work of art to the degree in which it supported his especial theory of progress."[36] Thus he was an opportunist in his criticism, and the Agrarians scolded him even though they did the same thing—they appreciated a work of art to the extent that it supported their special theory of Agrarianism. A further point against him was that he could not successfully transmute his sociology into poetry, he could not sublimate the one in the other. Here the Agrarians attacked Lanier for failing to do what on other occasions they had declared was impossible anyway: to make scientific objects suitable matter for poetic use.

In Warren's opinion, Lanier was didactic without ever understanding "the function of idea in art"; Lanier "regularly performed an arbitrary disjunction, both in creation and in criticism, between the idea and the form in which it might be embodied."[37] Despite Lanier's profession of having an extreme sensibility, he really lacked capacity for "aesthetic perception." As Ransom said, Lanier was "impressed unduly by mechanical products and the new applications of science. The taste for the mechanical is a taste for the abstract, but the philosophical status of agrarianism is that it is opposed to abstraction, and as an artist Lanier should have seen that his love of the Platonic abstraction was destructive to his poetry."[38] At one time in man's development the simple bull-tongued plow represented an advanced stage in "scientific development." The Agrarians did not object to this symbol of man's progress in the sturdy hands of a yeoman farmer, presumably because the plow had been sung about and written about in the poetic and social tradition; but they objected to the reaper and to the dynamo. Presumably, they represented the "mechanical products and the new applications of science" which Ransom disliked in the social philosophy of Sidney Lanier. And yet, might not future ages look back upon the reaper, the dynamo, and now, the primitive space ships, with the same nostalgic delight that Ransom felt about the simple, myth-laden tools of his beloved yeoman?

The controversy over Lanier which took place in 1933–34 did not end then. J. Atkins Shackford revived the whole affair in a series of three essays in the *Sewanee Review* several years later. Addressing himself to Ransom, Tate, and Warren, he asked the question: Who is a Southerner? And he answered caustically, "He must be a dyed-in-the-wool Secessionist, a fire-eating Agrarian, a whole-hearted devotee to whatever cause his section is involved or embroiled in at any given time, on the assumption that that cause is the right cause for his section."[39] But by then, 1940, the persons to whom he had addressed the question were themselves much less interested in the answer. Ransom, Tate, and Warren had already abandoned the sectional demand for a "restoration" in favor of a more specific literary crusade—to win over criticism, the teaching of English, and American literature itself to the New Criticism.

If the poet Sidney Lanier were the leading offender in the earlier undermining of the Southern tradition, the novelist T. S. Stribling was the leading offender in the thirties. As with Lanier, it was the scientific influence that destroyed Stribling as a proper Southern writer. The best study of how science vitiated Stribling's art was made by Warren in an essay published in the *American Review* in February, 1934. The following remarks from Allen Tate, however, seem to be an appropriate means of introducing Warren's criticism of Stribling. "Nineteenth-century science," Tate had written, "produced a race of 'problem' critics and novelists. The new 'social' point of view has multiplied the race. Literature needs no depth of background or experience to deal with problems; it needs chiefly the statistical survey and the conviction that society lives by formula, if not by bread alone."[40] Commenting on Stribling's novel *Unfinished Cathedral,* Tate called such books merely "inferior exercises in sensational journalism."[41] The South as a depressed area and the nation's "Economic Problem Number One" had indeed inspired a large number of humanitarian novels depicting the people's plight. Having those of Stribling in mind, Tate said:

It has been said that they are serious indictments of the South, but it must be remembered that although "social conditions" in the South are possibly even more desperate and corrupt than Mr. Stribling's representation of them, his earlier books cannot in the long run be understood as indictments of anything but the inferior sensibility and imagination of the author.[42]

Tate included Stribling among those "propagandists" who will be judged by the future "not on the abstract statement of a thesis but on their merits as writers."

Tate and Warren condemned Stribling for being in direct line of descent from the older naturalistic novelist who, as Warren said, "took science as a source of his method and his philosophy. His method was, professedly, objective and transcriptive; he was concerned with fact, not value."[43] In one sense the naturalistic novel was based on a science, biology, whereas "the realistic novel that we now know is based on a pseudo-science, sociology." Warren noted two issues arising in Stribling because of his devotion to this pseudo-science: "First, what is the actual content of his criticism; that is, what things in society does he dislike, and to what set of ideas do these likes refer? Second, what is the effect of this preoccupation on his work as an art form? From a given novel or given episode the two issues may be dissected out, in most cases, only by a certain exercise of violence."[44] Thus the content of the novel is at odds with its form: a Stribling type of novel contains more ideology than is required for an aesthetic effect. In fact, the tendentiousness of such a work makes a truly aesthetic result very doubtful if not impossible. Even if one assumes the objectivity of its survey, sociology lends itself to the "projects of reform." Sociology, therefore, does not enter the novel for an artistic purpose, but for something quite different—for satire, politics, revolution, and so on.

Stribling, a victim of this false science, allowed his novels to become saturated with a liberalism that was foreign not only to his art but also to the Southern tradition. Warren complained, for example, that the Southern whites in Stribling's fiction usually turned out to be mere "hicks."

If he [Stribling] is a hick-baiter and sometimes a snob, it is because American liberalism in its more sophisticated varieties has made such possible. The natural opposition to the liberal movement comes from the conservative country; therefore when the liberal loses his temper hick-baiting is his ordinary recourse. Liberalism flourished as the corollary to our great era of commercial expansion; therefore when the liberal loses his manners his ordinary recourse is snobbery.[45]

The liberal in writing a propaganda novel, Warren said, was haunted by sociological facts; he could not get close to his material because he was too much infatuated with a system of abstractions. He then feared that if he did get very close to his material—as William Faulkner had done, with significant success—the cherished factual "truths" perhaps might be absorbed in the complexity of the event itself. Characters and events interested the liberal novelist only as illustrations of his preconceived notions. Hence the novel created by him could be nothing more than a political pamphlet in disguise.

Warren went on to compare the modern sociological novel with the medieval morality play; the former, in his opinion, had all the stiffness, unreality, and abstraction that the comparison implies. "Event appears as a sort of allegory, a morality play of 'social forces.' " The plot of the novel dramatizes a "social proposition" which the author wishes to see "realized in actuality." Even the propaganda aspect of the work suffers.

Propagandist art is never pure propanganda in the first place, for something other than social conscience forces the choice of the art form, but the priority in this respect depends on the degree in which the author desires to see the practical triumph of his critical ideas and obtrudes that desire. In so far as this aim is possessed, and is obtruded, the work is scientific: it appeals to the scientist, the economist, the sociologist in us, and makes us say, we ought to do something about this.[46]

This response, however, is not the one that is evoked by a first-rate novel, play or poem. If the radical or proletarian novel of the thirties, for example, has already become an archaic literary form, then the basic aesthetic weakness which Warren describes may very well be an important reason for the demise. On the other hand, if a literary work saturated with Agrarian propaganda continues to live (Warren has never attacked Stark Young's *So Red the Rose* for being a poor novel), we must assume that such a work rises above its tendentious content to achieve a truly aesthetic effect.

A very important, although quite abstractly argued, exposition of the conflict between science and poetry may be found in Tate's first book of criticism, *Reactionary Essays on Poetry and Ideas* (1936). His earlier statements on the subject were here correlated and brought strongly to bear on the most central aspects of the aesthetic spirit. One of the theoretical structures which emerged took the form of a vast and somewhat ambiguous dichotomy—that between poetry of the *will* and poetry of the genuine *imagination*. Although Tate's ideas on the subject developed fully during his official Agrarianism, some scholars regard it as a vital contribution to the New Criticism.[47] After the Middle Ages, Tate asserted, the "cult of the will" emerged in Western civilization, and its growth endangered "imagination," the generative force of real poetry. It had existed before, this practical will, but in a form which allowed imagination to flourish. When science and rationalism arose to disparage and intimidate the older traditions, then the will began to be an enemy of poetry. "The first attitude," Tate wrote, "is the spirit of the practical will: in poetry until the seventeenth century it leaned upon morality and allegory; now, under the influence of science, it has appealed to abstract ideas."[48] The revival of Aristotle's rationalism during the Middle Ages was a notable factor in supporting the thinking "will" at the expense of the traditional, myth-nourished "imagination." Indeed, the attack on Aristotle and the Chicago school of critics which he inspired was a major indication of the Agrarian turn toward the New Criticism. Ransom in 1935 condemned Aristotle as a mere natural scientist. Writing rather bitterly against the concept of *catharsis* Ransom declared, "It reflects the patronizing view of certain natural scientists, who have strenuous programmes in view for humanity, and tolerate the arts only for medical or sanitary reasons, and in consideration of the present weak state of the racial mind."[49] As happened so often in their literary relationship, Tate echoed the thought of his older friend when he asserted: "We are aware of a greater range of experience. But it seems to me that purgation is a rather practical word. It is a medical term. We must not forget that Aristotle was a physician."[50]

The practical will when it served as a metaphysical context for Reason had its own brand of imagination, but it was a level too low and inferior to serve the aesthetic needs of the poet. This expression of conscious power, this will, according to Tate,

informs our criticism of society and the arts. For given the assumption that poetry is only another kind of volition, less efficient than science, it is easy to believe in the superiority of the scientific method. I myself believe in it. For the physical imagination of science is, step by step, perfect and knows no limit. The physical imagination of poetry, granting it an unlimited range, is necessarily compacted of futile and incredible fictions, which we summarily reject as inferior instruments of the will.[51]

The practical will's insistence upon the "truths" that will satisfy science cannot but condemn the "futile and incredible fictions" which alone can produce genuine poetry. In the course of time the will and the imagination have tragically tainted each other, to the decay of their respective essences. As for poetry, the practical and rational will with its aggressive and insatiable demands for empirical knowledge had deprived it of the traditional myths and other non-factual materials which inspire the imagination.

Until the seventeenth century, Tate wrote, the will sought poetic self-expression in morality and allegory, and even then it used whatever crude science was at hand. For the aesthetic reasons already given, Tate assumed that the poet should be blind to whatever scientific progress and discovery mankind was making. Spenser failed to be a poet of the highest order because his allegory, according to Tate, was motivated by other than aesthetic causes. The Elizabethan poet ruined his art by trying to prove the validity of assumptions that emanated from his will, his conscious thought, and not from his free-flowing, myth-haunted imagination. Since he lacked the freedom to explore reality in a purely artistic fashion, he only allegorized his notions and predetermined feelings. Hence all his characters appear sterile and wooden. "When the will supplants the imagination in poetry, the task of the poet, because his instrument is not adequate to his real purpose, is bound to be frustrated" (p. 99). The lofty aesthetic value to which poets aspired could be reached only when they ignored the rational climate of opinion which surrounded them, in whatever age. An excellent example of this type of poet was John Donne. Tate wrote:

Donne knew nothing of a scientific age, or of the later, open conflict between the two world-views, science and religion. Far from having a scientific attitude towards the problem of body and soul, he grapples with it, not to get any truth out of it apart from his own personality, but to use it as the dramatic framework of his individual emotion. (p. 66)

If Donne knew nothing of a scientific age, then it is surprising that he should often employ science-based metaphors in his best known poems, such as "The Compass" and "The Flea." Tate also implied that Milton chose to ignore science; yet Milton kept up as well as any other layman with the latest discoveries. Although a devout Christian —as devout as Newton—Milton believed in the validity of the Copernican system, a fact which Tate overlooked when he wrote, "It is this perfect divine order that makes Milton's mythology possible. It is the threat to such an order from the direction of the 'new cosmology' which 'calls all in doubt,' the new cosmology, that compelled Donne to ignore the popular pastoral convention of his time" (p. 70). The older convention of pastoral poetry had become so infiltrated with non-aesthetic matter that it could not be used by a poet as pure in his aims as Donne.

In its further desire to "prove" the truth about things and convince people through reason, the practical will eventually deserted allegory and morality. It turned to science as a better medium for serving its purposes; and in doing so, it appealed to abstract ideas in much the same manner as it had previously appealed to abstract characters and stylized emotions. Although Aristotle had been blamed for the medieval upsurge in rationalism, it was Plato whom Tate accused of the even more serious subversion of the poetic imagination by the practical will. By the end of the eighteenth century, he said, "the Platonic conquest of the world, the confident assertion of control over the forces of nature, had contrived a system of abstractions exact enough to assume the name of science" (p. 93). Tate called the scientific spirit, "without much regard for accuracy, a positive Platonism, a cheerful confidence in the limitless power of man to impose practical abstractions upon his experience" (p. 87). In the history of philosophy Plato is associated with the power and perfection and even the beauty of the idea. The idealist imposes his idea upon the imperfect, concrete, and contingent reality which he perceives with his senses. Through his mind, therefore, man the scientist and positivist imposes his "practical abstractions" upon his experience and nullifies his opportunity to develop his poetic imagination.

Poets require the sense of fruition, of concrete finality, and of traditional response; none of these is possible when the scientific method comes into use. Science never recognizes anything as final; it is forever mercurial and always finds one answer only to be able to ask another question. Tate repeated Schopenhauer in stressing the iconoclasm and mobility of science. The German philosopher had written:

While science, following the unresting and inconstant stream of the fourfold forms of reason and consequent, with each end attained sees further, and can never reach a final goal or attain full satisfaction any more than by running we can reach the place where the clouds touch the horizon; art, on the contrary, is everywhere at its goal. (p. 95)

The victims of this scientific iconoclasm and dynamism included the ancient myths and all other valuable "historic fictions." The deep conflict between rationalism and the poetic imagination, according to Tate, resulted in Romanticism. This rebellious movement, which questioned all authority by accepting reason, science, democracy and the perfectibility of man was in Tate's opinion a rebellion of the will in poetry as it faced the terrible consequences of having accepted the scientific spirit.

The poets, deprived of their historic fictions, and stripped of the means of affirming the will allegorically, proceeded to revolt, pitting the individual will against all forms of order, under the illusion that all order is scientific order. The order of the imagination disappeared. Thus arose romanticism, not qualitatively different from the naturalism that it attacked, but identical with it, and committed in the arts to the same imperfect inspiration. (p. 94)

Romanticism, therefore, was science, but without the "systematic method of asserting the will. Because it cannot participate in the infinite series of natural conquests, the romantic spirit impresses upon nature the image of its own passions" (p. 95). Specific aesthetic weaknesses followed. Among other faults, the style used by the Romantics was inflated and emotive; it lacked a definable objective. The poet could no longer fix his attention "upon a single experience," nor could he present objectively "the plight of human weakness." Instead, he fled from his situation into a "rhetorical escape" which gave his will "the illusion of power." Romanticism in a poet like Rimbaud led to the destruction of the will and to the surrender of the personality to extreme negativism.

A less extreme result of Romanticism was seen by Tate in the phrase "Romantic irony." This peculiar form of irony arose when the disordered imagination sought desperately and in vain to be "poetic" within the shackles of scientific rationalism. Tate said, "In the intervals when the illusion of individual power cannot be maintained, arise those moments of irony that create the dramatic conflict of romantic poetry" (p. 95). Such irony was a sign of "Negative Platonism," when the poet was compelled to state the opposite of what he meant, to surround his sterile abstractions with seemingly fertile and creative emotions. In the nineteenth century, Tate continued, Truth was felt to be "indifferent or hostile to the desires of men." These desires were formerly nurtured on "legend, myths, all kinds of insufficient experience; that Truth being known at last in the form of experimental science, it is intellectually impossible to maintain illusion any longer, at the same time that it is morally impossible to assimilate Truth." Trapped between these iron walls, the poet "revolts from Truth; that is, he defies the cruel and naturalistic world to break him if it can; and he is broken. This moral situation, transferred to the plane of drama or the lyric, becomes romantic irony" (p. 97). This matured view opposing Romanticism led Tate to an impression of Shelley which differed greatly from the one he had held a few years earlier. Shelley had now become a leading symptom of the general decadence in poetic values stemming from the incursions of science. Tate had powerful support from Ransom who had said of Shelley:

He never conceded that the health of poetry and the independent career of science were antithetical, and he could look to the future for the Golden Age. His program, with a little patting down and fixing, is like a premature piece of Marxianism, as follows. Production, under the law of maximum efficiency; what a desolate area of prose! Distribution, under the law of love; now we applaud. Consumption, under the law of beauty; which is very fine if we can believe in it.[52]

Although the dichotomies of production-efficiency, distribution-love, and consumption-beauty are intriguing, it is rather hard to relate them to any passages from Karl Marx. Ransom also elevated the Romantic poet to the first order of demons for his alleged revelation of the rational God of Science. Ransom said: "Shelley was the prophet of the new God, who anticipated the religious attitude of our leaders today with remarkable precision. He undertook, in his drama, to unbind Prometheus, the spirit of science, from his rock."[53]

Whereas Ransom had indicted Shelley as the prophet of the God of science, Tate now took him to task for being a Romantic in poetry. Lines such as "Life like a dome of many-colored glass/Stains the white radiance of eternity" were simply not poetic. They expressed "the frustrated individual will trying to compete with science. The will asserts a rhetorical proposition about the whole of life, but the imagination has not seized upon the materials of the poem and made them into a whole."[54] Shelley's famous "Ode to the West Wind" was an example of disillusionment arising from the defeat of the imagination by the practical will. Unable to face his future as a poet, Shelley asked the wind to waft him off to a *past* Golden Age, as Tate reads the poem. Scientific rationalism had thus succeeded in driving genuine values out of poetry and the poet out of the modern world. Shelley, the prophet of science, paid the immense price of losing his true worth as a poet by having a restless, revolutionary spirit.

A further effect of science was seen in the "crude optimism of a Victorian like Tennyson, a moral outlook that has almost vanished from poetry, and survives today as direct political and social propaganda supported by the sciences."[55] Against the romantic optimism of poets like Tennyson, the Agrarians posed the overwhelming aesthetic necessity of original sin. Several of Tate's "anti-science" poems plead for a recognition of this necessity. His "Last Days of Alice" deals with the death of the poetic imagination, with the dehumanization of man when denied his evil, and ends with the remarkable appeal:

> O God of our flesh, return us to Your wrath,
> Let us be evil could we enter in
> Your grace, and falter on the stony path![56]

The deeper spiritual meaning seems to be that God's grace is more significant when it is eventually won by a sinner; in a world run by scientific optimists, of course, God's grace might vanish altogether.

The drama, too, could not escape the chilling effects of science—of knowledge at the mundane level of *fact*. Nothing was regarded as sa-

cred anymore, Donald Davidson complained. The idea of divinity itself had more or less evaporated ever since the sixteenth century. In a
later book that still expressed strong Agrarian views, Davidson wrote:
"We are now predominantly a secular society, ruled by science, theoretical, applied, and 'social.' In a society ruled by science tragedy becomes an impossible conception. The pity and terror that belong to
tragedy by the Aristotelian definition are necessarily excluded from
the skeptical, inquiring, analytical processes of science."[57] Guided by
science, society was moving toward a pitiless and humorless future, a
society of pure and inhuman mechanism. Myth and religion, those two
great victims of the scientific method, could no longer adequately
nourish the poetic mind. Divested of their Agrarian economic and social context, the anti-scientific assumptions of Ransom, Tate, Warren,
and Davidson persisted throughout their coming identification with
the New Criticism.

Chapter VIII   Religion and Myth

MUCH HAS ALREADY BEEN SAID OR IMPLIED ABOUT AGRARIAN ATTITUDES toward religion and myth. Many of the social forces that others thought beneficial to mankind the Agrarians considered harmful to a proper religion. The industrial society seemed the culmination of the devil's work, for it concentrated all the related powers of evil: science, which destroyed religion by its constant search for factual truth; rationalism, which destroyed religion by crushing the old myths; modernism, which destroyed religion by doubting such "fundamentalist" concepts as creation according to Genesis; cosmopolitanism, which destroyed religion by admitting foreign elements into the organic Christian community; progress, which destroyed religion by scoffing at ancient traditions and by negating original sin, in its belief that man was perfectible; and liberalism, which destroyed religion by "softening down" the image of God, denying him his thunder, and turning him into a glorified Boy Scout, or at most a social worker rushing from case to case.

On the other hand, religious orthodoxy with its stress on dogma and ritual kept intact the image of a fierce and inscrutable God, one who was parsimonious in dispensing his grace; it kept man cursed with original sin, a miserable worm whom God could step on or save at his will. It would seem that only a reactionary could go to heaven; the liberal must go to hell. Furthermore, only a reactionary could write a proper novel or poem; and only a reactionary could be a proper literary critic. On these grounds, Allen Tate in calling his book *Reactionary Essays on Poetry and Ideas* was paying himself quite a compliment. He enjoyed a self-bestowed dispensation which, by being Southern, was also close to being divine.

We must go back beyond 1930 and *I'll Take My Stand* in order to place the Agrarian position on religion and myth in proper perspective and analyze it with some exactness. It was in this pre-Agrarian period—the Fugitive—that this position took shape. The earliest connection between religion and poetry—by no means an original idea—was made by John Crowe Ransom in 1919 when he entitled his first volume *Poems About God*. Here he presented in fragmentary fashion what eventually became a well-rounded theory on the relationship between religion and aesthetics. Ransom's Introduction began his long road to the eventual determinism which during the thirties made him demand an Agrarian society as a natural basis for a great literature. Now, in 1919, the classicist turned English teacher and Methodist minister's son turned poet declared:

The first three or four poems that I ever wrote were done in three or four different moods and with no systematic design. I was therefore duly surprised to notice that each of them made considerable use of the term God. I studied the matter a little, and to the conclusion that this was the most poetic of all terms possible; was a term always being called into requisition during the great moments of the soul. . . .[1]

During the twenties the one event which undoubtedly did most to engage the future Agrarians in religious polemics was the Scopes trial testing the proposition that Darwinian evolution could not be taught in Tennessee schools. In the end, the cynicism of writers like Mencken almost made the trial an occasion of honor, so deeply hurt was Southern sensibility by repeated charges of stupidity, illiteracy, and worse. To defend the Tennessee law was tantamount to a defense of the South as a region. That the issue was made to be "fundamentalism versus science" forced many combatants to be more extreme in their views than might otherwise have been the case. For example, some liberals saw the trial as an attempt by religious fundamentalists to capture another state government as part of a general conspiracy to establish a theocracy in the United States. On the other hand, conservatives like the Fugitives saw Clarence Darrow as the Anti-Christ himself who, having invaded the South from Chicago, was trying to vanquish God on the South's home ground. Scientific concepts like those of "evolution," and "geological time," were violating the fundamentalist belief in the origin of the earth and of man as described by the "revealed word of God," in Genesis. To the orthodox a disbelief in Genesis amounted almost to a disbelief in God; it could lead to agnosticism, and even to atheism. Once this fundamental basis of religion was abandoned in favor of geology, biology, and other sciences, little of religion remained that recognized the power and the glory of God and

His truth as revealed for all eternity by the Bible. Man could not split his faith between Genesis and Agassiz or Genesis and Darwin.

The Scopes trial brought many of Ransom's religious beliefs into a new focus against a background of hostility toward all the so-called modern ideologies, indeed, so much so that by the time of *I'll Take My Stand* he felt that religion and industrialism were mortal enemies. He wrote the following in the Statement of Principles prefacing the symposium.

Religion can hardly expect to flourish in an industrial society. Religion is our submission to the general intention of a nature that is fairly inscrutable; it is the sense of our rôle as creatures within it. But nature industrialized, transformed into cities and artificial habitations, manufactured into commodities, is no longer nature but a highly simplified picture of nature. We receive the illusion of having power over nature, and lose the sense of nature as something mysterious and contingent. The God of nature under these conditions is merely an amiable expression, a superfluity, and the philosophical understanding ordinarily carried in the religious experience is not there for us to have.[2]

Pursuing the idea of contingency, as opposed to the scientific attempt to discover and control the laws of nature, Ransom wrote, "I believe there is possible no deep sense of beauty, no heroism of conduct, and no sublimity of religion, which is not informed by the humble sense of man's precarious position in the universe."[3] In returning to the land, man would again sense the mystery and grandeur of nature; then the "old-time" religion would flourish. As Donald Davidson was to say, "My impression is that an anti-religious agrarian is a contradiction in terms, and that the education of nature, as Wordsworth vaguely held, must finally be a religious education, or nothing."[4]

It was Tate who delegated to himself the major task of writing on religion for *I'll Take My Stand*. He did so in relation to what he considered to be the religious tradition of the South. Resorting to metaphor for his definitions, Tate regarded true religion as a "whole horse," alive and kicking, seen cropping the bluegrass on the lawn. False religion, on the other hand, is not concerned with the whole horse, but with "that part of him which he has in common with other horses" and other vertebrates, and with that power of the horse which he shares with horsepower in general, its force. The whole horse, Tate asserted, exists whether we are able to discover it or not. Certainly religion as a total, living horse was hard to find nowadays, simply because the abstract and scientific mind cannot see him. Tate wrote:

This modern mind sees only half of the horse—that half which may become a dynamo, or an automobile, or any other horsepowered machine. If this mind had much respect for the full-dimensioned, grass-eating horse, it would never have invented the engine which represents only half of him. The religious mind, on the other hand, has this respect; it wants the whole horse, and it will be satisfied with nothing less.[5]

Mankind today is beset by adulterated faiths. Tate continued, "A religion of the half-horse is preeminently a religion of how things work, and this is the American religion." Functionalism, pragmatism, applied science—call them what you will—have divided the genuine religion so that the modern half-religionists believe in "omnipotent human rationality." They believe in a religion which can predict only success. Tate said: "The religion . . . of the whole horse predicts both success and failure. It says that the horse will work within limits, but it is folly to tempt the horse providence too far. It takes account of the failures—that is, it is realistic, for it calls upon the traditional experience of evil which is the common lot of the race" (pp. 158–59). Tate averred that such a "mature religion" was not very likely to suffer disillusion and collapse, whereas half-religion, which was not prepared for evil, supported a society which was riding for a crushing fall.

Having exhausted the horse metaphor, Tate shifted his argument to the image of history; he divided history into the Long View and the Short View. To the former he gave certain attributes of the half-horse, while the latter, the Short View, he more or less equated with the whole horse. The Long View, which had no real interest in particularity, had the fatal flaw of all the half-religions in that it resorted to rationality, to abstraction.

The Long View is, in brief, the cosmopolitan destroyer of Tradition. Or, put otherwise, since the Christian myth is a vegetation rite, varying only in some details from countless other vegetation myths, there is no reason to prefer Christ to Adonis. Varying only in some details: this assumes that there is no difference between a horse and a dog, both being vertebrates, mammals, quadrupeds, etc. The Short View holds that the whole Christ and the whole Adonis are sufficiently differentiated in their respective qualities (roughly details), and that our tradition compels us to choose more than that half of Christ which is Adonis and to take the whole, separate, and unique Christ. (p. 162)

Religious faith was inevitably weakened, in Tate's view, when man attempted to defend the Short View with its symbols and myths by the use of reason, which was an instrument natural to its enemy, the "scientific" Long View. Reason, science, nature—this hateful trinity forced even the medieval church to seek spiritual unity (through Thomism) by employing reason to support faith. "It has always seemed a scandal to us," Tate complained, "that Scholasticism should try to make rational all those unique qualities of the horse which are spirits and myths and symbols" (p. 164).

The main point which Ransom made in *God Without Thunder* was exactly this, that the "truth" in the Scriptures was a mythic truth, that this fact constituted its special value, and that any tampering with this truth by the Higher Criticism, Darwinism, science, or reason was meaningless. Other scholars have noted the similarity in the views of Tate and Ransom. Stewart reports that Tate had wanted to delay the publication of *I'll Take My Stand* because his essay for it, "Remarks on the Southern Religion," had too many ideas on religion similar to those in the soon-to-appear book written by Ransom. Robert Wooster Stallman observed that Geoffrey Stone in 1936 had pointed out the similarity between Ransom's views in *God Without Thunder* and Tate's stand in "Religion and the Old South." Stallman continued:

In *God Without Thunder,* Ransom defends the supernatural terms of religion by asserting that these terms are not intended to be taken as matters of fact, but rather as symbols, metaphors, fables, deliberate fictions which prescribe to us . . . an adequate way of looking at the whole of life in all its inexhaustible fullness and particularity.[6]

Still another critic, Delmore Schwartz, wrote that: "Tate takes over Ransom's view of the metaphorical character of religious belief and extends the notion to poetry."[7] We must emphasize at this point, however, that it was Ransom in *God Without Thunder* who offered the most complete and impressive Agrarian discussion of both religion and myth. In this respect Tate merely echoed his elder.

Before the publication of Ransom's "unorthodox defense of orthodoxy," the Agrarians were already engaged in a religious and literary debate with the Neo-Humanists; in this contest Tate took an important and lively part. The debate involved conservatives only; at stake was a profound and proprietary interest in religion, tradition, and literature. The issues raised in the debate greatly aid in further clarifying the religious assumptions held by the Agrarians.

During the twenties many others besides the Nashville group were searching for that inner conviction needed to fill the spiritual void revealed to them by such works as Eliot's *The Waste Land*. For the Marxist, this inner conviction seemed to be found in an ultimately benign teleology determined by dialectical materialism, by the inevitable play of historical forces. His "wholeness" centered on the justice of his cause, as he saw it, the validity of his "scientific" understanding of society, and the faith that through his ultimate victory in the struggle, his vision of a classless society would become a reality. In direct conflict with that of the Marxists, the "inner conviction" of the Neo-Humanists rested on the conservative, classical, and aristocratic tradition. They favored a self-control which set certain boundaries to the cultivated life; beyond these boundaries the true Humanist could not safely venture. Each man should in himself become a citadel of culture, a repository of gentility, urbanity, morality, and tradition. Morally and intellectually, he should keep company with such immortals as Confucius, Plato, Jesus, Shakespeare, and Goethe.

Led by Irving Babbitt and Paul Elmer More, the Neo-Humanists often clashed with rival contestants for domination of the conservative mind. They had much in common with the Southern Agrarians (the reactionary *American Review* welcomed both of them with equal delight), but the antagonism between them often seemed more bitter than that of either toward liberals and Marxists. We must assume that this bitterness prevailed precisely because they did have so much in common; therefore, they were both appealing to conservatives, whereas the leftists had more distant fields in which to forage. It is very hard to visualize Babbitt and More writing pamphlets, even with impressive erudition, to office clerks, coal miners, and dock workers. Such folk were too mundane for the Humanist culture.

Since both the Agrarians and the Humanists based themselves on tradition, they often expressed views which, out of context, could be taken as coming from either. Thus Babbitt in one instance declared, "The standards with reference to which men have discriminated in the past have been largely traditional."[8] Quite often the Humanists seemed to be using the same points of orientation, the same Index or list of heresies, for they too attacked industrialism, science, progress, naturalism, cosmopolitanism, and rationalism, to mention only a few. They also condemned Protestantism for its alleged betrayal of ritual and dogma. Speaking of the Protestant church in writing about the novel *Elmer Gantry*, Babbitt said:

The true reproach it has incurred is that, in its drift toward modernism, it has lost its grip not merely on certain dogmas but, simultaneously, on the facts of human nature. It has failed above all to carry over in some modern and critical form the truth of a dogma that unfortunately receives much support from the facts—the dogma of original sin.[9]

To Babbitt it was Rousseau who began the modernist corruption of taste and culture. Both Humanists and Agrarians agreed with the tenor of Spengler's *Decline of the West;* Babbitt echoed that Western culture "is now engaged in a sort of rake's progress that starts with Rousseau and his return to nature."[10] The strong trend toward naturalism in the nineteenth century had resulted in an "immense and be-wildering peripheral enrichment of life—in short, in what we are still glorifying under the name of progress."[11] No amount of this periph-eral progress, however, could atone for the void at the center. We all need conscious restraint, an "inner monitor" to guide our behavior. The Romantics, whom Rousseau helped to spawn, gave their passions free rein. Babbitt blamed Rousseau more than anyone else for being the "humanitarian Messiah" who sought to remake the world.[12] His philosophy had led directly to the French Revolution, that monstrous destroyer of ancient traditions. Ransom in *God Without Thunder* was to blame Shelley for being the new and despised Messiah of science; Babbitt also condemned Shelley, but for preaching so well the doc-trine of human equality. "In the realm of the human law," Babbitt wrote, "the nineteenth century, so far as it stood for a radical break with tradition, was, on the one hand, an age of rationalism, on the other, an age of romantic dreaming."[13]

We have seen how and why the Agrarians disapproved of rational-ism; the following is an example of Babbitt's attitude on the matter. He wrote: "Now it has been a constant experience of man in all ages that mere rationalism leaves him unsatisfied. Man craves in some sense or other of the word an enthusiasm that will lift him out of his merely rational self."[14] Freud with his id, his libido, his ego, and his dream life opened an entirely new world of the irrational, but it was not the frightening, and untraditional, irrationality of Freud that Babbitt had in mind. At any rate, he advised that reason should be abandoned be-cause it undermined tradition; it aided the social scientist in his at-tempts at humanitarian reforms. Such attempts, according to Babbitt, tended to constrict the personality. "It is self-evident," he wrote in a Humanist symposium, "that humanitarianism of the scientific or utili-tarian type, with its glorification of the specialist who is ready to sacrifice his rounded development, if only he can contribute his mite to 'progress,' is at odds with the humanistic ideal of poise and proportion."[15] Any one of the Southern Agrarians could have com-posed a similar passage.

Like the Agrarians, the Humanists also agreed with T. S. Eliot on the need for an organic society before a poet like Dante could emerge. In praising Giotto and other artists of the Middle Ages, Frank Jewett Mather, a leading Humanist, declared:

A humanistic criticism will hold . . . that an essential factor in the greatness of these artists was that, their themes coming almost ready made, they were spared the waste and perturbation of so called original invention and were free to face in tranquillity their real problem of transformation and execution.[16]

This idea, which is straight from Eliot, apparently won wide approval in the twenties; it crops up almost everywhere. It would seem that the loss of the Middle Ages—in religion as in all things—is a pervasive lament of the conservative mind. That medievalists of all ages recognize each other was shown again by the Humanist reference to fellow cultists of the Victorian period. Mather commented, "The gallant counter-attacks of a John Ruskin and a William Morris against modern industrialism show just how much and how little can be gained from a militant reaction."[17] Mather's opinions on aristocracy again compared favorably with those of the Agrarians. "In short," he wrote, "some aristocratic vision of the good life has always been the foundation on which great national art has been reared in the past."[18] He suggested that a proper way to solve the problem of restoring tradition and art would be to create the right kind of an aristocracy *within* our democracy.

Paul Elmer More quoted from Mather using phrases that the Agrarians were to echo quite often, in their joint attacks on the theories and achievements of Romanticism. The Humanists also felt this movement to be the aesthetic facade of the radical, scientific, and humanitarian culture of the Enlightenment—that force which shattered ancient patterns of ideas and art in as complete a manner as the French Revolution had shattered the inherited structure of society. Mather was quoted as saying that the end of expansive Romantic individualism was Romantic disillusionment and Romantic irony.[19] The concept of Romantic irony, greatly expanded and refined by Tate and others, appeared often in Agrarian arguments, and also became a much-used construction within the New Criticism.

Despite all the identity or near identity of view on so many topics, the Humanists and the Agrarians were open enemies. Their antagonism prevailed more during 1929 and the early thirties than later in the decade when both movements began to wane. It was in 1929 that Tate published "The Fallacy of Humanism," an essay disputing Babbitt's and More's philosophy on the uses of tradition and traditional religion. Robert Shafer, who answered Tate's attack, called the essay dogmatic and careless; moreover, he said it misquoted and misrepresented the Humanists. Shafer's rebuttal was titled, "Humanism and Impudence."[20] However impudent, Tate's essay was important because in it he had occasion to define more fully what he believed was the nature of traditional religion. The great virtue of such a religion was the "successful representation of evil." In Tate's estimate, not science but religion, or the dogmas thereof, could validate values.

In attacking the Humanists, Tate revealed some of his basic assumptions regarding the link between religion and literature. He excoriated the Babbitts and Mores on a number of issues, and quite pointedly on the question of this link. "Mr. More," said Tate, "entertains false hopes of literature; he expects it to be a philosophy and a religion because, in his state of 'independent faith,' he has neither a final religion nor a final philosophy prior to the book which he happens to be reading."[21] Expanding the implications of this serious indictment, Tate asserted that More could not find an adequate conception of tradition (experience) in terms of authority (reason), and therefore he gave us only "abstract, timeless, rootless, habitual ideas that closely resemble, in structure, the universe of the naturists; authority in More becomes the spectral sorites of infinite regress. There is no conception of religion as preserved, organized experience; you have a mechanism of moral ideas."[22] In other words, the Humanists in their eclecticism were incapable of having an organic religious philosophy; they put together so many twigs to make a tree.

The assumptions of his essay, Tate said, were that Humanism was not enough. If the values for which the Humanists pleaded were to be made rational, even intelligible, the prior conditions of an "objective religion" were necessary. Like Ransom in *God Without Thunder,* Tate declined to specify any particular church as the ideal example. Instead, he declared, "There is only one necessary religion, as Mr. Eliot has said, for men in the West. . . ."[23] Eliot, in the year before Tate's anti-Humanist essay appeared, had himself written on the subject in "The Humanism of Irving Babbitt." Robert Shafer believed that Eliot had been led astray on Humanism by T. E. Hulme. Various critics have noted that Tate based his own attack in part on hints furnished him by Eliot.

Eliot's primary criticism seemed to be that religion was a more traditional, more enduring, and more valuable experience than Humanism. In effect he distinguished between the two in order to dispel the confusion wrought by the alleged attempt to make Humanism itself a religion. Rather than having succeeded in this impossibility, the Humanist "has suppressed the divine, and is left with a human element which may quickly descend again to the animal from which he has sought to raise it."[24] Humanism and religion were not parallel entities; the first was sporadic, while the second was continuous. At another point Eliot accused Babbitt of trying to make Humanism work without religion—a problem involving the "inner conviction" or "control." Lacking a formal religious discipline, such control tended to vanish into a kind of spiritual quicksand. Eliot said, "And if you distinguish so sharply between 'outer' and 'inner' checks as Mr. Babbitt does, then there is nothing left for the individual to check himself by but his own private notions and his judgment, which is pretty precarious."[25] It has always been Eliot's contention that only an established church can adequately foster the genuine religious spirit.

Eliot and the Agrarians condemned the Humanists, mainly because their philosophy was too tolerant. To place men like Confucius, Jesus, Buddha, and Mohammed on the same plane of value disintegrated the traditional foundations of Western Christianity. The worst Humanist sin was a too promiscuous relativity, one that softened and blurred the differences among naturally hostile cultures. As Eliot was to declare in his Virginia lectures, such cultures must be fiercely self-conscious and defensive lest they become adulterated, lest they eventually dissolve into a common undifferentiated mass. On several occasions Tate wrote that a true religion "commands" us to consider the validity of absolutes. In 1936, he said, "The dominating structure of a great civilized tradition is certain absolutes—points of moral and intellectual reference by which people live, and by which they must continue to live until in the slow crawl of history new references take their place."[26] Tate was again referring to a necessary technique for the validating of values. He constantly maintained that a genuine religion could alone be that technique, and that its virtue was the successful representation of evil. Without such a concept of evil, and ultimately of original sin—concepts weakened by all theories of human perfectibility—there could be no reference by which to establish the concept of the pure, the good, the divine.

Tate insisted that religion imperiled itself when it ventured after rational knowledge of nature. Religious men, and all others as well, recommitted the original sin when they ate from the positivist and rationalist tree of knowledge. Ransom went so far, in this regard, as to state that religion existed not for the sake of its doctrines, but for the sake of its ritual. Thus he divested it of any temptation to deal with ideas and thought structures. Any ideational impulse could conceivably breach dikes for subversive doubts, agnosticism; it could sully the innocence of the symbolic ritual and dispel mystery with degrading scientific "truth." Religion's respect for the power of nature, Tate proclaimed, lay in her "contempt" for knowledge of it. He said, "Religion is satisfied with the dogma that nature is evil, and that our recovery from it is mysterious ('grace')."[27] Distant indeed is this view from that of Rousseau, who believed that nature was morally good, that the closer man got to nature the closer he got to a naturally benevolent God. The Southern Agrarians, insofar as Ransom and Tate were their spokesmen, strongly believed in a religion of dogmas; in *God Without Thunder* the preferred *form* was given to be ritual and myth rather than doctrine. Thus Ransom sought for religion as firm a *poetic* form as possible.

Tate had spoken of forms before. In 1926, in a review of *Decline of the West,* he had observed that for Spengler history was not a complex of laws but of forms which as organisms had to develop according to inherent properties. He wrote: "History should be the chronological study of these forms appearing in cultures as expression-media; it is not possible to control or alter them, but it is the business of history to predict their formal course."[28] The Agrarians found it easy to transfer to literature the relevance of the formal tradition in history and religion. This formalism came to be regarded as a major technique for the validating of aesthetic values, that is, for setting up standards and definitions for them. On the method of evaluating religion Tate wrote: "The organized meaning of the encounters of man and nature, which are temporal and concrete, is religious tradition, and its defense is dogma. The dogma acts for the recoil of the native from the snake: it is his technique for finding out the value of the encounter."[29] To be more specific, Tate could have said that dogma filled the vacuum left by the recoil of man from his encounter with rational knowledge. In the mythical Garden of Eden, the original sin had its genesis in the fateful quest of Adam and Eve for knowledge which was forbidden them. This was Satan's lure. Henceforth, man required some *form* through which to expiate his sin in his striving for grace—assuming that in his soul he had completely rejected the origina lure. That form was provided him by his traditional church through its elaborate structure of dogma, ritual, and myth.

The practice of a proper religious and aesthetic life required a place, and for the Agrarians the place most conducive to the purest results was the hinterland. As we have seen, they argued that industrial society herded people into cities, thus alienating them from nature; technology, deriving from the applied sciences, forced upon man a rapist's relationship with nature. He took what he wanted from nature with wanton brutality. The truly religious experience had its beginning and end in nature. Many others besides the Agrarians, of course, also held to this general belief. T. S. Eliot commented in this respect: "We may say that religion, as distinguished from modern paganism, implies a life in conformity with nature. It may be observed that a natural life and the supernatural life had a conformity to each other which neither has with the mechanistic life. . . ."[30] He only meant, he said, that a wrong attitude towards nature implied, somewhere, a wrong attitude towards God, and that the consequence was an "inevitable doom."

An examination here of some of Tate's arguments in behalf of a proper religion for Agrarians helps to prepare for the more complete explication of such a religion, or attitude toward religion, which appeared in Ransom's *God Without Thunder*. For whatever may be valid in the lofty estimate by Richard Weaver that the Agrarians may have invented a new metaphysic, Ransom and Tate deserve the major credit. It was they who probed most deeply into the philosophical implications of their stand. In this area of their thought it is more difficult to distinguish between them as Agrarians and as New Critics. In fact, we should jettison the labels altogether or say that in the metaphysics the labels tend to merge in a common significance. This uncertainty derives primarily from the absence of a comprehensive Agrarian book that records all the relevant details of the total social, aesthetic, and metaphysical outlook. Lacking such an official document and being wary of making too much of seeming contradictions, the literary historian is forced to synthesize from many and often minor writings all those views which he feels belong to Southern Agrarianism and to the New Criticism respectively. There was a definite Agrarian interpretation of nature, religion, and myth—and this trinity had a clear and organic relationship to a theory of literature. On the other hand, many of Ransom's and Tate's ideas on these matters extended without serious change into the period when they became primarily New Critics. Since neither developed with any marked exclusiveness into "textual critics," but remained essentially in what may be termed philosophical criticism (Ransom favored the word *ontology*), both he and Tate kept many of the attitudes toward literature which they formulated as Agrarians.

Ransom's *God Without Thunder* was the fullest Agrarian exposition of the trinity: nature, religion, and myth. In this book Ransom, with considerable fury, argued against every modernist, scientific, and humanitarian influence which had liberalized the Old Testament image of God as a stern potentate striking down sinners with a flick of his thunderbolts. It may be instructive at this point to mention some of the hostile reviews of *God Without Thunder,* not only because they refer to possible sources of Ransom's philosophy but also because they indicate the negative attitudes against which the logic of the book had to contend. For example, William S. Knickerbocker wrote in the *Sewanee Review:*

Only his "theological home-brew" smacks of Herbert Spencer's "Unknowable," aided and abetted in its establishment by the methods of David Hume, Immanuel Kant, and Sir William Hamilton—to say nothing of Dean Monsel of Oxford. A dash or two of the unorthodox suggestions of Henri Bergson makes it very attractive.[31]

Another hostile reviewer was Ernest Sutherland Bates. In the *Saturday Review of Literature* he made Ransom appear to be on an intellectual fox-hunt over badly broken terrain. He wrote:

One settles down comfortably at the beginning to enjoy an attack on modern science but almost immediately discovers that the attack is really on the Higher Criticism of the Bible; by the time the reader has brought up his memories of the Tübingen School, Strauss, Pfleiderer, Harnack, Cheyne, etc., to check the author's conclusions, he finds that Mr. Ransom has left him and is off on the trail of the anthropologists; following hot-footed, he next catches sight of the author pot-shotting mathematicians and philosophers; when he has finally caught up with the victor of so many fights and wishes to examine the loot, alas, the exhibition is over and the box is empty.[32]

Although himself an Agrarian, John Gould Fletcher was critical of Ransom's assertion that the fundamentalist was not an industrialist. Fletcher said that historically, "Fundamentalism in the Calvinist form in which Mr. Ransom upholds it led directly to industrialism, as both Catholics and Socialists, like the late Max Weber, have clearly shown."[33]

Tate, on the other hand, expressed a more favorable reaction—as would be natural because of the basic identity of view. He used the occasion of a review of Samuel Johnson's *London,* newly edited by Eliot, to comment: "An example of the material inevitability of social pressure is Mr. John Crowe Ransom's powerful defense of orthodoxy, which is somewhat embarrassed by his critical awareness that orthodoxy nowhere exists in a form acceptable to modern man."[34] Scott Buchanan in the *Virginia Quarterly Review* thought that the essential point of Ransom's book was that the Holy Trinity was still the pervasive mystery of contemporary Occidental life. He said that Ransom talked about "the lost paradise of the medieval synthesis, its disintegration into Protestantism and democracy, the stultification of the imagination in mechanical science, the collapse of the sentiments and affections in the commercial and industrial atmosphere, and the cultural chaos of rapidly shifting habits that never became customs."[35] This listing of factors which alienated the Agrarians from modern industrial society sounds familiar by now. Another critic of Ransom, Francis Fergusson, had the following to say in the *Bookman:*

In his defense of this orthodoxy, Mr. Ransom contrasts the pale theology of modernism with the rich myths of the Old Testament; he attacks the modern religion of science, both as an explanation of the universe and as a basis, in industrialism, for society; and finally he proposes the myth (elaborately defined) as a better basis for cosmology than scientific principles.[36]

Both Buchanan and Fergusson noted Ransom's book as a further contribution to the already deeply established conflict between religion and science. The extent of the conflict is readily seen in such a volume as Andrew Dickson White's *A History of the Warfare of Science with Theology in Christendom,* which came out in 1910. For two decades previous to *God Without Thunder,* White's book and others making a similar defense of science had had a great influence in spreading the latest brand of agnosticism. In defending science, White ridiculed the "older theologians" who learned nothing and forgot nothing, "sundry professors who do not wish to rewrite their lectures," and a "mass of unthinking ecclesiastical persons" who made up retrograde majorities on church tribunals. On the side of science, however, were "generally the thinking, open-minded, devoted men who have listened to the revelation of their own time as well as of times past, and who are evidently thinking the future thought of the world."[37] Just as Ransom wanted science to leave religion alone, so White wanted religion to leave science alone. "In all history," he wrote, "interference with science in the supposed interest of religion, has resulted in the direst evils both to religion and to science, and invariably; and, on the other hand, all untrammelled scientific investigation, no matter how dangerous to religion some of its stages may have seemed for the time to be, has invariably resulted in the highest good both of religion and of science."[38] In other words, science can be good for religion, but religion cannot be good for science. Edwin Mims, who dealt at some length in *The Advancing South* with the issues raised by the Scopes trial, reprinted a pertinent statement written in 1923 by a group of prominent scientists.

It is a sublime conception of God which is furnished by science, and one wholly consonant with the highest ideals of religion, when it represents Him as revealing Himself through countless ages in the development of the earth as an abode for man and in the age-long inbreathing of life into its constituent matter, culminating in man with his spiritual nature and all his God-like powers.[39]

Such attempts to attribute the sublimity of religion to science did not impress Ransom. As he saw the problem, religion had already surrendered altogether too much of its traditional, mythic, ritualistic, and faith-commanding power. Now that fear of punishment for original sin had all but vanished, God's grace had become easy of access and no longer a spiritual condition to be struggled and suffered for. In contrast with the modern God of the Social Gospel, Ransom's God was that of the Old Testament—omnipotent, inscrutable, and terrifying: "First, he was mysterious, and not fully understood; there was no great familiarity with him which might breed contempt. Second, he was worshipped with burnt offering and sacrifice. And third, he was the author of evil as well as of good."[40] Ransom's true God exercised his vast powers in the magnitude of the dark, beyond man's knowledge. God was very uncertain in betowing his favors. He was "fully equipped with his thunderbolts" and used them at will. When God lost these powers over the mind of man, he lost the respect of man. Ransom said, "This fact is proved today: the softer and more benevolent the representation of the God of Christendom, the more he is neglected, the less need of him the believers find they have."[41] The worship of such a soft and democratic God was actually, to Ransom, an act of irreligion. The New Testament, too, must be blamed for weakening God by recasting him in a more kindly, less threatening image. Ransom argued that this undermining of God's power had been the reason for the present "disintegration of the Kingdom of Heaven." The churches must revive "their old true Gods." Ransom was rather dubious whether the ends he desired could be attained at this late date in man's spiritual decay; he asked, "Or has Judaism softened him [the Old Testament God] down, and degraded him with its rather secular and commercialized existence?"[42]

Lacking all resemblance to man—and therefore indifferent to human problems—God, and religion, should be unconcerned with the material conditions of humanity, and with such things as social progress and reform. Ransom's idea of religious conformity implied elevation above the usual human problems; the only problem with which religion should be concerned was that of man's obedience to God. Logically, then, religion could not stand for a complex of moral principles; it disdained any "program" for social action. If such principles were allowed to exist, and if a conflict arose between them and their practical application, the result would necessarily be a kind of "religious irony" similar to the "romantic irony" which the poet had to suffer when his rationalism clashed with his aesthetics. In his orthodox doctrine Ransom plainly illustrated the fact that no such dilemma as religious irony could exist; in other words, no frustration could arise from the failure to achieve the translation of ethical desires into action. For Ransom the essence of religion did not live in its ideas, but in its ritual, its myth, its magic, and its spiritual "thunder." Three years after *God Without Thunder,* in a fine essay entitled "A Poem Nearly Anonymous," he reiterated his preference for ritual over doctrine.

Religion is an institution existing for the sake of its ritual rather than . . . for the sake of its doctrines, to which there attaches no cogency of magic, and for that matter a very precarious cogency of logic. The issues upon which the doctrines pronounce are really insoluble for human logic, and the higher religionists are aware of it. The only solution that is possible, since the economic solution is not possible, is the aesthetic one.[43]

Ransom composed this passage in 1933 during the major phase of the Agrarian movement. The quotation below indicates that Ransom's concern for the value of the myth and the ritual, as they appeared in both religion and in poetry, strongly persisted to the time when Ransom fully emerged as a New Critic. He wrote in his famous work, *The New Criticism,* in 1941:

Orthodox religious dogma is closely comparable with some body of Platonic or poetic "myth"; it is poetry, or at least it once was poetry; and again and again it is poetically experienced afresh, in the official pageantry and rituals of the public occasions. But it differs radically from the merely poetic myth in the hard and systematic use intended for it. . . .[44]

Only by resorting to the rigid formalism demanded by Ransom could religion exist as a worthy structure of rituals and myths. Thus religion and poetry were joined together in their fundamentally metaphorical natures.

The humanitarianism of the New Testament, Ransom declared, had replaced the older ritual and myth in religion; this fact had eventually assisted the penetration of religion by scientific rationalism, which in turn had replaced wonder with utility, fear with familiarity, and obedience with apathy. Speaking of the New Testament, Ransom said, "Such a religion as this is clearly the one which adapts itself to the requirements of our aggressive modern science." This religion is "characteristically Occidental and modern. But as far as a religion can be, it is fundamentally irreligious, or secular, both in its doctrines and in its works."[45] Too much *reason* in either religion and poetry destroyed their aesthetic power, and in both the process of destruction was well advanced.

After the New Testament, Ransom asserted, the next big infusion of rationalism came with the Protestant Reformation. This statement did not mean that Ransom, who had grown up a Methodist, was turning Catholic. Even the traditional medieval Church, and St. Thomas Aquinas himself, were not without blemish. Tate, too, had condemned the effort made by the Middle Ages to explain the Catholic faith through reason; according to Tate, "dogma as rationality is certainly a half-religion and is on the way to becoming a science or practicality."[46] Ransom, for his part, criticized St. Thomas for his pioneering and prodigious labor in convincing his church to bestow sanctity on Aristotle. Besides condemning both the "cathartic" and "mimetic" principles, Ransom called Aristotle the "father of the natural sciences" who was "not much of a humanist, and no sort of a religionist." As for the great Thomist contribution to theology, Ransom wryly complained, "The principle of reason and the principle of faith were wedded."[47] Protestantism, which grew as a response to rationalism and individualism, received from Ransom an even more serious rebuke. Not only had the Reformation disrupted a long religious formal tradition, but it also emerged, in almost Machiavellian fashion, alongside the early rise of modern science. Protestantism was a "naturalized religion" which, because of its respect for reason and progress, did away with myth, ancient ritual, and the older concept of God. Toward the end of this historic process, Protestantism became a rationale for industrialism, creating a pseudo-religious and pseudo-democratic halo around materialism and the profit motive.

Ransom in *God Without Thunder* gave much attention to the loss in spiritual values which followed the demise of the myths, religious and otherwise. Richard Weaver has praised Ransom for his "brilliant exposition of the myth as an expression of essential truth."[48] Literature on the myth, and especially on various aspects of the New Criticism in relation to the myth, has become very extensive. No attempt can be made here to relate to this wide literature the mythic views of Ransom and Tate. Both discussed the myth in religious and aesthetic contexts—the two often seemed to be identical—and found it useful to define myth as in severe struggle with science. Ransom said, "Science is professionally opposed to myths."[49] Myths are, in his opinion, "construed very simply by the hard Occidental mind: they are lies. It is supposed that everything written in serious prose ought to be historical or scientific. . . . Myths, like fairy tales, like poems, are neither.

They are therefore absurd" (p. 55). Ransom had answers for the higher criticism which in the nineteenth century had begun to question, with scholarly and scientific methods, the validity of the Bible. He wrote:

I believe that religious myths, including those of the Bible, are unhistorical and unscientific, precisely as our gallant historians and higher critics have recently discovered; but that their unhistorical and unscientific character is not their vice but their excellence, and that it certainly was their intent. (p. 56–57)

Poetry for Ransom and Tate came to be regarded as a superior form of knowledge; the myth, as usually objectified in ritual, was a superior form of worship, of faith, of religion. A myth could be felt intuitively by the inmost soul; it required no mind-consuming ratiocination. At best a reasoned doctrine could only be understood, with cold logic, by the mind. In commenting on *God Without Thunder*, while again criticizing the rationalist tampering with religion, Ransom declared: "It is as if I had said of the sacred objects and the supernaturalism of the faith: Behold these myths! Then I have defined the myths, in the cold and not very fastidious terms of an Occidental logic" (p xii). Before coming to Ransom's definition of the myth, it might be instructive to refer to Eliot on the same subject. Eliot was writing about Blake.

We may speculate, for amusement, whether it could not have been beneficial to the north of Europe generally, and to Britain in particular, to have had a more continuous religious history. The local divinities of Italy were not wholly exterminated by Christianity, and they were not reduced to the dwarfish fate which fell upon our trolls and pixies. The latter, with the major Saxon deities, were perhaps no great loss in themselves, but they left an empty place; and perhaps our mythology was further impoverished by the divorce from Rome.[50]

Ransom, for his part, was quite selective when he granted to the myth its essential qualities. He analyzed each of these qualities for a page or two in *God Without Thunder*. It should be understood at the outset that by implication he excluded those myths whose basic "truth" did not conform with the conservative tradition that he supported. None of the myths and legends created by folk imagination could be accepted as valid if their heroes were democratic, liberal, or national. The legendary character of Abraham Lincoln, for example, was pointedly condemned, while the powerful myth-making faculty of the Negro slave (recalling his tradition or dreaming of freedom), was not mentioned. Some writers have noted the status or class consciousness underlying Ransom's idea of mythology. In 1934 Henry Nash

Smith, in "The Dilemma of Agrarianism," saw the then current struggle between Agrarianism and industrialism as a clash between two ancient myths. The first believed in the victory of evil; the second, in the eventual triumph of good. Ransom had chosen the first, and in its behalf he became a persuasive apostle. "This sense of irreparable loss," Smith wrote, "of a rapid increase of evil and diminution of good in the world, is among the oldest of human experiences. Mr. Ransom has given a beautiful description of it in *God Without Thunder*, interpreting the story of expulsion from the Garden of Eden as an early formulation of this ancient and basic belief." Smith went on to enlarge his analysis of the dual nature of myths, citing "the curious contrast between two myths which have found widespread acceptance over long periods of time: the myth which implies that evil is constantly intruding itself into the universe, 'the longer the worse,' as Wulfstan put it; and the myth which implies that the universe is steadily moving toward some far-off divine event."

He continued:

The first of these myths, in some form or other, almost always underlies the conservative attitude: a fear of change, a desire to lay hold upon the past. The second, the myth of progress, underlies the various forms of Utopianism, and nourishes reformers like Shelley: the people whom the Agrarians lump together under the scornful name of Liberals.[51]

In his listing of the qualities necessary to the genuine myth, Ransom applied rather rigid criteria. The myth must be important, he said, and elucidate some great fundamental verity of the spirit. This demand accorded with the prior belief that faith was a matter for the soul and not the mind; it attached to intuition and the blood, not to reason and the brain. Furthermore, the myth must be vivid and energetic. Despite its possible exoticism (and the myth tended to get out of hand), it must be in strict keeping with our sense of taste and sensibility. Myths were, after all, the foundations of a fastidious gentleman's religion. They must not force him to defend what was spiritually untenable, crude, or ludicrous.

Once past these preliminary obstacles, the myth must be institutionalized, that is, made part of some inheritable practice. It could then become a social possession, preferably through an established church. Various forms of ritual could best preserve the myth for posterity. Not every myth, however, not even with the qualities mentioned, could serve and move mankind unless it was also alert to certain historical and psychic adjustments it had to make. We respond favorably to a myth, Ransom declared, only if it suits us racially and culturally. Ransom's dictum automatically ruled out myths created not only by the Negroes, Indians, and other non-whites, but also by liberals, humanitarians, and progressives—by everyone who lived primarily by reason. Their myths, if they could even be so named, were not mythic. Furthermore, even within the restricted area which Ransom designated, not every myth was to be accepted. At work was a cultural determinism which set still more limits on the myth's appropriateness. Urban dwellers, for instance, could not "accept with relish as the appropriate symbol of omnipotence a mere Rain-God, or a God of vegetation." Ransom continued, "We have no longer any particular relations with the beasts, and we could not care for totemism, or a myth which defined God as an animal."[52]

The true myth, according to Ransom's definition, possessed a quality which made it possible for aesthetics to solve the tough problem of belief. Neither the doctrines of the church nor the rationalism of science could perform this function. The unarguable plane of religion was its *ritual*; the ritual constituted its *form*; and the *myth* was its content. The salvation of the myth and the full restoration of its traditional power in religion could re-unify modern man's "divided sensibility." The modern dissociation had resulted, in part, from man's abandonment of the ancient myths which once helped so much in shaping his spiritual being.

Allen Tate also wrote at length on the value of myths. In several essays on modern poets he considered the loss of myth as a limitation on the artist. Writing about Hart Crane, Tate discussed the origin of myths and the paradox that Crane encountered:

If anthropology has helped to destroy the credibility of myths, it has shown us how they rise: their growth is mysterious from the people as a whole. It is probable that no one man ever put myth into history. It is still a nice problem among higher critics, whether the authors of the Gospels were deliberate myth-makers, or whether their minds were simply constructed that way; but the evidence favors the latter. Crane was a myth-maker, and in an age favorable to myths he would have written a mythical poem in the act of writing an historical one.[53]

Divided in sensibility, Crane could not overcome the paradox that his age presented him; therefore, he failed in his attempt to make a myth for America. Emily Dickinson, Tate found, approached the reality of myths more correctly. He wrote, "It is impossible to imagine what she might have done with drama or fiction; for, not approaching the puritan temper and through it the puritan myth, through human action, she is able to grasp the terms of the myth directly and by a feat that amounts to anthropomorphism, to give them a luminous tension, a kind of drama, among themselves."[54] And of Ezra Pound Tate wrote that he was a "powerful reactionary" who had a mind devoted to those ages "when the myths were not merely pretty, but true."[55] Tate made this outspoken commendation in the mid-thirties, but several years before he had been less kind to Pound; in fact, he hinted that Pound was already undergoing some kind of mental difficulty. In reviewing some of his poetry Tate wrote, "If Mr. Pound were not constitutionally unable to think, it would never have been conceived."[56] By the later period, thought and reason occupied a much lower position as factors required by the great poet.

How could modern man restore to himself his total sensibility, his complete personality? For the Agrarians naturally the answer lay in Agrarianism, or in those profound aspects of their ideology which touched upon the spiritual and aesthetic soul. Ransom saw in T. S. Eliot, an ideological ally, an excellent example of the complete personality in modern times. In his praise, Ransom wrote:

A natural affiliation binds together the gentleman, the religious man, and the artist—punctilious characters, all of them, in their formalism. We have seen one distinguished figure in our times pronouncing on behalf of all three of them in one breath. In politics, royalist; in religion, Anglo-Catholic; in literature, classical. I am astonished upon how comprehensively this formula covers the kingdom of the aesthetic life as it is organized by the social tradition.[57]

Ransom wrote this passage in 1933. Eight years later, in *The New Criticism,* he modified his opinion somewhat, declaring that while Eliot's famous series of alignments made the proper literary and religious affirmations, this series did not support the author's poetry nor even bear upon the great body of his criticism. In Ransom's opinion, "A public man could hardly have written a more conservative ticket."[58] Eliot's original presentation of his famous alignments in the introduction to *For Lancelot Andrewes* went as follows:

The general point of view may be described as classicist in literature, royalist in politics, and anglo-catholic in religion. I am quite aware that the first term is completely vague, and easily lends itself to clap-trap; I am aware that the second term is at present without definition, and easily lends itself to what is almost worse than clap-trap, I mean temperate conservatism; the third term does not rest with me to define.[59]

Ransom in 1933 adapted Eliot's formula to a Southern Agrarian context; after all, the word *royalist* was unsuitable to America, even to that part which lay south of the Mason-Dixon Line. The word *Catholic,* too, was hardly in keeping with the Southern tradition. Ransom's adaption took this form: "I would covet a program going something like this: In manners aristocratic; in religion, ritualistic; in art, traditional." He continued, "The word for our generation in these matters is 'formal,' and it might even bear the pointed qualification, 'and reactionary.' "[60]

Thus it probably followed that Tate three years later used the title, *Reactionary Essays on Poetry and Ideas.*Tate and Ransom seemed to have appropriated the term *reactionary* for literary usage. Ransom in *God Without Thunder* gave a reactionary interpretation even to the myths of the ancient Greek artistic tradition. "The lesson of the Greek myth and of Greek drama," he affirmed, "is what we would call in these days 'reactionary.' The Greeks were not yet indoctrinated with the Good God of the moderns, nor with industrialism, which is his cult." Ransom observed that the old Greek myth-maker, in binding Ixion to a revolving wheel, was saying "that men who have once committed themselves to industrialism will never escape from industrialism—wheels being perfect symbols of progress most uncomfortable for the human physiology that is bound to them."[61] Ransom was not opposed, as might be inferred, to the invention of the wheel by primitive man, nor did he object to the use of fire and metal; and yet, the Agrarian prejudice against progress could invite the idea that mankind should have remained in the Stone Age. In regard to the Ixion myth, Ransom failed to explain what kind of "industrialism" existed in ancient Greece or why the Gods (Zeus did not believe in original sin) should be so set against an order of society which was still, in economic and social terms, a few centuries in the offing.

As has already been indicated, another requirement for the complete personality, besides the practice of an orthodox religion, was the belief in the reality of original sin. Hulme's obsession with this concept has been mentioned. Among the Agrarians it was Robert Penn Warren who studied most profoundly the effects of original sin on human character and action, doing so mainly in his poetry and fiction. Ransom and Tate also examined its value to the fulfillment of both life and literature. According to the former, poets like Tennyson and Browning, by conforming to modern ideas of progress, could no longer divine the "inner meaning of experience" because of their disbelief in original sin. To strip man of the dubious blessing of this inherited guilt dehumanized him, and made him only a photographic image such as the "picture of the human body" with its parts divided and labeled—the picture that was usually shown in books on social hygiene. Scientific rationalism, when it entered and governed poetry, would not permit the imagination in creating its allegory of man to transgress the limits of reality as exhibited in the chart; for the chart was "science," and science failed to recognize sin, or spirit, or soul, or any supernatural power beyond discovery through reason. As Tate wrote:

The Seven Deadly Sins being now a little threadbare, our new allegorists are quite clear in their recognition that the arts, more especially poetry, have no specific function in society. The arts offer society a most pusillanimous instrument for the realization of the will. The better the art, one must add, the more pusillanimous. For art aims at nothing outside itself, and in the words of Schopenhauer, "is everywhere at its goal." There is no goal for the literature of the will, whose new objective must be constantly redefined in terms of the technology, verbal or mechanical, available at the moment.[62]

Original sin as an active concept with power to govern human action and give it spiritual meaning was therefore an element in the social and religious tradition; and if the above passage from Tate were any index, the concept of sin gives an internal meaning to art which it would otherwise not have. Tate's profound recognition of this alleged truth can also be seen in his one novel, *The Fathers,* which was published in 1936. In the story the narrator, remembering past events fifty years later, said:

Nobody today, fifty years after these incidents, can hear the night; nobody wishes to hear it. To hear the night, and to crave its coming, one must have deep inside one's secret being a vast metaphor controlling all the rest: a belief in the innate evil of man's nature, and the need to face that evil, of which the symbol is the darkness, of which again the living image is man alone.[63]

These words by Tate may express, as perfectly as is possible, the "inner meaning" of Warren's enigmatic novel *The Cave,* in which a man goes into the darkness, alone, and is not saved; but the ultimate test of his manhood, and its great value, derives from the courage that he acts upon in submitting to the encounter.[64]

Two of the major influences on the Agrarians, Hulme and Eliot, often addressed themselves to the need for original sin. In his famous essay on Baudelaire, Eliot had written that

the recognition of the reality of Sin is a New Life; and the possibility of damnation is so immense a relief in a world of electoral reform, plebiscites, sex reform and dress reform, that damnation itself is an immediate form of salvation—of salvation from the ennui of modern life, because it at last gives some significance to living. It is this, I believe, that Baudelaire is trying to express; and it is this which separates him from the modernist Protestantism of Byron and Shelley.[65]

Hulme whom Tate in 1927 called the "prophet of his generation," repeatedly deplored the decay of the modern temper. As we have seen, he also attacked the optimistic romanticism of poets like Byron and Shelley. He found the "root of all romanticism" to be the fallacious idea that individual man was an "infinite reservoir of possibilities," and that if "oppressive order" was destroyed, "these possibilities will have a chance and you will get Progress."[66] It is at this point that Hulme compliments the Catholic church for having defeated the Pelagian heresy and adopting the "sane dogma of original sin." Pelagius was a fourth century British monk who, as might be assumed, denied the validity of original sin and insisted upon man's having freedom of will.

The Agrarians and their followers found other relationships between religion and literature besides those touched upon above. Cleanth Brooks, Jr., made a further identification on the basis of hints provided for him by Ransom and Tate. For Brooks, too, the enemy of religion and art was science. "The qualities which art shares with religion," he wrote in the second Agrarian symposium, "are just those which Liberal Protestantism through its imitation of science has lost." Unlike religion, science could not prove its underlying assumptions; nor had science anything to say about values. These weaknesses of science came into religion through liberalism, with effects on art that were bad. "I am using art," Brooks wrote, "in the sense of a description of experience which is concrete where that of science is abstract, many-sided where that of science is necessarily one-sided, and which involves the whole personality where science involves one part, the intellect."[67] Brooks, of course, is better known as a New Critic than as an Agrarian; and as such a critic he is most renowned for his often brilliant textual analysis of poetry.

These opinions of his on religion and art recall those of Ransom in *God Without Thunder* where he said, "We do not make a sufficient contact with the world when we elect to be exclusively scientific, because that means blindness: that is the intellectual variety of anaesthesia."[68] The features disclosed by art "are those which render the fulness of the object and constitute a body of knowledge so radical that the scientist as scientist can scarcely understand it, and puzzles to see it rendered, richly, and wastefully, in a poem, or the painting."[69] By emphasizing religion as necessary to the total sensibility, Ransom and Tate established a major prerequisite of the traditional writer.

Richard Weaver, another one of their followers, praised them in this generous manner: "The great achievement of the Agrarians has been their achievement of a total awareness. By compelling us to see the price that is paid for severance from nature and for the ignoring of final design, they have made us realize why we today are partial men." In Weaver's opinion this enormous contribution resulted from the fact that the Agrarians went to God, a spiritual journey which brought about Ransom's "searching critique of humanized religion," Tate's premise that "man is by nature incurably religious," and Warren's subtle studies "of original sin and the problems of redemption."[70] When the religious artist rejected humanism in both his faith and his art and clung to his classical and formal tradition he was freed from all mundane matters which might otherwise inhibit his creativity. Brooks also mentioned the artist's greater scope.

And religion, again like art, is not man-centered in the same sense in which science is. To illustrate from art, the artist attempts something of a *rapprochement* with the universe outside him. Laying aside the practical motive, he tries to bring his interests into terms with larger, more universal matters.[71]

In *God Without Thunder* Ransom admired the simple idyllic life depicted in the poetry of Yeats; he contrasted this life with the progressive and scientific urge to go forward, "to improve the human position at the expense of nature as an enemy, to eat of the fruit of the tree of knowledge, to break from the definitive man-to-God relation, and to commit sin."[72] Critics hostile to the Agrarian position have attacked such a doctrine, when applied to the judgment of aesthetic value, as obscurantist. Weaver, on the other hand, has defended this attitude toward original sin, saying, "As soon as one begins to hint that the strain of wickedness in the human race recognized by Hebrew prophets and Greek philosophers long before Christian theologians is still with us, he is called an obscurantist and is disqualified from further public hearing."[73]

On many occasions the Agrarians made it quite clear that they regarded *abstraction* as an enemy of religion and poetry. It was the death of religion, Tate asserted, no less than the death of everything else of any value. Regarding the question of this death, Weaver connected religion and poetry as historic allies: "Poetry and religion have been too often conjoined in cultural history for the union to be fortuitous." Like the Agrarians, he too united the religious and poetic spirit, writing that if poetry were that which "has the most universal being, it is true that all poetry is a form of worship." He continued, "The practice of poetry amounts in effect to a confession of faith in immanent reality, which is the gravest of all commitments."[74] One is again reminded of Ransom's early assertion, made in 1919, that for him the most poetic word in the language was *God*. One is further reminded of Karl Shapiro's angry observation that too much modern poetry, influenced by Hulme and Eliot, attempts to *be* religion—to its self-mutilation as great art.[75]

In the Agrarian theory of literature, therefore, religion of a special orthodoxy occupied a prominent place of power. Religion won this position mainly because of Ransom's and Tate's concern with metaphysical values in nature, faith, ritual, and myth. It is not clear where the perfect form of religion has existed, although in his private practice Tate joined the Catholic church. Perhaps the closest to the ideal was the religion of the Old Testament, if *God Without Thunder* is to be the witness; yet Ransom hinted that even this religion as presently practiced might be contaminated by the excessive commercialism of the modern Jews. The religion of the Middle Ages suffered from the inroads of rationalism, made by the Scholastics and St. Thomas Aquinas; the Protestant Reformation was utterly wrong, as were all modern religions suffused with humanism and liberalism. Even the religion of the Old South, as Tate examined it, was outside the pattern of tradition. At one point in his writing, Frank L. Owsley was also disturbed by what he found in his region. "In sharp contrast to this religious sense," he said, "one who sojourns among these people long enough will find another characteristic: the decided tendency toward homicide as a mode of settling permanently certain types of personal differences."[76] Relative to this statement, Tate had explained that the resort to physical violence found in the South was residual from feudalism and the code of honor; yet in another context he found the Old South somewhat less than feudal. He wrote that the traditional forms of religion were not repeated there, and it is quite obvious that Catholicism, an orthodox religion, was never popular there. "This anomaly gave us," Tate wrote, "that remarkable society of the old South, which was a feudal society without a feudal religion."[77] From these and other views tending to disparage the religious quality of the South, it would seem that the Agrarians were somewhat dissatisfied with their tradition insofar as a proper spiritual life was concerned. Such a process of negation would seem to leave only fundamentalism, yet it seems certain that the highly cultivated Agrarians would eventually find its actual manifestations too crude, too lacking in form and taste. Herbert Agar did so in discussing certain religious practices to be found in the lower Mississippi Valley, the heart of the South. He wrote, "In the southern part of the Valley, among the poorest of the white tenant farmers, there have grown up a number of semi-savage cults, tragic in their degradation, farcical in their parody of Christian theology."[78] We are left, then, with the general strategy developed in Ransom's *God Without Thunder*, which favored no particular church over another, but which demanded return to ritual and orthodoxy, a *fundamentalism*, in all of them. He phrased his final admonition as follows: "With whatever religious institution a modern man may be connected, let him try to turn it back towards orthodoxy."[79]

Chapter IX   The End of Agrarianism

IN A COLLEGE ANTHOLOGY, "TOPICS FOR FRESHMAN WRITING," WHICH Ransom compiled in 1935, there is much evidence of his continued interest in Agrarianism. He used the opportunity, to include four pieces of his own: "Happy Farmers," "Shall We Complete the Trade?" and two selections from *God Without Thunder*. He also included articles by Troy J. Cauley, the author of *Agrarianism;* Herbert Agar, leader of the American Distributists; Stark Young, an original contributor to *I'll Take My Stand;* and Rexford G. Tugwell, who reviewed a book by Ralph Borsodi, a practicing Agrarian and subsistence farmer. Other articles dealt with machinery and civilization, overproduction, unemployment, the land, nationalism and foreign trade, religion and morals. However, three years later, 1938, when his own book *The World's Body* came out, he included only essays of literary criticism. Not a single one reflected specifically on his Agrarian past. This was merely another sign that by the later date Ransom and his associates had found a new interest. A decade earlier, Ransom and Tate had decided to "do something" about the South, and the result was the Agrarian ideology. Now, having lost hope of restoring a subsistence society, Ransom, Tate, Warren, and Brooks decided to "do something" about the teaching of college English. This time the result was that aesthetic phenomenon known as the New Criticism.

Some scholars have attempted to explain why the Southern Agrarians disintegrated as a movement. They were not, of course, "card-carrying members" of a fraternal society or political party. Only the bonds of ideology and friendship held them together; the mutual adulation in which they sometimes indulged has been noted on several occasions. In going from Agrarianism to the New Criticism, the four critics mentioned above developed what may be called—to use one of their favorite phrases—an "aesthetic distance" from the economics and sociology which they had previously espoused. This meant more a change in emphasis than in fundamental social outlook. To become more "aesthetic" or "formal" as critics did not necessarily demand a denial of the non-literary opinions which had composed their ideology. Indeed, a major reason advanced for the relatively poor sociology of the Nashville group as Agrarians was that they "thought in aesthetic and intellectual—rather than practical—terms."[1] It was always a question of which came first in importance, the Southern "restoration" for its own sake, as a "way of life", or the illustrious literature which it would presumably make possible. Thus, even as economists, the Agrarians were suffused with the aesthetic instinct. They tended to create their sociological "facts" through intuition and nostalgic feeling. Their ideal of a yeoman farming his land was, after all, a myth; and it seemed often to pain them that social scientists should, so unfairly, put the myth to a rational test.

What happened from about 1936 on was that the leading Agrarians stopped making a direct connection between their Southern ideology and their special theory of literature. They found that this theory could be considered apart, as an independent mode of knowledge, from the political economy on which it had been anchored. A number of essays that eventually added notably to their reputations as New Critics were actually written earlier, during their period as Agrarians. These essays reappeared (after initial publication elsewhere), in such books as Ransom's *The World's Body* (1938) and Tate's *Reason in Madness* (1941). For these critics, then, both the older and the newer labels are somewhat deceptive; they do not readily allow for crisscross of concepts that are equally valid under the two nomenclatures.

A brief glance at Ransom's and Tate's contributions to the *American Review*, which died in 1937, reveals their declining interest in the economics of Agrarianism. In 1935 and 1936 Ransom, for example, did not write a single economic article for this journal. Instead, he wrote on such purely literary topics as "The Cathartic Principle," "The Mimetic Principle," "Characters and Character," and "The Content of the Novel." That is not to say that Ransom wrote no more about Agrarianism. "What Does the South Want?" was printed both in the *Virginia Quarterly Review* and in *Who Owns America?* Allen Tate's last significant essay in the *American Review* was in 1936, "Notes on Liberty and Property," and was also reprinted in *Who Owns America?*. The last contribution by Tate to the *American Review*, in its February, 1937, issue, was on a literary subject, "Modern Poets and Convention."

The second symposium, *Who Owns America?*, represented the belated merger of Southern Agrarianism and American Distributism; but the merger came too late to save the former from distintegration, if indeed it could have been saved at all. Thomas J. Pressley in his caustic summary of the Agrarian movement said of this juncture: "The one 'victory' gained by the Agrarians in this decade was their union with the American Distributists in the publication of a second symposium in 1936. This symposium, entitled *Who Owns America?*, was edited jointly by Allen Tate, the Agrarian, and Herbert Agar, leader of the Distributists."[2]

Who Owns America? did represent a second major "stand" for Agrarian principles. Perhaps its most important new emphasis, derived in part from the alliance with the Distributists, was the idea that small ownership of property could insure the survival of individual liberty in an increasingly totalitarian world. Eight of the twelve contributors to *I'll Take My Stand* appeared in this second symposium. Lanier attacked the bigness of big corporations, showed how they endangered individual freedom, and suggested means to limit their power. Owsley wrote that private property, widely distributed, must be restored if America were to avoid fascist or communist totalitarianism. Tate analyzed the difference between corporations and "natural persons" and indicated how property concentrated in the former limited the freedom of the latter. Davidson concentrated on the need for political regionalism as the best means of insuring national stability. Ransom in "What Does the South Want?" assumed again that the South wanted Agrarianism. Lytle explained how the "livelihood farm" could secure the peace and welfare of the state. Wade contrasted the traditional values of country life with those of urban life. Warren, in "Literature as a Symptom," perceptively analyzed the current proletarian and regional trends in literature. Despite the work that went into it, *Who Owns America?* could not save the Agrarian movement from falling apart. The public had already examined the program and had found it wanting.

Tate's long essay, "The Profession of Letters in the South," embodied some of the reasons for his apparent disenchantment with the Southern literary tradition. It represented a public lack of faith in various aspects of the tradition which the Agrarians had been praising. Together with Ransom's "Modern With the Southern Accent," Tate's essay was published in 1935 in the Tenth Anniversary Number of the *Virginia Quarterly Review*—an occasion which involved six of the original contributors to *I'll Take My Stand*. Ransom had written in the special issue, "The Southern artists in going modern offer us their impression of a general decay, and that is not a pleasant thing to think about."[3] Apparently, the Southern writers were doing just that—going modern. Like Tate in the same number of the magazine, Ransom posed the unsolved problem of why the Southern tradition had provided such scant inspiration for literature.

There must be many Southerners waiting like myself to hear the right explanation of the skimpiness of Southern art in those very days when the Southern tradition was unquestioned; and we must feel chastened when we remark that an admired brilliancy in the contemporary display tends nearly always to coincide with a deep-seated decadence.[4]

Toward the end of his study of Southern reflections of modernism, Ransom blamed his region as follows: "There is little distinctively Southern poetry, then, because one of the peculiarities of the region is in the fact that it still conceives poetry as an adolescent function, and all adolescents are more or less alike."[5]

As for the Agrarian movement as a whole, the final commanding statement in its defense was Donald Davidson's *The Attack on Leviathan* (1938). It is Davidson who remained most persistent in his affiliation. Significantly perhaps, he stayed to teach English at Vanderbilt University. However, even his book, which stressed regionalism more than Agrarianism as such, was primarily a compilation of essays that he had previously published in the *American Review* and other journals. Along the way, as has been noted, the Agrarians had recruited their one professional economist, Troy J. Cauley, professor of economics at the Georgia Institute of Technology. However, his volume, *Agrarianism: A Program for Farmers* (1935), was not particularly convincing either as economics or as Agrarianism. Although for the most part the twelve original Agrarians made no direct disavowals of their lost economic cause, they did have one defection. In the late thirties Herman Clarence Nixon parted company with his old associates over disagreement with their program. He affirmed that he now sought a "broader program of agricultural reconstruction." After he examined several reasons for the failure of the Agrarians, Pressley declared, "The decade ended, as it had begun, with the Agrarians as separate individuals writing scattered protests against the dominant trends of Southern life."[6] Pressley was incorrect, of course, about both ends of the decade; at the beginning most of the Agrarians had been united as Fugitives;

at the end, they reunited as New Critics, and in this third phase they achieved their greatest fame.

In seeking to explain why a movement falls apart, we are always tempted to make surmises which can have no direct validation in existing documents. One of these unprovable surmises may be this: that the failure of a group such as the Agrarians to exert any great influence on society damages the pride of its leaders; thereafter, they may consider silence their only suitable recourse. The literary historian finds nothing when he seeks from the Agrarians themselves a set of reasons for the collapse of their social and economic movement. Certainly their own region, the South, did not greet their "stand" with any great enthusiasm. The lack of widespread support from those most calculated to respond, the southern youth, must have produced quite a sense of futility; and yet other zealous minorities have been able to sustain themselves even in the midst of outright persecution. Perhaps the worst form of tyranny meted to these sensitive poets and writers was ridicule; of this kind of rough treatment they got an ample portion from the very beginning, and not all of it came from the North.

I'll Take My Stand had incited a veritable stream of derision from fellow regionalists who refused to be represented before the nation by a bunch of "Reactionaries" and "Neo-Confederates." The Macon (Georgia) *Telegraph* scornfully titled its review of the symposium, "Lee, We Are Here." To the editors of this prominent regional journal the coming-out party of the Agrarians provided a "high spot in the year's hilarity." In the *Yale Review* the Southern historian Ulrich B. Phillips began his review of *I'll Take My Stand* with these mocking words: "In Dixie Land twelve take their stand and shed their ink for Dixie." Even the editor of the Nashville *Tennessean,* a hometown paper, was sharply hostile. It was his criticism which made Tate fear that the Agrarians might be made the subject of cartoons showing them cleaning the spring or plowing. Tate was also apprehensive of the "Alexanders"—the editors of the big Southern newspapers who took the Agrarians as a big bad joke. The laughter in New York, where the *Times* reviewer called their manifesto a "boy's Froissart of tales," was doubtless less hurtful to Agrarian pride; at least this response came from the enemy, the industrial and urban North. However, it was evident in a number of instances that the victims of the ridicule felt it rather keenly. The very magnitude of the economic proposals in *I'll Take My Stand* and in subsequent Agrarian works seemed to inspire unusually severe indictments. Among practiced politicians it is a common claim that any publicity, no matter how bad, is better than indifference. Thus it may be argued that the kind of ridicule cited above actually helped to create a national interest in the Agrarian program.

Perhaps even more cutting than ridicule were the serious appraisals of the social and political assumptions made by the Nashville coterie. This more balanced opposition took various forms, from the scorn of H. L. Mencken to the sober response of the liberal Southerners associated with the University of North Carolina. Mencken had been up in arms for some time about various aspects of the South. Some of his sharpest wit was directed against the backwardness and religious obscurantism which he felt was spotlighted by the Scopes trial. So fierce, however, was his attack on the Agrarians that few of them tried to reply; doubtless they felt that his emotionalism was beyond reach of reasonable rebuttal. However, Mencken, for all his theatrical bitterness, also regarded himself as a Southerner and a regionalist; as such he too made serious comments on the Agrarian position. Writing in the *Virginia Quarterly Review* in 1935, he said about Davidson and the Scopes trial: "He seems to believe in all seriousness that the Bryan obscenity at Dayton was a private matter, on which the rest of the country had no right to an opinion."[7] Mencken claimed to have been a regionalist long before the Nashville writers came forward. He expressed also a certain mild protest at being so solidly linked with New York cosmopolitanism by Davidson. In this respect Mencken pointed out that his native Maryland could qualify as part of the "hinterland" in which the Agrarians had taken such a proprietary interest. In his own peculiar fashion, however, Mencken defended the modernism of New York where "even the naughtiest atheism is measurably more consonant with civilization than the demonology prevailing in rural Tennessee, and that nothing advocated by the customers of Lawrence, Joyce, and La Stein is half so barbaric as the public frying of blackamoors."[8] As for the main challenge of the Agrarians—that of reversing the industrial process in favor of a subsistence economy— Mencken wrote with characteristic scorn mixed with reason:

Even the Agrarian Habakkuks themselves are the clients of industrialism, which supplies them generously with the canned-goods, haberdashery, and library facilities that are so necessary to the free ebullition of the human intellect. Left to the farmers of Tennessee, they would be clad in linsey-woolsey and fed on sidemeat, and the only books they could read would be excessively orthodox.[9]

Among the many groups whom they antagonized were the Southern liberals; this was natural, for the liberals were the most immediate rivals for control of the Southern mind. Working primarily at Chapel Hill, this group was deeply concerned with the practical solution to many of the region's social and economic problems. For one thing, it had done much to identify and examine these problems in the light of the latest social science. The more conservative Agrarians had shown no such practical concern. In his bitter book, *90° in the Shade*, Clarence Cason criticized this apparent unconcern as

a credo that takes no account of contemporary social evils so often traceable, in the opinion of other southerners, to the very way of life which the agrarians attempt to uphold. If, as Gerald W. Johnson once hinted, the Tennessee traditionalists do not consider the ravages of the loan-sharks, the unfairness of the tenant-farming system, and the Negro problem worthy of serious consideration at the present time, thereby exhibiting a willingness to ignore significant conditions which lie under their noses, how can they be trusted to maintain a clear-sighted perspective with reference to a ramified social structure that existed almost a century ago?[10]

Apparently the New Deal in Washington, which eventually developed a number of regional programs for recovery, was also aware of these Agrarian weaknesses. It was not to the Agrarians but to the liberals to whom the Roosevelt administration turned for guidance in trying to solve the South's pressing economic problems. The liberals accepted industrial America as an established fact; they regarded technological progress as a boon, not an evil; they felt that the "tradition" offered no leeway or release from the present critical dilemmas; and they wanted a New South to be both regionally strong and strongly integrated with a new and even more progressive nation.

The liberal symposium, or manifesto, was *Culture in the South* (1934); it was composed of essays written, with three exceptions, by prominent Southerners who had rejected the Agrarian lure. Its editor was W. T. Couch of the University of North Carolina. In the Preface to the book Professor Couch expressed the attitude of the majority of its contributors towards the Southern Agrarians.

One of the most thoughtful books on the South published in recent years, *I'll Take My Stand*, reveals clearly the fallacy of expecting a better way of life as a result merely of bigger and better business; but it falls into a more serious error of interpreting southern life in terms of industrialism *vs.* agrarianism.

Certainly in the present posture of affairs it is somewhat rash to assume, as these latest "agrarians" do, that farming in the South is a healthy and attractive occupation, peculiarly devoted to the service of genuinely human values, and that industry is necessarily a destroyer of human values.[11]

Couch also criticized the Agrarians for assuming that the South was a homogeneous region whereas life there, in fact, varied from class to class, and was further complicated by wide differences in political, economic, racial, educational, and religious faiths. Nor could the Nashville writers, according to Couch, point to a Southern past that was so much better than the present that it deserved to be restored.

Other arguments which the North Carolina group used against the Agrarians were that they based their concept of society on "economic obscurantism," that they did not understand the social realities in the South either past or present, and that they wanted an impossible revival of an irrevocably vanished tradition. The fact that the liberals led by Couch were now organized, with a symposium of their own, represented serious intellectual competition for the Nashville group.

Among the many contributors to *Culture in the South,* three were actually Southern Agrarians. They were Herman Clarence Nixon, John Donald Wade, and Donald Davidson. Of all the contributors, Tate in his long review of the book had praise for only Davidson. Tate felt that his essay, "The Trend of Literature," was the only intelligent one in the volume. He did not fail to comment, however, that Davidson was "ill at ease among his Liberal neighbors," but, be that as it may, he had put his finger

on a fundamental *malaise* of the modern Southern writer—his inability, for various reasons, to look upon his society as a normal manifestation of human life, with the consequent confusion of purpose that keeps his style and point of view on the defensive or satirical plane. Mr. Davidson, justly I think, makes exception in favour of the poets, who, however, standing outside this *Zeitgeist,* are unread. His essay brings to a head the whole cultural problem of the South, a problem that few of the other contributors seem aware of: that the basis of culture is a dignified local life resting upon the common people, who take all the props from under a genuine culture as soon as they are deprived of independence; hence the complete industrialization of the South, even if the perfect bungalow and kitchen sink of the industrial apologists were possible, would destroy the last stronghold of culture in the United States.[12]

By the mid-thirties the Agrarians were also being attacked for their publishing in the fascist-oriented *American Review.* Perhaps the phenomenon required no explanation beyond the fact that the *Review* willingly printed all kinds of rightist material. The editor, Seward Collins, scion of a wealthy family, used his inheritance to promote rightism in all its forms.[13] Collins favored an American form of monarchy, with the Middle Ages as a precedent, or else a compromise with fascism as its modern manifestation. In this brief definition of fascism by Collins may be heard overtones of various concepts that are readily identifiable with those of Ransom and his friends. "Fascism," Collins wrote, "betokens the revival of monarchy, property, the guilds, the security of the family and the peasantry, and the ancient ways of European life."[14]

In his monthly column Collins made his opinions evident from the first issue: "The Fascist economics, in particular, which has received scant treatment by our universally liberal and radical press, are badly in need of sympathetic exposition."[15] And in the second issue, of May, 1933, he stated, "When one turns to Italy, seeking to learn the nature of the new monarchies, one gradually comes to realize that Mussolini is the most constructive statesman of our age. Not only did he grasp the need of monarchy, but he joined to it a sound moral system." At any rate, as the decade passed, the *American Review* continued to publish essays praising fascism in Europe; and when the Spanish Civil War broke out in 1936, the journal was so forcefully a champion of General Franco's Nationalists that it organized the sale in America of books and other literature written in his behalf.[16]

At times Collins himself admitted being a fascist and at other times denied the allegation. In its May 27, 1936, issue the *New Republic* reprinted portions of an interview with Collins written by Grace Lumpkin for a journal called *Fight*. Miss Lumpkin, herself a Southerner, had also appeared in the Tenth Anniversary Number of the *Virginia Quarterly Review*, along with John Crowe Ransom and Allen Tate. In its editorial note the *New Republic* quoted some of her own generalizations about the Agrarians.

I do believe that after reading a number of books like 'God Without Thunder,' 'I'll Take My Stand,' and copies of the Southern Review and The American Review, that in those who write for them (some of them very sensitive and fine writers) there is the beginning of a group that is preparing the philosophical and moral shirt-front for fascism.[17]

During the interview Miss Lumpkin was represented as having asked Collins: "Some of the things you have said make me think you are a fascist. Are you?" His quoted reply was: "Yes, I am a fascist. I admire Hitler and Mussolini very much. They have done great things for their countries." The same page of the *New Republic*, a magazine for which Tate had written many reviews, carried a disavowal by him that he was a fascist. "First," Tate began, "I do not believe in fascism." Miss Lumpkin rejoined that he and the Southern Agrarians tended in that direction. Tate refused further rebuttal. As for Seward Collins, he made his own disavowal in the *American Review* in the summer of 1937, toward the end of the journal's life: "What they call 'Democracy' is in fact a 'Banker's Olympus'. It is operating under the instruments of 'Loan-Capital', more than anything else. Fascism is a revolt of the People. A revolt against debt. I am no Fascist. But I love Freedom. Also I hate usury."[18]

It is impossible to assess to what extent, if any, the affinity with fascism affected the internal unity and public image of the Agrarian movement. The surge of events leading them closer to an emerging political organization, represented by Collins, tended to contradict the position taken in *I'll Take My Stand* that they eschewed practical politics. At any rate, some of their hostile critics were not slow in making this political connection for them. Both the Marxists and the liberals did so. Speaking for the former, V. F. Calverton reported that Collins himself had put the fascist label on the Agrarians:

The editor of *The American Review*, Mr. Seward Collins, has definitely described this movement, which is familiarly known as *the new agrarianism*, "as fascist." Underlying this movement, as Mr. Collins pointed out in a debate with me on the issue, is the international fascist appeal to the farmers to fight the industrialists and financiers in an attempt to replace the power of Wall Street by that of Main Street.[19]

Ransom, employing a vehemence that was more characteristic of Tate than of himself, answered Calverton in "The South is a Bulwark."[20] That is, the South would be a sturdy fortress against Communism, the sort of program for America which Ransom accused Calverton of trying to promote.

In another later example of uneasiness on the part of critics, Peter A. Carmichael wrote for the *Sewanee Review* in 1940: "In that *REVIEW* [that of Collins] one will find remarkable proposals, some of which reek fascism and nazism, a shocking substitute for the pastoral view of life which we would naturally have supposed an authentic agrarianism to signify."[21] And F. O. Matthiessen, reviewing American poetry from 1920 to 1940, commented that "Tate has called himself a 'reactionary,' and some of the less clear minds of the group, taking their stand even against the racial reforms of the New Deal, have drifted dangerously close to native fascism."[22]

Other observers also dwelled upon the same problem of the fascist relationship. The period had become highly sensitized in terms of political belief . American writers by the score were joining leagues and congresses to combat whatever serious fascist threat might arise to endanger their freedom of expression. *It Can't Happen Here* was as symbolic of the thirties as *Babbitt* had been of the twenties. Whereas Babbittry had contributed to the exodus of literary expatriates to Europe seeking a climate more conducive to art, now in the new decade the rise of European fascism reversed the literary movement; to the very expatriates who had left in a huff the freedom of life and expression in America, their native land, now glowed with renewed luster. With them came dozens of European artists, writers, and thinkers, men like Thomas Mann and Albert Einstein, who had to go into exile when their very lives were in peril. For romantic as well as political reasons the Spanish Civil War made an especially strong impact on American writers. Most of them, it is correct to say, were opposed to the fascist gamble. Thus the Agrarians appeared in even greater isolation from the mainstream of American culture by their continued publication in the *American Review*.

Irrespective of what kinship with fascism did to hasten the dispersal of the Agrarians, other and perhaps more tangible factors existed to cause the break-up. One of them was the now apparent feeling that the South, both old and new, was really not so conducive to great literature as once it was felt or hoped to be. Tate especially showed keen disillusionment with the entire idea of the Southern tradition, and even with tradition as such.

His reservations emerged bluntly in the course of a paper, "Modern Poets and Convention," which he read in Richmond, in December, 1936, at a meeting of the Modern Language Association. Tate said:

I should like to glance at the related question of tradition in poetry. I seem to understand this problem a little less every day. I only know that there are certain effects in the poetry of the past that I cannot reproduce; nor do I see them successfully reproduced in other modern verse. It is a significant discrepancy that Mr. Paul Elmer More has found between the criticism and the poetry of Mr. T. S. Eliot. The criticism exhibits an insight into the poetry of the past that Mr. More, I believe, would call profound; but Mr. Eliot's own poetry seems to be quite different from the poetry that he admires. If Mr. Eliot is a traditionalist, and I think he notoriously is, why doesn't he write traditional poetry?[23]

Tate had previously shown a similar concern in one of his rare public disagreements with Ransom, who had written in the *Virginia Quarterly Review* about the evil influences of modernism on the South. By this time (1935 and 1936, in both of which years Tate allowed "The Profession of Letters in the South" to be printed) he was finding more than modernism to be wrong with the culture of his region. He wrote:

the arts everywhere spring from a mysterious union of indigenous materials and foreign influences: there is no great art or literature that does not bear the marks of this fusion. So I cannot assume, as Mr. Ransom seems to do, that exposure to the world of modernism . . . was of itself a demoralizing experience. Isn't it rather that the Southerner before he left home had grown weak in his native allegiance?[24]

A few lines later Tate asked, apropos of the above references to More and Eliot: "And, lastly, what shall we say of Mr. Ransom's own distinguished and very modern poetry?" Apparently neither Ransom nor Eliot was overly concerned with making his creative practice conform strictly with his announced critical theory. When Tate attempted such a conformity, the results were disappointing. As he stated, the best he was able to do in "support of an historical belief in the value of a strict form" was to write in the last fifteen years "about twenty bad sonnets."[25] These views of Tate, however, did not overtly weaken Ransom's conviction about the value of the formal tradition— nor that of Tate for very long—despite their failure to achieve positive results from its applications. Ransom defined in *The World's Body* what he meant by *formal* in relation to tradition.

By formal we are not to mean the metre only; but also, and it is probably even more important, the literary type, with its fictitious point of view from which the poet approaches his object. And by tradition we should mean simply the source from which the form most easily comes. Tradition is the handing down of a thing by society, and the thing handed down is just a formula, a form.[26]

In analyzing his difficulty, Tate indirectly revealed the trouble in maintaining a traditional Agrarian theory of letters in a society obviously and strongly committed to industrial progress. He was writing of poetic tradition, but the range of relevance can be extended to the entire Agrarian ideology. Tate also stated in his address to the Modern Language Association that no poet could give us a traditional experience unless he had available for his use some kind of traditional behavior. The failure of contemporary America to produce the types of human action desired by the Agrarians, despite their strenuous urgings, doubtless added to the conclusion that they were in stagnant if not poisoned waters.

Earlier that same year, 1936, in a Phi Beta Kappa address at the University of Virginia, Tate had already shown concern over the problem of keeping intact a traditional approach of life and art. He spoke of "week-end traditionalists" as a disappointed minister might speak of "Sunday Christians." Tradition as we find it today "has little to do with the real business of life." Tate included in his talk a pejorative

reference to John Ruskin, the Victorian medievalist and art critic; earlier in the Agrarian movement the ideas of Ruskin were highly
praised for their rejection of various aspects of modernism. Tate
claimed that we could not pretend to be "landed gentlemen two days
of the week if we are middle-class capitalists the five others." And then
he added:

You will remember Ruskin's objection to the Gothic factory-architecture of
his age—what ornamentation he urged should be used around the cornice of a
kind of building that was new in that time. Ruskin's stylized money-bags set
at the right rhythmic intervals around the cornices of the Bethlehem Steel
Corporation might be symbolic of something going on inside, but I think the
Chairman of the Board might rightly object that Ruskin was not a good sa-
tirist, but merely a sentimentalist, and the chairman would leave his cornices
bare.[27]

Tate's point was that a tradition cannot be grafted onto an untraditional way of life. Industrial society could not develop or venerate any
tradition because of its own insistent change and growth. In order to
support this view Tate cited Jefferson, "who would have known that
to revive something is to hasten its destruction," that is, if it is not *sufficiently* revived.[28] How could Agrarianism ever be sufficiently revived?
No doubt, as much as anything else, it was this impossibility which
forced Tate, Ransom, Warren, and Davidson to stop promulgating its
"restoration" with any vigor after 1936 or thereabouts. The Southern
social tradition had been exhausted even in the field of essays written
in its uncritical praise. By this year Tate seems to have shifted his emphasis from *restoration* of the past to the *creation* of something new
through what then became known as the Distributist-Agrarian program. In "A Traditionalist Looks at Liberalism," Tate modified the
concept of restoration as follows: "It is a special 'psychosis' of modern
man that impels him to 'restore the past.' Those ages of the past that
he cries for had restored nothing whatsoever; they created something,
and although they levied upon the past, they quickly transformed
their borrowings, and amalgamated past and present into a whole."[29]
How the Southern ante-bellum tradition would have merged, and
emerged, after such amalgamation (and with what) Tate did not specify.

The tension caused by clinging to a traditional sociology and to a
theory of literature that it supposedly nourished was best revealed in
Tate's long essay, "The Profession of Letters in the South." Some of
the assumptions in it are reminiscent of the "anti-Southernism" which
the author had expressed in the mid-twenties, yet the title itself was an

echo of a statement which Tate made in 1932, at the highest point of the Agrarian crusade. We might infer, at least to some degree, that Tate suffered from a latent crisis in regional loyalty throughout his public career as an Agrarian. In an Editorial Note written when he edited a Southern Number of *Poetry*, Tate said, "There was never a profession of letters in the South. There were, and perhaps here and there still are, ladies and gentlemen."[30] He did not stop there but went on to heap more doubt upon the Southern literary tradition: "The historian of Southern poetry must constantly pause to inquire into the causes of our thin and not very comprehensive performance. . . ." In the same issue of *Poetry* he condemned quite sharply the contemporary Southern poets; earlier, at the turn of the decade, he noted that the poetry of the Fugitives had been the best poetry composed in the whole nation. Now he reported, "It almost amounts to this: that a poet cannot be 'Southern' without behaving like a fool; and if he tries not to be a fool, he will not be recognizably 'Southern.' "[31] These words do not testify to any strong expectations from his own region.

In "The Profession of Letters" Tate expanded on these negative attitudes. Although he again attacked science and capitalism, he stressed the deficiencies of the Old South in artistic matters. "By glancing at the South," he candidly admitted, "we shall see an important phase of the decline of the literary profession."[32] After a number of years of eulogy of the region for its supposed value to the arts, Tate now regretfully said that the Southern tradition had "left no cultural landmark" so evident that the people could see themselves in it. He continued: "We lack a tradition in the arts; more to the point, we lack a literary tradition. We lack even a literature. We have just enough literary remains from the old regime to prove to us that, had a great literature risen, it would have been unique in modern times" (p. 149). Unlike the Dark Ages of England, which had at least a *Beowulf*, the Old South produced no typical masterpiece, no great epic in which the society found itself mirrored. Whereas the Agrarians had previously praised social laggardism as beneficial for life and art, now Tate disparaged it, saying "The South clings blindly to forms of European feeling and conduct that were crushed by the French Revolution and that, in England at any rate, are barely memories" (p. 149). Either Tate was off his guard in denigrating memories, or he had revised his basic attitude toward their value to aesthetic theory; for it was precisely such memories, with their long and fertile associations, that were once presumed to be fundamental to a proper literature. Now the rich traditional memories deriving from the Old South seemed to have lost their power.

. In addition, Tate seemed to feel that the idea of progress, so frequently linked with science and industrialism as an evil, was irrelevant to Southern literature. The question to ask, in his opinion, was not whether a society was progressive or traditional, but "Was the structure of society favorable to a great literature? Suppose it to have been favorable: Was there something wrong with the intellectual life that cannot be blamed upon the social order?" There was. The region's intellectual life was "hag-ridden with politics," a fact "partly rooted in the kind of rule that the South had, which was aristocratic rule," that is, rule by a class, and "the class must fight for interest and power" (p. 152). Earlier in his career Tate had said that politics had brought out the "genius" of the South; the Agrarians in general had glorified aristocratic rule and called Southern political oratory a fine art.

Tate now said that the spiritual deficiencies of the Old South were "more serious even than those of the debased feudal society of eighteenth-century rural England. With this society the ante-bellum South had much in common" (p. 161). Bearing in mind how the Agrarians had so highly praised the resemblance between the South and this "feudal" England in *I'll Take My Stand*, the scholar must surmise that the above grim criticism, coming from so important an Agrarian, would have a rather chilling effect on the movement. Tate continued in the same vein: "For the genteel tradition has never done anything for letters in the South; yet the Southern writers who are too fastidious to become conscious of their profession have not refused to write best-sellers when they could, and to profit by a cash nexus with New York. I would fain believe that matters are otherwise than so: but facts are facts."

In the past the Agrarians had roundly condemned the culture of big cities. Tate now recognized to what extent the lack of publishing centers had hurt Southern writers. It contributed greatly to their ultimate inability to remain Southern. Without a great regional metropolis for writers to gather, work, and thrive, Tate said, the "Southern writer, of my generation at least, went to New York. There he was influenced not only by the necessity to live but by theories and movements drifting over from Europe" (p. 162). As for critical writing, which Tate affirmed did have distinction, it could never be a Southern criticism as long as it had to be "trimmed and scattered" in Northern periodicals.

In more than a superficial sense, then, Tate's essay on the past and present status of Southern literature could serve as a swan song for Agrarianism as the social and economic system essential to a proper aesthetic achievement. If in the past it had not really produced, it was quite futile to base an ideal literature on its restoration, especially when this restoration itself seemed so impossible. Other Agrarians besides Tate noted contradictions between their theory and the reality. Indeed, there were certain ambivalences in the theory which vitiated it as a thoroughly organic body of doctrine. As early as 1933, Ransom had sought to explain with qualifications the Agrarian attitude toward big cities, since critics like Mencken had been unkind to their eulogy of the static rural life. To offset criticism of the bitter Mencken type, Ransom offered a plan for "a new capital city for the Union, deep in the interior where our capital city ought to be, and be larger, more modern, and more beautiful than any city on earth."[33] The building of this metropolis was Ransom's solution for the economic crisis which was then at its depth. Another solution he thought of was war, but this was "too heroic a stimulus; not much relished by democracies." When Ransom sought to justify his proposal—which certainly seemed odd coming from the foremost Agrarian—he seemed for a moment to be betraying his basic philosophy. He said, "Agrarians may not like cities temperamentally . . . yet they too go to cities . . . and it is a matter of fact that the city focuses all the features of a culture as nothing else does." And in the same general trend of thought he continued, "The meanest tillers of the olive groves had an Athens to go to when they went to a city, and its beauty acquainted them by its persuasive symbolism with the character of their empire and their civilization."[34]

These lapses in absolute conviction eventually became rationalizations for that exodus from the South which Richard Weaver carefully analyzed in "Agrarianism in Exile." Other scholars found additional reasons for the dispersal. Pressley spoke of the Agrarian inability to reach the common man. Their opinions were too sophisticated for their own good. Though allegedly presented in his behalf, the Agrarian program was not actually directed at the common man, but at the intellectuals of the South who were themselves groping for solutions to new problems. The Agrarians were able to win over very few intellectuals either. They were weak in their basic diagnosis of social change, of history itself. They thought more in moral than in scientific constructions at a time when other kinds of historiography has been losing prestige. Their picture of the Old South, for example, was emotional rather than historical. Pressley felt there was no unity or clarity, "either in their picture of the ideal Agrarian society or of the programs necessary for its achievement."[35] Finally, according to Pressley, they did not "really *evaluate* industrialism" since they refused to take into account its positive triumphs. Nor did they do the same, it may be added, in regard to science, urbanism, and progress.

Charles Glicksberg in "Allen Tate and Mother Earth" suggested the Agrarians did not quite understand what they were up against when they first announced their campaign against modern society. He wrote, "What these embattled Southern intellectuals, led by John Crowe Ransom and Allen Tate, have in mind is nothing less than the reversal of history so that the truth, their way of life, may prevail."[36] As Professor Couch of the North Carolina liberals had scolded the Agrarians for their economic obscurantism, so Glicksberg attacked their "aesthetic mysticism." He said of Tate, "By a kind of mysterious alchemy of the imagination, he distils the essence of experience and thus reports the total reality rarefied and quintessential. Allen Tate is frequently guilty of this sort of aesthetic mysticism."[37]

Of sympathetic critics, it is perhaps Weaver who has given the best analysis of why the Agrarians dispersed. He did so in 1950 after a number of years had elapsed. Among the various causes he gave was the fact that the Agrarians had become homeless in their own region. They enjoyed no real following, nor were they at all typical of the kind of folk whose leaders they purported to be. Their philosophical ideas were "as far above the average Southern farmer as the empyrean."[38] Facts were facts, as Tate had said, and the South was already embarked upon industrialism, so much so that no group of poets and critics, no matter how potent their metaphors, was able to stem the tides of change. For both general and individual reasons, then, many of the Agrarians took the path of exile for which they had long been critical of Southern writers from Lanier to Stribling. After the emigration had occurred, the words by Ransom on Lanier, "He did not remain in the South; he got out as soon as he could," seemed self-condemnatory.

Other opinions by the Agrarians themselves relevant to the exodus included the idea stated by Robert Penn Warren that the South "insisted on being the tail of a kite [industrial society] that was going down."[39] Donald Davidson explained the extension of their careers northward by saying that "we never imagined that Southern principles, once defined, would apply just as benevolently in New York City as some wise men thought that Eastern metropolitan principles would apply in the South."[40] Besides the fact that the Agrarians were not adequately appreciated by their own region, Weaver cited what he felt were other reasons for the "fairly general exodus" which he dated as having taken place from 1938 on. Describing this "ironic circumstance," he said, "For a time it seemed that a good record as a Southern Agrarian was all that one needed for a call to some Northern institution with good salary and honorable status. It seemed indeed that the unreconstructed Southerner was preferred."[41]

Weaver's justification for this academic preference was the fact that the universities were "engaged in a critical battle to save the humanities," and that the Agrarian ability to scout and attack the influences of science would be invaluable to such a salvation. In the initial stage of Agrarianism, Davidson had affirmed that perhaps only the English teacher could restore the traditional humanities to their old respected position in the curriculum. Weaver might also have added that the former Agrarians were "safe" politically; unlike some other professors on the campus, they were not likely to embarrass college administrations by becoming "test cases" for academic freedom. Thus by the end of the thirties, when the economics of Agrarianism had obviously crumbled, Ransom, Tate, Brooks, and Warren turned to a new task: the reformation of college English studies and the revamping of literary criticism.

As an ideology, Agrarianism had many enduring aspects; as a social movement, it had to fail. By 1936 it was clear that the Agrarian leaders were generals without an army. No significant section of the people, North or South, had been convinced to abandon their money-based industrial economy, nor could the Agrarians seem to find new and compelling arguments to make further debate profitable. Gifted in various ways, they had careers as educators, artists, and critics to pursue; their continued stubborn adherence to the Agrarian myth would have indelibly dubbed them as cranks and eccentrics. They might have aroused more popular interest had they entered politics and run for office in espousal of their philosophy, but they were armchair philosophers first and last, and not practical politicians.

By mid-decade a new challenge presented itself which seemed more congenial to their manifold talents. If they could not alter the course of American society as a whole, they might at least alter the direction of criticism and change it from what they deemed the sterile, archaic, historical method to the dynamic, aesthetic, and textual methods of what was soon to be celebrated as the New Criticism. Many of the principles that were seen in this new light, however, had already been substantially developed and aired during Agrarianism.

Chapter X   The New Criticism

FROM THE FOREGOING DISCUSSION OF AGRARIAN DISPERSAL, WE MIGHT assume that the ideology initiated by *I'll Take My Stand* had no further life; but that would not be so. No literary movement of significance ever completely dies, if for no other reason than that historians continue to evaluate its achievement. The Agrarian stand, in addition, has a more dynamic and topical reason to be invoked: many of the issues which it reflected have not been resolved. The South as a region is still divided between Old and New; with slight changes in emphasis, the internal social and cultural conflict is still between reaction and progress. For a movement abandoned by its leaders more than two decades ago, Agrarianism still has an amazing power to stir the feelings of both conservatives and liberals.

For example, two important books on the South involve *I'll Take My Stand* in their own special up-to-date polemics. The conservative side is represented by *The Lasting South* (1957), a symposium edited by Louis D. Rubin, Jr., and James Jackson Kilpatrick. The book, though disclaiming any specific purpose, is clearly one of the region's negative responses to the Supreme Court's opinion on school desegregation. As stated in the Preface, the fourteen contributors hold in common that "in an increasingly modern and cosmopolitan world, there is more than ever the need for the persistent individuality of the South, and the need for Southerners to think long before bartering that individuality for the dubious advantages of conformity."[1] The editors of *The Lasting South* say of their co-contributors: "With some regret, perhaps, they do not offer to the South a specific platform and bill of particulars such as was so memorably presented nearly three decades ago in that brilliant book *I'll Take My Stand*." Much had changed in the South in thirty years, but enough of the old "way of life" remained to warrant a new stand by the modern conservative.

One of the ways in which liberals refer to *I'll Take My Stand* is well exemplified by William H. Nicholls' *Southern Tradition and Regional Progress* (1960). Because of the race antagonism over the school issue, he writes, "I completely lost any residual belief that the South could successfully reconcile tradition and progress."[2] The authors of *I'll Take My Stand* sought no such reconciliation; they supported tradition, they despised progress. Their candor appeals to Nicholls, and he states that he finds "the Vanderbilt Agrarians more instructive than their more moderate successors," that is, the contributors to *The Lasting South*.[3] The Agrarians combined in their ideology everything which Nicholls regards as impediments to Southern social and economic advance; his book, therefore, begins with a detailed critique of Agrarianism. The tenacity of traditional values, though often subjective and hard to fathom, is for Nicholls the main reason for a stubbornly retrograde and stagnant South.

He specifies how the Agrarians enhanced these values and why this course tends to discourage growth of the industrial-urban complex which in our technological age seems to provide best for the general welfare. Had the Agrarian program succeeded, it "would have segmented a national economy whose major asset had been its vast free-trade area; it would have revived and strengthened the South's negative and destructive spirit of sectionalism; and it would have reduced to an even slower pace the industrial-urban development and agricultural progress which are essential if we are to solve the South's serious problem of poverty."[4] Nicholls further condemns the Agrarian prospectus because it favored a rigid social structure, an undemocratic political system, a weak sense of social responsibility, and conformity in thought and behavior.

This brief mention of two typical references to *I'll Take My Stand* has been made in order to correct any possible impression that Agrarian ideas lost all their impact when the movement itself fell apart. The major Agrarians, of course, went on to even greater fame and influence as New Critics. If we could clearly and conclusively define what the New Criticism was, we could more easily assess their role in its origins and growth. Some observers regard the entire Agrarian ideology as part of the New Criticism. Others separate the sociology from the aesthetics, although the Agrarians themselves usually indicated an organic relationship. On one point all the commentators agree: the ritual of naming was performed by John Crowe Ransom. The occasion was a book entitled *The New Criticism*, which appeared in 1940, ten years after the Agrarian symposium. A new literary era was recognized to be at hand.

Ransom's book altered the perspectives of criticism and, by retroaction, suddenly made critics "new" who had simply been critics before. Not all the established critics qualified, however. Those with a strong liberal or sociological bent, like Edmund Wilson or Malcolm Cowley, were not regarded as sufficiently formal or aesthetic. The traditionalists and rightists, like T. S. Eliot, qualified easily, even though some of them did not become typical New Critics, that is, explicators of the text. Virulent clashes over the underlying politics of the New Criticism abounded during the forties and fifties. It origins, of course, cannot be attributed to one man, not even to Ransom. In fact, he did not even have to invent the name. "The New Criticism" was also the title of a lecture delivered by Joel E. Spingarn at Columbia University on March 9, 1910 and reprinted subsequently in a number of books. One of these books was a collection of essays edited by Edwin Berry Burgum in 1931 and called *The New Criticism*. When Ransom used the same title, it immediately caught fire.

It did so not only because a richly creative body of criticism had already been written in the twentieth century but also because the status of the critic himself had been greatly enhanced. As never before, he could play for the highest literary stakes. No longer was he a peripheral figure—a Dick Minim in Dr. Samuel Johnson's wry sense—but rather a veritable potentate of culture. We might mention any Big Name critic at random—Trilling, Eliot, Barzun, Brooks, Wilson, Ransom, Tate, Warren—and briefly note the familiar avenues open to him for fame and fortune.

First of all, he can usually have a full professorship at some renowned college or university, there to enjoy a regular salary, universal prestige, and, as W. H. Auden once wrote, the adulation of the immature. No matter how naive the disciples, it is always pleasing to be regarded as God with infallible judgments on poetry and prose. Then, of course, the Big Name critic publishes constantly in several categories, all of them useful to his career. For prestige, the critic writes articles and explications for the learned journals; when he has enough he brings them out as another "book in criticism." Also primarily for prestige is the volume that issues from a series of lectures that bear the name of some distinguished benefactor. The book itself may not be very profitable, but the initial stipend for the lectures could run to several thousand dollars. The most lucrative jackpot is the popular textbooks, for example, *Understanding Poetry,* by Brooks and Warren. Excellent and lucky textbooks go on from edition to edition down through the years. Some critics blessed with great creative talent, like Eliot and Warren, also write successful poems, novels, and plays. In addition, the Big Name critic can be a busy editorialist, serving magazines and publishers in several capacities. He can prepare anthologies, review books, edit new editions of classics, serve as a consultant, judge literary contests, and sit on editorial boards. Finally, the Big Name critic can be a public figure, a celebrity called upon to speak before important gatherings; he can perform as a panelist on radio and television shows, be lionized at cocktail parties, and even serve his country through such media as cultural exchange. He has other opportunities almost too numerous to mention. In short, the Big Name critic is always close to whatever big money there is in modern letters. His very name is symbolic of power. For the past two decades or more no literary group has enjoyed more power and influence than those known as New Critics. Among the most prominent, and the most engaged in debate, were Ransom, Tate, Brooks, and Warren.

Disagreement still exists among scholars regarding the origins of the New Criticism. Some believe with Howard Mumford Jones that it may have started with T. S. Eliot's memorable little book, *The Sacred Wood* (1920). Others like to credit I. A. Richards with having intensified and deepened the study of literature by use of the methods of psychology. Still others feel that the alleged novelty of the criticism was merely a revival of the textual analysis long practiced by critics in France. Malcolm Cowley expressed this belief when he said, "The New Criticism is a very old criticism. I had a brain-and-bellyful of it at the University of Montpellier in 1921. There it was called *explication du texte.*"[5] Part of the uncertainty derived from the fact that various types of critical approach were termed "new" whereas the concept of *tradition,* the assigning of value to aesthetic forms associated with the past, strongly obsessed some of the New Critics. What could be new, we might ask, about something that was very old?

Be that as it may, a certain chronology of events took place in the late thirties which helped to make Ransom's *The New Criticism* seem very timely and wise. Its own contribution to aesthetic theory actually turned out to be rather insubstantial; some observers of the critical scene have termed its message foggy and obscurantist. Other writings by the former Agrarians, however, including Ransom himself, can more readily be understood as contributions to something "new" in criticism. In several early but vital essays the Agrarians discussed the tradition of literary forms, the function of criticism, and the proper aims of the critical quarterly. These and other formal and more purely aesthetic matters appeared prominently in Ransom's own *The World's Body* (1938), a compilation of essays showing his critical views rather than his political economy. Also in 1938, Warren and Brooks put out their anthology, *Understanding Poetry*, an event which perhaps marked the first time in literary history that a textbook has also been a potent force in criticism. The following year Brooks published his *Modern Poetry and the Tradition*. Allen Tate, too, after his *Reactionary Essays on Poetry and Ideas* appeared in 1936, was very active in promoting the new critical-versus-historical emphasis by writing the additional essays included in *Reason in Madness* (1941). In the two reviews which they controlled, the *Southern* and the *Kenyon*, the former Agrarians published article after article inspired by their new aesthetic cause.

Meanwhile, outside the Agrarian ranks, other significant events were happening. One of the most noteworthy was an article by Professor Ronald S. Crane, of the University of Chicago, which appeared in *The English Journal* in October, 1935, under the title, "History Versus Criticism in the University Study of Literature." Perhaps more than any other single document, this one by Crane set the aesthetic tone of the ensuing controversy. In behalf of a specialized formalism deriving from Aristotle, Crane established the basic contrast which subsequently compelled a choice of approach on the part of the teacher (or scholar and critic). In 1938 Ransom also condemned that type of scholar who thought it enough "to spend a lifetime in compiling the data of literature and yet rarely or never commit himself to a literary judgment.[6] Nevertheless, it was from the professors of literature that Ransom hoped, eventually, for "the erection of intelligent standards of criticism." As it turned out, these were prophetic words. "He argues there," Ransom said, referring to Crane's article, "that historical scholarship has been overplayed heavily in English studies, in disregard of the law of diminishing returns, and that the emphasis must now be shifted to the critical." Under the impact of the New Criticism—including the Chicago tangent of it—the "reform of the courses in English," which Crane asked for, occurred everywhere in varying degree.

The former Agrarians who became New Critics eagerly joined the academic battle to turn the universities toward *criticism*, doing so in lively competition with other rival aesthetic doctrines. Ransom declared, "Criticism must become more scientific, or precise and systematic, and this means that it must be developed by the collective and sustained effort of learned persons—which means that its proper seat is in the universities." By the dropping of *history* from the valuation of literature, the Agrarians had a rather convenient reason for abandoning their previous sociology. They could now say that the relationship between literature and an Agrarian society, or any kind of society, was irrelevant to the structure of a formalist criticism, the only type capable of arriving at aesthetic judgment. In attacking the older methods of teaching, Tate wrote, "The historical method will not permit us to develop a critical instrument for dealing with works of literature as existent objects; we see them as expressions of substances beyond themselves."[7] In another essay, in which he echoes Ransom, he spoke of the function of criticism as being equivalent to the knowledge of aesthetic form.

This, doubtless, is the perennial hope of criticism—to know more; a hope perpetually achieved and defeated, when the knowledge of one generation becomes useless for the next; for in criticism there is none of the "progress" of accumulated knowledge that we enjoy from science. I mean here by "knowledge" the understanding of styles and forms.[8]

This formalism, and its brilliant application, illuminated the sections in *Understanding Poetry* written by Warren and Brooks. In some respects the individual explications may be said to have "overguided" both the teacher and student, but it is precisely the force of example which gives a book such as this its exceptional influence in the classroom. The actual choice of poems, too, was excellent and calculated to give the formalist approach its fullest and most advantageous play. At the beginning of a long Letter to the Teacher, the editors immediately declare the formal approach by rejecting the traditional "substitutes" for the poem as the object of study. They continue, "The substitutes are various, but the most common ones are:

1. Paraphrase of logical and narrative content.
2. Study of biographical and historical materials.
3. Inspirational and didactic interpretation."[9]

As is clear, the authors relegate to the realm of heresy, a term later often employed, the materials which are crucial to the historical, the biographical, the sociological, and the ethical critic. After such elimination, the only type of critic left who can evaluate the poem itself (*qua* poem, as the Aristotelians are wont to say) is the formal/aesthetic critic, i.e., the New Critic. He does not entirely neglect the logical, narrative, biographical, historical, inspirational, and didactic elements, but they become mere aids for his primary purpose. When these extra-literary elements are made the focus of criticism, they represent "confused approaches" to the study of poetry.

According to Brooks and Warren, a "satisfactory method of teaching poetry" should embody the following maxims:

1. Emphasis should be kept on the poem as a poem.
2. The treatment should be concrete and inductive.
3. A poem should always be treated as an organic system of relationships, and the poetic quality should never be understood as inhering in one or more factors taken in isolation.[10]

A multiplicity of individual elements *fuse* in the making of the artistic object; in the total "poetic statement," which is the poem, this fusion must constitute the aesthetic achievement that most interests the critic. How well and in what distinctive manner the technical elements fuse is the business of the critic to discover and evaluate. In a long Introduction dealing with the general nature of poetry, Brooks and Warren find occasion for another attack on the old enemy, science. This time, however, the point at issue is *language*—and not rationalism, or the fate of myth, or the way in which science helped industrialism destroy the Southern tradition. It is now a question of the "language of science" versus the "language of poetry," and when the former enters into a discourse about the latter, the critic again finds himself in the realm of heresy. The beginning of aesthetic wisdom, which is the same as saying critical judgment, is the ability to distinguish between these two basic kinds of language. Only on the basis of this distinction can a critic evaluate the function of idea, or any other singular element, in a poem. Perhaps the most dramatic word in the New Critic's vocabulary is "organic," which implies the total view. As Ransom was to assert, it is this fused completeness that embodies the ontology of poetry, the essence of its being what it is, or, as the existentialists might say, the poem's *withness*.

Various scholars have from time to time sought to establish a kind of priority of importance among the former Agrarians. There have been some, for example, who tend to place Allen Tate above Ransom in the leadership of the New Critics. Robert Wooster Stallman did so in "The New Critics," published in *Critiques and Essays in Criticism,* a volume which he edited in 1949. In his essay he commented on the strategy of the four Agrarians who became leading aestheticians.

While Brooks and Warren have brought the New Criticism into the universities, it is Tate and Ransom who have furnished it with systematic aesthetic studies. Their critical ideas constitute a single doctrine, their critical positions being basically identical. . . . Tate stakes out the issues more resolutely, and without Ransom's ironic detachment. As the spokesman for the Southern school of poet-critics, he has the greatest eye for the facts of the times and he is downright and persuasive in declaring them. It is this which accounts for my placing of Tate at the center of this present perspective.[11]

One instance of how Tate staked out the issues became an important event in the strategy of the New Criticism. In the March 8, 1940, issue of the *Princeton Alumni Weekly* he published an essay in which he noted the then current university conflict between the historical and the aesthetic literary critics. Ransom immediately added his support in the Summer, 1940, issue of the *Kenyon Review,* which he had founded and edited. His essay was entitled, "Mr. Tate and the Professors." At the same time Ransom announced a symposium, which was significant to the ensuing academic battle, to be held jointly in the Autumn numbers of the *Kenyon* and *The Southern Review*. Its contributors were to defend the teaching of *criticism* rather than *history* in college English courses. Yvor Winters, to whom Ransom devoted a long chapter in *The New Criticism,* referred to this event by saying, "In the autumn of 1940 *The Southern Review* and the *Kenyon Review* published a joint symposium attacking the methods commonly in use in teaching English. The chief complaint of the contributors was this: that the departments of English in the main teach history instead of criticism, whereas they should teach criticism instead of history."[12] The seeds sown by Ronald Crane were bearing fruit. Since its inception in 1935 at the Louisiana State University, *The Southern Review* has regularly published the Agrarians, which was logical with Warren and Tate active in its editorship; and it continued to do so after they separated as a social movement. As might be assumed, the *Review* also enthusiastically sponsored the New Criticism.[13]

The symposium that was held was entitled "Literature and the Professors." In his essay for the *Princeton Alumni Weekly,* Tate had favored what Ransom termed the "structural" criticism of literature. In his essay for the symposium itself, "The Present Function of Criticism," Tate severely condemned the historical approach for having attempted to be a scientific method. Leaning on the ideas of Hulme, he said: "The point of view of this essay . . . is influenced by the late, neglected T. E. Hulme (and not this essay alone). It is a belief, metaphysically demonstrable, in a radical discontinuity between the physical and the spiritual realms."[14] Criticism should try, therefore, to present the metaphysical knowledge of forms, for only then would the aesthetic spirituality of art be revealed to the cognoscenti. Historical scholars had shown no functional awareness of this fundamental requirement of aesthetics. Indicative again of the continuing hostility to science was the inclusion by Ransom in *The New Criticism* of an important quotation from Tate's essay. Ransom praised his friend's assertion that "historicism, psychologism, scientism, in general the confident application of the scientific vocabularies to the spiritual realm, has created a spiritual disorder that may be briefly described in terms of a dilemma." Condemning the *doctrine of relevance* as employed by the historical scholars, Tate had said of this practice: "It means that the subject-matter of a literary work must not be isolated in terms of form; it must be tested (on an analogy to scientific techniques) by observation of the world that it represents" (p. 243). Such a practice, of course, minimizes the special genius of the poet, his particularity as an artist.

The function of criticism should have been to demonstrate what Tate again referred to as "the special, unique, and complete knowledge which the great forms of literature afford us" (p. 240). However, the contemporary scholars in the universities had not maintained the tradition of literature as a unique form of knowledge. Once the honored bearers of the humane tradition, they had now "merely the genteel tradition; the independence of judgment, the belief in intelligence, the confidence in literature, that informed the genteel tradition, have disappeared. . . ." Only the hollow shell of the great tradition remained.

Ransom in his essay for the symposium, "Strategy for English Studies," stated flatly that "scholarship" had finished its job. "The work accomplished," he wrote, "has been historical, linguistic, editorial."[15] The classics of criticism that have been bequeathed to us "do not provide us with a standard for poetic theory nor for actual criticism." Unless a new approach were found and applied, the professors would not be needed much longer, since "the handbooks are there." Employing a somewhat different connotation of science from that of Tate, Ransom said, "The critical attitude is tough, scientific, and aloof from the literary 'illusion' which it examines." Science, a word hitherto much reviled by all the Agrarians, was used now in the sense of formally *objective*. This last citation reveals how far Ransom had gone by 1941—a distance in emphasis mainly—from the older position that a proper society was requisite for a proper literature. Now he stressed, "In strictness, the business of the literary critic is exclusively with an aesthetic criticism."[16]

The year after the symposium, *The New Criticism* appeared and gave the latest aesthetic doctrine both a name and a more definite direction. Reversing Stallman's view and assigning the leadership to

Ransom, William Elton in his quaint but rather genuine guide to the New Criticism placed Tate in the direct line of descent from Ransom in a genealogical map of the influences at work among the New Critics.

> J. C. Ransom (1888–   )
> (Formal; Non-Organic;
> Traditional; earlier,
> Southern Agrarian)
> A. Tate (1899–   )
> (Similar to Ransom but
> transition to:
> C. Brooks/R. P. Warren)[17]

In Elton's concept of genealogy, Ransom in turn is one of the lines of descent stemming from T. S. Eliot, who is called "Classical: Formal; Traditional." All these are considered approximate relationships.

It is rather futile to attempt to estimate the relative value of leadership in the New Criticism. Of more significance are those aspects of Agrarianism, those literary formulations, which survived the collapse of the sociology and functioned without radical change in the new aesthetic emphasis. In making such a judgment we can employ the criteria of the New Critics themselves. Stallman, for one, spoke of this criticism in such a way as to include most of the Southern Agrarian theory of literature within its province. He found a unifying theme in the idea of "dissociation of sensibility." It this were *new*, although it derived from Eliot, then Ransom and Tate were performing an important task of the New Criticism as early as the late twenties—before they even announced themselves as Agrarians. Stallman also mentioned what he considered to be variations on this central theme: loss of tradition, loss of a fixed convention, loss of belief, and loss of a world order.[18] At any rate, concern over these losses seems quite removed from *textual analysis*, or *artistic autonomy*, or *formal aesthetics*—three of the major locutions with which the New Critics are usually identified.

Regarding tradition—insofar as it involved the Agrarians—if we take away the qualifying adjective *Southern* we have the general noun *tradition*, which remained in their critical arsenal after they abandoned stress on the aesthetic value of their region. In fact, tradition gained in importance when its meaning was applied to the history of literary *forms* that existed quite apart from the social tradition that may have been their basis. Thus certain formal precedents existed to help guide the modern poet in the artistic handling of his subject matter, just as under the Agrarian system, the "way of life," there were certain formal *social* precedents.

Stallman included as another theme of the New Criticism the loss of a homogeneous society, with a consequent loss of belief in religion and myth. He follows Eliot on Blake when he says: "The concentration resulting from a framework of mythology and theology and philosophy is one of the reasons why Dante is a classic, and Blake only a poet of genius."[19] Stallman wrote at some length on Ransom and Tate in his essay for the anthology of New Criticism which he edited. Of the latter he said, "Eliot's theme informs Tate's standard for judging such poets as Robinson, MacLeish, and Cummings."[20] Somewhat further on he wrote that "Tate sets down Crane's career as a 'vindication of Eliot's major premise—that the integrity of the individual consciousness has broken down.' "[21] Interestingly enough, Tate composed these judgments while still a very prominent Agrarian. They appeared in *Reactionary Essays on Poetry and Ideas,* after having been published even earlier as book reviews.[22]

If we were to use the broadest frame of reference for the new body of criticism—following the standards set by Eliot, Ransom, Tate, Stallman and others—then we must conclude that a substantial part of the Agrarian ideology must be placed within its limits. What mainly has to be cast aside is the adherence to the Southern sociology, with its related antagonism to modern industrial America. The older concept of regionalism and its aesthetic reflection must also be minimized, although now and then it rose to the surface. For example, Tate referred to it in 1940 when discussing the achievement of Thomas Hardy. He wrote:

He had had in him from birth an immense, almost instinctive knowledge of the life of the people rooted in ancient folk-tradition and fixed, also, in the objective patterns of nature and of the occupations close to nature. This knowledge of a provincial scene . . . must have toughened his scepticism against the cruder aspects of Victorian thought, liberalism, optimism, and the doctrine of progress, and he could concentrate with a sort of classical purity upon the permanent human experience.[23]

On the whole, however, the previous sociological approach to the study of literature lost out to the aesthetic; the tension that seemed always to exist in Ransom and Tate between the two poles was resolved in favor of the second. Solomon Fishman touched upon the nature of this tension in *The Disinherited of Art.* "The seeming paradox," he wrote, "arises from the conjunction of two incompatibles: a doctrine that assigns the highest value to the local, indigenous charac-

ter of culture; and a criticism that, adjuring historical and environ-
mental relativism, postulates absolute literary standards."[24]

The term *absolute* is quite familiar to anyone who has closely
studied Tate's literary career. On it hinges the belief of John Bradbury, for instance, that Tate has a good claim to being the founder of
the new critical approach. In his book *The Fugitives,* Bradbury intro-
duces a brief chapter entitled "Aesthetic Formalism" in which he
makes the following bow to Tate as the founder.

At the close of his essay "Poetry and the Absolute," published in 1927,
Tate had issued what amounted to a call for a new school of critics, who, "by
attending exclusively to the properties of poetry as a fine art," could develop
"an elaborate aesthetic attitude . . . enabling them to isolate explicitly the
absolute quality of particular poets and to reject a poetry from which the
quality is missing."[25]

While Tate was acquiring the Southern consciousness that led to the
social determinism of Agrarian aesthetics, he was simultaneously interested in an absolutist, purist, formalist attitude which, in time,
qualified him as a leading New Critic. Bradbury credits *Hound and
Horn* with being the first organ of aesthetic formalism treating art
from a "technical" point of view. Tate became a regional editor of
this journal in 1931. Upon its demise in 1934, *The Southern Review,*
founded by Brooks and Warren at Louisiana State University, became
its distinguished successor. According to Bradbury, its tenor strongly
reflected the aesthetics of Tate, and its career coincided with the
"golden era" of criticism written by Ransom, Tate, Warren, and
Brooks. Another journal directly associated with the latest formalism
was the *Kenyon Review*; it was founded by Ransom when he went to
teach at Kenyon College in Gambier, Ohio.

Had not the idea occurred sometime in 1928, as Donald Davidson
informs us, to publish a manifesto for a definitely Southern movement, it is quite likely that Ransom and Tate would have been considered "pure" or "absolute" critics much sooner than was the case.
Nothing was necessarily lost, of course, by such a delay. Actually, in
many obvious ways, they gained a great deal by their Agrarian experiment—for one thing, a national reputation. But even a cursory examination of Tate's book reviews during the mid-twenties, for instance,
proves him heavily under the influence of T. S. Eliot; and insofar as
Eliot was then already a New Critic, then Tate also must be regarded
as being deeply affected. Echoes of Eliot appeared in review after review during this time. They reveal the young Tate constantly using
the new critical phrases invented or stressed by Eliot.

In a 1926 essay on Conrad Aiken's poetry Tate wrote, "Too often Mr. Aiken discards his sensibility to meet the demands of this pattern. . . ."[26] He was referring to the external pattern of a theme; in other words, the poetic form. No doubt a good poet does not sacrifice that subtle sense of rightness, that delicacy of insight—or whatever *sensibility* really is—for the sake of having something in the structure appear "right" to the casual eye. Other evidence proves that sensibility was of major interest to Tate in the twenties. Of *Manhattan Transfer* he said, "But since Mr. Dos Passos has limited his sensibility to the diligent illustration of appearance and has not proposed an aesthetic problem, you will find that none is solved."[27] Tate seemed unwilling to admit, in this case, that aesthetic value could inhere in the experimental form of the novel. The definition of sensibility itself seemed to be limited to such elements as point of view, subject matter, and superficial structure.

His review in March, 1926, of the poetry of Léonie Adams contained references not only to sensibility but also to *impersonality* and the *objective correlative*. The lady's sensibility, Tate found, was metaphysical in Dr. Johnson's sense, for "she expresses herself in her best poems in terms of something impersonal and beyond convictions. . . ."[28] He mentioned the "objective reference" in her poetry; and, having "a distinguished limited sensibility, she is a distinguished minor poet." How Tate measured the various degrees of sensibility in different talents he never revealed. Writing of Santayana's *Dialogues in Limbo,* as a further example, Tate discovered that "it is an organization of the total sensibility into a mode of self-sufficient contemplation."[29] In the same year Tate had the opportunity to review a book of poetry by Eliot himself—poetry which, in Tate's critical view, "has attempted with considerable success to bring back the total sensibility as a constantly available material, deeper and richer in connotation than any substance yielded by the main course of English poetry since the seventeenth century."[30] The last part of Tate's remark referred obviously to the position taken by Eliot favoring the metaphysical poetry of the age of John Donne.

Other examples of Tate's concern with sensibility exist in these early writings, along with other influences of Eliot. Of Hemingway's *The Torrents of Spring* Tate said that "like 'Pamela', it contains emotions in excess of the facts."[31] That which was often cited by Eliot as dissociation of sensibility was somewhat altered by Tate, at times, to *dissociated intelligence*. In examining Edwin Muir's *Transition*, he wrote that "the comprehensiveness of his treatment [of idealism] is nevertheless to be wondered at in an age of dissociated intelligences."[32] Muir was a Scottish traditionalist who nevertheless did not develop any traces of Agrarian-like distaste for science.

Several years later, in the midst of his Southern Agrarianism, Tate made an observation that differentiated the critical method of Eliot from his own and Ransom's. The procedure of Eliot was to go from aesthetics to religious, moral, and social matters; on the other hand, he and Ransom took the opposite course and went from the social to the aesthetic. To justify his own method Tate quoted from Belgion, the critic whose book, *The Human Parrot*, he was reviewing: "But nobody can ever learn from a poem itself that the emotions it imitates are profound and serious. To recognize this, one must already know what is profound and serious."[33] It would seem that insofar as its emotions were concerned, a poem could not be *autonomous*, or have a completely separate formal being apart from the reader; nevertheless the concept of autonomy was soon to predominate in Tate's aesthetic theory, when the poem became an absolute object in itself, bearing a special kind of sensuous, psychological, and even ideational knowledge— all subsumed in the *art*.

Since there was no organized gradualism in Tate as he progressed towards a renewed aesthetic emphasis during and after his Agrarianism, many rather abrupt signs were present to reveal the tension in his mind. Commenting on Horace Gregory's *Chelsea Rooming House*, he made a separation between the social and the aesthetic which seems at odds with the above opinion that poetic emotion must be judged for its seriousness and profundity by external criteria. Tate now believed that Gregory

was tempted to identify his experiments in the poetic value of common speech with one of the numerous causes of the People. These causes are good, but there is no necessary connection between them and the art of verse. Mr. Gregory was only doing what Wordsworth did—reforming not society but his language under the spur of social passion; when the reform is accomplished the poet, being a poet and desiring to wear the ribbon of craft on his coat, tends to forget the passion and settles down to his specific task of writing.[34]

Southern Agrarian criticism as a whole faced a problem posed by the differentiation between form and content. It seemed difficult—if not actually contradictory and insincere—to praise the aesthetic form of a work whose content was prejudicial to the Agrarian philosophy. This was the same kind of trap into which Matthew Arnold sometimes fell when he over-praised or under-praised something on the basis of its "Celtic" or "Teutonic" character. Whitman was thus rejected by the Agrarians for his content—and for his poetic form, also, which was "untraditional"—since his content was taken to reflect the ideology of industrial democracy, and hence it was Northern and hostile to the South. Benét's *John Brown's Body* would have been "better" aesthetically had it been written by an Agrarian, say by Robert Penn Warren, who wrote a biography of Brown. As for Sidney Lanier, Tate wrote that the usual criticism of Lanier was motivated by a desire to "give Lanier a 'rank' and to worry his poetry into some kind of 'social significance,' rather than the critical impulse to estimate the exact quality of his work."[35] This had kept Lanier high in the order of American poets. According to Tate, Lanier was a mediocre poet who was both a confused thinker and a literary opportunist. Lanier allowed moral abstraction to vitiate what might have been a purer aesthetic achievement. Tate wrote:

As he failed to present one clear image in his verse, so he failed to see through a single leading idea of his age. And this failure, as in the case of his poetry, betrayed him into large abstractions with moral names; he identified with "truth" those political notions, those public movements, those theories of art, which promised success to his career.[36]

A term later to be frequently used by the New Critics was *heresy of the didactic*. In regard to poetic content the word *heresy* appeared in Tate's essay, "Poetry and Politics," written about the time he was attacking the use of political ideas by Lanier. Speaking of political art, Tate declared, "We get neither art nor politics; we get heresy." He praised poets like MacLeish and Ransom because "their job is praise of the Virgin, not the display of Romantic personality."[37] Tate employed the entire locution in February, 1934, while reviewing John Peale Bishop's poetry. Here he presented the problem of content and form, and especially with the diffusion in the content of a dominating idea; in the New Criticism this would be called the *prose statement*, the "something less" than the poem itself. He wrote:

If the "social" point of view can subdue the philosophy of the material, and close the disjunction between experience and form, power and ritual, the literature of the future belongs to that point of view; but it will still be a nice question then whether it will still be the social point of view. There is no evidence that this will happen; for communist poetry at present is an aggravated case of one symptom of the right-wing disease—the "heresy of the didactic," which the communists undertake as enthusiastically as their opponents deplore it. We are now all necessarily moralists.[38]

The indecision shown here over the possible value of the social point of view in poetry was eventually resolved in the doctrine of the *fallacy of communication;* this, in turn, may be directly related to the Agrarian antagonism to "poetry of the will," of scientific rationalism. It was a fallacy for the poet to use his poem as a vehicle for ideas and public emotions which could, perhaps, be better carried by a scientific or some other prose discourse. Tate came to believe that all nineteenth-century poetry—that written after 1798, the year of the *Lyrical Ballads* —was bad because it sought to be a poetry of communication.[39]

Tate's early and important essay on formalism, "Poetry and the Absolute," was published in 1927. In it he developed a concept of formalism which was later part of the basis for the accusation that Tate believed in "art for art's sake." He wrote, "And of all the ends toward which poetry as an art strives, the most important is a signification of experience that becomes absolute, within the dimensions of the poem."[40] Poetry, therefore, was the fusion of "an intensely felt ordinary experience, an intense moral situation, into an intensely realized art." He also proposed a construction which was to resound during the later Agrarian period when he said, "Romantic German aesthetics, through Hegel, collapses as the fallacy of abstraction. . . ."[41] The key negative term, of course, is *abstraction,* that accursed offspring of science.

For a moment in the late twenties, Ransom seemed to take an opposite view of Romanticism; instead of equating it with abstraction, which he soon did in *God Without Thunder,* he did the reverse and spoke of its particularity. He believed that the Classical and Romantic moods were two forms of the artistic revulsion against science. The first was faulty since it was a criticism which used the very methods of science, whereas "In romantic art we revel in the particularity of things, and feel the joy of restoration after an estrangement from nature."[42] These are strange words from Ransom in view of the basic attack on Romanticism soon to be made. At this time Ransom may have been acting upon the "new criticism" of the previous generation —that outlined by Joel Spingarn in 1910 when he mentioned Carlyle's observation that criticism in Germany was on "the essence and peculiar life of the poetry itself."[43] For that matter, Tate's doctrine of absolute poetry was not far removed from this German aesthetic view; nor was it too distant from another dictum of the older dispensation as defined by Spingarn, who proclaimed: "We have done with the race, the time, the environment of a poet's work as an element in Criticism."[44] Such a dictum would not apply to the more consciously Agrarian part of the Southern Agrarian theory of literature; however, it would apply to the more deliberately aesthetic part; and it would apply even more clearly to Ransom and Tate when they severed their literary aims from the aim of restoring a traditional society. Tate's persistent opposition to Romanticism, to poets like Shelley and Lanier, re-emerged in the New Criticism in the form of *emotive use of language*—to mention one of the pejorative terms—which in turn was related to the *impersonal theory of art*. Unlike the Romantics, the modern poet should not be compelled to respond emotionally and mechanically in certain prescribed ways. This desideratum seems to contradict the praise by both Eliot and the Agrarians of traditional behavior, arising from a settled society like that of Dante's, which was felt to be vital to the creation of the highest poetry.

The theoretical contradiction between these two views resulted, we might infer, from the limitation in the context of relevant value which came during the transition to the new formalism. The aesthetic sense was enlarged at the expense of the social; that is, critical appraisal became more poem-bound, autarchic, and the previous line of thought from the social to the aesthetic was broken. The Agrarian rejection of scientific rationalism developed into the doctrine called the *heresy of paraphrase* by the New Critics; the analysis of a poem involved more than a logical restatement of its idea pattern. Tate's specific amplification of the attack on rationalism, on Platonism and abstraction, had already set up in poetry the dichotomy between the *practical will* and the *imagination*. This was another element accepted as characteristic of the New Criticism by Stallman, Elton, and others.

In his later and more exclusively aesthetic position, Tate condemned the making of value judgments on the thought content of poetry, saying, "We know the particular poem, not what it says we can restate. In a manner of speaking, the poem is its own knower, neither poet nor reader knowing anything that the poem says apart from the words of the poem."[45] To repeat a basic dogma: Any usual paraphrase of the ideas (the prose statement) was deceptive, even irrelevant, to the aesthetic evaluation; a real analysis must presuppose that poetry had an independent, absolute existence and exhibited a special knowledge with its own criteria of value. In a poem, which was autonomous, the only relevance of the subject-ideas was to each other "within the formal meaning of the work itself." As a New Critic, Tate regarded as mere expressionists "the writers who see in works of literature not the specific formal properties but only the amount and range of human life brought to the reader."[46]

The leading Agrarians who became New Critics dealt fully with formalism in literature. Indeed, concern with form was one of the bridges connecting the two phases of their career. They related the problem of form to science and tradition, and to contemporary society.

For example, Ransom in 1933 had written in "A Poem Nearly Anonymous," an essay on *Lycidas,* that "our modern societies, with their horror of 'empty' forms and ceremonies, and their invitation to men to be themselves, and to handle their objects as quickly and rudely as they please, are not only destroying old arts and customs . . . but exposing their own solidarity to the anarchy of too much individualism."[47] At the same time he asserted: "The formal tradition in art has a validity more than political. . . . What I have in mind is an argument from aesthetics which will justify any formal art, even a formal literature." And finally, he said, "I suggest . . . that art is usually, and probably of necessity, a kind of obliquity; that its fixed form proposes to guarantee the round-about of the artistic process, and the 'aesthetic distance.' " Thus the form dominated the content and permitted nothing extraneous in idea or emotion to threaten the poem's integrity as art. A year later, in an article called "Poets Without Laurels," Ransom said:

There is yet no general recognition of the possibility that an aesthetic effect may exist by itself, independent of morality or any other useful set of ideas. But the modern poet is intensely concerned with this possibility, and he has disclaimed social responsibility in order to secure this pure aesthetic effect. He cares nothing, professionally, about morals, or God, or native land. He has performed a work of dissociation and purified his art.[48]

Back in his time, Spingarn had also affirmed, "We have done with all moral judgment of art as art."[49] Roger Fry, too, had written, "For the moment I must be dogmatic and declare that the esthetic emotion is an emotion about form."[50]

Tate commented on Ransom's essay for the *Yale Review* in his own essay on Bishop, wherein he asked, "Where shall the poet get a form that will permit him to make direct comprehensive statements about modern civilization?"[51] He discovered that Bishop had studied the poets of the present age who, "like Yeats, seem to have achieved, out of the galvanized mythology or by means of a consciously restricted point of view, a working substitute for the supernatural myth and the concentration that a myth makes possible."[52] Tate blamed society itself for the absence of form. "It is probable," Tate said, "that there is an intimate relation between a generally accepted 'picture of the world' and the general acceptance of a metrical system and its differentiation into patterns."[53] Modern society, with its hatred for any kind of *status quo,* permits neither a social nor an aesthetic stability. Tate continued, "So the modern poet, struggling to get hold of some kind of meaning, blunders into the *impasse* of form, and when he finds no usable form he finds that he has available no metrical system either." Tate's mention of Ransom at this point was related to still another attack on science. He wrote:

The specialization of scientific technique supplanting a central view of life has, as Mr. John Crowe Ransom showed in a recent essay (*The Yale Review,* Spring, 1935), tended to destroy the formal arts; poetry has in turn become a specialization of aesthetic effect without formal limitations.[54]

Besides stressing the values of form as an Agrarian, Ransom also stressed *ontology,* the element which emerged in the forefront as a critical strategy in *The New Criticism.* One of his most brilliant essays, "Poetry: A Note on Ontology," was composed in 1934 during his Agrarian period; like a number of his essays representing this period, it was reprinted in *The World's Body.* That this essay has been deemed a prime example of New Criticism is proved by its inclusion by Stallman in his anthology. The word *ontology* as used in aesthetics was not invented by Ransom. Ramon Fernandez had used it as far back as 1927, and Tate had quoted him in a review of his book *Messages.*

Allowing that the visions of art are by definition imaginative, we can say that aesthetics must be an imaginative ontology, that is to say that the fundamental problem of aesthetics is no other than the metaphysical problem of being, but translated to the plane of the imagination.[55]

Ontology in relation to poetry was also mentioned by Charles Maurras in the preface to the *Musique Interieure.* Speaking of Maurras, Stallman commented, "Poetry . . . is ontology, 'for poetry strives . . . towards the roots of the knowledge of Being.' Ransom transposes the problem of being, which is for him the basic problem in aesthetics, to the plane of the imaginative content of literature and art."[56] As we can readily see, this is a strong echo of Ramon Fernandez.

In pursuit of further aesthetic clarity, Ransom in 1934 distinguished between a poetry of *things* (Physical Poetry, like that of the Imagists) and a poetry of *ideas* (Platonic Poetry), and spoke in favor of the first. He made the notable statement that "science gratifies a rational or practical impulse and exhibits the minimum of perception. Art gratifies a perceptual impulse and exhibits the minimum of reason."[57] That the ontology in a poem involved its formal existence was evident from Ransom's assertion that "art always sets out to create an 'aesthetic distance' between the object and the subject, and art takes pains to announce that it is not history."[58] In repeating Kant's doctrine that the aesthetic judgment was unconcerned with "the existence or nonexistence of the object," Ransom was closely paralleling Tate's appraisal of poetry as an entity absolute unto itself.

As was the case with Tate, Ransom's denial of poetic relevance to scientific rationalism, Platonic abstraction, and just plain ideas led him to place aesthetic value on more metaphysical and abstract elements. Much as he opposed the alleged abstractions of scientists, he himself formulated abstract doctrines about the aesthetic value that inhered in myths, nature, regionalism, and God. Poetry alone, as a humanizing force in our culture, might possess the power of re-unifying man's divided sensibility. During his entire Agrarian period there was always evident in Ransom a striving for an aesthetic reality superimposed on physical reality, a reaching beyond and through the concrete object to arrive at its aesthetic essence. Even the eating of a good formal meal could be a fastidious and "rich, free, and delicate aesthetic experience."[59] Both the genuine Agrarian and the genuine poet had this sensibility, which Ransom defined as follows: "It is the complicating factor in man which raises him above the status of a rational animal, and allows him a special kind of knowledge and of pleasure." In the poet, particularly, it was his *form* which crystallized and revealed the quality of his sensibility. Ransom praised T. S. Eliot's triple-based foundation for the proper aesthetic life; one of the bases was formalism, the concern with the structure which the content received from the poet's skill and imagination. To Ransom this increment of value was the "necessary difference of artifice, convention, and formality to which the artist submits his imitation of reality."[60] Form, which embodied the poet's total aesthetic *being,* was thus a requirement beyond the mere immediacy of imitation. When he came to write *The New Criticism,* Ransom proposed ontology as the central evaluating technique for the critic. He examined intensively the alleged limitations of several other types of critics whom he termed *new:* the psychological (Richards); the historical (Eliot); and the logical (Winters). Then he presented his own choice of the modern ideal, presumably represented by himself, in the final section entitled, "Wanted: An Ontological Critic." What he meant, unfortunately, did not come through with sufficient clarity to enable critics actually to practice the "ontological" approach. Throughout his book Ransom again stressed heavily the difference between poetry and science, in much the same manner in which he and his associates had done during the thirties; but now were added such critical terms as *structure* and *texture* which had received no previous emphasis. He wrote, "We sum it up by saying that the poem is a loose logical structure with an irrelevant local texture."[61] This may be a shrewd observation, but it could not suffice as a basis for a critical theory. Antagonism to scientific rationalism, the old Agrarian bugaboo, appeared in statements such as this: "I suggest that the differentia of poetry as discourse is an ontological one. It treats an order of existence, a grade of objectivity, which cannot be treated in a scientific discourse."[62] Brooks and Warren had said about the same thing in their introduction to *Understanding Poetry*. Ransom's repetition had gained importance because now, in 1940, it helped to define the New Criticism.

The critical debates which ensued—often engaging political ideologies as well—proved as effectively as anything else could that the New Criticism had succeeded. In the universities it challenged the established historical and scholarly methods of teaching literature. In time many English departments split into militant factions as a result of struggles for power between the "historical scholars" and the "New Critics." The former were often made to appear ignorant of or indifferent to the purely "aesthetic" values in literature. Their rebuttal included the possibility that textual criticism, though it properly emphasized the poem as a poem, nevertheless could lead to obscurantist mumbo jumbo when the critic performing the explication had an excess of method but very little solid knowledge.

The perennial conjunction of aesthetic formalism and reactionary social ideology made the New Critics, including the former Agrarians, subject to charges of going to extremes in both categories. A too rarefied explication, with layers upon layers of meanings and multiple alternatives set in mystical or symbolic structures and textures of form, lent itself to the scornful label, the "new scholasticism." As for the reactionary ideology supported by many New Critics, it inspired attacks such as that of Robert Gorham Davis who wrote: "Over the last two decades, in the journals of the New Criticism, *authority, hierarchy, catholicism, aristocracy, tradition, absolutes, dogma, truths* became related terms of honor, and *liberalism, naturalism, scientism, individualism, equalitarianism, progress, protestantism, pragmatism* and *personality* became related terms of rejection."[63]

Nevertheless, the Agrarian–New Critics and their methods of evaluation became the most exciting subject of comment on the literary scene. Their textbooks were adopted by colleges and universities. They and their followers published voluminously. They have since taught, lectured, judged writing contests, taken part in conferences, reviewed books, and reaped all the rewards reserved for the highest authorities in literature. More important perhaps, they have greatly influenced the standards by which all literature, past and present, is judged. In general, these standards have been such as to denigrate the democratic and popular authors of the past and to discourage such writers in the present. No Whitman, Dreiser, or Sandburg, for instance, has been deemed worthy of consideration as a genuine artist by the New Critics. Citing an extreme case of anti-democratic bias, Davis singled out an article in which Robert Heilman, a New Critic, held that "liberal-democratic-progressive views," if believed in with conviction, "made one incapable of appreciating imaginative literature at all."[64]

We might ponder how in a generally democratic culture, a group of critics so obviously alien to democracy could gain such a strong position in literature? The answer is not simple. Part of it might be their dazzling array of supposedly new approaches in the critical analysis of literary texts. By comparison, the older historical scholars seemed dull and irrelevant; the Marxist critics were dangerous as well. Part of the answer might also lie in the preoccupation of the liberal-left critics with the defense of democracy against fascism, first in Spain and then throughout the world. While they spoke at rallies, issued manifestoes, and signed protest letters, the New Critics quietly established beach-heads in the English departments of American colleges and universities.

During the past two decades the New Criticism has had a rich and complex internal life. The leading practitioners themselves have had to respond to the dynamics of time and change. A few years after *The New Criticism* appeared, John Crowe Ransom felt obliged to jettison his own original contribution—the notion that the essence of a poem exists in the relationship between its structure and its texture. Unfortunately, he himself wrote few more poems to add to the delightful little classics composed earlier in his career. Robert Penn Warren has concentrated on his series of impressive novels; he seems destined to live on in our literature no matter what happens to his fame as a critic. The most accomplished explicator of all, Cleanth Brooks, Jr., often exhibits in his criticism an astonishing amount of historical knowledge; his scholarship is invariably superb. Allen Tate has brought new emotional power to bear upon his abiding first love, the writing of poetry; and he has done so with an intensity of feeling that he used to find objectionable in a romantic like Shelley.

As Southern Agrarians they may have failed in effecting one kind of restoration; but as New Critics they succeeded very well in another—in restoring to the poem, the story, and the play an intrinsic aesthetic vitality. It is a rare scholar who teaches today without a keen sense of the aesthetic attributes stressed by the New Critics. They gave new duties to the modern critic, a higher status to poetry as a special type of knowledge, and won for themselves a permanent place in our literary history.

Reference Material

CHAPTER I

1 "The Southern Renaissance," *American Heritage*, II (1955), 744.
2 "The Tennessee Poets," *New Republic*, LIV (March 7, 1928), 25.
3 "On Leaving the South," *Scribner's*, LXXXIX (January 1931), 25.
4 Berkeley and Los Angeles, 1953, p. 5.
5 "The Fugitive—1922–1925," *Princeton University Library Chronicle*, III (April 1942), 81.
6 Ransom mercilessly attacked *The Waste Land* in "Waste Lands," *Literary Review*, III (July 14, 1923), 825–26.
7 Cowan, *The Fugitive Group*, p. xv.
8 Eds. Louis D. Rubin, Jr., and Robert D. Jacobs (Baltimore, 1953).
9 "The South," *Forum*, LXXIX (February 1920), 178.
10 "The Tennessee Poets," p.103.
11 "Notes on the Changed South," *New Republic*, XLVI (April 28, 1926), 300.
12 Editorial, "The New South," *Saturday Review of Literature*, VI (October 26, 1929), 309.
13 "The Literary Awakening in the South," *Bookman*, LXVI (October 1927), 138.
14 "The Southern Legend," *Scribner's*, LXXXV (May 1929), 542.
15 *Ibid.*, p. 540
16 See Donald Davidson, "I'll Take My Stand: A History," *American Review*, V (Summer 1935), 301–21.
17 *Ibid.*, p. 307.
18 In *Twentieth Century Authors*, eds. Stanley J. Kunitz and Howard Haycraft (New York, 1955), p. 350.
19 See Ransom, "The South Old or New?" *Sewanee Review*, XXXVI (April 1928), 139–47, and Davidson, "First Fruits of Dayton," *Forum*, LXXXIX (June 1928), 896–907.
20 *I'll Take My Stand*, eds. Twelve Southerners (New York, 1951), p. 264
21 *American Review*, IV (March 1935), pp. 529–47.
22 Stewart, "The Fugitive Agrarian Writers," p. 295.
23 *Ibid.*, p. 296.
24 *Ibid.*, p. 297.
25 *Ideas in America* (Cambridge, 1944), p. 210.

CHAPTER II

1 "Last Days of the Charming Lady," *The Nation,* CXXI (October 28, 1925), 485–86. The following quotations from Tate are from this article.
2 *Ibid.,* p. 486
3 "The Poet Laureate," *Literary Review,* IV (March 1924), 626.
4 "Last Days of the Charming Lady," p. 486.
5 "The Lost Poet of Georgia," *New Republic,* LXIII (July 23, 1930), 294.
6 "The Artist as Southerner," *Saturday Review of Literature,* II (May 15, 1926), 781.
7 *Ibid.,* p. 782.
8 *Ibid.*
9 "First Fruits of Dayton," *Forum,* 79 (June 1928), 903–4.
10 Chicago, 1925, p. vii.
11 *Ibid.,* p. 2
12 Tate himself gave an interpretation of this poem in "Narcissus as Narcissus," *Virginia Quarterly Review,* XIV (Winter 1938), 108–22.
13 *Lee in the Mountains* (New York, 1949), pp. 80–81.
14 John L. Stewart, "The Fugitive Agrarian Writers: A History and a Criticism," unpublished Ph.D. dissertation, Ohio State University, 1947, p. 289.
15 "The Fugitive—1922–1925," *Princeton University Library Chronicle,* III (April 1942), 82.
16 John M. Bradbury, *The Fugitives* (Chapel Hill, 1958).
17 "The Serpent in the Mulberry Bush," *Southern Renascence,* p. 355.
18 Quoted in Mims, *The Advancing South,* p. 157.
19 *Ibid.,* p. 249.
20 "First Fruits of Dayton," p. 898.
21 *Ibid.,* p. 905.
22 These quotations come from *The Fugitives,* pp. 10–11.
23 *The Advancing South,* p. xi.
24 *The Last of the Provincials* (Boston, 1947), p. 217.
25 *The American Heresy* (London, 1927), p. 10. The following page references are also from the same source.
26 *Jefferson Davis* (New York, 1929), p. 303.
27 *Ibid.,* pp. 301–2.
28 *Ibid.,* p. 87.
29 *Stonewall Jackson: The Good Soldier* (New York, 1928), p. 39.
30 "Life in the Old South," *New Republic,* LIV (July 10, 1929), 211–12.
31 *Speculations,* ed. Herbert Read (London, 1954), p. 117.

CHAPTER III

1 See Donald Davidson, "I'll Take My Stand: A History," *American Review,* V (Summer 1935), 315.
2 *I'll Take My Stand,* ed. Twelve Southerners (New York, 1930), p. xviii. The following quotations and page references are from the same source.
3 "Land!" *Harper's,* CLXV (July 1932), 223.
4 "The American Review's First Year," *American Review,* III (April 1934), 124.

5 John Crowe Ransom, "Happy Farmers," *American Review*, I (October 1933), 529. The following quotations and page references are also from this source.

6 Troy J. Cauley, *Agrarianism: A Program for Farmers* (Chapel Hill, 1935), p. 100. The page references in the following paragraphs are to the same source.

7 "Land!" pp. 221–22.

8 "Happy Farmers," p. 527.

9 *American Review*, IV (March 1935), 546.

10 Rupert B. Vance, "Is Agrarianism for Farmers?" *Southern Review*, I (July 1935), p. 43.

11 *Agrarianism* (Chapel Hill, 1935). The following quotations and page references are also from Cauley.

12 XXIV (October 1931), pp. 178–88.

13 "The Foundations of Democracy," *Southern Review*, I (Spring 1936), 718.

14 "The Integration of Agrarian and Exchange Economies," *American Review*, V (October 1935), 586. The following quotations and page references are from the same source.

15 *Agricultural Reform in the United States* (New York, 1929), p. 3.

16 *Ibid.*, p. 13.

17 Cauley, *Agrarianism*, pp. 55–56.

18 "Is Agrarianism for Farmers?" p. 52.

19 *Ibid.*, p. 50.

20 *Culture in the South*, ed. W. T. Couch (Chapel Hill, 1935), p. viii.

21 New York, 1946, pp. 76–77.

22 *Agrarianism*, p. 68.

23 *Ibid.*, p. 69.

24 *The Advancing South*, p. 69.

25 *Ibid.*, p. 66.

26 *Ibid.*, p. 73.

27 *Land of the Free* (Boston, 1935), p. 162.

28 Oliver Carlson, "The Southern Worker Organizes," *The Nation*, CXXXIX (September 26, 1934), 354.

29 *American Review*, II (January 1934), 314–15.

30 "The Restoration of Property," *American Review*, I (April 1933), 3.

31 *American Review*, I (May 1933), 207.

32 *American Review*, I (Summer 1933), 347.

33 *Ibid.*, p. 350.

34 "John Strachey, Marx, and Distributism," *American Review*, V (May 1935), 184.

35 *American Review*, II (November 1933), 46.

36 *Ibid.*, p. 56.

CHAPTER IV

1 The intellectual and political tyranny which settled over the land has been brilliantly described by C. Vann Woodward in "The Irony of

Southern History," *Southern Renascence,* pp. 63–79.

2 These figures are from W. E. B. DuBois, *Black Folk: Then and Now* (New York, 1939), pp. 200, 203.

3 *The Rise of Cotton Mills in the South* (Baltimore, 1921), p. 10.

4 Clement Eaton, *A History of the Old South* (New York, 1949), p. 252.

5 *Ibid.,* p. 253.

6 *Essays in the History of the American Negro* (New York, 1945), p. 11.

7 *Ibid.*

8 *Ibid.,* p. 62.

9 *A History of the Old South,* p. 490.

10 *Ibid.,* p. 495.

11 Richmond, 1854, p. 662.

12 *Agriculture in the Southern United States to 1860* (New York, 1941), I, 502. The following page references are to the same source.

13 Quoted from Fanny Kemble in Broadus Mitchell, *The Rise of Cotton Mills,* p. 95.

14 *Agriculture in the Southern United States to 1860,* p. 456.

15 *Ibid.,* p. 793.

16 *A History of the Old South,* p. 431

17 *William Gregg, Factory Master of the Old South* (Chapel Hill, 1928), p. 60.

18 New York, 1936, p. v.

19 Quoted in Willard Thorp, *A Southern Reader* (New York, 1955), p. 571.

20 James D. B. DeBow, *The Industrial Resources of the Southern and Western States* (New Orleans, New York, 1852–53).

21 *William Gregg,* p. 60.

22 See *A Southern Reader,* p. 260.

23 *A History of the Old South,* p. 431.

24 *Agriculture in the Southern United States to 1860,* p. 935.

25 *Ibid.*

26 *Ibid.,* p. 928.

27 *Ibid.,* p. 932.

28 *Origins of the New South* (Baton Rouge, 1951), p. 140.

29 *Ibid.,* p. 224.

30 *The Rise of Cotton Mills in the South,* p. 95.

31 Woodward, *Origins of the New South,* p. 206.

32 *Black Reconstruction in America* (New York, 1935), p. 705.

33 *Origins of the New South,* p. 211.

34 *Ibid.,* p. 249.

35 "Dilemma of the Southern Liberals," *American Mercury,* XXXI (February 1934), 233.

36 *Ibid.,* p. 227.

37 Both *The Advancing South* by Mims and *Liberalism in the South* by Dabney contain valuable material on the New South.

38 "Dilemma of the Southern Liberals," p. 233.

39 Walter Hines Page, *The Rebuilding of Old Commonwealths* (New York, 1902), p. 20. The following page references are also to this source.

40 *The Advancing South,* p. 112.

CHAPTER V

1   *Latter-Day Pamphlets* (Boston, 1850), p. 26.
2   Arthur J. Penty, "Means and Ends," *Criterion*, XI (October, 1931), 9.
3   *Ibid.*, p. 23.
4   *Ibid.*, p. 1.
5   *Ibid.*, p. 5.
6   "Reconstructed But Unregenerate," *I'll Take My Stand*, p. 15.
7   *God Without Thunder* (New York, 1930), p. 212.
8   "Reconstructed But Unregenerate," p. 19.
9   "A Century of Progress," *American Review*, IV (January 1935), 383.
10 "Ruskin," *American Review*, IV (February 1935), 509.
11 *Ibid.*, pp. 509–10.
12 *I'll Take My Stand*, p. xv.
13 "A Mirror for Artists," *I'll Take My Stand*, p. 28.
14 *Ibid.*
15 *Ibid.*, p. 31.
16 *Ibid.*, pp. 46–47. Ransom in *God Without Thunder* had already detailed this point in a brilliant chapter entitled "Satan as Science."
17 *Ibid.*, p. 38.
18 *Ibid.*
19 *Ibid.*, p. 51
20 "The Trend of Literature," *Culture in the South*, pp. 198–99.
21 "Not in Memoriam, But in Defense," *I'll Take My Stand*, p. 358.
22 "A Statement of Principles," *I'll Take My Stand*, p. xvi.
23 *Ibid.*
24 Young, "Not in Memoriam, But in Defense," p. 339.
25 "Regionalism and Education," *American Review*, IV (January 1935), pp. 311–12.
26 "Education, Past and Present," *I'll Take My Stand*, pp. 98–99. The following page references are to the same source.
27 "The Briar Patch," *I'll Take My Stand*, p. 250.
28 See Frederic E. Faverty, *Matthew Arnold the Ethnologist* (Evanston, 1951).
29 "The Profession of Letters in the South," p. 155.
30 *Ibid.*, pp. 156–57.
31 "The Irrepressible Conflict," *I'll Take My Stand*, p. 77.
32 "A View of the Whole South," p. 424.
33 "Reconstructed But Unregenerate," *I'll take My Stand*, pp. 10–11.
34 "T. S. Stribling: A Paragraph in the History of Critical Realism," *American Review*, II (February 1934), 469.
35 For a bitter attack on Northern interference with the South's race problem, see Frank L. Owsley's "Scottsboro, The Third Crusade," *American Review*, I (Summer 1933), 257–85.
36 Warren, "The Blind Poet: Sidney Lanier," *American Review*, II (November 1933), 341.
37 Warren, "T. S. Stribling: A Paragraph in the History of Critical Realism," p. 484.
38 *Sherwood Anderson's Memoirs* (New York, 1942), p. 459.

39 "Tradition and Orthodoxy," *American Review*, II (March 1934), pp. 516–17.
40 *Points of View* (London, 1941), p. 140.
41 *Ibid.*, p. 141.
42 Davidson, *The Attack on Leviathan* (Chapel Hill, 1938), p. 73.
43 "The Stieglitz Spoof," *American Review*, IV (March 1935), 591.
44 "A View of the Whole South," p. 424.
45 "Not in Memoriam, But in Defense," *I'll Take My Stand*, p. 250.
46 "Where Are the People?" *American Review*, II (December 1933), p. 232.
47 *The Fathers* (New York, 1936), p. 210.
48 "A View of the Whole South," *American Review*, II (February 1934), 425.
49 Tate *et al.*, "The Question of the Pound Award," *Partisan Review*, XVI (May 1949), 520.
50 "What is a Traditional Society?" *American Review*, VIII (September 1936), 377
51 *The Attack on Leviathan*, p. 94.
52 *Notes on the State of Virginia* (Richmond, 1853), pp. 173–74.
53 *Ibid.*, p. 175.
54 *Ibid.*
55 Davidson, *The Attack on Leviathan*, p. 178.
56 *Notes on the State of Virginia*, p. 175.
57 I'll Take My Stand: A History," p. 312.
58 Tate, "Lincoln? Lee?" *New Republic*, LV (June 6, 1928), 75.
59 *The Attack on Leviathan*, p. 217.
60 "Where Are the People?" p. 234.

CHAPTER VI

1 "Regionalism and Sectionalism," *New Republic*, LXIX (December 21, 1931), 158.
2 *American Regionalism* (New York, 1938), p. v.
3 *Ibid.*, pp. 44–46
4 *Ibid.*, p. 168.
5 *Ibid.*, p. 175.
6 *Race Questions and Other American Problems* (New York, 1908), p. 61.
7 *Ibid.*, p. 74.
8 Owsley, "The Historical Philosophy of Frederick Jackson Turner," *American Review*, V (Summer 1935), 370.
9 Vernon L. Parrington, *Main Currents in American Thought*, II (New York, 1927), v.
10 "Regionalism and Folk Art," *Southwest Review*, XIX (July 1934), 433.
11 *American Regionalism*, p. 171.
12 *Technics and Civilization* (New York, 1934), p. 292
13 *American Regionalism*, p. 175.
14 Agar, *Land of the Free*, pp. 135–36.
15 "A Sociologist in Eden," *American Review*, VIII (December 1936), 177–204.

16 *Southern Regions of the United States* (Chapel Hill, 1936), p. 253. The following page references are to the same source.
17 Odum and Moore, *American Regionalism*, p. 618.
18 *Ibid.*, p. 631.
19 Tate, *"Regionalism and Sectionalism,"* p. 160. The following quotations are from pp. 158–60 of the same article.
20 Davidson, *The Attack on Leviathan*, p. 408.
21 "Regionalism and Sectionalism," p. 159.
22 *Ibid.*, pp. 159–60.
23 "The Aesthetic of Regionalism," *American Review*, II (January 1934), 301. The following page references are to the same source.
24 "Some Don'ts for Literary Regionalists," *American Review*, VIII (December 1936), 146.
25 "Characters and Character," *American Review*, VI (January 1936), 146.
26 Fishman, *The Disinherited of Art*, p. 84.
27 "Some Don'ts for Literary Regionalists," p. 150.
28 Austin Warren, quoted by Odum in *American Regionalism*, p. 182.
29 "Literature as a Symptom," *Who Owns America?*, p. 271.
30 *Ibid.*, p. 273.
31 *Ibid.*, p. 270.
32 "Some Recent Novels," *Southern Review*, I (Winter 1936), 624.
33 Warren, "Literature as a Symptom," p. 276.
34 *Ibid.*, p. 278.
35 *Saturday Review of Literature*, XVI (June 12, 1937), 3.
36 "Regionalism and Nationalism in American Literature," *American Review*, V (April 1935), 53.
37 *The Attack on Leviathan*, p. 81.
38 *Ibid.*, p. 84
39 *Ibid.*, p. 85.
40 *Ibid.*, p. 86.
41 New York and London, 1935, p. 9.
42 *The Attack on Leviathan*, p. 126.
43 *Ibid.*
44 *Ibid.*, p. 86.

CHAPTER VII

1 *I'll Take My Stand*, pp. xi–xii.
2 *Ibid.*
3 "A Critique of the Philosophy of Progress," *I'll Take My Stand*, p. 122.
4 *The Idea of Progress* (London, 1920), p. 7.
5 *Ibid.*, p. 323.
6 For a full discussion of this topic see Frederick Stocking, "Poetry as Knowledge: The Critical Theories of John Crowe Ransom and Allen Tate," unpublished dissertation, University of Michigan, 1946.
7 Tate, "Literature as Knowledge," *The Man of Letters in the Modern World* (New York, 1955), p. 52. This essay also appeared in Tate's *On the Limits of Poetry* (New York, 1948).

8   "John Crowe Ransom: A Study in Irony," *Virginia Quarterly Review*, II (January 1935), 94.
9   *God Without Thunder*, p. 190.
10 "Tiresias," *The Nation*, CXXIII (November 17, 1926), 509.
11 Tate, "The Revolt Against Literature," New Republic, XLIX (February 9, 1927), 330. The following page references are to the same source.
12 *Ibid.*, p. 329.
13 *Ibid.*
14 "Poetry and the Absolute," *Sewanee Review*, XXXV (January 1927), 47–48.
15 "Critical Responsibility," *New Republic*, LI (August 17, 1927), 340.
16 "A Philosophical Critic," *New Republic*, XLVI (April 21, 1926), 281
17 "The Present Function of Criticism," *On the Limits of Poetry* (New York, 1948), p. 9.
18 "A Defense of Order," *New Republic*, LIV (May 16, 1928), 281.
19 "Poetry in the Laboratory," *New Republic*, LXI (December 18, 1929), 112.
20 Tate, "The Bi-Millennium of Virgil," *New Republic*, LXIV (October 29, 1930), 298.
21 "Taste and Dr. Johnson," *New Republic*, LXVIII (August 19, 1931), 24.
22 *Ibid.*, p. 23
23 "Flux and Blur in Contemporary Art," *Sewanee Review*, XXXVII (July-September 1929), 362–63.
24 "Poetry: A Note on Ontology," *American Review*, III (May 1934), 193–94.
25 *Southern Review*, IV (Summer 1938), 104.
26 "Edith Rickert: On the Sublime," *New Republic*, L (April 27, 1927), 281.
27 J. W. N. Sullivan, "Art and Reality," *The New Criticism*, ed. Edwin Berry Burgum (New York, 1930), p. 190.
28 "Friction of Powder-Puffs," *Sewanee Review*, XLVII (July 1940), 321.
29 Benedetto Croce, "Intuition and Art," *The New Criticism*, ed. Burgum, p. 47.
30 Aubrey Starke, "The Agrarians Deny a Leader," *American Review*, II (March 1934), 539.
31 *Ibid.*, p. 537.
32 "A Southern Romantic," *New Republic*, LXXVI (August 30, 1933), 70.
33 Ransom, "Hearts and Heads," *American Review*, II (March 1934), 568.
34 *Ibid.*, p. 567.
35 Warren, "The Blind Poet: Sidney Lanier," *American Review*, II (November 1933), 35.
36 *Ibid.*, p. 38.
37 *Ibid.*
38 Ransom, "Hearts and Heads," p. 567.
39 J. Atkins Shackford, "Sidney Lanier as Southerner," *Sewanee Review*, XLVIII (April-June 1940), 154.
40 "The Profession of Letters in the South," p. 146.
41 "T. S. Stribling," *The Nation*, CXXXVIII (June 20, 1934), 709.
42 *Ibid.*

43 Warren, "T. S. Stribling: a Paragraph in the History of Critical Realism," p. 464.
44 *Ibid.*, p. 465.
45 *Ibid.*, p. 476.
46 *Ibid.*, p. 483.
47 See William Elton, *A Guide to the New Criticism* (Chicago, 1951), p. 36.
48 *Reactionary Essays on Poetry and Ideas*, p. 83.
49 "The Mimetic Principle," *American Review*, V (October 1935), 536.
50 In *Invitation to Learning*, ed. Huntington Cairns (New York, 1941), p. 218.
51 *Reactionary Essays on Poetry and Ideas* (New York, 1936), p. 99. The following page references are to the same source.
52 Ransom, "The Tense of Poetry," *Southern Review*, I (Autumn 1935), 229.
53 *God Without Thunder*, p. 190.
54 Tate, *Reactionary Essays on Poetry and Ideas*, p. 85.
55 *Ibid.*, p. 103.
56 "Last Days of Alice," *Poems: 1922–1947* (New York, 1947), 116.
57 Davidson, *Still Rebels, Still Yankees* (Baton Rouge, 1957), p. 125.

CHAPTER VIII

1 *Poems About God* (New York, 1919), p. x.
2 *I'll Take My Stand*, p. xv.
3 "Reconstructed But Unregenerate," *I'll Take My Stand*, p. 16.
4 "Agrarianism For Commuters," *American Review*, I (May 1933), 241.
5 "Remarks on the Southern Religion," *I'll Take My Stand*, p. 157. The following page references are to the same source.
6 "John Crowe Ransom: A Checklist," *Sewanee Review*, LVI (Summer 1948), 445.
7 *Ibid.*
8 "The Critic and American Life," *Forum*, LXXIX (February 1928), 163.
9 *Ibid.*, p. 166.
10 *Democracy and Leadership* (Boston and New York, 1924), p. 20.
11 Babbitt, "Humanism: An Essay at Definition," in *Humanism and America*, ed. Norman Foerster (New York, 1930), p. 23.
12 *Democracy and Leadership*, p. 132.
13 *Ibid.*, p. 145.
14 *Ibid.*, p. 68.
15 "Humanism: An Essay at Definition," p. 34.
16 "The Plight of Our Arts," in *Humanism and America*, p. 117.
17 *Ibid.*, p. 119.
18 *Ibid.*, p. 121.
19 Paul Elmer More, "The Humility of Common Sense," in *Humanism and America*, p. 117.
20 *Bookman*, LXX (January 1930), 489–98.
21 "The Fallacy of Humanism," *Hound and Horn*, III (January-March 1930), 247.

22 *Ibid.*, p. 249.
23 *Ibid.*, p. 253.
24 "The Humanism of Irving Babbitt," *Forum*, LXXX (July 1928), 38.
25 *Ibid.*, p. 41.
26 "A Traditionalist Looks at Liberalism," *Southern Review*, I (Spring 1936), 735–36.
27 "The Fallacy of Humanism," p. 255.
28 "Fundamentalism," *The Nation*, CXXII (May 12, 1926), 532.
29 "The Fallacy of Humanism," p. 255.
30 *Points of View*, p. 151.
31 "Theological Homebrew," *Sewanee Review*, XXXIX (January-March 1931), 109.
32 "Swinging Round the Circle," *Saturday Review of Literature*, VII (February 28, 1931), 627.
33 *Criterion*, XI (October 1931), 131
34 Quoted in "Taste and Dr. Johnson," *New Republic*, LXVIII (August 19, 1931), 23.
35 "The Search for Trinity," *Virginia Quarterly Review*, VII (July 1931), 451.
36 Untitled review of *God Without Thunder*, *Bookman*, LXXIII (March 1931), 100.
37 *A History of the Warfare of Science with Theology in Christendom* (New York and London, 1910), pp. 318–19.
38 *Ibid.*, p. viii.
39 Mims, *The Advancing South*, p. 280.
40 *God Without Thunder*, p. 312.
41 *Ibid.*, p. 89.
42 *Ibid.*, p. 354.
43 *American Review*, I (September 1933), 457.
44 Norfolk, Connecticut, 1941, p. 205.
45 *God Without Thunder*, p. 5.
46 Tate, *Reactionary Essays on Poetry and Ideas*, p. 177.
47 "The Cathartic Principle," *American Review*, V (Summer 1935), 295.
48 "Agrarianism in Exile," p. 593.
49 *God Without Thunder*, p. 70. The following page references are to the same source.
50 *The Sacred Wood* (New York, 1921), p. 157.
51 "The Dilemma of Agrarianism," *Southwest Review*, XIX (April 1934), 230.
52 *God Without Thunder*, p. 92.
53 *Reactionary Essays on Poetry and Ideas*, p. 35.
54 *Ibid.*, p. 13.
55 *Ibid.*, p. 50.
56 "Beyond Imagism," *New Republic*, LIV (March 21, 1928), 165.
57 "The Poet and Tradition," *American Review*, I (September 1933), 346.
58 *The New Criticism*, p. 137.
59 *For Lancelot Andrewes* (Garden City, New York, 1929), p. vii.
60 "The Poet and Tradition," p. 456.

61 *God Without Thunder,* p. 134.
62 "Beyond Imagism," p. 101.
63 Tate, *The Fathers* (New York, 1936), pp. 218–19.
64 Warren, *The Cave* (New York, 1959).
65 "Baudelaire," *Selected Essays* (New York, 1950), pp. 378–79.
66 "Romanticism and Classicism," in *Critiques and Essays in Criticism,* p. 4.
67 "A Plea to the Protestant Churches," in *Who Owns America?,* p. 326.
68 *God Without Thunder,* p. 217.
69 "The Poet and Tradition," p. 459.
70 "Agrarianism in Exile," p. 605.
71 "A Plea to the Protestant Churches," p. 328.
72 *God Without Thunder,* p. 129
73 "Agrarianism in Exile," p. 606.
74 *Ibid.,* p. 590.
75 *In Defense of Ignorance* (New York, 1960). In particular, see the chapter entitled "W. B. Yeats: Trial by Culture," pp. 87–113.
76 "The Old South and the New," *American Review,* VI (January 1936), 476–77.
77 "Remarks on the Southern Religion," *I'll Take My Stand,* p. 166.
78 *Land of the Free,* p. 33.
79 *God Without Thunder,* p. 357.

CHAPTER IX

1 "Agrarianism: An Autopsy," *Sewanee Review,* XLIX (April-June 1941), 161.
2 *Ibid.,* p. 158.
3 "Modern with the Southern Accent," *Virginia Quarterly Review,* XI (April 1935), 185. The original Agrarians included in this issue were Tate, Lytle, Wade, Young, Warren, and Ransom.
4 *Ibid.,* p. 186.
5 *Ibid.,* p. 200.
6 Pressley, "Agrarianism: An Autopsy," p. 161.
7 "The South Astir," *Virginia Quarterly Review,* XI (January 1935), 55.
8 *Ibid.,* p. 58.
9 *Ibid.,* p. 53.
10 Chapel Hill, 1935, p. 49.
11 *Culture in the South,* p. vii.
12 "A View of the Whole South," *American Review,* II (February 1934), 415.
13 See *Who's Who in America,* 1944–45, XXIII, 411, for a biographical sketch of Seward Bishop Collins.
14 *American Review,* III (April 1934), 124.
15 "Editorial Notes," *American Review,* I (April 1933), 127.
16 An advertisement for "The American Review Book Shop" on the back cover of the September, 1937, issue offered "A number of the latest books on Nationalist Spain: *A Nation on the March* by Harold Cardozo; *Span-*

ish Rehearsal by Arnold Lunn: *Correspondent in Spain* by E. Knob-laugh; *Heroes of Alcazar* by R. Rimmermans; *The Seige of Alcazar* by H. R. Knickerbocker. . . ."

17 *New Republic,* LXXXVII (May 27, 1936), 75.
18 "Count Your Dead: They are Alive!" *American Review,* IX (Summer 1937), 269.
19 "The Bankruptcy of Southern Culture," *Scribner's,* XCIX (May 1936), 298.
20 *Scribner's,* XCIX (May 1936), 294–98.
21 "Jeeter Lester," *Sewanee Review,* XLVIII (January-March 1940), 22.
22 "American Poetry, 1920–1940," *Sewanee Review,* LV (Winter 1947), 39–40.
23 "Modern Poets and Convention," *American Review,* VIII (February 1937), 429.
24 Tate, *Reactionary Essays on Poetry and Ideas,* p. 163.
25 "Modern Poets and Convention," pp. 429–30.
26 *The World's Body,* p. 432.
27 "What is a Traditional Society?" *American Review,* VIII (September 1936), 377.
28 *Ibid.,* pp. 377–78.
29 "A Traditionalist Looks at Liberalism," *Southern Review,* I (Spring 1936), 741.
30 *Poetry,* XL (May 1932), 92.
31 *Ibid.,* p. 96.
32 "The Profession of Letters in the South," *Reactionary Essays on Poetry and Ideas,* p. 148. The following page references are to the same essay.
33 "A Capital for the New Deal," *American Review,* II (December 1933), 136.
34 *Ibid.,* pp. 137–38.
35 "Agrarianism: An Autopsy," p. 162.
36 *Sewanee Review,* XLV (July-September 1937), 287.
37 *Ibid.,* p. 290.
38 "Agrarianism in Exile," pp. 597–98.
39 *Ibid.,* p. 599
40 "I'll Take My Stand: A History," *American Review,* V (Summer 1935), 308.
41 "Agrarianism in Exile," p. 596.

CHAPTER X

1 *The Lasting South,* eds. Louis D. Rubin and James Jackson Kilpatrick (Chicago, 1957), p. ix.
2 *Southern Tradition and Regional Progress* (Chapel Hill, 1960), p. x.
3 *Ibid.,* p. 8.
4 *Ibid.,* p. 33.
5 "Forum on the New Criticism," *American Scholar,* XX (Winter 1950–1951), 88.

6   *The World's Body* (New York, 1938), pp. 328–30.
7   Quoted by Elton, *A Guide to the New Criticism* (Chicago, 1951), p. 39.
8   "Two Orders of Knowledge," *New Republic*, LXXIV (May 10, 1939), 23.
9   *Understanding Poetry* (New York, 1938), p. iv.
10 *Ibid.*, p. ix.
11 "The New Critics," *Critiques and Essays in Criticism* (New York, 1949), p. 496.
12 *In Defense of Reason* (New York, 1947), p. 564.
13 Another journal that published the Agrarians as individuals was *Review of Politics,* sponsored by the University of Notre Dame.
14 "The Present Function of Criticism," *Southern Review,* VI (Autumn 1940), 236. The following page references are also to this article.
15 These quotations are taken from "Strategy for English Studies," *Southern Review,* VI (Autumn 1940), 226–35.
16 "Criticism as Pure Speculation," in *The Intent of the Critic,* ed. Donald A. Stauffer (Princeton, 1941), pp. 101-2.
17 Elton, *A Guide to the New Criticism,* p. 2.
18 "The New Critics," p. 489.
19 *Ibid.*
20 *Ibid.*
21 *Ibid.*, p. 490
22 Some of Tate's favorite essays kept reappearing in his later books.
23 "Hardy's Philosophic Metaphors," *Southern Review,* VI (Summer 1940), 101.
24 *The Disinherited of Art,* p. 95.
25 *The Fugitives,* p. 102.
26 "Conrad Aiken's Poetry," *The Nation,* CXXII (January 13, 1926), 39.
27 "Good Prose," *The Nation,* CXXII (February 10, 1926), 160.
28 "Distinguished Minor Poetry," *The Nation,* CXXII (March 3, 1926), 237.
29 "Complex Melancholy," *The Nation,* CXXII (April 14, 1926), 418.
30 "A Poetry of Ideas," *New Republic,* XLVII (June 30, 1926), 173.
31 "The Spirituality of Roughnecks," *The Nation,* CXXIII (July 28, 1926), 90.
32 "Tiresias," *The Nation,* CXXIII (November 17, 1926), 509.
33 "A New English Critic," *New Republic,* LXX (March 16, 1932), 133.
34 "Gregory's New Poems," *New Republic,* LXXIV (April 12, 1933), 255.
35 "A Southern Romantic," p. 67.
36 *Ibid.*, p. 70.
37 "Poetry and Politics," *New Republic,* LXXV (August 2, 1933), 310.
38 "John Bishop's Poems," *New Republic,* LXXVII (February 21, 1934), 52.
39 See Tate's essay "Tension in Poetry," *Southern Review,* IV (Summer 1938), 101–15.
40 "Poetry and the Absolute," p. 46.
41 *Ibid.*, p. 52.
42 Ransom, "Classical and Romantic," *Saturday Review of Literature,* VI (September 14, 1929), 127.
43 Spingarn, "The New Criticism," in *The New Criticism,* ed. Burgum, p. 10.

44 *Ibid.,* p. 22.
45 Quoted by Elton, *A Guide to the New Criticism,* p. 35.
46 *Ibid.,* p. 39
47 *American Review,* I (September 1933), 446–47.
48 *Yale Review,* XXIV (Autumn 1934), 505.
49 "The New Criticism," p. 18.
50 "The Artist and Psycho-Analysis," *The New Criticism,* ed. Burgum, p. 198.
51 Tate, "Note on Bishop's Poetry," *Southern Review,* I (Autumn 1935), 361.
52 *Ibid.,* p. 360.
53 *Ibid.,* p. 359.
54 *Ibid.*
55 Tate, "Critical Responsibility," *New Republic,* LI (August 17, 1927), 340.
56 "The New Critics," p. 499.
57 "Poetry: A Note on Ontology," *American Review,* III (May 1934), 189.
58 *Ibid.,* p. 190.
59 Quoted by Elton, *A Guide to the New Criticism,* p. 40
60 *Ibid.,* p. 10
61 *The New Criticism,* p. 280.
62 *Ibid.,* p. 281.
63 "The New Criticism and the Democratic Tradition," *American Scholar,* XIX (Winter 1950–51), p. 10.
64 *Ibid.*

Selected Bibliography

MAJOR AGRARIAN SOURCES

DONALD DAVIDSON

"The Artist as Southerner," *Saturday Review of Literature*, II (May 15, 1926), 781–83.
"First Fruits of Dayton," *Forum*, LXXXIX (June 1928), 896–907.
"A Mirror for Artists," *I'll Take My Stand*, ed. Twelve Southerners, pp. 28–60.
"Criticism Outside New York," *Bookman*, LXXIII (May 1931), 247–56.
"The Rise of the American City," *American Review*, I (April 1933), 100–104.
"Agrarianism For Commuters," *American Review*, I (May 1933), 238–42.
"Dilemma of the Southern Liberals," *American Mercury*, XXXI (February 1934), 227–35.
"Lands That Were Golden," *American Review*, III (October 1934), 545–61.
"The Trend of Literature," *Culture in the South*, ed. W. T. Couch, pp. 183–210.
"Regionalism and Education," *American Review*, IV (January 1935), 310–25.
"The Returning Frontier," *American Review*, IV (March 1935), 622–27.
"The First Agrarian Economist," *American Review*, V (April 1935), 106–12.
"Regionalism and Nationalism in American Literature," *American Review*, V (April 1935), 48–61.
"I'll Take My Stand: A History," *American Review*, V (Summer 1935), 301–21
"A Note on American Heroes," *Southern Review*, I (Winter 1936), 436–48.
"A Sociologist in Eden," *American Review*, VIII (December 1936), 177–204.
"Howard Odum and the Sociological Proteus," *American Review*, VIII (February 1937), 385–417.
"Gulliver With Hay Fever," *American Review*, IX (Summer 1937), 152–72.
"Where Are the Laymen?" *American Review*, IX (October 1937), 456–81.
The Attack on Leviathan. Chapel Hill: University of North Carolina Press, 1938.
"The Traditional Basis of Thomas Hardy's Fiction," *Southern Review*, VI (Summer 1940), 162–78.
Lee in the Mountain. New York: Charles Scribner's Sons, 1949.
"Theme and Method in *So Red the Rose*," *Southern Renascence*, eds. Louis D. Rubin and Robert D. Jacobs, pp. 262–77.
Still Rebels, Still Yankees. Baton Rouge: Louisiana State University Press, 1957.

JOHN CROWE RANSOM

Poems About God. New York: Henry Holt & Co., 1919.
"Waste Lands," *Literary Review,* III (July 14, 1923), 825–26.
"The Poet Laureate," *Literary Review,* IV (March 29, 1924), 625–26.
Grace After Meat. London: Hogarth, 1924.
Chills and Fever. New York: Alfred A. Knopf, 1924.
"A Man Without a Country," *Sewanee Review,* XXXIII (July 1925), 301–307.
"The Poetic Discontent," *The Calendar of Modern Letters,* I (August 1925), 461–63.
"Freud and Literature," *Saturday Review of Literature,* I (October 4, 1924), 161–62.
Two Gentlemen in Bonds. New York: Alfred A. Knopf, 1927.
"The Poet and the Critic," *New Republic,* LI (June 22, 1927), 125–26.
"The South—Old or New?" *Sewanee Review,* XXXVI (April 1928), 139–47.
"The South Defends Its Heritage," *Harper's,* CLIX (June 1929), 108–18.
"Flux and Blur in Contemporary Art," *Sewanee Review,* XXXVII (July 1929), 353–66.
"Classical and Romantic," *Saturday Review of Literature,* VI (September 1929), 125–27.
"Reconstructed But Unregenerate," *I'll Take My Stand,* eds. Twelve Southerners, pp. 1–27.
God Without Thunder. New York: Harcourt, Brace & Co., 1930.
"The Realm of Matter," *New Republic,* LXIV (October 22, 1930), 262–63.
"The State and the Land," *New Republic,* LXXI (February 17, 1932), 8–10.
"Land!" *Harper's,* CLXV (July 1932), 216–24.
"The Poet and Tradition," *American Review,* I (May 1933), 179–203.
"A Poem Nearly Anonymous," *American Review,* I (September 1933), 444–67.
"Happy Farmers," *American Review,* I (October 1933), 513–35.
"A Capital For the New Deal," *American Review,* II (December 1933), 129–42.
"The Aesthetic of Regionalism," *American Review,* II (January 1934), 290–310.
"Hearts and Heads," *American Review,* II (March 1934), 554–71.
"Poetry: A Note on Ontology," *American Review,* III (May 1934), 172–200.
"Poets Without Laurels," *Yale Review,* XXIV (Autumn 1934), 503–18.
"Sociology and the Black Belt," *American Review,* IV (December 1934), 147–54.
Topics for Freshman Writing. New York: Henry Holt & Co., 1935.
"Modern With the Southern Accent," *Virginia Quarterly Review,* II (April 1935), 184–200.
"Mr. Pound and the Broken Tradition," *Saturday Review of Literature,* XI (January 19, 1935), 434–35.
"The Cathartic Principle," *American Review,* V (Summer 1935), 287–300.
"The Mimetic Principle," *American Review,* V (October 1935), 536–51.
"The Psychologist Looks at Poetry," *Virginia Quarterly Review,* II (October 1935), 575–92.
"The Tense of Poetry," *Southern Review,* I (Autumn 1935), 221–38.

"Characters and Character," *American Review*, VI (January 1936), 271–88.

"The Making of a Modern: The Poetry of George Marion O'Donnell," *Southern Review*, I (Spring 1936), 864–74.

"What Does the South Want?" *Virginia Quarterly Review*, XII (April 1936), 180–94.

"The South is a Bulwark," *Scribner's*, V (May 1936), 294–98.

"The Content of the Novel: Notes Toward a Critique of Fiction," *American Review*, VII (Summer 1936), 301–18.

"Contemporaneous Not Contemporary," *Southern Review*, II (Autumn 1936), 399–418.

"A Cathedralist Looks at Murder," *Southern Review*, I (Winter 1936), 609–623.

"Sentimental Exercise," *Yale Review*, XXVI (December 1936), 353–68.

"The Poet as Woman," *Southern Review*, II (Spring 1937), 783–88.

"Shall We Complete the Trade?" *Sewanee Review*, XLV (April 1937), 182–90.

"Art and Mr. Santayana," *Virginia Quarterly Review*, XIII (Summer 1937), 420–36.

"Criticism, Inc." *Virginia Quarterly Review*, XII (Autumn 1937), 586–602.

The World's Body. New York and London: Charles Scribner's Sons, 1938.

"Mr. Empson's Muddles," *Southern Review*, IV (Autumn 1938), 322–39.

"Yeats and His Symbols," *Kenyon Review*, I (Summer 1939), 309–22.

"The Aesthetic of Finnegan's Wake," *Kenyon Review*, I (Autumn 1939), 424–28.

"The Teaching of Poetry," *Kenyon Review*, I (Winter 1939), 81–83.

"Mr. Tate and the Professors," *Kenyon Review*, II (Summer 1940), 348–350.

"Old Age of a Poet," *Kenyon Review*, II (Summer 1940), 345–47.

"Strategy for English Studies," *Southern Review*, VI (Autumn 1940), 226–35.

The New Criticism. Norfolk, Conn.: New Directions, 1941.

"Criticism as Pure Speculation," *The Intent of the Critic*. ed. Donald A. Stauffer. pp. 91–124.

The Kenyon Critics. ed. John Crowe Ransom. Cleveland and New York: The World Publishing Co., 1951.

ALLEN TATE

"In the Classical Tradition," *Guardian*, I (November 1924), 25.

"The Persistent Illusion," *The Nation*, CXIX (November 19, 1924), 549.

"Last Days of the Charming Lady," *The Nation*, CXXI (October 28, 1925), 485–86.

"Conrad Aiken's Poetry," *The Nation*, CXXII (January 13, 1926), 38–39.

"Good Prose," *The Nation*, CXXII (February 10, 1926), 160–61.

"Distinguished Minor Poetry," *The Nation*, CXXII (March 3, 1926), 237–38.

"Complex Melancholy," *The Nation*, CXXII (April 14, 1926), 416–18.

"A Philosophical Critic," *New Republic*, XLVI (April 21, 1926), 594.

"Fundamentalism," *The Nation*, LXXII (May 12, 1926), 532–33.

"A Poetry of Ideas," *New Republic*, XLVII (June 30, 1926), 172–73.

"Literary Criticism in America," *New Republic*, XLVII (July 28, 1926), 283.

"The Spirituality of Roughnecks," *The Nation*, CXXIII (July 28, 1926), 89–90.

"Tiresias," *The Nation*, CXXIII (November 17, 1926), 509.

"The Revolt Against Literature," *New Republic*, XLIX (February 9, 1927), 329–30.

"Toward Objectivity," *The Nation*, CXXIII (February 16, 1927), 185–86.

"The Eighteenth-Century South," *The Nation*, CXXIV (March 30, 1927), 346.

"Poetry and the Absolute," *Sewanee Review*, XXXV (January 1927), 41–52.

"Edith Rickert: On the Sublime," *New Republic*, L (April 27, 1927), 281–82.

"Critical Responsibility," *New Republic*, LI (August 17, 1927), 339–40.

Stonewall Jackson: The Good Soldier. New York: Minton, Balch & Co., 1928.

"Beyond Imagism," *New Republic*, LIV (March 21, 1928), 165–66.

"A Defense of Order," *New Republic*, LIV (May 16, 1928), 395–96.

"Lincoln? Lee?" *New Republic*, LV (June 6, 1928), 75–76.

"The Presidents' Wives," *New Republic*, LX (June 20, 1928), 127.

"The Irrepressible Conflict," *The Nation*, CXXVII (September 19, 1928), 274.

"Mr. More, the Demon," *New Republic*, LVII (December 12, 1928), 116–17.

Jefferson Davis: His Rise and Fall. New York: G. P. Putnam's Sons, 1929.

"American Poetry Since 1920," *Bookman*, LXVIII (January 1929), 503–08.

"Life in the Old South," *New Republic*, LIX (July 10, 1929), 211–12.

"The Fallacy of Humanism," *Criterion*, VIII (July 1929), 661–81; and *Hound and Horn*, III (January-March 1930), 234–58.

"Poetry in the Laboratory," *New Republic*, LXI (December 18, 1929), 111–13.

"Remarks on the Southern Religion," *I'll Take My Stand*, eds. Twelve Southerners, pp. 155–75.

"Mr. Cabell's Farewell," *New Republic*, LXI (January 8, 1930), 201–202.

"The Same Fallacy of Humanism," *Bookman*, LXXI (March 1930), 31–36.

"A Distinguished Poet," *Hound and Horn*, III (July-September 1930), 580–85.

"The Lost Poet of Georgia," *New Republic*, LXIII (July 23, 1930), 294–95.

"More About the Reconstruction," *New Republic*, LXIII (August 13, 1930), 376–77.

"The Bi-Millennium of Virgil," *New Republic*, LXIV (October 29, 1930), 296–98.

"Ezra Pound's Golden Ass," *The Nation*, CXXXII (June 10, 1931), 632–34.

"Taste and Dr. Johnson," *New Republic*, LXVIII (August 19, 1931), 23–24.

"Regionalism and Sectionalism," *New Republic*, LXIX (December 23, 1931), 158–61.

"A New English Critic," *New Republic*, LXX (March 16, 1932), 89–90.

"Editorial Note," *Poetry*, XL (May 1932), 90–94.

"In Memoriam: Hart Crane," *Hound and Horn*, V (July 1932), 612–19.

"Hart Crane and the American Mind," *Poetry*, XL (July 1932), 210–16.

"Gregory's New Poems," *New Republic*, LXXIV (April 12, 1933), 255–56.

"The Problem of the Unemployed," *American Review*, I (May 1933), 129–49.

"Poetry and Politics," *New Republic*, LXXV (August 2, 1933), 180–82.

"Where Are the People?" *American Review*, II (December 1933), 231–37.

"A Southern Romantic," *New Republic*, LXXVI (August 30, 1933), 67–70.

"A View of the Whole South," *American Review*, II (February 1934), 411–32.

"John Bishop's Poems," *New Republic*, LXXVII (February 21, 1934), 52–53.

"Spengler's Tract Against Liberalism," *American Review*, III (April 1934), 41–47.

"Poetry Supplement," ed. Allen Tate, *American Review*, III (May 1934), 171–265.

"T. S. Stribling," *The Nation*, CXXXVIII (June 30, 1934), 709–10.

"The Profession of Letters in the South," *Virginia Quarterly Review*, XI (April 1935), 161–76.

"A Note on Bishop's Poetry," *Southern Review*, I (Autumn 1935), 357–64.

"The Function of the Critical Quarterly," *Southern Review*, I (Winter 1936), 551–59.

"Notes on Liberty and Property," *American Review*, VI (March 1936), 596–611.

"A Traditionalist Looks at Liberalism," *Southern Review*, I (Spring 1936), 731–44.

The Fathers. New York: G. P. Putnam's Sons, 1936.

Reactionary Essays on Poetry and Ideas. New York: Charles Scribner's Sons, 1936.

Who Owns America? ed. with Herbert Agar. Boston: Houghton Mifflin Co., 1936.

Letter, *New Republic*, LXXXVII (May 27, 1936), 75.

"Mr. Burke and the Historical Environment," *Southern Review*, I (Autumn 1936), 363–62.

"Modern Poets and Convention," *American Review*, VIII (February 1937), 427–35.

"What Is a Traditional Society?" *American Review*, VIII (September 1936), 376–87.

"R. P. Blackmur and Others," *Southern Review*, III (Summer 1937), 183–98.

"Tension in Poetry," *Southern Review*, IV (Summer 1938), 101–15.

America Through the Essay. ed. with A. Theodore Johnson, New York: Oxford University Press, 1938.

"Narcissus as Narcissus," *Virginia Quarterly Review*, XIV (Winter 1938), 108–122.

"Two Orders of Knowledge," *New Republic*, LXXXIV (May 10, 1939), 23.

"Hardy's Philosophic Metaphors," *Southern Review*, VI (Summer 1940), 99–108.

"The Present Function of Criticism," *Southern Review*, VI (Autumn 1940), 236–46.

"Yeats's Last Friendship," *New Republic*, CIII (November 25, 1940), 730–32.

Reason in Madness. New York: G. P. Putnam's Sons, 1941.

A Southern Vanguard. ed. Allen Tate. New York: Prentice-Hall, Inc., 1947.

Poems, 1922–1947. New York: Charles Scribner's Sons, 1948.

On the Limits of Poetry. New York: The Swallow Press and William Morrow & Co., 1948.

"The Question of the Pound Award," *Partisan Review*, XVI (May 1949), 512–22.

The Forlorn Demon. Chicago: Henry Regnery, 1953.

The Man of Letters in the Modern World. New York: The Noonday Press, 1955.

ROBERT PENN WARREN

John Brown. New York: Payson & Clarke Ltd., 1929.

"The Briar Patch," *I'll Take My Stand,* eds. Twelve Southerners, pp. 246–64.

"The Blind Poet: Sidney Lanier," *American Review,* II (November 1933), 27–45.

"T. S. Stribling: A Paragraph in the History of Critical Realism," *American Review,* II (February 1934), 463–86.

"John Crowe Ransom: A Study in Irony," *Virginia Quarterly Review,* II (January 1935), 93–112.

"A Note on the Hamlet of Thomas Wolfe," *American Review,* V (May 1935), 191–208.

"Some Recent Novels," *Southern Review,* I (Winter 1936), 624–49.

"Some Don'ts For Literary Regionalists," *American Review,* VIII (December 1936), 142–50.

"Literature as a Symptom," *Who Owns America?* eds. Allen Tate and Herbert Agar. Boston: Houghton Mifflin Co., 1936.

Understanding Poetry. ed. with Cleanth Brooks, Jr. New York: Henry Holt, & Co. 1938.

Night Rider. Boston: Houghton Mifflin Co., 1939.

Selected Poems, 1923–1943. New York: Harcourt, Brace & Co., 1944.

All the King's Men. New York: Harcourt, Brace & Co., 1946.

World Enough and Time. New York; Random House, 1950.

The Cave. New York: Ransom House, 1959.

OTHER AGRARIAN SOURCES

Brooks, Cleanth, Jr. "A Note on Symbol and Conceit," *American Review,* III (May 1934), 201–211.

———. "The Modern Southern Poet and Tradition," *Virginia Quarterly Review,* XI (April 1935), 305–20.

———. "The Christianity of Modernism," *American Review,* VI (February 1936), 435–46.

———. *Understanding Poetry,* ed. with Robert Penn Warren. New York: Henry Holt & Co. 1938.

———. *Modern Poetry and the Tradition.* Chapel Hill, N. C.: University of North Carolina Press, 1939.

Cauley, Troy Jesse. *Agrarianism: A Program for Farmers.* Chapel Hill, N.C.: University of North Carolina Press, 1935.

———. "The Integration of Agrarian and Exchange Economies," *American Review,* V (October 1935), 584–602.

Fletcher, John Gould. "Education, Past and Present," *I'll Take My Stand,* eds. Twelve Southerners. New York: Harper & Bros., 1930.

———. Review of John Crowe Ransom's *God Without Thunder, Criterion,* XI (October 1931), 127–31.

———. "Section Versus State," *American Review,* I (September 1933), 483–89.

———. "Regionalism and Folk Art," *Southwest Review,* XIX (July 1934), 429–34.

———. "A Century of Progress," *American Review,* IV (January 1935), 377–84.

———. "Ruskin," *American Review*, IV (February 1935), 504–12.

———. "The Stieglitz Spoof," *American Review*, IV (March 1935), 588–602.

———. "An Aesthetic Humanist," *American Review*, V (May 1935), 238–42.

———. "A Stone of Stumbling," *American Review*, V (Summer 1935), 379–84.

———. *Life is My Song*. New York: Farrar & Rinehart, 1937.

Fugitives: An Anthology of Verse. New York: Harcourt, Brace & Co., 1928.

I'll Take My Stand, eds. Twelve Southerners. New York: Harper & Bros., 1930.

Lanier, Lyle H. "A Critique of the Philosophy of Progress," *I'll Take My Stand*, eds. Twelve Southerners. New York: Harper Bros., 1930.

Lytle, Andrew Nelson. "The Hind Tit," *I'll Take My Stand*, eds. Twelve Southerners. New York: Harper & Bros., 1930.

———. *Bedford Forrest and His Critter Company*. New York: Minton, Balch & Co., 1931.

———. *The Long Night*. Indianapolis, New York: Bobbs-Merrill Co., 1936.

Nixon, Herman Clarence. "Whither Southern Economy?" *I'll Take My Stand*, eds. Twelve Southerners, New York: Harper & Bros., 1930.

———. "Colleges and Universities," *Culture in the South*, ed. Couch. Chapel Hill, N.C.: University of North Carolina Press, 1935.

Owsley, Frank Lawrence. *State Rights in the Confederacy*. Chicago: University of Chicago Press, 1925.

———. "The Irrepressible Conflict," *I'll Take My Stand*, eds. Twelve Southerners. New York: Harper & Bros., 1930.

———. *King Cotton Diplomacy*. Chicago: University of Chicago Press, 1931.

———. "Scottsboro, The Third Crusade," *American Review*, I (Summer 1933), 257–85.

———. "The Pillars of Agrarianism," *American Review*, IV (March 1935), 529–47.

———. "The Historical Philosophy of Frederick Jackson Turner," *American Review*, V (Summer 1935), 368–75.

———. "The Old South and the New," *American Review*, VI (February 1936), 475–85.

———. *Plain Folk of the Old South*. Baton Rouge: Louisiana State University Press, 1949.

"A Statement of Principles," *I'll Take My Stand*, eds. Twelve Southerners. New York: Harper & Bros., 1930.

Young, Stark. "Not in Memoriam, But in Defense," *I'll Take My Stand*, eds. Twelve Southerners. New York: Harper & Bros., 1930.

———. *So Red the Rose*. New York: Charles Scribner's Sons, 1934.

———. "Strange Shade," *New Republic*, LXXXIII (June 19, 1935), 170.

SECONDARY SOURCES

Agar, Herbert. *Land of the Free*. Boston: Houghton Mifflin Co., 1935.

———. "John Strachey, Marx, and the Distributist Ideal," *American Review*, V (May 1935), 168–84.

———. "Culture Versus Colonialism in America," *Southern Review*, I (July 1935), 1–19.

Allen, James S. *Reconstruction*. New York: International Publishers, 1937.

Allen, W. E. D. "The Fascist Idea in Britain," *American Review*, II (January 1934), 328–49.

American Heritage. eds. Leon Howard, Louis B. Wright, and Carl Bode. Vol. II. Boston: D. C. Heath & Co., 1955.

Anderson, Charles R. "Violence and Order in the Novels of Robert Penn Warren," *Southern Renascence*, eds. Louis D. Rubin and Robert D. Jacobs. Baltimore: The Johns Hopkins Press, 1953.

Anderson, Sherwood. *Memoirs*. New York: Harcourt, Brace & Co., 1942.

Aptheker, Herbert. *Essays in the History of the American Negro*. New York: International Publishers, 1945.

Arnold, Willard Burdett. *The Social Ideas of Allen Tate*. Boston: Bruce Humphries, Inc., 1955.

Ayres, C. E. *Science the False Messiah*. Indianapolis: Bobbs-Merrill Co., 1927.

Babbitt, Irving. *Rousseau and Romanticism*. Boston and New York: Houghton Mifflin Co., 1919.

————. *Democracy and Leadership*. Boston and New York: Houghton Mifflin Co., 1924.

————. "The Critic and American Life," *Forum*, LXXIX (February 1928), 161–76.

————. "Humanism: An Essay at Definition," *Humanism and America*, ed. Foerster.

Baker, Joseph E. "Regionalism in the Middle West," *American Review*, IV (March 1935), 603–14.

————. "Four Arguments For Regionalism," *Saturday Review of Literature*, XV (November 28, 1936), 3–4, 14.

Barr, Stringfellow. "Shall Slavery Come South?" *Virginia Quarterly Review*, VI (October 1930), 481–94.

————. "No North, No South!" *The Nation*, CXXXII (January 21, 1931), 67–68.

Basso, Hamilton. "Letters in the South," *New Republic*, LXXXIII (June 19, 1935), 161–63.

Bates, Ernest Sutherland. "Swinging Round the Circle," *Saturday Review of Literature*, VII (February 28, 1931), 627.

Beath, Paul Robert. "Four Fallacies of Regionalism," *Saturday Review of Literature*, XV (November 28, 1936), 3–4, 14, 16.

Beatty, Richard C. "Donald Davidson as Fugitive-Agrarian," *Southern Renascence*, eds. Louis D. Rubin and Robert D. Jacobs. Baltimore: The Johns Hopkins Press, 1953.

Belloc, Hilaire. *The Servile State*. London: Constable & Co. Ltd., 1950.

————. "The Restoration of Property," *American Review*, I (April 1933), 1-16; (May 1933), 204–19; (Summer 1933), 344–57; (September 1933), 468–82; (October 1933), 600–609; (November 1933), 46–57.

————. *The Restoration of Property*. New York: Sheed & Ward, 1936.

Black, John D. *Agricultural Reform in the United States*. New York: McGraw-Hill, 1929.

Blackmur, R. P. "In Our Ends Are Our Beginnings," *Virginia Quarterly Review*, XIV (Summer 1938), 446–50.

Bliven, Bruce. "Away Down South," *New Republic*, L (May 4, 1927), 269–98.

Botkin, Benjamin. *Folk-say, a Regional Miscellany.* Norman: University of Oklahoma Press, 1929.

Bowers, Claude G. *The Tragic Era.* Boston: Houghton Mifflin & Co., 1929.

Bradbury, John M. *The Fugitives.* Chapel Hill, N.C.: University of North Carolina Press, 1958.

Brickell, Herschel. "The Literary Awakening in the South," *Bookman,* LXVI (October 1927), 138–43.

Brinton, Crane. "Who Owns America?" *Southern Review,* II (Summer 1936), 15–21.

Buchanan, Scott. "The Search for Trinity," *Virginia Quarterly Review,* VII (July 1931), 451–57.

Burgum, Edwin Berry, ed. *The New Criticism.* New York: Prentice-Hall, Inc., 1930.

Burns, Aubrey. "Culture in California. Regionalism on the West Coast," *Southwest Review,* XVII (Summer 1932), 373–94.

Bury, J. B. *The Idea of Progress.* London: Macmillan & Co., 1920.

Cairns, Huntington, ed. *Invitation to Learning.* New York: Random House, 1941.

Calverton, V. F. "The Bankruptcy of Southern Culture," *Scribners,* XCIX (May 1936), 294–98.

Canby, Henry Seidel. "A Prospectus for Criticism," *Saturday Review of Literature,* XVIII (May 21, 1938), 8–9.

Carlson, Oliver. "The Southern Worker Organizes," *The Nation,* CXXXIX (September 26, 1934), 353–55.

Carmichael, Peter A. "Jeeter Lester," *Sewanee Review,* XLVIII (March 1940), 21–29.

Cash, W. J. "The Mind of the South," *American Mercury,* XVIII (October 1929), 185–92.

———. *The Mind of the South.* New York: Alfred A. Knopf, 1941.

Cason, Clarence E. "Retreat From the Southern Mills," *Southwest Review,* XVIII (Winter 1933), 97–107.

———. *90° in the Shade.* Chapel Hill, N.C.: University of North Carolina Press, 1935.

Chase, Richard. *Quest For Myth.* Baton Rouge: Louisiana State University Press, 1949.

Collins, Seward. "Editorial Notes," *American Review,* I (April 1933), 122–27.

———. "Editorial Notes," *American Review,* I (April 1934), 118–28.

———. "Three Important Books," *American Review,* VII (October 1936), 601–04.

———. "Count Your Dead: They Are Alive!" *American Review,* IX (Summer 1937), 266–95.

"Contributors," *New Republic,* LXIII (August 13, 1930), 379.

Couch, W. T., ed. *Culture in the South.* Chapel Hill, N.C.: The University of North Carolina Press, 1935.

———. "An Agrarian Programme for the South," *American Review,* III (Summer 1934), 313–26.

Cowan, Louise. *The Fugitive Group.* Baton Rouge: Louisiana State University Press, 1959.

Cowley, Malcolm. *Exile's Return*. New York: The Viking Press, 1934.
———. "A Game of Chess," *New Republic*, LXXXVI (April 29, 1936), 348–49.
———. In "Forum on the New Criticism," *American Scholar*, XX (Winter 1950–51), 86–104.
Crane, Ronald S. "History Versus Criticism in the University Study of Literature, *The English Journal*, XXIV (October 1935), 645–67.
Croce, Benedetto. "Intuition and Art," *The New Criticism*, ed. Edwin Berry Burgum. New York: Prentice-Hall, Inc., 1930.
Daniel, Robert. "Modern Poetry and the Tradition," *Sewanee Review*, XLVIII (July-September 1940), 419–24.
Davis, Robert Gorham. "The New Criticism and the Democratic Tradition," *American Scholar*, XIX (Winter 1949–50), 9–19.
———. In "Forum on the New Criticism," *American Scholar*, XX (Winter 1950–51), 86–104.
Dawson, Christopher. *The Making of Europe*. New York: Sheed & Ward, 1932.
DeBow, James D. B. *The Industrial Resources, etc., of the Southern and Western States*. New Orleans, New York: DeBow's Review, 1852–53.
Donahoe, Wade. "Allen Tate and the Idea of Culture," *Southern Renascence*, eds. Louis D. Rubin and Robert D. Jacobs. Baltimore: The Johns Hopkins Press, 1953.
DuBois, W. E. B. *The Souls of Black Folk*. Chicago: A. C. McClurg & Co., 1903.
———. *Black Reconstruction in America*. New York: Russell & Russell, 1935.
———. *Black Folk: Then and Now*. New York: Henry Holt & Co., 1939.
Eaton, Clement. *A History of the Old South*. New York: Macmillan Co., 1949.
Editorial. "The Boom in Regionalism," *Saturday Review of Literature*, X (April 7, 1934), 606.
Editorial Comment. *New Republic*, LXXXVII (May 27, 1936), 75–76.
Eliot, T. S. *The Sacred Wood*. New York: Alfred A. Knopf, 1921.
———. "The Humanism of Irving Babbitt," *Forum*, LXXX (July 1928), 37–44.
———. *For Lancelot Andrewes*. Garden City, N.Y.: Doubleday Dorn, 1929.
———. *The Use of Poetry and the Use of Criticism*. London: Faber & Faber Ltd., 1933.
———. "Tradition and Orthodoxy," *American Review*, II (March 1934), 513–28.
———. *The Idea of a Christian Society*. New York: Harcourt, Brace & Co., 1940.
———. *Points of View*. London: Faber & Faber Ltd., 1941.
———. *Selected Essays*. New York: Harcourt, Brace & Co., 1950.
Elliott, William Y. *The Pragmatic Revolt in Politics*. New York: Macmillan Co., 1928.
———. *The Need for Constitutional Reform*. New York, London: Whittlesey House, 1935.
Elton, William. *A Guide to the New Criticism*. Chicago: Modern Poetry Association, 1951.

Faverty, Frederic E. *Matthew Arnold the Ethnologist.* Evanston, Ill.: North-western University Press, 1951.

Fergusson, Francis. Review of John Crowe Ransom's *God Without Thunder, Bookman,* LXXIII (March 1931), 100–101.

Fishman, Solomon. *The Disinherited of Art.* Berkeley and Los Angeles: University of California Press, 1953.

Fitzhugh, George. *Sociology for the South.* Richmond: A. Morris, 1854.

Foerster, Norman, ed. *Humanism and America.* New York: Farrar & Rinehart, 1930.

——. "Tradition Versus Revolution," *American Review,* II (November 1933), 107–11.

Fry, Roger. "The Artist and Psycho-Analysis," *The New Criticism,* ed. Edwin Berry Burgum. New York: Prentice-Hall, Inc., 1930.

Geismar, Maxwell. *The Last of the Provincials.* New York: Hill & Wang, 1959.

Gerould, Katherine F. "A Yankee Looks at Dixie," *American Mercury,* XXXVI (February 1936), 217–20.

Glicksberg, Charles I. "Allen Tate and Mother Earth," *Sewanee Review,* XLV (July 1937), 284–95.

Gray, James. "The Minnesota Muse," *Saturday Review of Literature,* XVI (June 12, 1937), 3–4, 14.

Gray, Lewis Cecil. *Agriculture in the Southern United States to 1860.* Vol. I. New York: Peter Smith and Carnegie Institution of Washington, 1941.

Handy, William J. *Kant and the Southern New Critics.* Austin: University of Texas Press, 1963.

Hardy, John Edward. "The Achievement of Cleanth Brooks," *Southern Renascence,* eds. Louis D. Rubin and Robert D. Jacobs. Baltimore: Johns Hopkins Press, 1953.

Harris, Corra. "The South," *Forum,* LXXIX (February 1928), 177–80.

Hesseltine, W. B. "Look Away, Dixie," *Sewanee Review,* XXIX (January-March 1931), 97–103.

Hicks, Granville. *The Great Tradition.* New York: Macmillan Co., 1933.

Hollis, Christopher. *The American Heresy.* London: Sheed & Ward, 1927.

Hulme, T. E. "Romanticism and Classicism," *Critiques and Essays in Criticism,* ed. Robert Wooster Stallman. New York: The Ronald Press, 1949.

——. *Speculations.* ed. Herbert Read. London: Routledge & Kegan Paul Ltd., 1954.

——. *Further Speculations.* ed. Sam Hynes. Minneapolis: University of Minnesota Press, 1955.

Jefferson, Thomas. *Notes on the State of Virginia.* Richmond: J. W. Randolph, 1833.

Johnson, Thomas Cary, Jr. *Scientific Interests in the Old South.* New York: D. Appleton-Century, Inc., 1936.

Jones, Howard Mumford. "The Southern Legend," *Scribner's,* LXXXV (May 1929), 538–42.

——. "Is There a Southern Renaissance?" *Virginia Quarterly Review,* VI (April 1930), 184–97.

———. "The Future of Southern Culture," *Southwest Review,* XVI (January 1931), 142–63.

———. "On Leaving the South," *Scribner's,* LXXXIX (January 1931), 17–27.

———. *Ideas in America.* Cambridge Mass.: Harvard University Press, 1944.

———. *The Theory of American Literature.* Ithaca, N.Y.: Cornell University Press, 1948.

Karanikas, Alexander. "John Crowe Ransom and Allen Tate: A Study of the Southern Agrarian Theory of Literature." Unpublished Ph.D. dissertation, Northwestern University, 1953.

Kendricks, Benjamin B. "A Southern Confederation of Learning. Higher Education and the New Regionalism," *Southwest Review,* XIX (Winter 1934), 182–95.

Key, V. O. *Southern Politics in State and Nation.* New York: Alfred A. Knopf, 1949.

Keyserling, Hermann Alexander, *graf* von. *America Set Free.* New York: Harper & Bros., 1929.

Knickerbocker, William S. "The Fugitives of Nashville," *Sewanee Review,* XXXVI (April 1928), 211–24.

———. "Theological Homebrew," *Sewanee Review,* XXXIX (January-March 1931), 103-111.

———. "Mr. Ransom and the Old South," *Sewanee Review,* XXXIX (April 1931), 222–39.

———. "Friction of Powder-Puffs," *Sewanee Review,* XLVII (July 1940), 315–21.

Krutch, Joseph Wood. *The Modern Temper.* New York: Harcourt, Brace, & Co., 1929.

Kunitz, Stanley J., and Haycraft, Howard, eds. *Twentieth Century Authors.* New York: The H. W. Wilson Co., 1955.

Lanier, Sidney. *Retrospects and Prospects.* New York: Charles Scribner's Sons, 1899.

Lindeman, E. C. "Notes on the Changing South," *New Republic,* XLVI (April 28, 1926), 299–300.

Lumpkin, Grace. Letter in "Correspondence," *New Republic,* LXXXVII (May 27, 1936), 76.

Mather, Frank Jewett, Jr. "The Plight of Our Arts," *Humanism and America,* ed. Norman Foerster. New York: Farrar & Rinehart, 1930.

Matthiessen, F. O. "American Poetry, 1920–1940," *Sewanee Review,* LV (Winter 1947), 24–52.

———. "Primarily Language," *Sewanee Review,* LVI (Summer 1948), 391–401.

Meiners, Roger K. *The Last Alternatives: A Study of the Works of Allen Tate.* Denver: Alan Swallow, 1963.

Mencken, Henry L. "Uprising in the Confederacy," *American Mercury,* XXII (March 1931), 379–81.

———. "The South Astir," *Virginia Quarterly Review,* XI (January 1935), 47–60.

Mills, Gordon H. "Ontology and Myth in the Criticism of John Crowe Ransom." Unpublished Ph.D. dissertation, University of Iowa, 1943.

Mims, Edwin. *The Advancing South*. Garden City, N.Y.: Doubleday Page, 1926.

------. "Intellectual Progress in the South," *American Review of Reviews*, LXXXIII (April 1926), 367–69.

Mitchell, Broadus. *The Rise of Cotton Mills in the South*. Baltimore: The Johns Hopkins Press, 1921.

------. *William Gregg, Factory Master of the Old South*. Chapel Hill, N.C.: University of North Carolina Press, 1928.

------. "Survey of Industry," *Culture in the South*, ed. W. T. Couch. Chapel Hill, N.C.: University of North Carolina Press, 1935.

Molyneaux, Peter. "Land of Cotton," *Southwest Review*, XVI (July 1931), 437–59.

More, Paul Elmer. "The Humility of Common Sense," *Humanism and America, ed.* Norman Foerster. New York: Farrar & Rinehart, 1930.

Morrow, Felix. "Unorthodox Orthodoxy," *The Nation*, CXXXI (December 24, 1930), 711.

Morton, Inez. "A Critical Study of the Fugitive Poets." Unpublished Ph. D. dissertation, New York University, 1936.

Mumford, Lewis. *Technics and Civilization*. New York: Harcourt, Brace, & Co., 1934.

Munro, William Bennet. "Do We Need Regional Governments?" *Forum*, LXXIV (January 1928), 108–12.

Munson, Gorham B. "The Young Critics of the Nineteen-Twenties," *Bookman*, LXX (December, 1929), 369–73.

Murchison, Claudius. "Depression and the Future of Business," *Culture in the South*, ed. W. T. Couch. Chapel Hill, N.C.: University of North Carolina Press, 1935.

"The New South." Editorial, *Saturday Review of Literature*, VI (October 26, 1929), 309–10.

Nicholls, William H. *Southern Tradition and Regional Progress*. Chapel Hill, N.C.: University of North Carolina Press, 1960.

Odum, Howard W. *Southern Regions of the United States*. Chapel Hill, N.C.: University of North Carolina Press, 1936.

------. "From Sections to Regions," *Saturday Review of Literature*, XVI (June 12, 1937), 5.

------. "On Southern Literature and Southern Culture," *Southern Renascence*, eds. Louis D. Rubin and Robert D. Jacobs, pp. 84–100.

Odum, Howard W. and Moore, Harry Estill. *American Regionalism*. New York: Henry Holt & Co., 1938.

Ostrolenk, Bernhard. *The Surplus Farmer*. New York and London: Harper & Bros., 1932.

Overall, John Hubert, "A Review and Critical Study of the Fugitives." Unpublished dissertation, George Peabody College, 1928.

Owen, William V. *Labor Problems*. New York: Ronald Press, 1946.

Page, Walter Hines. *The Rebuilding of Old Commonwealths*. New York: Doubleday Page, 1902.

Parks, Edd Winfield. *Segments of Southern Thought*. Athens, Ga.: University of Georgia Press, 1938.

Parrington, Vernon Louis. *Main Currents in American Thought*. Vol. II. New York: Harcourt, Brace, & Co. 1927, 1930.

Penty, Arthur J. "Means and Ends," *Criterion*, XI (October 1931), 1–24.

———. "The Jettisoning of Adam Smith," *American Review*, IV (January 1935), 326–36.

Phillips, Ulrich Bonnell. *Life and Labor in the Old South*. Boston: Little, Brown & Co., 1930.

Pipkin, Charles W. "The Southern Philosophy of States' Rights. The Old Sectionalism and the New Regionalism," *Southwest Review*, XIV (Winter 1934), 175–82.

Pockwinse, Florence Beth. "A History of the Fugitives and *The Fugitive*." Unpublished Ph. D. dissertation, Boston University, 1938.

"Points of View." A symposium on Southwestern culture. *Southwest Review*, XIV (Summer 1929), 474–94.

Pressley, Thomas J. "Agrarianism: An Autopsy," *Sewanee Review*, XLIV (April 1941), 145–63.

Richards, I. A. *Principles of Literary Criticism*. New York: Harcourt, Brace, & Co., 1928.

Rock, Virginia Jean. "The Making and Meaning of I'll Take My Stand: A Study in Utopian-Conservatism, 1925–1939." Unpublished Ph.D. dissertation, University of Minnesota, 1961.

Rowe, John C. "Agrarianism: The Basis for a Better Life," *American Review*, VI (December 1935), 176–92.

Royce, Josiah. *Race Questions and Other American Problems*. New York: Macmillan Co., 1908.

Rubin, Louis D. and Jacobs, Robert D., eds. *Southern Renascence*. Baltimore: The Johns Hopkins Press, 1953.

Rubin, Louis D. "The Serpent in the Mulberry Bush," *Southern Renascence*. 352–367.

Rubin, Louis D. and Kilpatrick, James Jackson, eds. *The Lasting South*. Chicago: Henry Regnery, 1957.

Shackford, J. Atkins. "Sidney Lanier as Southerner," *Sewanee Review*, XLVIII (April-June 1940), 153–73; (July-September 1940), 348–55; (October-December 1940), 480–93.

Shafer, Robert. "Humanism and Impudence," *Bookman*, LXX (January 1930), 489–98.

———. "The Definition of Humanism," *Hound and Horn*, III (July-September 1930), 533–56.

Shapiro, Karl. *In Defense of Ignorance*. New York: Random House, 1952.

Shields, James W. "Woes of a Southern Liberal," *American Mercury*, XXXIV (January 1935), 73–79.

Smith, Bernard. *Forces in American Criticism*. New York: Harcourt, Brace, Inc. 1939.

Smith, Henry Nash. "The Dilemma of Agrarianism," *Southwest Review*. XIX (April 1934), 216–32.

Spingarn, Joel E. "The New Criticism," *The New Criticism,* ed. Edwin Berry Burgum. New York: Prentice-Hall, Inc., 1930.

Stallman, Robert Wooster, ed. *Critiques and Essays in Criticism.* New York: The Ronald Press, 1949.

——. "The New Critics," *Critiques and Essays in Criticism,* pp. 488–506.

——. "The New Criticism and the Southern Critics," *A Southern Vanguard,* ed. Tate. New York: Prentice-Hall, Inc., 1947

——. "John Crowe Ransom: A Checklist," *Sewanee Review,* LVI (Summer 1948), 442–76.

Starke, Aubrey. "The Agrarians Deny a Leader," *American Review,* II (March 1934), 534–53.

Stauffer, Donald A., ed. *The Intent of the Critic.* Princeton, N.J.: Princeton University Press, 1941.

Stearns, Harold E., ed. *Civilization in the United States.* New York: Harcourt, Brace, & Co. 1922.

Stewart, John Lincoln. "The Fugitive Agrarian Writers: A History and a Criticism." Unpublished Ph.D. dissertation, Ohio State University, 1947.

——. *John Crowe Ransom.* Minneapolis: The University of Minnesota Press, 1962.

Stocking, Fred H. "Poetry as Knowledge: The Critical Theory of John Crowe Ransom and Allen Tate." Unpublished Ph.D. dissertation, University of Michigan, 1946.

Stone, Geoffrey. "It is the Virile Part to React," *American Review,* VIII (Summer 1936), 341–52.

Stribling, T. S. *The Sound Wagon.* New York: Literary Guild, 1936.

——. *The Store.* New York: Literary Guild, 1937.

Sullivan, J. W. N. "Art and Reality," *The New Criticism,* ed. Edwin Berry Burgum. New York: Prentice-Hall, Inc., 1936.

Thorp, Willard. "Allen Tate: A Checklist," *Princeton University Library Chronicle,* III (April 1942), 85–90.

——. ed. *A Southern Reader.* New York: Alfred A. Knopf, 1955.

Turner, Arlin. "Fiction of the Bayou Country," *Saturday Review of Literature,* XVIII (April 30, 1938), 3–4, 16.

Vance, Rupert B. "The Profile of Southern Culture," *Culture in the South,* ed. W. T. Couch. Chapel Hill, N.C.: University of North Carolina Press, 1935.

——. "Is Agrarianism For Farmers?" *Southern Review,* I (July 1935), 42–57.

——. "Little Man, What Now?" *Southern Review,* I (Winter 1936), 560–67.

——. *All These People.* Chapel Hill, N.C.: University of North Carolina Press, 1945.

Weaver, Richard M. "Agrarianism in Exile," *Sewanee Review,* LVIII (Autumn 1950), 586–606.

White, Andrew Dickson. *A History of the Warfare of Science with Theology in Christendom.* New York and London: D. Appleton, 1910.

White, William Allen. "Racy of the Soil," *Saturday Review of Literature,* X (April 7, 1934), 607.

Wilson, Edmund. "The Tennessee Poets," *New Republic*, LIV (March 7, 1928), 103–4.

Witcutt, W. P. "William Morris: Distributist," *American Review*, II (January 1934), 311–15.

Winters, Yvor. *In Defense of Reason*. New York: The Swallow Press and William Morrow, 1947.

Woodward, Barbara. "Theories of Meaning in Poetry, 1915–1940." Unpublished Ph.D. dissertation, University of Michigan, 1946.

Woodward, C. Vann. *Origins of the New South*. Baton Rouge: Louisiana State University Press, 1951.

———. "The Irony of Southern History," *Southern Renascence*, eds. Louis P. Rubin and Robert D. Jacobs. New York: Prentice-Hall, Inc., 1953.

Wynn, Dudley "A Liberal Looks at Tradition," *Virginia Quarterly Review*, XII (January 1936), 60–79.

Index

Abercrombie, Lascelles, 129
Abolitionism: in South, 61; views on, of Fitzhugh, 64
Abolitionists: attacked by Hollis, 29
Adams, Léonie, 201
Agar, Herbert: as recruit to Agrarianism, 32; views on land, 41, 42; on the New South, 53; on Marx, 57; cites Carlyle, 80; on regionalism, 106; on primitive religion, 169, 190; in Ransom's anthology, 171; in *Who Owns America?*, 173
Agrarianism: and Neo-Humanism, 17, 80, 86, 148, 149, 151, 152; and fundamentalism, 26, 27, 29, 169; defined, 34; models for, 34, 35; in Old South, 36; and the depression, 38; and subsistence farming, 38–43, 66, 67; and distributism, 39, 49, 55–58 *passim;* defined by Ransom, 39–40; and the New Deal, 40; defined by Cauley, 43–49; in colonial days, 66; and education, 77, 86, 87, 88; benefits of, to art, 85; Negro's status in, 88, 94; related to New Criticism, 172, 188, 199, 204, 205, 207; reasons for failure of, 175; and Fascism, 179, 180, 181. *See also* Agriculture; Old South; Regionalism
Agrarians: the Twelve Southerners, 2; reasons for coherence, 4–7; major influences on, 8; influence of Eliot on, 8, 81, 200; activities of, in twenties, 13–16; early criticism of South, 19–23; and Parrington, 28; and Hollis, 28, 29; and Hulme, 30, 31; and Jefferson,

47, 95, 96, 97, 98; and Carlyle, 81, 82. *See also* Agrarianism
Agriculture: crisis in, in twenties. 33, 49, 50, 54; role in South, 37; commercial and subsistence types, 39, 46; stagnation of, 49; low income from, 50; condition of, 52; reforms in, proposed by Poe, 53; changes in, in Old South, 69. *See also* Tenant farmers
Aiken, Conrad, 201, 202
Alderman, Edwin A., 74
American Review: as supporter of Franco, 39; cited by Cauley, 42; as ultra-rightist journal, 55; Fascist views in, 178–80
Anderson, Sherwood: chairs Richmond debate, 17; quotes Ransom on anti-Semitism, 92
Anglo-Saxons: as exclusively fitted for freedom, 63, 64
Anti-Semitism: as aspect of racism, 89, 91, 92, 93, 169; Agrarian attitude toward, 89, 93, 94
Aptheker, Herbert: on instability of plantation system, 62, 63
Aquinas, St. Thomas, 160; mentioned, 169
Aristocracy: relation of, to South, 35, 60, 94; views on, of Keyserling, 95; its code of honor and Tate, 94, 95. *See also* Gentleman
Aristotle, 138, 160; mentioned, 139, 193
Arnold, Matthew: on Romantic poets, 128; mentioned, 77, 89, 126, 202
Auden, W. H., 191

Commonsense

Cataloging

Commonsense

Cataloging

A Manual for the Organization of Books and
Other Materials in School and
Small Public Libraries

Esther J. Piercy
CHIEF OF PROCESSING
ENOCH PRATT FREE LIBRARY, BALTIMORE

THE H. W. WILSON COMPANY, NEW YORK, 1965

Preface

This book is designed to be practical, to serve as a manual or handbook for the beginning cataloger, trained or untrained. If used as suggested, with the information and decisions of the individual library recorded in the checklist provided in Appendix VII, it should also serve as the manual of practice for that library. Even though the author may prefer or recommend certain practices (indicated by starred items in the checklist), inevitably there will be local situations which make other practices preferable or necessary. For the sake of consistency within an institution and to speed succeeding catalogers' learning the history and procedures, recorded decisions are necessary.

In the subtitle, "the organization of books and other materials" is admittedly a lengthy phrase; nevertheless there is no shorter way to say what is meant. Libraries are no longer solely collections of books: books must be supported by other materials, including pamphlets, maps, records, periodicals, pictures, films, and other forms of communication. And, while cataloging and classification are the basic means of organizing materials, they are not the only methods of dealing with books, let alone the other materials. A library's collections should be as easily and fully used as possible, but the arrangements for this use should be made in the most expeditious way possible, that is, the most economical in time.

The terms "Processing," "Technical Services," and "Technical Processes" do not appear in the title since many of the services generally included in these terms are not considered here. Excluded, for instance, are the selection and acquisition of materials; their shelving, care, and housing; and their control (circulation, registration, etc.). The physical preparations (pasting, stamping, lettering, jacketing, etc.) *are* included because this work is part of cataloging in many libraries and because many questions of cataloging and preparations are solved together.

The school libraries for which this manual is intended include those in elementary, junior high, and senior high schools, general and special. Defining "the small public library" is more difficult, but in general the concern is primarily with those libraries in communities of 10,000 or fewer people and those not expected to expand greatly in the foreseeable future. Actually, however, the cataloging is appro-

5

priate for public libraries much larger. Whether the organization or processing is done within the walls of the individual library or done for it in some processing center, the *kind* of cataloging will be the same. Church libraries were not included in the original planning of this manual, but it developed that, with few exceptions, the practices recommended would also be suitable for church and parish libraries; these exceptions are therefore noted in the text.

The word "commonsense" is used because the hope is to dispel some of the fears, mystery, superstitions, and mystique which sometimes surround the word "cataloging." After all, all the librarian has to do is decide, first, what purposes the collection is intended to serve, and then how best to organize the materials to perform the services.

In making such decisions he is conforming with recent movements and evaluations. The last few years have seen the publication of many sets of standards, the most pertinent being those for school libraries, public libraries, and the small public library. The American Library Association rules for form of entry, the ALA-LC rules for descriptive cataloging, and the ALA rules for filing are in the process of revision. The practices recommended herein observe the principles enunciated for these revisions, but are adapted to conform with the best practices developed for school and public libraries over the past twenty years.

COMMONSENSE CATALOGING differs from many similar works in this field not only in the features which make possible its adoption as a manual for each library, but also in its over-all arrangement. It is deliberately designed to go from the general to the specific, and from principles to practices, in the belief that before one can work effectively, one must have one's purposes clearly defined, that one must see the picture whole before undertaking the specific tasks. An attempt has been made to keep the text less tedious by removing routine matters and incorporating them in the Appendices; thus it is hoped that the prospective cataloger will be persuaded to read the entire text before starting work—he will surely save time in the long run by doing so.

As usual with even so simple a work, many people have become involved at various stages and have made contributions. From the Wayne County Public Library have come some of the card samples used. And gratitude must be expressed to those who have read different drafts of the work and made careful suggestions; they have eliminated many mistakes and strengthened the whole. People who took the time to give this generous help include Virginia Drewry of the

Georgia State Department of Education; Claribel Sommerville and the catalogers at the Public Library of Des Moines, Iowa; Eloise Rue and James Krikelas of the University of Wisconsin, Milwaukee; Mary V. Gaver and Paul S. Dunkin of the Graduate School of Library Service of Rutgers—The State University, New Jersey; Ruth French Strout of the Graduate Library School of the University of Chicago; and Audrey Smith of the Free Library of Philadelphia. Gertrude Samuels, Marian Sanner, and the other catalogers at the Enoch Pratt Free Library have, of course, talked out many points and answered endless questions.

It would be difficult to find more congenial people to work with than the officers and executives of The H. W. Wilson Company; Howard Haycraft, Edwin B. Colburn, and Thomas E. Sullivan have contributed encouragement, expressions of faith, and valuable assistance. Most of all, John Jamieson has been patience itself and has demonstrated what being a really good editor means.

ESTHER J. PIERCY

Baltimore, Maryland
April 1965

Table of Contents

CHAPTER 1

Procedures and Preliminaries

Background Information

Anyone planning to make use of this book would be well advised to read it through, noting that there is more than one way to do most things in cataloging and in organizing a collection. After a careful reading of the whole, one is ready to start over, studying each chapter and the corresponding checklist in Appendix VII. Whether the individual library is a new one just being organized or an older one with records and procedures established, it is advisable to think through the whole procedure, decide what is best, and make plans to act accordingly. No procedure is ever so perfect as not to profit from searching inspection, and no change can be made in the future so well as in the present since it is assumed that any library worth organizing is going to grow and keep on growing.

The procedures and decisions chosen for each particular library are those best for that library, and to decide what is best (that is, what is wanted and needed and economically sound), the catalog must be looked at in terms of its place in the library and the library's place in its institution or community. Therefore some preliminary information is needed, gathered through consultation with co-workers, authorities, the administration, and the governing body; through study of the community; and through concentrated thought. Such background information should include:

1. The present size of the community served (town, county, school, or church, as the case may be)
2. The community's potential size. Is it growing rapidly, steadily, or not at all?
3. The size and potential size of the library. What is its organizational pattern? Is it now, or is it likely to become, part of a larger system? What is its relationship to the system? What is likely to be its relationship? Does the system now have centralized processing? If not, is it being planned, or does it seem to be a logical future development?
4. The circulation system employed. Is any change contemplated? (Much of the work of preparing books and materi-

13

als for use must be coordinated with the way they are charged out.) Are book cards used? Date-due slips?

5. The policy regarding lost books. Is the borrower charged for the loss? Is he charged actual library cost, the list price, or something more than list price to pay for processing? Or is a flat charge made? Is this policy the same for adults and children?

6. Any city, school, or church restrictions (established by law or policy) affecting the work. For instance, is an accession record required? Special accounting? Inventory accounting? Report or other forms prescribed? What statistics are required? Is there a manual or record of procedural decisions or recommendations?

7. The people served. Does the library serve primarily (or only) adults or children? If children are served, of what age?

8. Type of service. Is the library used primarily (or exclusively) either for reference or for circulating materials? Does it take an active part in educational activities, directly or indirectly?

9. The other library resources of the community.

10. The library's relationship to school supervisors, county or state library agencies, or other supervisory and advisory bodies.

11. Shelving policies. Are all books on open shelves or is part of the collection in closed stacks? If the latter, what proportion? What categories?

12. The book-buying policy. Are books bought on contract? Bids? Ordered once a year? Twice a year? Monthly? Weekly?

13. The policies on accepting gifts of books; of other materials.

14. Special collections or rooms. Are any special collections maintained? If so, are they separately housed or shelved? Separately indexed or cataloged?

15. Audio-visual and other non-book materials. What types are acquired? How are they used? Do they circulate? To whom?

16. The library's discard and replacement policies. For example, does it keep only latest editions of informational books?

17. Duplication of material. Is the policy to have many copies of few titles or few (even single) copies of many titles? Are paperbacks used as duplicates?

After the prospective cataloger has collected and thought through such information and decisions, he is ready to read through this book, record his decisions in Appendix VII, and thus convert the book into a manual for his own library. The process should prepare him for more intelligent work and should make for more uniform and consistent practice, both for himself and his successors. It is very easy to forget details and impossible to pass all of the information on to others if it is not written down. Furthermore, writing procedures down requires sharper thought and more definite decisions.

Planning the Work

Ideally, establishing cataloging procedures and decisions is best done at the beginning, that is, with a new library or a new collection. However, the cataloger (the term "cataloger" is used for anyone doing the work even though the cataloging is only a part of his work) nearly always must do his work in a library in which practices have been established, must decide what is best for the library, and then consider his strategy. He has several choices: (1) he can follow precedent, (2) he can "adapt" old practices to new (that is, compromise or combine), (3) he can do over what has been done, or (4) he can ignore the old (expecting it to be discarded ultimately) and start anew.

His decision as to the course to be followed is based on the questions listed at the beginning of this chapter, and also on the size of the collection, how appropriate and competent has been the former work, and what is feasible in time and money. Although it is foolish to continue bad practices, compounding the errors and building toward future recataloging, it is also unwise to assume immediately that all of the past is bad and begin something one cannot finish or something which will keep the catalog in a turmoil for a long period.

Sometimes shortcuts can be employed in adapting old to new. For instance, one can line out old subject headings on cards and write in new ones above, assuming that such unsightly cards will sooner or later be withdrawn. Sometimes a history card or a cross reference (see pages 145-148) will tie the old and new together. The important thing is to decide why things were done as they were, what will be gained by a change, and what is the best and simplest way to effect the change. If one is a newcomer to cataloging or new to the library, it is safest to wait a few months for self-education before making drastic changes.

It is also necessary to keep in mind the possibilities of the individual library's becoming part of a larger system or joining a processing center. No cataloging or preparations procedures should be adopted which will make future cooperation difficult. It is wise to adopt the practices of the nearest libraries of similar type and size. Perhaps it is best to do no cataloging until the pattern is clear. In the interim the books could be arranged in large groupings, such as "literature," "sports," "religion," and so forth, with no catalog.

The public library standards recommend that a library not undertake its own processing if it is not large enough to keep a full-time cataloger busy, and the school standards recommend that a system of three or more schools centralize the processing work. The centralized processing movement is growing so rapidly and being pushed so unanimously that it may be considered inevitable. So it cannot be stressed enough that centralization should always be considered in terms of "when," not "if."

Tools for the Work

After the preliminary study, the librarian is ready to acquire the necessary tools for cataloging. The minimum for even the smallest library includes:

a list of subject headings
a classification schedule
a cataloging manual
the handbook of directions for ordering prepared cards

The cataloger should have access to a good unabridged dictionary, an up-to-date encyclopedia, appropriate foreign dictionaries, and such book selection aids as the appropriate *Standard Catalog*, the appropriate ALA *Basic Book Collection*, the ALA *Booklist and Subscription Books Bulletin*, *Book Review Digest*, and *Publishers' Weekly*. Larger libraries buying more adult books will also need a manual for applying the classification numbers, fuller rules of cataloging, more advanced cataloging texts, trade bibliographies, etc. (See Appendix VI.)

This manual touches only briefly on the classifying of materials and the application of subject headings, because the standard guides are necessary to have, and each has a good introduction explaining its use. The introductions must be studied carefully before any attempt is made to use the schemes.

Physical Organization

The next preparatory steps are acquiring the necessary equipment and supplies and organizing the work.

A desk and posture chair are necessary. If this is a one-man library, a separate desk should be provided in addition to the one on which orders are prepared, reports drafted, letters written, magazines and bibliographies checked, and all other work done. Even if the second "desk" is a kitchen table, it should be there in a quiet corner where the work can be spread out, and, in case of interruption, returned to. A typewriter is needed with a card platen. If one typewriter must serve all purposes, an extra platen can be purchased. (See Chapter 11 for further discussion.)

The work space should be not only comparatively secluded, but near a sink with running water. A second work table for preparing materials is also desirable. A catalog case is necessary (two if children and adults are served with separate catalogs), the size depending on the size of the library, and the material and style depending on the library decor. In estimating the size of the catalog, one may figure a thousand cards to a drawer and five cards for each title. It must be a standard library card catalog, made by a regular library supply house. The work area should have additional files for the shelf-list record, authority cards, order records, etc. A paste pot and shellac pot, a small pasting machine, a sponge, a book truck or two, and some handy shelves and cupboards should round out the minimum equipment requirements.

As regards supplies, the most important are the catalog cards (see Chapter 11 for a discussion of size and kind). As an estimate of the number of cards needed, it takes about five per volume (*not* title) to be added in a year's time. (There will be some duplication of titles, but the round number of five allows for shelf-list cards and for spoilage.) Of course, if printed cards are to be purchased, the number of plain ones needed will be proportionately smaller. Transparent book jackets, if used, must be selected and ordered (see Chapter 13); book cards, pockets, and date-due slips must be purchased—all are described in catalogs from library supply houses (see Appendix IV). Pens, pencils, inks, brushes, paper labels, paste, shellac, steel and other erasers, alcohol, discs or "spots" necessary for marking books, rubber stamps, and mending and other supplies can be purchased as needed from the library supply houses or from a local stationery store.

Organization of the Work

If the staff has more than one member, one person should have the responsibility for the cataloging and one for the typing and other clerical work under the cataloger's supervision. Definite time should be scheduled for the work, based on the pattern of ordering. That is, if books are ordered once or twice a year, full time may be needed to work on them when they arrive; if the flow is thin and spread throughout the year, a few hours a week may serve. Even in a one-man library, the librarian should schedule definite time to do the work, preferably when the library is closed. If he tries to attend to the public's needs and catalog at the same time, both activities suffer.

He should assemble his material in one place and plan to have the work move in a methodical way through the steps. For instance, he should have the books to be cataloged arranged alphabetically by author on a truck, and checked all at one time against the necessary files. If cards are being purchased but have not yet arrived, the books can either be put on a "wait" shelf (kept in alphabetical order) until the cards arrive, or, better, they can be classed and the order cards used as temporary records, releasing the books for use. In schools they can sometimes be held; in public libraries they will have to be prepared and released for circulation at once.

If all cards are to be typed, a work slip is prepared, written or typed, indicating the information to be carried on the completed catalog card. Or, if the information on the order card is full enough to indicate the necessary information, it may serve as a work slip. When a sufficient number of books are assembled with the work slips or printed cards, they are ready for the cataloger. (The preliminary steps of ordering cards, preparing work slips, and assembling them with the matching books can be done by a clerical, student, or volunteer assistant.)

The cataloger checks the slips or cards aganst the books, indicating any corrections or changes, then assigns classification numbers from the classification scheme and assigns subjects from the headings book. Then, working with half a dozen at a time, he checks the work slips or cards against the catalog and the shelf list to make sure that the suggested entries, subjects, and classification numbers conform with previous practice. (See Chapters 3, 5, 7, and 8 for details of these processes.) When he has completed this work, the truckload of books is turned over to the typist for completion. The cataloger "revises" the work (that is, reads proof and indicates corrections) and removes the catalog and shelf-list cards from the books. The truckload of books is then ready for the page or student assistant who prepares the books: pasting in pockets, lettering the spines, stamping ownership, applying jackets, etc. This work is also checked by the cataloger or by an experienced clerk. These steps may be summarized:

Clerical or student assistant

1. Checks proposed order in catalog, indicating call number for duplicates
2. Prepares order card

4. Completes and places order for books
5. Orders printed cards for books
6. When cards arrive, checks against books or records on hand, arranges cards for books not received alphabetically in card file
7. When books arrive, separates duplicates from new titles
8. Draws order cards; shelf-list cards for duplicates, printed catalog cards for new titles
9. Stamps or letters accession numbers in books
10. Arranges books on truck with cards in books

Cataloger

3. Reviews order

11. Checks cards against books, indicating changes or indicating information for typing cards
12. Assigns classification number for each book
13. Assigns subject or subjects
14. Indicates other cards
15. Checks slips against shelf list and catalog

Clerical or student assistant	*Cataloger*
	16. Pencils call number in book
	(11-16 alternative if catalog cards have not yet arrived: Assigns classification number
	Writes call number on order card and in book
	Records statistical count
	Sends book to Step 25)
17. Types headings and call numbers on printed cards or types full sets of cards	
18. Enters accession information on shelf-list card	
19. Types book card, pocket, and label	
	20. Revises typing of cards and label
	21. Removes catalog, shelf-list, and order cards from books
	22. Records statistical count
	23. Files shelf-list cards
	24. Discards order cards if no longer needed
25. Pastes pocket and date-due slip in book	
26. Applies label to book jacket Applies jacket to book *or* Letters spine of book Shellacks book	
27. Files cards in catalog above rod or with filing cards	
	28. Checks lettering and other preparations work
	29. Revises filing in catalog
30. Shelves books	

The work space should be carefully planned for this progression. Every waste step is wasted time, and running back and forth checking one book at a time here and there is not only wasteful but tiring. *If* sized plastic jackets are used (see page 92), the measuring gauge should be attached to the wall near the jackets, which are grouped by size; a group of books is measured, the jackets pulled and laid in the books (the proper one in each), the books stacked on the work table, then all the jackets applied and pasted (or taped) in one sitting. Every step (no matter how trivial) should be planned with the same care. Doing half a dozen things at once on a cluttered work table or desk is inefficient and nerve-wracking.

Aids and shortcuts should be used freely, but big machines to do small jobs make no sense. If there is a choice in procedures, a few minutes of timing the different ways will usually provide the answer. Printed or processed forms and rubber stamps are true gold if used wisely. For instance, if reference books are cataloged but shelved behind the desk and the clerk must type or write again and again, "Ask at desk for this book," get a stamp. A small library, however, has neither time nor money nor facilities for testing more elaborate equipment or products; it is much wiser to read what has been done or to ask for advice. (See Chapter 13.*)

Library Publishers

Appendix IV gives a list of library supply houses and publishers specializing in library publications; for the latter some background information is required:

1. The Library of Congress (commonly spoken of as LC) is the library organized for the use of the United States Congress in Washington. It is one of the largest libraries in the world, and the institutions it services have grown to include not only other government agencies, but also practically every library in the country; it is, in fact, the unofficial national library. Its librarians participate in all major library planning in the country; it publishes many aids and tools; and it offers various direct services, including the sale of printed catalog cards.

2. The American Library Association (ALA), as the largest association of American librarians, necessarily takes the lead in establishing library goals and standards, in urging governmental legislation for improving libraries and library services, in establishing and unifying library practices, and in conducting institutes and workshops. It also publishes reports, periodicals, studies, aids, and tools. Three

* Also to be consulted is D. D. Dennis, *Simplifying Work in Small Public Libraries.* Philadelphia, Drexel Institute of Technology, 1965.

of its divisions are particularly concerned with matters which are also of concern to users of this manual: the American Association of School Librarians, the Public Library Association, and the Resources and Technical Services Division. The last includes a Cataloging and Classification Section which speaks for ALA in this area of work.

3. The H. W. Wilson Company was founded in 1898 to serve libraries and the book world, first through its indexes (including, among many, the *Readers' Guide to Periodical Literature* and the *Cumulative Book Index*), then through other publications (including the *Standard Catalog* series and the *Wilson Library Bulletin*) and other services, among them the sale of printed catalog cards. The company, its officers, and its employees work closely with libraries and library organizations for general library improvement and the improvement of its own services.

4. The R. R. Bowker Company is a publishing house which has served the book world, including libraries, since 1872. Its publications include *Publishers' Weekly*, the *American Book Publishing Record*, the *American Library Directory*, the *Library Journal*, and many other books and serials.

5. Others. The F. W. Faxon Company, the Scarecrow Press, the Shoe String Press, and the Special Libraries Association are among the other publishers who specialize in library aids. In addition, library schools are responsible for many magazines, serials, institutes, studies, and publications.

CHAPTER 2

The Card Catalog

The library catalog need not be a frightening thing, and its preparation should not be a goal in itself. It is a tool to serve the librarian and the library user; although it is the library's most important reference tool, it is still a tool. This means that it should contain only what is of predictable need and should eliminate all unnecessary embellishments, both as to what cards are included and what information is carried on the cards. No more time should be spent on it than necessary, but no information of value should be omitted.

There are various types of catalogs, but the type most widely used in the United States is the dictionary card catalog. Schools, public libraries, and other small libraries use the dictionary catalog almost without exception, and it is the one with which we are concerned here. In this type of catalog all cards (or "entries") are in one file, alphabetically arranged by the first or filing name or word.

The Catalog as Holdings Record

The catalog is not new; almost from the time that man, singly or in groups, started collecting books or their forerunners, he has felt the need to list the works to show him what he has. This remains the primary purpose of the catalog: to show what the library has. This the catalog does, and it must be prepared to do so, regardless of which of several pieces of information the user may have. He may know:

the author of a work;
the title of a work;
the editor of a work;
some other name or term associated with a work.

For each of these designations a card is made and filed in its alphabetical place under the key name or word. Thus the reader seeking a specific work quickly discovers whether or not it is in the library's collections.

The Catalog as Location Record

After the reader learns what the library has, the next information needed is: where is the desired book located? Libraries have found the easiest way to answer this need is to assign a symbol to each book; the symbol will then serve as a device for shelving it in the desired order. If this symbol or device is carried on both the book and the catalog cards relating to it, the user may then be led directly from catalog card to book. It has also been found that by employing a subject classification scheme (see Chapter 8) books on the same subject can be brought together on the shelves, with books on related subjects close by. Thus the symbol, a subject classification number, serves two purposes: it locates a specific work and it brings it together with like materials. The user is led to the desired specific book, or he may browse through the books on the shelf which relate to the subject in which he is interested.

Reference Uses of the Catalog

Library practice has also discovered many reference uses for the card catalog, implicit both in deciding what cards are needed and in determining what information is to be included on the cards.

As to what cards are needed, the catalog may be expected to tell, in addition to the information discussed above: (1) what does the library have on a specific subject? and (2) what titles by a given author does the library have? Answers to the first question are provided by the use of subject headings (names, words, or phrases). Showing what the library has by a given author is done by providing cards under the name or names he has used in his works.

The information on the card supplies a description of the individual work, such as who was responsible for its contents, who published it, its age, its size, what it is about, and its relation to other works. (See Chapter 6.)

Cards in Sets

For each separate work cataloged a set of cards is prepared. Ordinarily, these will all be alike except for the top line, which carries the name, word, or phrase under which each card is filed. This use of a set of like cards is called the "unit" card system. One card is prepared which is called the "main entry"; this is usually the author card, and other cards are made which are exact copies of it except for the addition above the author's name of the various names, words, or phrases under which the additional cards will be filed. All cards other than the main entry card are "added entry" cards. The number of cards required depends on the book itself (see Chapter 4) and may vary from one to twenty-five, three to five being the average. A set may look like this:

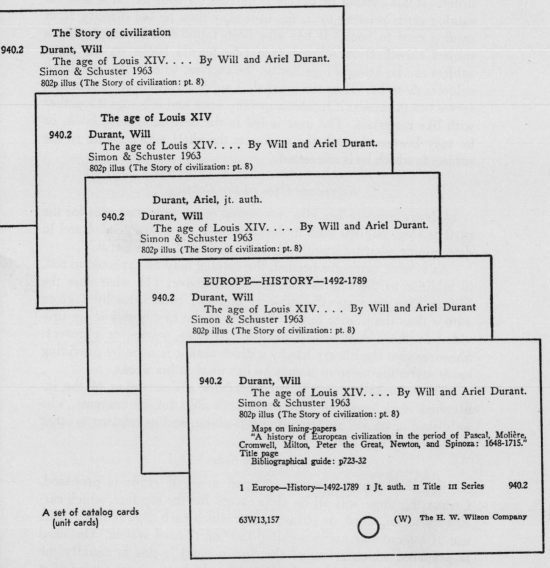

The Story of civilization

940.2   Durant, Will
        The age of Louis XIV. . . . By Will and Ariel Durant.
    Simon & Schuster 1963
    802p illus (The Story of civilization: pt. 8)

The age of Louis XIV

940.2   Durant, Will
        The age of Louis XIV. . . . By Will and Ariel Durant.
    Simon & Schuster 1963
    802p illus (The Story of civilization: pt. 8)

Durant, Ariel, jt. auth.

940.2   Durant, Will
        The age of Louis XIV. . . . By Will and Ariel Durant.
    Simon & Schuster 1963
    802p illus (The Story of civilization: pt. 8)

EUROPE—HISTORY—1492-1789

940.2   Durant, Will
        The age of Louis XIV. . . . By Will and Ariel Durant
    Simon & Schuster 1963
    802p illus (The Story of civilization: pt. 8)

940.2   Durant, Will
        The age of Louis XIV. . . . By Will and Ariel Durant.
    Simon & Schuster 1963
    802p illus (The Story of civilization: pt. 8)

        Maps on lining-papers
        "A history of European civilization in the period of Pascal, Molière,
Cromwell, Milton, Peter the Great, Newton, and Spinoza: 1648-1715."
Title page
        Bibliographical guide: p723-32

1 Europe—History—1492-1789 I Jt. auth. II Title III Series   940.2

63W13,157   (W) The H. W. Wilson Company

A set of catalog cards
(unit cards)

FIGURE 1

The set above shows examples of printed cards purchased for use.
If printed cards are not used in the library or not available for a
title, the cards must then all be typed. In this case, shorter forms may
be used for all of the cards except the main entry.

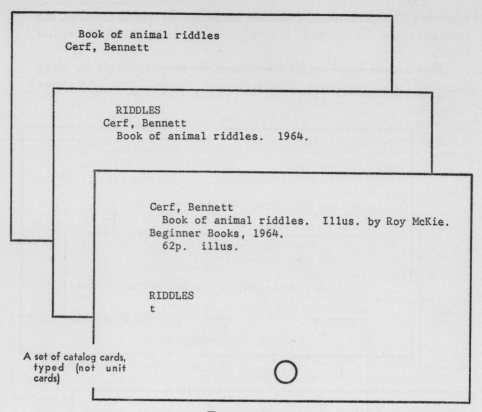

Book of animal riddles
Cerf, Bennett

RIDDLES
Cerf, Bennett
    Book of animal riddles. 1964.

Cerf, Bennett
    Book of animal riddles. Illus. by Roy McKie.
Beginner Books, 1964.
    62p. illus.

RIDDLES
t

A set of catalog cards,
  typed (not unit
  cards)

FIGURE 2

Tracings on Cards

The cards will be scattered throughout the catalog, each under its
own key filing or "entry" word. It is necessary therefore to know how
many and what cards exist for each work in order to find them again
to make corrections or to withdraw them when the title is no longer
in the library. Therefore a means of finding or tracing these cards
must be provided. This is done by listing all of the clues (filing
names, words, or phrases) on the main entry card. These listings are
called "tracings," appropriately enough. They appear on the face of
the card if there is room, otherwise on the back.

There is an established practice for this listing. If on the face of
the card, they are at the bottom and are arranged in paragraph or
column form. If there is not room on the front, they are typed, one
below the other, on the lower part of the back of the card (see Appendix I for typing directions). Tracings for subject entries come
first, and on printed cards are designated by Arabic numbers, with all

other headings indicated by Roman numbers. In typing tracings, the numbers may be omitted, but subjects are then typed in capital letters.

That a card exists under the title of the work is shown by using the word "title" or simply "t" as a tracing. Other abbreviations may also be used (see page 159).

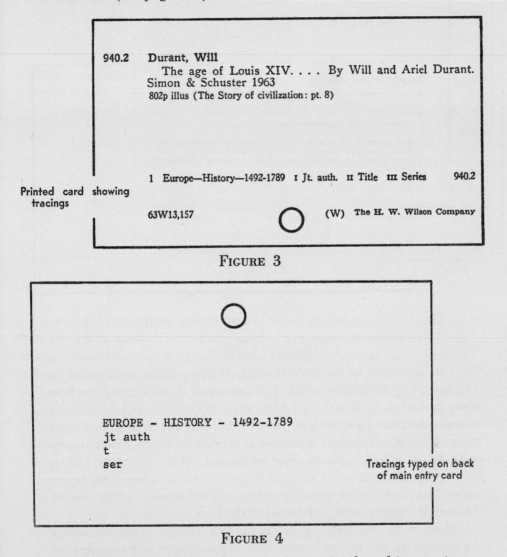

940.2   **Durant, Will**
        The age of Louis XIV. . . . By Will and Ariel Durant. Simon & Schuster 1963
        802p illus (The Story of civilization: pt. 8)

1 Europe—History—1492-1789 ɪ Jt. auth. ɪɪ Title ɪɪɪ Series   940.2

Printed card showing tracings

63W13,157   (W) The H. W. Wilson Company

FIGURE 3

EUROPE – HISTORY – 1492-1789
jt auth
t
ser

Tracings typed on back of main entry card

FIGURE 4

A new practice which makes sense is to raise the subject tracings on the card and precede them with a note saying something like: "Related books in Catalog under——." This is to lead the reader from one subject to related ones. (See Figure 5.)

Tracings used as lead
to related subjects
(reprinted courtesy
of Wayne County
Public Library)

370.973   RAFFERTY, Max Leivis, 1917-
Related   *Suffer, little children.* New York, Devin [c.]1962.
Books In   166p.   3.00
Catalog   *1. Education—U.S.—1945- —Addresses, essays, lec-*
Under   *tures.*
              Critical commentary on the state of American schools.

Title.   Mr 63

617.6   GREENBERG, Saul N.
           So you want to be a dentist, by Saul N. Greenberg,
           Joan R. Greenberg. New York, Harper [c.1963]
Related   168p. illus.   3.50
Books In   *1. Dentistry as a profession.*
Catalog
Under   Career guide. Covers predental requirements, curriculum and
           training, starting a practice, and specialization. With a chap-
           ter on women in dentistry and a list of dental schools in
           America.

Title.   Mr 63

FIGURE 5

Form of the Catalog Card

The decision as to how much and what information to supply on a card depends on its proposed use and hence on the size and service pattern of the individual library; but the form of the card itself, that is, the sequence of the information, follows uniform practice (see Chapter 6). This practice has been established through the years and has proved satisfactory. It takes into consideration readability, ease of preparation, assistance in preparing bibliographies, emphasis, and the requirements for adding necessary information as it later becomes available. (See Chapter 6 and Appendix I.)

If libraries follow the same form, it makes it easier to instruct people in the use of the catalog; it helps people in using different libraries; and it aids in the exchange of information between libraries. Also, it means that cards from various sources may be interfiled in the same catalog; future combining of library collections is possible with minimum effort; and later plans for cooperation between libraries are simplified.

Actual arrangement of information on the card (spacings, indentation, and so forth) has also established a pattern, as detailed in

Appendix I. However, with the widespread practice of machine copying and with cataloging information appearing in various sources (e.g., *Publishers' Weekly*) these arrangements give way, and no great harm is done. Thus, although it is simpler for a typist to have only one pattern to follow, the form is not sacrosanct. The cards pictured in Figure 5 were made by enlarging and photographing the LC cataloging information from *Publishers' Weekly*.

The amount of bibliographic information (the book description) depends on the size of the collecton (potential as well as present), a definition of its chief users (age, reading ability, interests), and its primary uses (school assignments, independent study or research, recreational reading, information reading, quick reference, etc.)

Organization Other than Cataloging

Although the dictionary catalog is the type of organization of material primarily discussed in this manual, it must always be kept in mind that there are other ways of organizing or controlling library collections. The ALA standards for small libraries recommend book cataloging for all public libraries, but there is wide variation in the handling of materials other than books and of different collections. For some materials or collections it is best to classify and not catalog, to catalog and not classify, or to do neither. Although proposed use and best ways of service are the primary considerations, costs and time must also be considered. It is poor planning to spend a great deal of time on an elaborate control when a simpler method will serve equally well. To do so not only means waste but often means withholding material from use.

For example, such publications as college catalogs, trade catalogs, publishers' catalogs, and courses of study may well be shelved without any treatment except, perhaps, being stamped with the library's ownership. Only the latest edition of each is kept, older editions being discarded as they are superseded by new ones. Many reference books (encyclopedias, atlases, dictionaries, almanacs, directories, yearbooks, etc.) will be kept in one collection or else on stands and tables. Neither cataloging nor classification is necessary, although some marking (such as "R") is helpful for shelving purposes.

Audio-visual and other non-book or near-book materials and their treatment are discussed in Chapter 14.

CHAPTER 3

The Main Entry

An entry is the name or word or phrase under which a card is filed or a bibliographic listing made. There are author entries, title entries, subject entries, illustrator entries, series entries, editor entries, etc.

The "main entry" is that name or term under which the work is primarily entered both on a catalog card and in a bibliography. The selection and the determination of the form in which it will be used (see Chapter 5 for form) are the most important parts of descriptive cataloging. It is by this main entry that a work will principally be known, and should most frequently be sought. If a book must be entered only once, as in a bibliography or union catalog, it will be by this main entry. All other names or phrases used as filing terms for that work then become "added entries."

The starting place for cataloging a book, then, is determining the main entry, and the starting point for doing this is the title page, which carries the title, customarily including the author statement. Further information, if needed, is gained by reading the preface, the introduction, and the table of contents; by checking the cover of the book and the information on the paper dust jacket; and, if necessary, by scanning the book itself.

Author as Main Entry

If it is decided that one person wrote the book, his name is used as the main entry. Since he is the author, this is the author entry. Happily, most main entries *are* author entries.

For example:

> *A title reads:* Flood, A Romance of Our Times. Robert Penn Warren.
> *The main entry would be:* Warren, Robert Penn

If there are two or three authors, the first name on the title page is usually selected as the main entry.

Examples:

Title: Who's Who in Faulkner. Margaret Patricia Ford.
Suzanne Kincaid.
Main entry: Ford, Margaret Patricia

Title: The Call of the East; Stories by Mary and Robert
Nyberg.
Main entry: Nyberg, Mary

If, however, it is obvious that another person listed elsewhere on
the title page is primarily responsible for the work, *his* name is used.

Title: Sears List of Subject Headings. Sixth edition by
Bertha Margaret Frick. With Practical Suggestions
for the Beginner by Minnie Earl Sears.
Main entry: Sears, Minnie Earl

For a collection of works or an anthology, such as a collection of
poems, essays, stories, or plays by different authors, the name of the
editor or the compiler becomes the main entry.

Title: Eat, Drink and Be Buried. Edited and with an Introduction by Rex Stout. (The contents are by many
different writers.)
Main entry: Stout, Rex, ed.

A bibliography, index, etc., prepared by one person is entered
under his name.

Title: A Concise Bibliography of the Works of Walt Whitman, by Carolyn Wells and Alfred F. Goldsmith.
Main entry: Wells, Carolyn

A translated or revised work is entered under the author of the
original work if the text is essentially unchanged; but if the work is
rewritten or "adapted" so much as to constitute a new work, the
adapter becomes the author.

Examples:

Title: The Bedside Bunyan; an Anthology of the Writings
of John Bunyan. Selected and Edited by Arthur
Stanley.
Main entry: Bunyan, John

Title: Owen Wister Out West; His Journals and Letters.
Edited by Fanny Kemble Wister.
Main entry: Wister, Owen

Title: The Pajama Game. Book by George Abbott and
Richard Bissell based on Mr. Bissell's Novel, 7½
Cents. (Rewritten in a different form)
Main entry: Abbott, George

Title as Main Entry

Occasionally a work is published anonymously with no author indicated anywhere in the book; if the cataloger has no knowledge of its authorship, he must then use the title as the main entry.

> *Title:* The Art of Cookery. By a lady.
> *Main entry:* The Art of Cookery

Or, different authors or editors may prepare different editions of a work; in this case, also, the title is the main entry.

> *Title:* Best Plays of the Year. (Edited in different years by
> Burns Mantle, John Chapman, and others)
> *Main entry:* Best Plays of the Year

If many individuals have prepared the work or parts of it and there is an editor, the editor's name is treated as if he were the author. If four or more wrote the work or different parts of it and there is no editor or no one person is indicated as primarily responsible, the title must be the main entry.

> *Title:* Philosophy and History, Essays Presented to Ernst
> Cassirer.
> *Main entry:* Philosophy and History

Almanacs, yearbooks, encyclopedias, dictionaries, and most periodicals are other examples of types of materials cataloged under title.

> *Title:* The American College Dictionary, ed. by Clarence L.
> Barnhart with the Assistance of 355 Authorities
> and Specialists.
> *Main entry:* The American College Dictionary

Anonymous Works, Sacred Works, and Other Special Headings

An anonymous classic is defined by the *A.L.A. Glossary of Library Terms* as "a work of unknown or doubtful authorship, commonly designated by title, which may have appeared in the course of time in many editions, versions, and/or translations. The term includes . . . poems, epics, romances, tales, plays, chronicles, . . . sacred literature. . . ." These include Mother Goose, the Arabian Nights, Beowulf, Robin Hood, King Arthur, and others. For these works, a standard heading is established and employed. (See Chapter 5 for the form of these special headings.)

The Bible and its parts and other sacred works are also entered under a standardized form.

> *Title:* The Holy Bible, a New Translation by James Moffatt.
> *Main entry:* Bible

Under names of countries or other political units certain publications (such as laws, constitution, etc.) are provided with a "made-up" or "form" heading. (See Chapter 5.)

> *Title:* Internal Revenue Code. Full Text of the 1954 Internal Code.
> *Main entry:* U.S. *Laws*

Corporate Body as Main Entry

Sometimes a work is issued by an institution, organization, government body, or other collective group. Examples are the Boy Scouts of America, the National Education Association, Johns Hopkins University, and the United States Office of Education. If there is no personal author, the name of the group is used as the author; this is called a "corporate author," and is the main entry.

If the institution or body is serving as the publisher and there is an identifiable personal author, the work is entered under his name with, perhaps, the corporate name used as an added entry. (See Chapter 4.)

> *Title:* Subject Headings; a Practical Guide by David Judson Haykin, Chief, Subject Cataloging Division, Library of Congress. (Published by the Library of Congress)
> *Main entry:* Haykin, David Judson

If the publication is nonpersonal and has an official relationship to the group, the corporate entry is used as the main entry. Or, if a publication of a body is one that may be issued repeatedly or revised often with the author varying from edition to edition, the corporate main entry is chosen.

> *Title:* The Cubmaster's Packbook, Boy Scouts of America.
> *Main entry:* Boy Scouts of America

Thus, for an annual report of the Boston Public Library, "Boston Public Library" becomes the author and the main entry even though the librarian may have signed the report. However, if John Smith makes a study or survey of the Boston Public Library, for the resulting publication John Smith is the author, and the Boston Public Library the subject. Or if the Boston Public Library employs John Smith to make a study for it, John Smith will be the author and main entry, but an added entry (not subject) will be made under the Library's name.

CHAPTER 4

Added Entries

The name (personal or corporate) or term under which a work is best known is the main entry (see Chapter 3). All other catalog cards prepared for that work and carrying at their tops other filing names, words, and phrases, become added entries.

Added entries fall into three groups: subjects, titles, and other added entries. Many librarians say "added entries" when they mean all *except* subjects and titles. (As so often happens in library work, the terminology is confusing.) But strict accuracy or logic makes every entry an added entry if it is not the main one; and the form of the card (indention, arrangement, emphasis, etc.) makes only the one distinction.

Subject Entries

Subject entries are made for all subjects discussed at some length in a work (see Chapter 7).

Title Entries

Title cards are made for most or, in some libraries, all titles. Larger libraries do not make title entries for titles beginning with overused and nondistinctive phrases such as *History of, Story of, Philosophy of, Report of, Bulletin of, Proceedings of,* etc. Others (particularly small libraries) make entries for titles of all works. The latter practice is probably best since it is both consistent and automatic, and calls for no mind-reading or special decisions. The few necessary exceptions are noted below.

Any part of a title may also be used as an entry if it is felt that a particular word or phrase will be that most likely to be remembered. This is called a "catch title." Thus, a title *The Parable of Sticks and Stones* might well be remembered as "Sticks and Stones"; and so that book might have two title cards, one for the full title and the other for the catch title, "Sticks and Stones." Or, for a title beginning with the author's name, a shortened title (catch title) is made. For instance, a work entitled *Shakespeare's Romeo and Juliet* would have only one title entry, *Romeo and Juliet.*

A former practice was that of using inverted headings; thus the *Parable* title above would have a card under *Sticks and Stones, the Parable of.* This is awkward, is not actually needed, makes extra work, and can lead to complications; so it is no longer recommended.

If a title is the same word or phrase as a subject heading, the subject heading is preferred with no title card being made. Thus, for a book entitled simply *Arithmetic* there would be a subject entry consisting of that word and no entry would be made under title. (This means that the entry is lost if the subject is later changed unless care is taken at the time of change.)

See Appendix I for directions for making the title card.

Other Added Entries

If a publication is the joint work of two or three people, the first named, or the one indicated as most responsible for the work, is selected as the main entry; but additional cards are used for the second and third names. These additional entries are known as "joint authors" or "joint editors," as the case may be. The book *Modern Physics*, by Charles E. Dull, H. Clark Metcalfe and John Williams, would be entered under Charles E. Dull as the main entry, but it would have an added entry for H. Clark Metcalfe as joint author and one for John Williams as joint author. (If more than three people are named, the title is used as main entry, and an added entry is made only for the first name.)

If a work is done for an organization or institution, the author is named as main entry, but the name of the organization or institution, if important to the work, is used as an added entry.

Sometimes it is necessary to make an additional card under an illustrator, an editor, the author of an important introduction, a translator, a compiler, or a sponsor, or to show other important relationships to the work. The relationship to the publication if other than author or joint author, is shown in abbreviated form, such as "ed.," "jt. ed.," "illus." This relationship must also be shown in the description of the book in the body of the card, or in a note on the card, as:

"Critical introduction" by Charles Bradley, p.3-40.

Added entries other than subjects or titles should be kept to a minimum. Very real chance for confusion over responsibility or real need in the specific library are the only reasons for making them. They should not be allowed to multiply just on the off-chance that someone someday might use them, or just because some other library has used them.

Analytics

Parts of some works are of sufficient importance to require cards to bring them out in the catalog. Cards for such entries are called *analytics* since they analyze the contents of the book or set of books.

There are subject analytics, title analytics, author analytics, author-title analytics, and title-author analytics. They are used most often for composite works, collections, compilations, and so forth.

For instance, a group of plays by different authors is bound in one volume under a collective title. Each play and each author may be requested; therefore cards are made under the author and title and, in reverse, under the title and author. For example, for a volume of plays compiled and edited by Bennett Cerf, each play should be brought out:

Sherwood, Robert
    The petrified forest   *author and title analytic*
Cerf, Bennett, ed.
    Sixteen famous American plays

    The petrified forest
Sherwood, Robert   *title and author analytic*
Cerf, Bennett, ed.
    Sixteen famous American plays

These entries appear above the main entry (compiler, editor, author, or title) of the book.

For a collection of works by one author, we may need a title analytic for each individual work, even though analytics are not needed for the author. His name, of course, is the main entry for the volume.

Example:

    Romeo and Juliet
Shakespeare, William
    Shakespeare's tragedies

It is less usual to have author analytics without accompanying titles; but it is possible, for instance, for a collection of speeches or essays, written by different people but with nondistinctive titles.

Lincoln, Abraham
Perkins, George, ed.
    Inaugural addresses of George Washington, Abraham
Lincoln, and Woodrow Wilson

(Author analytics would be made for each person.)

Subject analytics may be used for parts of a collection or even for a section of a single work. Thus a collection of biographies may have names as subjects; or a book may have a separate section on a subject.

ART, FRENCH
Johnson, Harold
Modern European painting
GLENN, JOHN
Smith, James E.
The astronauts

A collection of essays or a book, parts of which are written by different authors, may require subject analytics. It may also possibly need author analytics. It could conceivably have all three: author, subject, and title.

Any book which has a separate part or a prominent section of many pages devoted to a subject different from the subject used for the entire book may need a subject analytic.

The decision regarding when and for what works to use analytics depends on such factors as (1) the size and nature of the collection, (2) the amount of material in the library on a subject or by an author, (3) the unusualness of the material, and (4) whether or not the information as to the book's contents is available elsewhere. (For instance, reference books such as the *Essay Index*, the *Standard Catalogs*, play indexes, etc., analyze the contents of many books.) Small libraries generally analyze their materials more than do large ones, since they do not always have so many reference books, and since the reference books (indexes, bibliographies, and so forth) are usually not published until some months or even years later than the books being indexed. However, it would seem much more efficient and effective to buy more reference books and do less catalog analyzing.

Every analytical card made must be traced on the main entry card for the volume. The tracing may be only the words "auth anals" or "t anals" or "a and t anals," if every author or title listed on the unit card in contents note is used. Or the tracing may say, if necessary, "author anals: Smith, Taylor, Jones," etc. Otherwise the exact tracing for each analytic is listed along with the other tracings. (See Chapter 2 and Appendix I for information on tracings.)

The former practice of including inclusive paging in the analytic entry at the top of the card is no longer recommended. If the exact paging is needed, it is included in the contents note, in a separate note on the unit card, or at the left-hand side of the analytic card below the call number. For subject analytics whose page numbers are not shown elsewhere on the card, page numbers may be added as part of the call number on the analytic card. If the contents note is long,

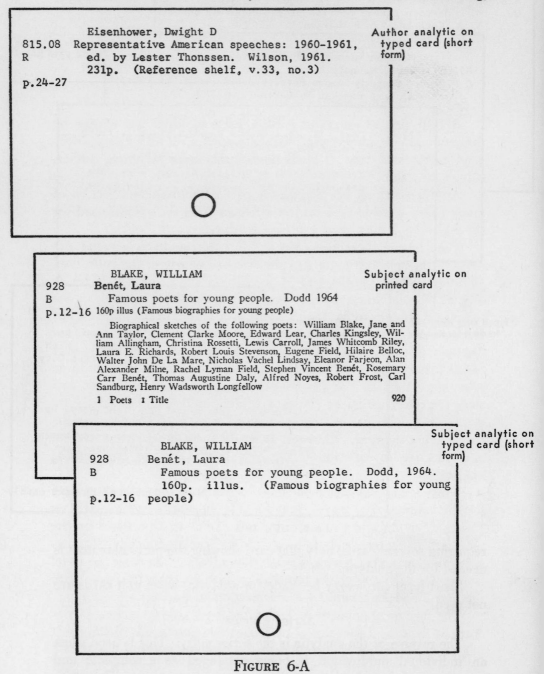

FIGURE 6-A

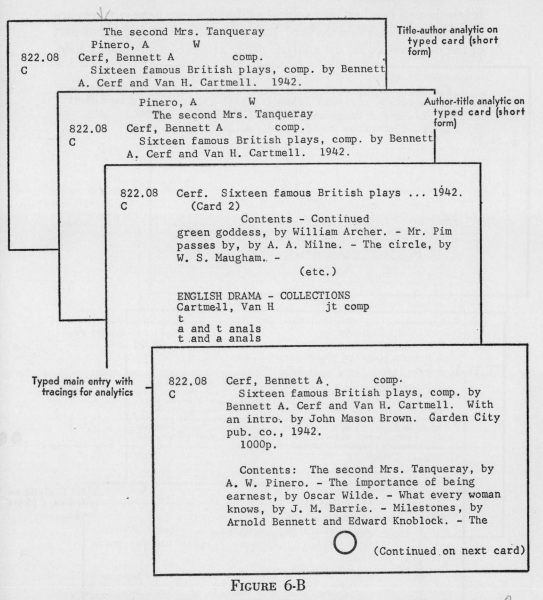

The second Mrs. Tanqueray
Pinero, A   W
822.08   Cerf, Bennett A   comp.
C   Sixteen famous British plays, comp. by Bennett
          A. Cerf and Van H. Cartmell. 1942.

Title-author analytic on typed card (short form)

Pinero, A   W
The second Mrs. Tanqueray
822.08   Cerf, Bennett A   comp.
C   Sixteen famous British plays, comp. by Bennett
          A. Cerf and Van H. Cartmell. 1942.

Author-title analytic on typed card (short form)

822.08   Cerf. Sixteen famous British plays ... 1942.
C   (Card 2)
                   Contents - Continued
          green goddess, by William Archer. - Mr. Pim
          passes by, by A. A. Milne. - The circle, by
          W. S. Maugham.. -
                        (etc.)

          ENGLISH DRAMA - COLLECTIONS
          Cartmell, Van H   jt comp
          t
          a and t anals
          t and a anals

Typed main entry with tracings for analytics

822.08   Cerf, Bennett A.   comp.
C   Sixteen famous British plays, comp. by
          Bennett A. Cerf and Van H. Cartmell. With
          an intro. by John Mason Brown. Garden City
          pub. co., 1942.
              1000p.

              Contents: The second Mrs. Tanqueray, by
          A. W. Pinero. - The importance of being
          earnest, by Oscar Wilde. - What every woman
          knows, by J. M. Barrie. - Milestones, by
          Arnold Bennett and Edward Knoblock. - The

          (Continued on next card)

FIGURE 6-B

requiring several cards, only that card showing the particular item is
needed for the analytic.

Short-form cards may be made for analytics when unit cards are
not used.

Series Entries

The reverse of the analytic is the series entry. This is used when
an individual publication is being cataloged as a complete and
separate work but also belongs to a series of importance. The series

may be an annual, a monographic series, a publisher's series, or one of several other kinds. If there is likely to be a need for knowing what the library holds in the series or if the series volumes are going to be used or asked for under the series name, an added entry is made carrying the name of the series. Most series are indicated by a note on the unit card following the collation. (See Chapter 6 and Appendix I.)

Fuller, Muriel, ed.
    More junior authors.   Wilson, H.W. 1963
235p illus (The Author ser)

    "This work is designed to be a companion volume to 'The Junior Book of Authors,' second edition, revised, edited by Stanley J. Kunitz and Howard Haycraft and published in 1951. . . . [It] includes biographical or autobiographical sketches [arranged alphabetically] of 268 authors and illustrators of books for children and young people. The great majority are authors and illustrators who have become prominent since the publication of the second edition." Preface

1 Authors   2 Illustrators ɪ Title   920.03

Printed card showing series note (no series entry indicated)

       The Reference shelf

301.43 Horowitz, Alice H   ed.
    The outlook for youth.   Wilson, H.W. 1962
216p (The Reference shelf v34, no. 1)

    "The articles in the first three sections deal with subjects of major importance to young people—education, employment, and marriage. . . The concluding section, 'Present Trends,' offers some general comments on the attitudes of high school and college students and outlines several ways in which young Americans have participated in public affairs in their own country and abroad." Preface
    Bibliography: p206-16

1 Education — U.S.   2 Marriage   3 Vocational guidance
4 Youth ɪ Title ɪɪ Series   301.43

Series entry

       Second World War

940.53 Churchill, Sir Winston Leonard Spencer
    Hinge of fate.   Houghton 1950
1000p illus maps (Second World War v4)

    "The Prime Minister tells of the year 1942 that led to the invasion of Sicily, through the ebb and flow of warfare in Africa, and the discouragingly slow job of reconquest. There are revealing accounts of meetings with F.D.R., and determined efforts at collaboration with Stalin." Retail bookseller
    Condensation of this title appeared in the "New York Times"

    1 World War, 1939-1945   2 World War, 1939-1945—Great Britain
ɪ Title ɪɪ Series   940.53

    4-16-54   (W) The H. W. Wilson Company

Series entry

FIGURE 7

A series entry must be traced on the main entry card for the work. This may be the designation: "ser" or "ser: (the name of the series)."

Restraint should be practiced in making series cards. Entries for publishers' series (e.g., Landmark Books) are rarely made, and there are reference books (such as the *Cumulative Book Index*, publishers' catalogs, and Baer's *Titles in Series*) which supply the information.

CHAPTER 5

Form of the Entry

Kinds of Entry

Not only is it important to determine which name or word is selected as the entry, it is important to follow established practice as to the form used. Roughly, the forms of entry fall into ten categories:

1. The personal name. May be used as main entry, or as subject or other added entry.
2. The corporate name. May be used as main entry, or as subject or other added entry.
3. The name of an object. May be used as main entry (though rarely), or as subject or other added entry.
4. The "form" or made-up entry. May be used as main entry or added entry.
5. The standard heading. Used as main entry for classical or other standard works; may also be used as subject or title.
6. The conventional title. Used with author, in which case it precedes the book's printed title.
7. The real title. Used as main entry or title added entry.
8. The catch title. Used as title added entry.
9. The word as subject (noun). Used only as subject entry.
10. The phrase as subject. Used only as subject entry.

Title entries (7-8) are discussed in Chapter 3, and subjects (9 and 10) fall in Chapter 7; the present chapter deals only with the first six forms of entry.

Personal Name

The personal name may be one of several types.

The easiest to work with is the type we are most accustomed to, such as John Clark Jones. This is entered under surname, followed by given name, as: Jones, John Clark. Unfortunately, our mythical Mr. Jones may vary his usage, at one time publishing under his full name, another time under John Jones, another time using J. C. Jones or J. Jones, Clark Jones, J. Clark Jones, or even just Jones or Mr. Jones. There was a time when catalogers did research on every name, exhausting every available source to "establish" the man's full name along with his birth and death dates. Even research libraries have had to give this up as too costly and not justified by need.

The current practice for small libraries is to use the name as it appears on the title page. If the name is the same as one already in a specific catalog for a different person, some distinguishing information is added for the new one. This may be a fuller name or the inclusion of birth and death dates or some other feature. If the person is already in the catalog under a different form of name, the earlier form is used unless there is some pressing reason to prefer the new one. If the newer one is used, it means recataloging all of the materials already cataloged or tying the two forms together through cross references or history cards. (See Appendix I, pages 145-148.)

If a printed card is being used and the name given on it is fuller in form than that given on the title page and it is a name new to the catalog, nothing is gained by cutting it back. If the printed card has a shorter form than that previously used, the additional information can be added to the new cards. For most personal names, the more information given, the better, for it is less likely to bring about later adjustments; however, it is not worth while to search for the information if it is not in the book, except when there is another person in the catalog with the same name. Another exception to this general statement occurs in cataloging for elementary school libraries or for children's rooms: it is felt best to omit all dates in these cases to avoid confusing the child.

Library of Congress cataloging often uses a name in a form fuller than that on the title page and fuller than that needed for the small library. If the individual library uses LC printed cards, it must decide when it must cut the names back or use a simpler form.

The H. W. Wilson cards now being made use the title-page form of the name in every case, without regard to consistency. In some libraries this may not matter, but others may want to establish one form for each writer so as to keep all his works together. There are good arguments on both sides of this question and the decision—an administrative one—should be made only after careful consideration and with good cause, not just on the basis of what the cataloger is used to doing or used to seeing other libraries do. The strongest argument for each author's having the same form, different from all others, is that it provides for the reader who wants to find all works of an author together. This is necessary in research libraries. The public library patron and usually the school library user much more often seek the individual title and find it more easily if the title-page form is used; even if several authors have the same name (e.g., John Smith), the user (who seldom understands the librarian's arbitrarily established items of differentiation) finds the title more easily if all works of all John Smiths are interarranged by title.

Personal names bring other questions and variations, among them: pseudonyms, forenames, changing names, compound names, names with prefixes. In general, the title-page form is used or the form most generally used or best known. But some further comments may be helpful.

A pseudonym is generally preferred, particularly for current and popular material, if it is generally used and known. Books are published, advertised, and sold under the pseudonym, and it is the name used in reviews and discussions. Why make it difficult for the reader to find the book? Public libraries (large and small) have been swinging to the use of pseudonyms for some years, and the schools are also turning in this direction. If an author uses both his real name and a pseudonym, or two or more pseudonyms, enter each book as its title page indicates. If it is desired, the individual's works may be tied together by means of references or history cards (see Appendix I).

Forenames are used for royalty, popes, saints, members of religious orders, etc. The small library has few of their works to worry about; those few can be handled simply by using the name followed by a designation, word or phrase (in English), to identify him.

Examples:

> Elizabeth II, Queen of Great Britain
> John XXIII, Pope
> Benedict, Saint
> Napoleon I, Emperor of the French
> Margaret, Princess of Great Britain
> Edward, Brother

People sometimes change their names: women marry, people change nationality and language form, etc. Use the name best known (e.g., Pearl Buck) or follow the title page. Following the title page too slavishly may occasionally give trouble since different printings or editions of the same work may be published under different names, but it doesn't happen often enough to weaken the principle.

For compound names or names with prefixes, the practice of the language in which the author writes is observed. Hyphenated names are treated as one name. References from the unused forms are made, if needed.

Examples:

> Fitzmaurice-Kelly, James (reference from Kelly, James Fitzmaurice.)
> FitzGerald, Edward
> De Morgan, Augustus (reference from Morgan, Augustus de)
> Du Maurier, Daphne (reference from Maurier, Daphne du)
> De la Mare, Walter (reference from La Mare, Walter de and from Mare, Walter de la)
> Le Sage, Alain René
> La Fontaine, Jean de
> Goethe, Johann Wolfgang von

Classical writers are entered under the names best known in English, as: Horace, Cicero, Virgil.

Corporate Name

Corporate bodies were discussed as authors in Chapter 3 and as added entries in Chapter 4. The form to be used for a corporate name is, again, that of the title page, or that best known or most used as:

> Boy Scouts of America
> American Library Association
> Library of Congress
> Chicago Museum of Natural History
> San Jose State College

(Note that articles "a" and "the" are not used at the beginning.)

If the name of the corporation is in a foreign language, the English form is used unless the foreign name does not translate well or is extremely well known. Thus:

> National Socialist Party, Germany, *but*
> Bibliothèque Nationale, Paris

If it is necessary to differentiate between two or more institutions or organizations of the same name, the place is added:

> Hawthorne school, Caldwell
> Hawthorne school, Springfield, Ill.
> Hawthorne school, Springfield, Mass.
> First Presbyterian Church, Indianapolis

If a work is produced by a section, chapter, division, or other part of a body, this is ignored in the entry; the main body is sufficient to identify the work except in very large libraries. Thus, a publication of the Reference Services Division of the American Library Association is entered only under American Library Association. If the division has a distinctive name, the name is used by itself, e.g. American Association of School Librarians (a division of ALA).

The corporate body may be a governmental agency. These are entered under the name of the governmental jurisdiction followed by a period, if no other mark of punctuation is present, and then by the department or bureau, all in the English form:

> Illinois (State) Department of education
> U.S. Office of education (U.S. is always used for the United States)
> Chicago, Ill. Police department
> Germany. National economic council
> Great Britain. Foreign office

The abbreviation for the state name is used after cities and counties of the United States, and "(State)" is added for states; the name of the country is added for foreign place names. Thus:

> Springfield, Ill.
> Springfield, Mass.
>
> New York, N.Y.
> New York County, N.Y.
> New York (State)
>
> Paris, France
> Montreal, Canada

These additions serve two purposes: to distinguish two places or bodies with the same name and also to differentiate official governmental publications.

Library of Congress entries for corporate bodies are most complex, using foreign language forms and many subdivisions; thus these cards are usually unsuitable for the small library. In some cases it is possible to line out the undesired subdivisions, but it is better not to use the cards at all.

Name of Object

Occasionally the name of an object is used (particularly as subject). The best-known form is used, followed by a descriptive word in parentheses if necessary:

> Plymouth Rock
> Leaning Tower of Pisa
> Eiffel Tower (Paris)
> Liberty Bell (Ship)
> U.S.S. Constitution (Ship)

Form Entries

For some entries extremely vague or variable in form, stylized forms have been established. Those used as authors ("form headings") are limited to "Laws," "Treaties, etc.," "Constitution," "Courts," "Charter." They follow the appropriate geographical name:

Ohio (State) Laws.
U.S. Courts.
Chicago, Ill. Charter.

The small library will have little need for such entries.

Anonymous Standard Works

Some works ("classics," epics, folk stories, etc.) have come down to us through the ages and have no known authors; or they are de-

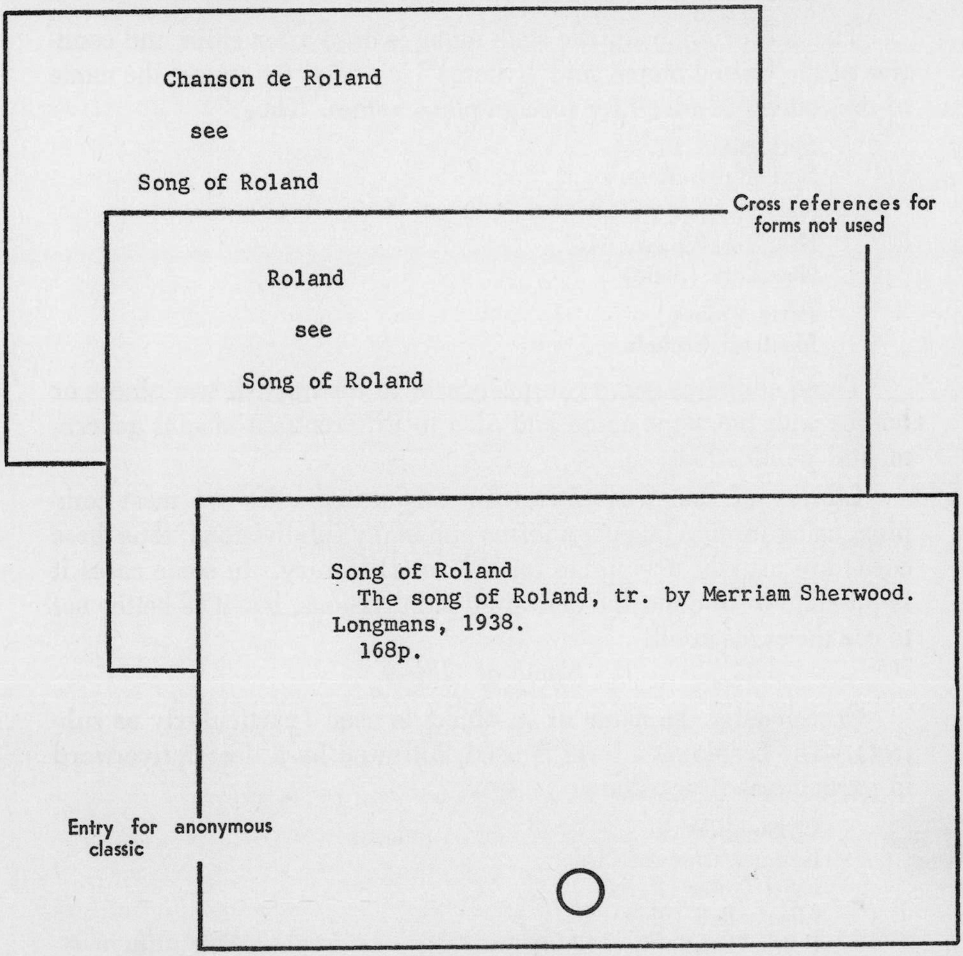

Chanson de Roland

    see

Song of Roland

Cross references for
forms not used

Roland

    see

Song of Roland

Song of Roland
    The song of Roland, tr. by Merriam Sherwood.
Longmans, 1938.
    168p.

Entry for anonymous
classic

FIGURE 8

rived from cycles of tales and are published under various titles. These include Mother Goose, the Pearl, Reynard the Fox, the Song of Roland, the Arabian Nights, Beowulf, the Fall of the Nibelungen, the Book of the Dead, Cynewulf, etc. For these, the English form is used with "see" references from well-known titles in foreign languages, as illustrated in Figure 8.

In some cases, an author is identified with groups of folk or epic stories even though these stories also exist separately. Best known of these are (1) the stories of Arthur and the Knights of the Round Table, which may or may not stem from the writings of Malory, and (2) Aesop's fables. If the book is definitely identified as the work of one man, his name is used as author; otherwise the standard name is used, as:

King Arthur

The Bible

The Bible constitutes a problem all its own. The ALA rule reads: "Enter the Bible or any part of it (including the Apocrypha) under the word Bible. Include as subheading, "O.T." (Old Testament), "N.T." (New Testament), the name of the book or group or books, as the case requires. . . ."

Bible.
Bible. N.T.
Bible. N.T. Mark
Bible. O.T.
Bible. O.T. Kings

Form or Conventional Titles

Even works of known authors may appear under many titles. *Don Quixote*, for instance, in addition to all its editions in Spanish and other languages, has been published in English under the titles *The History of the Valorous and Witty Knight-Errant, Don-Quixote of the Mancha, The Life and Exploits of the Ingenious Gentleman Don Quixote de la Mancha, The History of the Renowned Don Quixote de la Mancha, Don Quixote de la Mancha, The Adventures of Don Quixote, The History of the Ingenious Gentleman, The Ingenious Gentleman Don Quixote de la Mancha*, and many more.

If the library has several editions of such a work, it is easiest to adopt one form and use it at the beginning of the title, in brackets to show it does not appear on the title page. (This is one of the few times the use of brackets is recommended.) This device should not be used unless the library has several editions of the title or there is good reason to think it will have many and that following the title pages would result in the editions' being separated.

Example:

> Cervantes Saavedra, Miguel de
> [Don Quixote]
> The adventures of Don Quixote . . .

In this case, instead of making title references for unused forms or title cards for each form, one title reference is made, reading:

> Don Quixote
> Cervantes Saavedra, Miguel de
> For all entries of this work see entries under author

Form titles may also be used to bring together collected works of a prolific author. For instance, the library may have several books by Shakespeare with titles beginning with such phrases as "Complete Works," "Shakespeare's Tragedies," "Plays," "Four Comedies," etc. For these the form title "Works" will bring the titles together in one place without leaving interpretation and decision to the filer in such directives as, "File all collected works of an author together followed by titles of individual works." The entry looks like this:

> Shakespeare, William
> [Works]
> Complete works

In this case no title cards or title references are needed.

CHAPTER 6

Descriptive Cataloging

The term *cataloging* is sometimes employed inclusively to cover all of the activities involved in organizing library materials. It is also the term used for any specific part of the work such as establishing the form of entry. Catalogers themselves most often speak of cataloging in relation to its professional aspects as distinguished from the administrative and clerical ones of implementation. The professional work may be divided into two parts: (1) descriptive cataloging, which includes establishing the entries (main and added entries), both as to choice and form, and the descriptive information carried on the cards; (2) subject cataloging, which includes assigning classification numbers and subject headings to material.

This may be shown in outline form:

Cataloging in Its Broadest Sense

I. Administration of the catalog work
    A. Establishing goals of service
    B. Planning and establishing procedures and flow of work
    C. Selecting and providing care for supplies and equipment
    D. Supervising personnel, including assignment of tasks
    E. Coordinating cataloging with the other library activities
    F. Maintaining the catalog or catalogs
        1. Acquiring and/or making cards
        2. Filing cards
        3. Arranging for number and kinds of catalogs
        4. Providing aids for catalog use
        5. Keeping catalog or catalogs up to date
    G. Shelf-listing and maintaining the shelf list
    H. Physically preparing the materials
    I. Maintaining statistics and making reports

II. Professional cataloging
    A. Descriptive cataloging
        1. Choosing entries
            a. Main entries
            b. Added entries

2. Establishing form of entries
3. Selecting descriptive information carried on the card
4. Arranging information on the card

B. Subject cataloging
1. Assigning subject classification numbers (or call numbers)
2. Selecting subject headings

This chapter deals with parts 3 and 4 of II A of the outline.

Information on the Catalog Card

The items of information, any of which may appear on a full unit catalog card, include:

1. The call number
   a. Location symbol or designation
   b. Subject classification number
   c. Letter for main entry (author's surname, first word of corporate entry, or first word—not an article—of the title)
   d. Cutter number
   e. Work letter
   f. Edition designation (number or date)
   g. Volume or publication number

2. The main entry
   a. Personal name
   b. Corporate name
   c. Form name
   d. Title

3. The title statement
   a. Form title
   b. Main title
   c. Subtitle or alternate title
   d. "By" statement
   e. Statement of joint responsibility
      (1) Joint author
      (2) Joint editor
      (3) Editor
      (4) Translator
      (5) Illustrator
      (6) Sponsoring or collaborating body
   f. Edition statement

4. Imprint
   a. Place of publication
   b. Publisher's name
   c. Date of publication (or copyright date)
5. Collation
   a. Paging or volume numbering
   b. Size
   c. Illustrative information
6. Series note
7. Other notes
   a. Bibliography
   b. Contents
   c. Publication history
   d. Relation of work to other works
   e. Annotation
   f. Other explanatory information
8. Tracings
   a. For subjects (designated by capital letters or Arabic numerals)
   b. For other added entries (designated in entry form or by Roman numerals)
      (1) Joint author or other joint responsibility
      (2) Sponsoring or collaborating body
      (3) Titles

No library includes all of this information on any one card; small libraries never use all of it, and what they do use is in an abbreviated form.

Arrangement of Information

There is an accepted order for arranging the information on the card. Other things being equal, it is well to follow the form, but rigid conformity is no longer considered essential. The placement is indicated by (1) the left-hand edge of the card, (2) the "first indention," (3) the "second indention," etc. (see Appendix I for spacing).

On the main entry line (which is the top line of the main entry or unit card) appear from left to right: the classification number, the author's name, and his birth and death dates, if used. If the main entry is an editor or illustrator, etc., the relationship is shown after the name or dates, for example, "ed." or "illus." One line below the author or main entry and at the second indention begins the title. The title is generally taken from the title page of the book, unnecessary or repetitive information being eliminated, and other information being added if needed. It is in paragraph form if more than one line is required. (If a form or conventional title—see pages 48-49—is used, it appears one line below the author at second indention, and the title page title drops to the next line, second indention.)

The title page is not followed closely, and the use of dots and brackets for omitted or supplied information is no longer observed. (We are cataloging the book, not the title page.) The title includes the "by" phrase if, for any reason, the author statement differs from the name used as the main entry. Among the differences to be brought out on the card is joint or multiple authorship. Not more than three names are given, the rest being indicated by "and others." The title transcription also includes information about the edition, and any information necessary to distinguish the work from others.

Following the title transcription, in the same paragraph, is the imprint: place of publication, publisher's name, and date. The place is not necessary for general publishers, nor for publishers in New York, nor at all in the case of small libraries; if used, only the first-mentioned place is named. The publisher's name is shortened to the prominent name ("Scribner," "Little, Brown"). The date preferred is the copyright date (usually found on the back—or "verso" —of the title page). A small "c" precedes the copyright date. If no copyright date is shown, the imprint (title page) date is used. Fiction and children's books may not need any date (see page 59), or the earliest publishing date is used. If that date is old (as for standard works), a note may be added: "First published 1878," etc.

Below the title paragraph come the collation (paging, illustrative matter, size) and the series note. If collation is included (and it is recommended for nonfiction though not for fiction or for children's picture books), it is restricted to the last Arabic numeral printed in the book's paging and to the word "illus." or "map" for any illustrative material. Size is not noted. If Library of Congress cards are used, the size (or any of the above information) may be left on the cards even though it is not noted on typed or other locally prepared cards.

If the book is part of a series, that information follows the collation or is located where the collation would be.

Bibliographic information or other notes follow in lines below, each note being a separate paragraph. These include calling attention to a distinctive feature of the book, listing the contents, or giving information relating the book to others, such as change of title or a sequence. Wilson cards carry annotations (brief, noncritical descriptions of the content and coverage of the works), and this practice is being adopted by some schools and public libraries. (For examples of contents notes see Appendix I.)

Figure 9 illustrates a Wilson card, with the parts indicated:

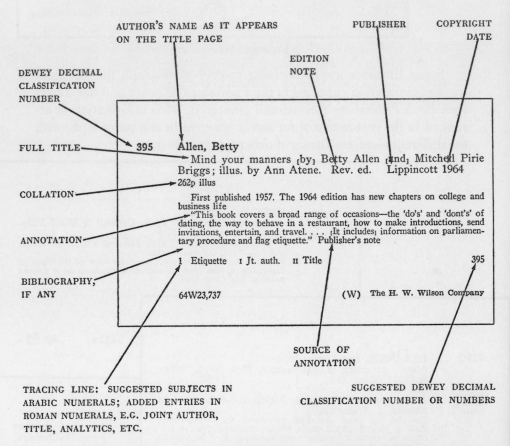

FIGURE 9

If there is no author and the work is entered under title, a "hanging indention" is used; that is, the title starts at the first indention on the top line, and the full title transcription and imprint all stay within the second indention.

Title main entry showing hanging indention

913.03 The concise encyclopedia of archaeology; ed. by Leonard
Cottrell. The contributors: P. J. Adams [and others].
Hawthorn Bks. 1960
512p illus maps

"Forty-eight of the world's leading authorities have recorded their
knowledge of every society and civilization that the world has known.
The articles are arranged alphabetically and more than 150 photographs
illustrate the informative text. A. J. Arkell, Thor Heyerdahl, J. Alden
Mason, and J. M. Cook are only a few of the contributors." Huntting
For further reading: p501-09
Quarto volume

1 Archeology—Diction-   aries i Cottrell, Leonard, ed. 913.03

60W10,493   ◯   (W) The H. W. Wilson Company

FIGURE 10

Some libraries and processing centers photograph the LC cataloging information supplied in the *Publishers' Weekly* and the *American Book Publishing Record* and enlarge it. This information is arranged in the customary order but is grouped in one paragraph, with the different elements shown in different type faces.

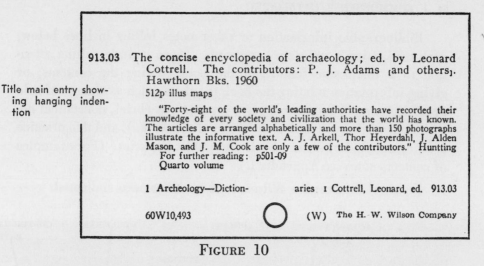

Fiction   BRESLIN, Howard
A hundred hills. New York, Crowell [c.1960] 300p.
illus.   4.50
*1. Vicksburg, Miss.—Siege, 1863—Fiction. 2. U. S.
—Hist—Civil War—Fiction.*
Romantic and dramatic novel from the days of the siege of
Vicksburg. A love story as well as a portrayal of a turning
point in the Civil War.

Title.   Ap 63

729.2   BERANEK, Leo Leroy, 1914-
Music, acoustics & architecture. New York, Wiley
Related
Books in
Catalog
Under [c.1962] 586p. illus.   17.50

*1. Architectural acoustics. 2. Music—Acoustics and
physics. 3. Music-halls.*
Text by the chief acoustical consultant for Philharmonic
Hall in New York's Lincoln Center. Features detailed statistics, acoustical evaluations, and illustrations of 54 halls in
all parts of the world.

◯   Mr 63

Cards photographed
from Publishers'
Weekly
(reprinted courtesy
of Wayne County
Public Library)

FIGURE 11

Books in Series

Books and other publications often have a direct relationship to other publications. For cataloging, these can be grouped as books in series, sets, serials (including periodicals), and variant editions. Sometimes it is difficult to distinguish among some of them.

Books in series follow one another in progression or sequence, or are closely related in content, and are grouped under an inclusive name. There are publishers' series (usually a group of books planned to meet a certain demand or age level) such as the Landmark Books or the Little Golden Books. There are information books or texts which progress in difficulty, such as numbered arithmetic books or readers; these are usually designated by volume or "book" number. There are true series related by subject and format which may or may not be numbered; examples are The Chronicles of America and The Reference Shelf. Lastly, there are works (usually fiction) in which the story and the characters are carried from volume to volume, as in the Jalna books or the Babar stories. Books in such series are generally cataloged separately but tied together by a series note or by a "Preceded by" and "Followed by" note; if important, they may have series entries (see pages 39-41).

If the volumes are numbered and the series is classified as a set (see below), it may have one inclusive cataloging as for a serial, or the volumes may be separately cataloged with the series note and with the volume number made part of the call number (see page 69).

Books in Sets

Some works are issued in sets: the collective works of an author, collections of types of materials, reference works, etc. If each volume is a separate title (such as a play or novel), it is best to separate the volumes and catalog and classify them separately. If they cannot be broken up, as in the case of an encyclopedia or separate works continued from volume to volume, they are cataloged and classified as a set. The publication dates (if more than one) are inclusive (e.g., 1950-55), and, instead of paging, the number of volumes is indicated (3 v., 2 v., etc.). If the set is cataloged before publication is completed, it is done as an "open entry"; that is, the imprint shows the earliest date followed by a dash, leaving space to fill in the last date when the set is completed, and the collation shows just "—v." with space for completion.

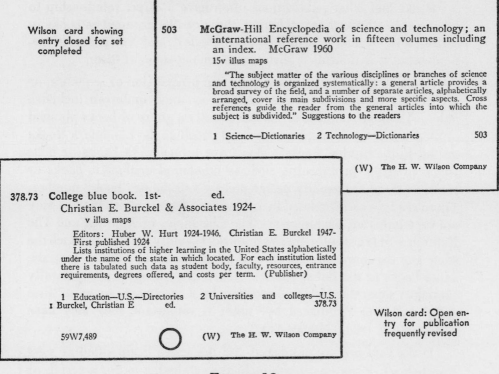

Wilson card showing entry closed for set completed

503   McGraw-Hill Encyclopedia of science and technology; an international reference work in fifteen volumes including an index.   McGraw 1960
       15v illus maps

       "The subject matter of the various disciplines or branches of science and technology is organized systematically: a general article provides a broad survey of the field, and a number of separate articles, alphabetically arranged, cover its main subdivisions and more specific aspects. Cross references guide the reader from the general articles into which the subject is subdivided." Suggestions to the readers

       1 Science—Dictionaries   2 Technology—Dictionaries   503

                                                 (W) The H. W. Wilson Company

378.73 College blue book. 1st-   ed.
        Christian E. Burckel & Associates 1924-
          v illus maps

          Editors: Huber W. Hurt 1924-1946. Christian E. Burckel 1947-
          First published 1924
          Lists institutions of higher learning in the United States alphabetically under the name of the state in which located. For each institution listed there is tabulated such data as student body, faculty, resources, entrance requirements, degrees offered, and costs per term. (Publisher)

        1 Education—U.S.—Directories   2 Universities and colleges—U.S.
        ɪ Burckel, Christian E   ed.   378.73

        59W7,489   ◯   (W)   The H. W. Wilson Company

Wilson card: Open entry for publication frequently revised

FIGURE 12

Serials, Including Periodicals

A serial is "a publication issued in successive parts, usually at regular intervals, and, as a rule, planned to be continued indefinitely." (See *A.L.A. Glossary*.) Serials include such materials as periodicals, reports, yearbooks, memoirs, proceedings, bulletins, and transactions. The small library has few of these and seldom catalogs those it has—periodicals, almost never. A few rules are sufficient for this type of material (see Chapter 14).

A serial is entered under the title, with hanging indention and, if incomplete, with an open entry (see above). If the serial is ended or completed, the cataloging is closed; that is, the concluding dates are indicated and the total number of volumes given. If the publication changes title, each part is cataloged under the title at time of publication, and the records of parts are brought together on the catalog cards by means of notes: "Preceded by . . ." and "Continued as . . . ."

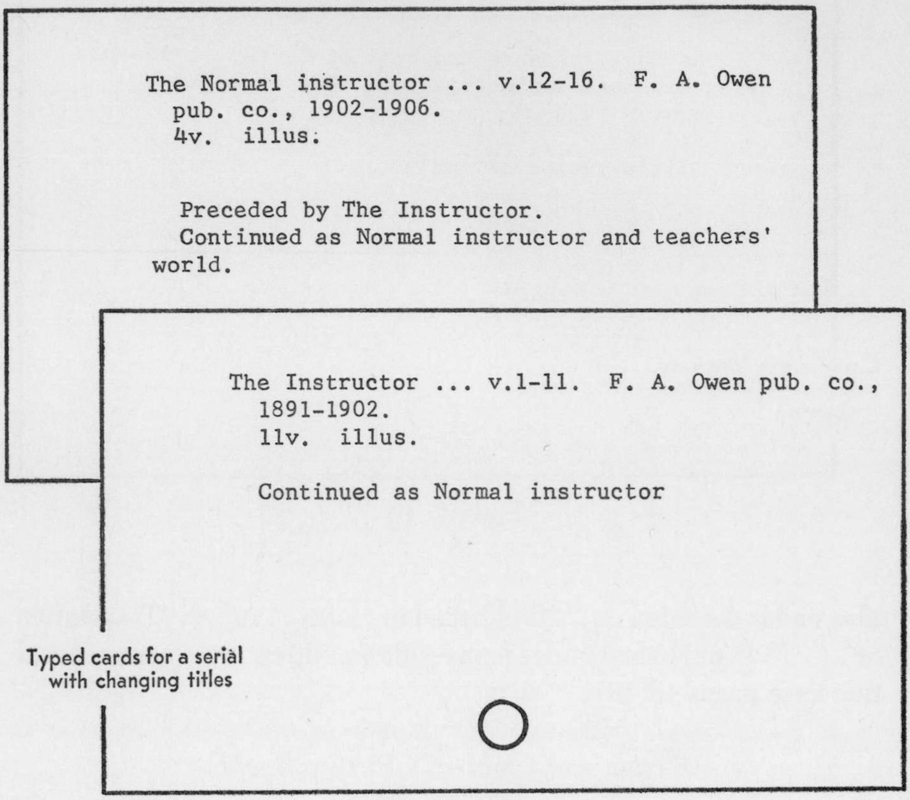

```
        The Normal instructor ... v.12-16.  F. A. Owen
          pub. co., 1902-1906.
          4v.  illus.


        Preceded by The Instructor.
        Continued as Normal instructor and teachers'
      world.
```

```
          The Instructor ... v.1-11.  F. A. Owen pub. co.,
            1891-1902.
            11v.  illus.

          Continued as Normal instructor
```

Typed cards for a serial
with changing titles

FIGURE 13

Variant Editions

Generally a new edition of a book is cataloged separately if it varies in content from the preceding one. Some works are frequently revised or issued at frequent intervals with different contents (such as almanacs, yearbooks, "Best plays," etc.); public and school libraries find it helpful to catalog these as open entries (like true serials), thus avoiding much recataloging. In research libraries many more editions of works are retained, and details of edition variation are important. For this reason those LC cards which catalog each edition separately are not followed by small libraries.

Different editions of a work may sometimes be published under different titles. For these, catalog under the title page for version (or versions) in the library, indicating variations with a note: "Published

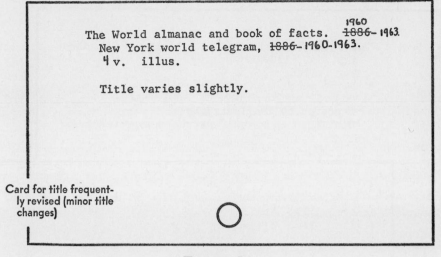

The World almanac and book of facts. ~~1886~~ 1960- 1963.
New York world telegram, ~~1886-~~ 1960-1963.
4 v. illus.

Title varies slightly.

Card for title frequent-
ly revised (minor title
changes)

FIGURE 14

also under the title . . . ," "Published in . . . as . . . ," or "Translation
of . . . ." If published under many different titles, use a conventional
title (see pages 48-49).

Fiction and Children's Picture Books

For nonfiction (adult or juvenile) more information is needed
about the work than for fiction. For factual material, the edition, the
editor, the publisher, the publication date, and the paging are important as showing the age of the information, the authority, etc.
Since the cataloging is exact, a separate set of catalog cards is
required for each edition or version except for the frequently revised
works noted in the section above.

Fiction and children's picture (or "easy") books do not require
such exact identification; in fact, all that is required is the name of
the author, a short title, and the copyright date. For older, standard
fiction, the date may be omitted, or the note "first pub. . . ." may
be used (see Figure 15). Thus one cataloging will take care of all
printings and editions of a work of this type. This method of handling
the material saves much time since fiction and picture books have the
heaviest duplication and discard pattern.

If the name of the illustrator is important (as it sometimes is in

jF   Stevenson, Robert Louis
                 Treasure Island. first pub. 1883.

**Shelf-list entry for title
showing the date of
original publication**

Figure 15

identifying different editions of children's books), this information
may be indicated on the shelf-list card, relating it to the individual
copies. (See Chapter 10.)

CHAPTER 7

Subject Cataloging

Subject Entries

As indicated in Chapter 2, one of the important reference services of the catalog is to show what material the library has on different subjects. Classification locates the book by subject, but each book can stand in only one place, and subject entries in the catalog bring out other subject facets, and also relate subjects to one another and suggest new approaches. Even the tracings are helpful in this. Specialists may often seek a specific title under author or title entry, but students and laymen (and even specialists are laymen in all but their own specialties) lean heavily on the subject approach.

Subjects are shown by using names, words, or phrases as filing terms or entries. These are added (one card for each subject entry) in capital letters at the top of the unit card. (Formerly subjects were typed in red, but in the present age of rapid copying machines, printing, and photographic copying of cards, red is no longer practical.)

A subject card is made if an entire work is about one subject or if a major part or section of a book is about one subject. To bring out different facets or relationships, several subject entries are sometimes needed. The number used depends on the complexity and importance of the book, the size and goals of the library, and the amount of material available on the subject. A small library will make more subject entries on general topics than will a large one; the larger one may be more interested in bringing out a new or little-known topic of interest to only a few specialists. The beginning cataloger tends to make too many subject entries. He should not try to analyze every thought in the book but should deal only with its major contributions. Subjects go out of date quickly, in both terminology and concepts, and the cataloger who is overgenerous in assigning them finds recataloging more difficult.

Any person—real, mythological, or fictional—may be a subject. The form for his name is the same as that for an author. Any object, institution, organization, or governmental or other body can become a subject for discussion or study; here again the form follows that of the other entries.

Words and phrases, however, are so varied in form and arrangement and their meanings so overlapping, that special guidance is needed to insure uniformity and consistency. For this reason, lists of subject headings have been prepared, and a selected one is followed. There are literally dozens of these lists, most for use with certain subject fields or specialties such as medicine, aeronautics, music, and law. The school library and the public library, however, need consider only the general lists.

Lists of Headings

The largest and fullest of these is *Subject Headings Used in the Dictionary Catalogs of the Library of Congress.* Designed for use in cataloging collections running into the millions, this list is not needed for children's books or for school libraries (with the possible exception of large technical or college preparatory high schools). Larger public libraries use LC subjects for adult books, but smaller ones do not need them. These subjects are the ones indicated on LC cards. The small library using LC cards may find that it must use shorter, simpler, or more general terms and will therefore not follow all LC suggestions for subjects.

For children's books, Elva Smith's *Subject Headings for Children's Materials* was very good at one time but has been out of print and out of date for many years. In 1952 the ALA published *Subject Headings for Children's Materials,* by Eloise Rue and Effie LaPlante, which was designed especially for school libraries, observing the philosophy of the educational institution. This, too, has become dated, and at present there are no plans for revising it. Moreover, it is difficult to use it in conjunction with other lists, since it reverses in some places the principles followed by LC, Smith, and Sears.

Sears List of Subject Headings, revised by Bertha Frick, is designed on the same principles and follows in general the practices of the LC list; the two can be used to supplement each other with some alteration. Sears can also be used to supplement Smith. Sears is revised every five or six years with emphasis on updating terminology; it contains terms simple enough for children's cataloging and subjects adequate for most adult materials. In addition, it indicates the Dewey Decimal class numbers for the terms used. Sears headings, moreover, are used on Wilson cards. For these reasons it is recommended for supplementing older lists and for full adoption whenever possible. Before using it, the cataloger should study carefully both the preface and the introductory section, "Suggestions for the Beginner in Subject Heading Work."

It has sometimes been argued that school libraries should use terminology which follows the curriculum. This is not recommended by experienced librarians since it confuses the child who has to use different libraries. It is better to make references from educational terms to equivalent headings in the list.

References

There is need for a network of "see" and "see also" references to lead the user from terms he may think of to those used in the card catalog. These references must be kept accurate; they must not refer to terms no longer used or away from those which *are* in use. Thus, one looking under ANIMAL STORIES will be told to look under ANIMALS—STORIES (a "see" reference). At the end of all of the cards headed ANIMALS—STORIES, there should be a card saying:

> ANIMALS—STORIES
> see also
> ANIMALS—HABITS AND BEHAVIOR
> ANIMALS IN LITERATURE
> (etc.)

The references to be made are indicated in the subject headings list, and a record of those used in the individual library is made by checking these items. Additional references are sometimes made if they are found to be needed.

Subjects in Regional Processing

It is in subject work that a cooperative or regional processing center is most helpful; but, paradoxically, it is in subject work that the center leaves most work to be done in the individual library. The centralized work is helpful because it is done by experienced people who have adequate tools available, and also because the work is suitable (assuming that the cooperative venture comprises libraries of comparable sizes and goals). But subject cards, even from these centers, must be consistent with those in the individual catalog and must be reinforced by the proper references. Ideally, perhaps, the cataloger from the center visits the cooperating libraries to advise and check on the work. In a school system, the communication can be much closer and more uniform than in public libraries located in different towns. But even a large public library system in a single city finds it difficult to keep branch catalogs up to date and accurate, so the problem is always present.

Subject work is most important and most difficult, calling for a wide background of information and knowledge and also for judgment. It cannot be done thoughtlessly or slapdash or turned over to a typist. It requires careful study of methods and principles, complete comprehension of the information contained in the introductory material of the list employed, careful study of each publication, and thoughtful consideration of the work in relation to the library's collections, clientele, and goals. Nor may a subject, once selected, be forgotten; each new book or new term calls for reevaluation of older usage, possibly for recataloging.

CHAPTER 8

Classification of Books

As noted in Chapter 2, most books in the collection require some classification in order to lead the user from the card catalog to a specific subject, and also to group together the books on the same or related subjects.

Classification Schemes

If there are only a few appropriate lists of subject headings, there is even less choice for the classification scheme or schedule to be followed. Only two general classification schemes are widely used in America today: the Library of Congress classification (LC) and the Dewey Decimal classification (DC). Although LC is superlative for very large or for special or research libraries where there is a concentration of many books in a subject area, the Dewey Decimal classification is the overwhelming choice for schools and public libraries and should be adequate for most church libraries. (A genuine research collection of theological materials would do better with LC, however.) Dewey is the classification most used in general libraries and best known to library users. It is also followed by many printed bibliographies and library tools, both in arrangement and in indicating classification numbers for individual titles. Its "Relative Index" and its mnemonic features (certain numbers carrying the same meaning throughout) make it easier to learn and to use. But perhaps its strongest point is its adaptability to the size and nature of a collection.

Reader Interest Classification

Some libraries have experimented with reader-interest classification, that is, large groupings of material around general interest topics such as "The Home," "Hobbies," "The Job," etc.

There are several ways to manage the details of establishing such groupings. One is to use the group term in place of the classification on book and on all catalog cards; this commits one to leaving books in this arrangement permanently or to reclassifying them later if the arrangement should be changed. Another method is to classify regularly, then add to the catalog cards the group name by means of a stamp or penciled notation; this also means removing the marks if books are removed from their groups. The simplest way is to pencil the information opposite the accession information on the shelf-list card; this makes it possible to put different copies in different places (one in the large grouping and one in its regular class number, for instance) and means that only one change needs to be made when the book is removed from the group.

The books must also be flagged or marked in some way to insure their being returned to the desired shelves. This can be done by using colored dots on the spine—nail polish does this effectively—or by using special book cards; the latter slows up shelving, of course, since it requires the shelver to open every book.

Most libraries find following a standard subject classification best for the bulk of the collection, and cater to special interests (which change from year to year) by means of exhibits or by setting up temporary groupings. Reference work and finding the individual title are easier when each book has a definite location.

Dewey Classification

Dewey divides all knowledge into nine subject classes (100-900) with a tenth (000) for general materials. Each class number is subdivided by 10, these 10 again by 10, and then each whole number by decimals for specific breakdowns (see Appendix V). This allows the individual library to classify as broadly or as specifically as its collections and purposes demand. This feature is reflected in the Dewey publishing pattern; there is a full edition and an abridged one for libraries up to 20,000 titles. Each starts with summary tables. While it is possible to assign to certain books classification numbers of seventeen or more digits, each representing a refinement, it is just as correct to use, when appropriate, a much shorter number for the same book. Elementary schools and very small public libraries will seldom if ever need to go beyond three or four digits. Larger high schools and medium-sized public libraries may need to expand in certain subjects to four or five figures (one or two beyond the decimal point) and in a few subjects even to six figures. The abridged edition is adequate for small libraries; it expands where expansion is needed and is the safest guide to follow.

The ten classes of Dewey are:

000   General works
100   Philosophy

200 Religion
300 Social sciences
400 Language
500 Pure science
600 Technology
700 The arts
800 Literature
900 History

One subject may be traced through its steps, with intervening numbers omitted, to illustrate flexibility:

600 Technology
  620 Engineering
    621 Mechanical engineering
      621.3 Electrical engineering
        621.38 Electronic and electric communication engineering
          621.384 Radio communication engineering
            621.3848 Radar

Thus a book on radar engineering might be classed in any one of these seven numbers depending on the size of the collection and the degree of specificity needed. If the library has twenty or thirty books in its entire technology group, all engineering books could be put in the general engineering number 620; if it had a large collection on engineering, the seven digits might be employed, thus locating the book on radar in its precise slot.

For the inexperienced classifier the danger is in being too specific. It is wasted effort and only confusing to use the most specific (longest) number for each book in a small collection. The numbers on Wilson cards are safe to follow. The suggested numbers on Library of Congress cards usually need to be shortened. The classifiers at LC deliberately carry numbers to the farthest possible subdivision, taking it for granted that individual libraries will cut them to suit their needs.

Fiction, Juvenile Books, and Other Variations

Simpler and shorter numbers can be used for children's books than for those in adult collections since there is much less material available in each subject field. And certain kinds of materials for either adults or children can be given group designations. "F" has been used in many libraries for fiction and "B" or 92 for individual biography. "Easy" or picture books can also be grouped under a single symbol such as "E." Or, preferably, fiction, at least fiction in English, is not classed at all, but simply shelved in a separate, author-arranged collection. In this case, it has been found helpful to have the word "Fiction" appear on the catalog cards where the classification number usually appears—since the users have been instructed to get a "number," they sometimes select any item on the card if the call-number space is blank.

A public library or church library needs to differentiate between adult and juvenile materials and uses a small "j" before the class number for children's books, as j530, jB, jF. Public libraries usually classify a title which appears in both adult and juvenile collections with the same number, but some compromise may occasionally be necessary for certain types of material. Children's librarians, for instance, may want to classify fictionalized biography with biography, whereas librarians working with adults treat it as fiction. Legends, folk stories, and fairy stories may be made a separate collection in the children's room or kept with fiction; in the adult collection they may be classified as folklore. Titles which go only into the children's collection can, of course, be classified as simply as possible and in the class where they are the most useful in work with children.

Classifying a Book

A manual to explain the Library of Congress application of Dewey numbers is available, but small libraries will find the introduction to the abridged edition of the Dewey Decimal classification scheme an adequate preparation; a careful reading of it is essential before any attempt is made to classify.

Classification is a third area, along with establishing the main entry and subject cataloging, which calls for knowledge, experience, and judgment. The cataloger must study the book being classified, the classification scheme, and the individual library's collection. He must class each book in relation to what has been done before but must also face a world where knowledge is growing and changing at a dizzy pace.

He can get help from printed cards, and from such book reviewing tools as the *Standard Catalogs, Book Review Digest,* the ALA *Booklist and Subscription Books Bulletin, Publishers' Weekly,* the ALA "Basic Book" lists, *Children's Catalog,* etc., all of which give suggested classifications.

Call Numbers and Cutter Numbers

A call number is a number assigned to a book to distinguish it from others. It got this name because in former days books were kept in stacks or shelves inaccessible to the public, and the patron requested or "called for" the book he had selected by means of the catalog. This is still true, of course, of any part of the collection which is closed to the reader.

A full call number may include a subject classification number, a letter or letters plus a number representing the author's name, a "book" or "work" letter indicating the title, and designations as needed for edition, volume or copy number, special location symbol, and size indication. Thus, an arithmetic book entitled *Playing with Numbers*, by Becker, might have a number like

511
B39p3
v.2

This shows that the book is on arithmetic (511) and will be shelved with other arithmetic books. The author number (B39) is obtained by combining the initial letter of the author's last name with a number from a numerical table so designed as to insure, through its use, an alphabetical arrangement. This is also called a Cutter number since the tables were devised by C. A. Cutter; they were later expanded from two to three figures by Kate Sanborn and are called the Cutter-Sanborn tables. For most names, one initial and two numbers are used; for names beginning with vowels or S, two letters and one number are needed, thus: Sm5, An3.

The "p" in the Becker call number derives from the title, and the 3 following shows it to be the third edition of this work. The third line is for cases of works of two or more volumes. The call numbers on the catalog cards do not, as a general rule, include volume numbers, since the cards apply to all volumes of the set. The volume number does appear on the back (spine) of the book, on the book card, and the book pocket.

Not all of this call number is needed for the small public library, still less for the school or church library. The usual practice is to use just an initial for the author, thus:

511
B

The book is then shelved with other books with the same classification number, alphabetically by the author's name (except for biography, described below). This sometimes means lettering the author's name on the spine of the book, if it does not already appear there or if the name printed is not the one used in cataloging.

How large a library should be before it considers the use of Cutter numbers is a question debated among librarians. If there are so many books in one class as to make shelving or finding individual titles difficult, there are two ways to break up the group: closer (more exact) classification or the use of Cutter numbers. Generally, the first is preferable since it can be employed only where needed.

A second criterion for considering Cuttering is the need for differentiation among various editions of a work. Each edition of a nonfiction book requires separate cataloging; so if multiple editions of a title are kept, the need arises to differentiate. This may be done by using a full call number or by making the publication date part of the number, thus:

511
T
1963

Some librarians use Cutter numbers only for the more crowded classes of material, such as 398.2 (legends) or biography, and use just initials elsewhere.

Whether classified (in 920-929), kept in 92, or B, individual biography is cataloged by author but arranged according to biographee. If a Cutter number is used, it is the number for the subject, and it is followed by a letter for the author, with a second letter, if needed, for the title. Thus, Sloane's life of Robinson is

B
R65s

If Sloane writes a second book on Robinson, another letter is added after the "s," as "sc." If there are biographies on other Robinsons, different numbers are used, as: R651, R652.

Special Markings or Symbols

Size creates a need for another symbol in libraries where very large or very small books are separately shelved. It is a saving of space to do so, for shelves can be placed nine or ten inches apart to accommodate most books. Very small books (under three inches in height) are not shelved in place because they are too easily lost or mislaid. The few small books may be kept in a drawer or cupboard and the catalog and shelf-list cards stamped "Shelved separately. Ask at desk." Books too large for standard shelving can be shelved, according to number, in a special section with high shelves. (They should never be turned on their fore-edges, as this practice breaks the backs.) For these a "q" may precede the class number (q759) on all cards and on the book itself. The letter stands for "quarto," a term adapted from the rare book trade and in general usage. Some libraries even have groupings by size, e.g., those up to nine inches, those nine to eleven inches in height, and those over eleven inches. In this case, "q" is used for the second size, and "f" ("folio") for the largest. But this adds to the confusion of the public and should be done only for the most pressing of reasons.

Reference books must also be identified by printing "R" or "Ref" or some such symbol above the class number on the spine of the books and, if the books are cataloged, on the catalog cards. The cards may also be stamped in the left margin to indicate location, e.g., "Reference book. Inquire at desk."

Other symbols are also used. Reader interest classification was mentioned above. Most public libraries have special collections for young adults; these may be marked "Y" on the spine. Public libraries also mark spines to indicate mysteries, westerns, collections of short stories, etc. These are not necessarily separated from other fiction; and if they are not, the mark on spine (with a colored disc or "spot") is all that is needed. Special collections such as those on local history, if separately housed, must be marked by a symbol. Books in foreign languages may be kept separate; in this case letters ("G" for German, "F" for French, "R" for Russian, etc.) designate language, as well as location. Audio-visual and other non-book materials are usually designated by letters: "R" or "P" for recordings or phonodiscs, "S" for slides, etc. (see Chapter 14).

Use of symbols requires careful planning. A list of all those used must be compiled and made available to the public. The same symbol cannot have two meanings: thus "R" cannot stand for Reference, Russian, and Records; nor "S" mean short stories, Spanish, and Slides.

To complicate the picture further, elementary school libraries frequently grade their materials for appropriate age level or school grade. The grade numbers may appear only at the upper right-hand corner of the shelf-list card.

The following rule of thumb may be helpful: If the symbol designates a separate shelving or housing for all copies of the work, it must appear on the catalog and shelf-list cards as well as on the materials themselves. If the symbol is used for separate shelving of only some copies (as perhaps for "Y"), it must appear on the material and on the shelf-list card but need not show on catalog cards. If the symbol does not disturb the shelf arrangement of the material, it appears only on the material itself and a notation is made on the shelf-list card to insure that all copies are marked uniformly.

CHAPTER 9

Copy Identification

Every copy of every publication which is circulated or loaned for use must have its own distinguishing designation to keep the holdings and circulation records accurate.

Copy Numbers

If there is only one copy of a title, the author and title or call number distinguish it. For a volume of a set of books or magazines the number of the volume and/or issue sets it apart from other pieces with the same title.

But as soon as two or more copies of the same work are acquired, another means of identification becomes necessary. The simplest method in a single collection is to use copy numbers—the first copy of a title has no number, the second becomes copy 2, the third copy 3, etc. To apply this system effectively, all copies must be acquired at the same time, a record must be maintained of the number of copies the library holds of every title, or some other device must be evolved. The shelf list (see Chapter 10) keeps the record of cataloged books. However, if the library is or is likely to become part of a system of libraries or if the cataloging is done centrally for several libraries, the shelf-list record for all of the agencies may not be handy to the cataloging office. Even if it is, the copy assigning becomes involved and adds another step to the work. Copy numbering, furthermore, must be done as part of cataloging, whereas accessioning can be done wherever it fits best in the procedures.

Accession Numbers

For these reasons, the employment of a "copy identification" (or "accession") number is recommended. In this procedure, every book or piece to be cataloged is given a sequential number; the number is stamped or written in the book and is used in shelf-list and circulation records. The number may be a continuing sequence: the first book ever acquired is number 1, the next 2, and so on forever. The disadvantage of this is that unbroken numbers are more difficult to type and to check accurately than those with some kind of break.

Such a break can be made by incorporating the year into the number. Thus the first book acquired in 1965 is given the number 65-1, the second 65-2, etc. If possible, an automatic stamping machine should be acquired. Larger libraries or processing centers handling many volumes use a seven- or eight-digit numbering machine—whichever length seems appropriate to the library's or system's annual acquisitions. In this case the first number is 65-0001 or 65-00001. The machine works by tens from the right-hand side, the tenth number in each row tripping the change in the next row; thus the number of digits is always the same. The same practice can be used for smaller numbers; 65-001, etc. Incorporating the date also gives additional information: it shows how many books were added in a given year and also the approximate age of each book. By recording in a small notebook the last number used each day—or week —or month, statistics and age can be more closely pinpointed. It is possible, of course, to combine numerals and letters in an accession number, but the last two advantages are then lost.

If stamping is done, the number is stamped on the book card and pocket and in the book, preferably on the first right-hand page following the title page. It is unsightly on the title page, and it should not be on the back of the title page because the stamping breaks the back if pressure falls on the back of the book rather than on the bulked pages. Sometimes it is also possible to stamp the number directly onto the shelf-list card. Machines rarely have more than triple automatic repeats, but if a book card is not used or the pocket is not stamped, one stamping is saved. A large operation, such as a processing center, may use a second machine for shelf-list stamping. It is also possible to buy a machine which repeats until hand-triggered to change to the next number.

The numbering is done where it best fits in the procedural chain. For an individual library or one with a central shelf-list record, it is perhaps best done before the cataloging starts so that the record on the shelf list can be typed as the rest of the typing is done. If the work is being done for a system of many libraries and the shelf-list cards are stamped, the stamping can come last in the process. Or the stamping (or copy assignment) can be done by the individual library after receiving the book from the center.

The Accession Book

The term "accession number" is an inheritance from the old accession book and continues to be used by librarians even though "copy identification" is more accurate, if more unwieldy. Not too many years ago every library maintained a large book in which were recorded (by hand, alas), for every book received, the author, title, publisher, source, date of acquisition, and the amount paid. The accession book still exists in some libraries, but the only reasons for it would seem to be (a) to serve as a substitute for the catalog in a very small collection, or (b) to meet some legal or regulatory requirement. If the latter is the case, it would be well to work to remove the regulation.

Use of Copy or Accession Numbers

In discussing copy numbers and accession numbers, the important point is that although the system may change (from accession number to copy number or from copy number to accession number), only one system of identification should be used at one time. It is nothing but waste motion to use both an accession number and a copy number on the same book. Volumes of a numbered set, of course, carry both the volume number and the accession (or copy) number, since it is entirely possible to acquire two or more copies of any volume.

Accession or copy numbers are never re-used, e.g., for a book replacing one lost or discarded. Re-use of numbers would throw the statistics off and also mislead as to the age of the new copy. Besides, one cannot be confident that a withdrawn book will never reappear.

Accession or copy numbers, to repeat, are stamped or typed or written in the book, on the book card and pocket, and on the shelf-list card. They are not shown on catalog cards and are not lettered on the spine of the book, since they are of no interest to the patron. They are not even needed for shelving, for it makes no difference which copy comes first if there are two or more.

CHAPTER 10

The Shelf List

The shelf list is a file of cards, one entry for each title in the
cataloged collection, arranged in the same order as the books on
the shelf, that is, according to classification. On the shelf-list card,
in addition to the call number and cataloging information, is a notation of every copy and every volume the library holds of the title.

Value and Use of the Shelf List

The shelf list becomes the inventory record and, as such, is possibly the most valuable record in the library. It is the basis for
establishing the value of the collection, and sometimes is even insured
itself. In case of fire or other catastrophe, it provides the basis both
for rebuilding the collection and for damage claims. The shelf list is
also one of the most useful records for the librarian's work. In book
selection it is necessary to know the amount of material in a given
subject area as well as how many copies there are of each title. In
order work the shelf list is a handy source of information on bibliographical details and prices.

The classifier works constantly with the shelf list to see how
books in certain subjects have been classed, to see how different class
numbers have been applied, and also to determine when certain
classes are getting too full and hence need to be subdivided. If the
collection uses full call numbers (that is, uses Cutter numbers—see
Chapter 8), the classifier also must check the number considered for
a new book to make sure that it has not been used for another. And,
of course, the shelf list is used in assigning copy numbers if they are
used (see Chapter 9). In preparing bibliographies the shelf list is
sometimes helpful. And it is used for statistical counts and records
and as the tool in taking inventory. A very small library might get
along without a catalog, but it would have difficulty in functioning
without a shelf-list record.

Arrangement and Location of the Shelf List

The nonfiction entries in the shelf list are arranged according to
classification number and then, within the same number, alphabeti-

cally by author. The numbers follow numerically up to the decimal point, then in decimal arrangement after the point. Thus, 620 precedes 621, but 621.24 precedes 621.3, and 621.99 precedes 622. Cards for fiction are kept separate (unless classified in 813, 823, etc.), arranged alphabetically by author and then, under author, by title. Individual biography may be inserted between 919 and 920 or kept separate, arranged first by the subjects' names, then by author, and then by title of the book. It is helpful to type the shelf-list card with the name of the biographee at the top of the card above the author's name; this makes it easier to use and file this portion of the list. Other nonclassed books (picture books, etc.) are kept in separate files, alphabetically by author, then by title. Separate shelf-list files are kept for non-book materials, such as recordings, slides, etc. (see Chapter 14).

If books are Cuttered and a full call number is used, the shelf-list arrangement is exact: first by class number, then by author's letter, then author number, next by title, then by edition. The earliest edition comes first, the others following in chronological order. If the call number includes a date, the arrangement is also chronological.

The shelf-list cards are kept in easy-to-use file drawers of the same quality as those for the catalog, and, for easy consultation, the drawers should never be more than two-thirds full. The shelf list is kept handy to the area where the cataloging is done. It also helps to have it as accessible as possible to the reference and circulation work but never where it can be used by the public without close supervision. (Its records are too important to risk being marked, ink-spattered, rearranged, or otherwise tampered with.) And *no one* except the cataloger is ever authorized to remove a card or change a card or record in the shelf list.

Information on the Shelf-List Card

The actual information included on a shelf-list card varies from library to library and from one era to another. Formerly it was considered time-saving to prepare the card with the briefest possible cataloging information. Recently, however, libraries have had occasion to regret this, and opinion now favors using a full catalog card, giving all of the information included on the main entry card —in other words, using a unit card. Having this full information aids in classification and cataloging, often saving an extra checking in the catalog. Tracings, in particular, are needed. If printed cards are purchased or cards are machine-produced, it is actually quicker to acquire an extra card than to type a short-form shelf-list card; but even if the cards are typed, the extra minutes required to type a full card are saved over and over. An "S" penciled over the hole in the card or a stamped "Shelf list" identifies the shelf-list card so that it will not get into the catalog by mistake.

All copies and all volumes of a title are shown on the shelf-list card. If there is room on the face of the card, the holdings record is added there; otherwise, or when the space runs out, the card is flipped and the record goes on the back. If needed, additional cards may be prepared and tied to the first.

Examples of holdings records for a public library:

60-3	3.00	Each accession number indicates a copy followed by
62-76	3.25	the price of the book at time it is added.
63-60	3.25	

cop 1	3.00	If copy numbers are used instead of accession num-
cop 2	3.25	bers.

1959	59-7	3.00	For an annual or added volume or edition identified
1960	60-10	3.25	by date. Note 2 copies of 1960 volume, the second
1960	60-175	g	a gift.
1962	62-20	3.25	

v 1 58-7 6.50 v 1-3   For a set with volume numbers. Note 2
~~v 2 58-7~~   copies of v.2, the first having been with-
v 3 58-7   drawn (lost or worn out).
v 2 61-15

Every unnecessary stroke of pen or typewriter is eliminated, so "cop" is used for copy, "v" for volume, "g" for gift, and the dollar sign is omitted. The letter "c" is not used for copy, since "c" generally means copyright.

A school or church library will omit the price if borrowers are not charged for lost books.

The price indicated is that charged the borrower who loses the book. If the actual (i.e., discount) cost is charged (as it is in some schools), the price given is that of actual cost; if the price charged is the list (retail) price, that is the one shown. A public library may charge its adult borrower the list price and the child a set price; in that case, the list price is used throughout; it is consistent and also is more helpful as ordering information. It is possible in a public library to charge more than the list price to pay for the costs of replacement. In such a case, it is sometimes advisable to code the price, raising it, say, to the next even dollar and giving it a symbol. Thus, books priced at $2.01 to $3.00 could be P3; $3.01 to $4.00,

P4, etc. This coded price can then be included on the book card, and thus when a book is lost, the information is immediately available to the assistant responsible for overdues.

The price has to be noted on shelf-list cards, at least in the public library, in order to establish quickly the amount to be charged for lost books. It is also an aid in estimating the value of the collection for insurance purposes. And since in preparing a replacement order the shelf list must be checked to determine holdings in the library, jotting down the price at the same time saves looking it up in trade sources and helps to indicate the desired edition.

In Chapter 6 it was said that all editions of a fiction title or picture ("easy") book could be recorded on the same shelf-list record. If it is also necessary to identify variations among individual copies, this information can be included in the accession record thus:

59-621	2.00	(Heath)	or	59-621	2.00	(Heath ed.)
60-15	2.25	(Doubleday)		60-15	2.25	(Doubleday,
60-78	2.25	″				Peters illus.)
62-153	3.50	(Follett)		60-78	2.25	″
				62-153	3.50	(Follett, preb.)

Or the name of the publisher of the first copy received may be included in the imprint on the shelf-list card only, in which case only variations from the first copy are noted in the accession information.

Inclusive listing, such as "cop 1-3," or "v 1-4," is never used, for if one copy or volume is withdrawn, complicated notation then becomes necessary to indicate what has been withdrawn and what remains. Taking inventory is also made more difficult if there is inclusive listing. Ditto marks can be used as indicated.

Formerly it was the practice to include in the accession information the date and source of acquisition. This does not serve any apparent need. If reordering, the library places the order with its current dealer regardless of the source of the copies previously acquired. There is some argument for including the date of acquisition if the copy-numbering system is used, but an accession number which includes the date shows the book's age closely enough.

CHAPTER 11

Catalog Cards and Catalog Maintenance

Preparation of Cards

Catalog cards are made by individual libraries or library processing centers, using typewriters or other machines, or they are purchased ready-made. (See Chapter 12 for a discussion of card services.) Even if prepared cards are acquired, there is still some work to be done on them by the individual library. Therefore it is necessary to have available a typewriter with a card platen, preferably one with an immovable steel strip inserted the length of the platen rather than a smaller clamp which rises and closes on a spring. The latter gets out of order frequently, wears out the platen more quickly, and does not permit rolling the platen backwards. But to get the strip one must be very firm with typewriter salesmen, who are invariably reluctant to supply this item.

Typing directions for making cards are given in Appendix I. But it is well to keep in mind that the more hand typing employed, the simpler should be the cards, for it takes time not only to type, but to proofread, and all typing must be revised letter by letter. Some information which can be accepted and used when found on a printed card can be omitted in typing. (See Chapter 6.)

Many copying machines have been tried by libraries in making their own catalog cards, but none are really successful in small operations. The inexpensive machines (such as the automatic typewriter, small mimeographs, etc.) require one full manual typing of stencil or master or copy plus more or less satisfactory reproduction. It has not proved to be efficient or economical to use machines for fewer than five copies per card; and since single, small libraries rarely need more than this, they are left with but three choices: to type all of their cards, to join a processing center or other cooperative operation, or to purchase printed cards—or to combine two or all three of these methods. Some libraries have occasional access to a duplicating machine outside the library or have one machine for all library work; but arrangement for its use means fitting the card work into other schedules, sometimes means transporting material from one work area to another, and generally does not produce acceptable work since different adjustments are required for cards and for paper work.

Catalog cards should be of good stock, exactly (preferably rotary) cut, and exactly punched with the hole in lower center. The so-called 3 x 5 card (which is actually 7½ x 12½ centimeters) is standard everywhere now, and no good can come of varying the size. Librarians no longer insist on a 100 per cent rag card, for it is more expensive, thicker, less flexible, and more difficult to use in a typewriter or copying machine than part-rag. It also soils just as quickly and, in time, tends to "fuzz" at the top. (Some soiling can be avoided by painting the tops of the cards with red ink. This is done by pushing all of the cards, purchased unbanded, tightly together in a box and applying the ink with a brush; it takes only a moment and is considerably cheaper than buying cards already edged.) Some of the library supply houses now sell a card which has no rag content but is acid free; this is cheaper even than part-rag, stands up well in tests, and, so far, in use. It is best to use unlined, plain white cards of medium weight.

Catalog Maintenance

A school library may need to maintain just one catalog and one shelf list; a public library needs at least two catalogs and two shelf lists, one each for adult and children's materials. The children have their own catalog for several reasons. If they have their own, on their eye level, they use it more easily, take a proprietary interest in it, and learn from it. Sometimes they experiment (rearranging or removing cards or guide cards) and this is easier to correct in the smaller catalog. They are not always deferential to adults if sharing the same one, and besides the children's and the adult collections are usually in separate areas. Most important, simpler entries and subjects are used for children, thus making interfiling with the adult cards difficult. There are other, more subtle, differences between cataloging for children and for adults. For instance, "Juvenile literature" is a legitimate subheading for a subject assigned to a book, but it is not one used in a child's catalog—it is redundant since all of the material in the juvenile collection is for children, and the child will *not* be drawn to any book so described.

The catalog case should be expertly made by experienced library suppliers so that the drawers move easily and are neither too long nor too short; the rod holding the cards is true and strong; the cards move easily in the drawer; smoothly-sliding shelves are provided at the proper place; and the hardware (windows for labels, rod locks, and handles) is attractive, strong, easy to use, and rust-proof. All of the drawers should be near eye-level and easily reached. It is better to have fewer drawers per vertical row and to spread them farther in width, both for ease of use and to enable more people to use the catalog at the same time.

Cards should never fill a drawer more than three-quarters full; this allows enough space for them to be pushed back and forth and remain fully exposed without having to be held. Proper allowance should be made for growth, so new cases will start with only a few inches of cards per drawer. The adjustable back block is moved to keep cards upright. When a case is outgrown, new sections are acquired (another reason for using standard makes which provide for expansion), and the cards are redistributed. This is done by pushing all cards of each drawer to the front and, holding them tightly together and upright, measuring them with a ruler. The total inches of the measurement of all cards is divided by the number of drawers now available to give the number of inches of cards to be allotted to each. A blank card should be placed at the front and back of each drawer to absorb dust and dirt. The number of cards assigned to each drawer cannot be exactly the same, because the break between drawers should come at a convenient place in the alphabet: between "Def" and "Deg," for instance, rather than between "Defen" and "Defeo."

The labels for each drawer will show the contents of that drawer, and the whole alphabet must be covered though there may not be entries for every combination of letters shown. Thus, one drawer label would not end with "Debt" and the next start with "Deep" even though these are the key words on the cards at the break; the labels would in this case end with "Deb" and start with "Dec" or end with "Ded" and start with "Dee."

Strong and attractive guide cards should be interspersed among the cards approximately 1 to 1½ inches apart—less to start with since they get farther apart as the number of cards increases. If they can be afforded, titled guides with printed strips to be cut and inserted in window slots are most usable and attractive. There is a new guide card available, made of Mylar; it is attractive, takes far less space, and is reported to be as durable as that made of cardboard. The word appearing on the guide should, for the most part, be a simple, short one which is likely to be used for a long time. For instance, one selects "Farm" rather than "Farm Animals," "Johnson" rather than "Johnson, Robert M.," or "Johanesen." (There will probably always be a Johnson in the catalog, but not always a Johanesen or a Robert M. Johnson.) It is simplest to use half-cut guides and alternate right- and left-hand ones.

For spots where the filing is complicated and difficult to understand, guides may be used to show the arrangement. Thus:

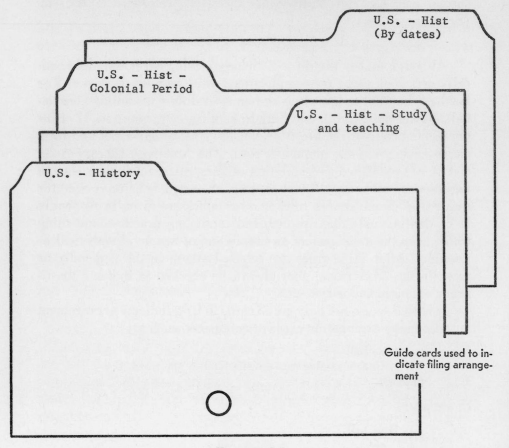

Guide cards used to indicate filing arrangement

FIGURE 16

"How-to-use" cards should also be scattered through the catalog, one or two to a drawer. And directions for use of the catalog should be posted nearby. They should be in large print and should have diagramed card information, demonstrating what is an author, a title, a subject. Such aids are available from library supply houses.

The catalog should be kept clean, attractive, and up to date. If cards or labels become soiled, they should be replaced. Isinglass or other transparent material can be cut and inserted in the drawer windows over the labels. Colored labels to match the decor of the room are effective and attractive, and can be a help in keeping drawers in order since one color can be used for all drawers in a horizontal row. It is possible to obtain plastic covers to use over cards in sections getting very heavy use; these are also available with colored top borders, as are catalog cards with different-colored top edges for special use, e.g., for audio-visual materials, reference books, etc. (See Chapter 14.)

Filing

Although we say that in a dictionary catalog cards are alphabetically arranged, there are complications which require decisions. For instance, how do we file words or names of different spelling (basketball, basket ball; Smith and Smyth; catalog, catalogue; etc.)? How do we file prefixes (de, Mc, Mac, von)? What of surnames and forenames, abbreviations, numerals, etc.? The American Library Association has published a compilation of filing rules which gives enough variations to allow any library to select its own; it is being revised for easier use. Some simple rules and examples are given in Appendix II of this manual; these recommend cataloging practices and filing which keep the arrangement as simple and as nearly alphabetical as possible. After filing rules are selected (those in the Appendix or those in the ALA rules) they should be checked to indicate the library's choices and usage.

It is well to use not only guide cards to help indicate arrangement but also many explanation cards or references, such as:

> Base ball
>> In this catalog this term is filed as one word. See
> Baseball

or simply:

> Base ball
>> see
> Baseball

The more cards which are filed at one time, the less time is taken per card; therefore it is efficient to keep new cards arranged in a separate file (at the end or beginning of the catalog), interfiling when several hundred have accumulated. However, some libraries prefer more frequent filing, sacrificing some efficiency for the sake of improved service. The cards can and should be arranged and filed in the preliminary file by clerks, pages, volunteers, or student assistants. When the time comes to file into the main part of the catalog, the clerk or student does the preliminary filing, either leaving the cards above the rods or inserting a "filing" card before each card filed. This filing card should be heavy, of a bright color, cut one quarter of an inch taller than the catalog cards, and with a keyhole notch in the bottom center permitting it to be lifted out without removing the rod. The advantage of using such a device is that it is the filer who takes the time to remove and replace the rods; it also means that the drawers can be put back into the case without cards being lost or damaged. Further, service is not interrupted, and the revising can be done when convenient. The filer keeps a list of the drawers in which new cards have been filed. The filing cards can be used over and over again since the reviser removes them as he corrects the filing. These filing cards are available from library supply houses.

Filing should be revised by the librarian responsible for the cataloging, for he is not only checking the proper arrangement but is also watching for errors in cataloging, noting where guides or references are needed, looking for "dead" or questionable cards, watching for subjects requiring subdivision, etc.

CHAPTER 12

Cataloging Services

A librarian in the United States need not feel he is alone or has to pioneer; there is abundant help and advice all about him. First, there is much in print designed to inform him, and often there is an experienced librarian in the community or nearby who will be only too happy to help a newcomer or a beginner. Most important, a great many states have a state library or state library extension service to advise public libraries, and state or regional school library supervisors to help school libraries; this is the primary concern of these offices. Many churches foster church libraries, preparing guidance manuals and offering advice from their central offices. Information is supplied through the mail by library schools and large libraries, as well as by the Library Services Branch of the United States Office of Education. Salesmen from library supply houses can be helpful; most of them sincerely want to assist each library to find the supplies and equipment that are best for its needs. Moreover, studying supply-house catalogs is an education in itself.

Published Cataloging Information

In addition to the essential cataloging tools cited in Chapter 1, there are many other publications which give help to the cataloger and classifier. No matter how small it is, the library will undoubtedly subscribe to the ALA *Booklist and Subscription Books Bulletin;* this carries a selected list of new books in each issue, showing for each an annotation, the proper author and title, the Dewey Decimal classification, the Library of Congress card number (for ordering cards from LC), an indication as to whether Wilson cards are available (W), and suggested subjects. The *Standard Catalog* series, which includes *Standard Catalog for High School Libraries* (available also with a *Catholic Supplement*), *Children's Catalog, Fiction Catalog,* and *Standard Catalog for Public Libraries,* gives complete Wilson company cataloging and classification information, and any library should have at least one of them. The suggestions made in all of these tools are appropriate for small libraries, including school libraries, and can be followed if they agree with the individual library's cataloging policies.

Library of Congress cataloging is now given in full in the weekly listing of new books in *Publishers' Weekly*, and this information is cumulated in the monthly *American Book Publishing Record* (BPR), as well as in the LC catalogs of printed cards. The last mentioned will probably not be in the small library, but may be available in another local library. *Book Review Digest* and *Cumulative Book Index* also carry helpful information, matching that of LC. The LC cataloging is most helpful in indicating authors and in suggesting classification and subjects; however, the small library should not follow it blindly—the classification is often too detailed, the authors (particularly corporate authors) too complex, the subjects too specific or too technical. Publishers' catalogs usually provide information on the subject coverage of the books listed, and so, of course, do all reviewing magazines. The cataloger of the small library must learn to check all sources of information but must use them judiciously.

Printed Cards

Printed (or processed) catalog cards are available from many sources. The Library of Congress, as it catalogs books for its collections, prints extra copies of the cards and sells them. This cataloging is for a very large library which includes materials from all over the world in every language, so that the cataloging is appropriate only for the largest high schools and the adult collections of public libraries of some size. Some publishers now obtain LC cards for their books and distribute a set in each copy; but there is no way to know this in advance. Some of these cards can be used as they are, some can be adapted, all will give some help to the cataloger.

The H. W. Wilson Company has been printing and selling cards since 1938, and these cards are designed specifically for the school and small public library. Entries are simple, descriptive cataloging is brief, appropriate subjects and classification are indicated, and annotations are included on the cards. They are available only in sets and can be ordered either with or without subject headings and Dewey classification numbers printed at the top. Since other added entries are already printed, the individual library needs to type only the subject and classification number, at most. A set of cards includes one author or main entry card, one card for each added entry indicated, and one author card for shelf-list use.

Printed cards, either LC or Wilson, will take some time to get—two weeks to several months, depending on the location of the library (mails take as much as a week from the West to the East Coast), and whether or not the cards are available when the order is received. Both institutions keep millions of cards printed and ready, but even so, cards for a specific book are not always immediately available. Some libraries order cards when ordering a book even though it results in some wasted cards if the book is not received. Ordering cards also takes time on the library's part: the catalogs or lists must be searched to locate card numbers or to see if cards are available; orders must be prepared; and the cards, when received, checked against the order, and brought together with the books. Records must be maintained for unfilled orders. Then in some cases adjustments must be made in accordance with local policy, and cards changed or retyped. If all of this holds up cataloging the books and interferes with service, particularly for adult books in a public library, the books should be classified with the help of printed information and released, after a brief penciled record has been made for a temporary file. If needed, temporary cards can even be made for the catalog and shelf list; such cards should be flagged, or colored cards should be used, so that they will not be overlooked indefinitely. Occasionally, a change in author may require rehandling a book so prepared —correcting the entry on book card and pocket, relettering the spine, etc.—but such occasional rehandling is not so serious as holding the book out of circulation. The lists of Wilson cards available now include the classification number for each title. The books can therefore be classified correctly even though the cards have not yet come.

The time and cost of purchasing cards must be weighed against the greater cost of doing all of the work in the library. Nor is cost the only consideration; the caliber of the work and the appearance of the cards are also important.

Centralized or Cooperative Services

Cards are sometimes available from sources closer to the library. For many years the Library Services Division of the Georgia State Department of Education has produced cards for the small libraries of that state. These are made specially for schools and small public libraries. Recently, other states have started similar services. Springing up all over the country are centralized processing centers for cataloging and making cards plus various other services such as buying, lettering, and jacketing. These are varied in organization—

single counties, groups of counties, regions, sections. Some are cooperative, with all libraries in a group combining their resources; some are organized so that one library supplies the service to others on a contract basis; some are part of a central unit such as a state or country library or a school system. These cooperative or centralized ventures do not necessarily save a great deal of money, but being able to afford specialists, better equipment, better tools, they provide more uniform and better work than the single library, and their services enable the individual librarians to devote more time to serving their patrons in reference, reader advisory guidance, book selection, and community work.

Commercial Services

There are also commercial firms (such as Alanar, affiliate of the Bro-Dart Industries, Inc., of Williamsport, Pennsylvania, and the Professional Library Service of Santa Ana, California) which will do any or all of the processing steps for a fee. Some studies have shown these services to be more expensive than centralized or co-operative processing organizations, but the latter are not always available, and, in each case, it is worth while to see what the services have to offer. Even if not used all of the time, they certainly can help in such emergencies as critical staff shortages, opening a new library or enlarging or reorganizing one, periods of rush spending, etc. They will do as much or as little as the library asks (Alanar even sets up a whole school library—books, furniture, catalog), but there are always some things that only the individual library itself can do: checking names and subjects against its own usage, making necessary cross references, accessioning or assigning copy numbers, adding accession information to its shelf list, and filing the cards.

CHAPTER 13

Physical Preparation of Materials

Books and other library materials must be physically prepared for the shelves and for circulation. They require marks of ownership, circulation provisions (book cards, if used, and pockets to carry them, and date-due slips), lettering and other spine markings, jacketing, and, for unbound materials, special strengthening. These procedures, like all others, must be fitted into the work where they can be done most efficiently and most expeditiously. It is work which can and should be done by the lowest-salaried assistants—student assistants (volunteer or paid), pages, or clerks. With careful planning it can be done quickly but exactly; bad or careless work can result in defacing the material, spoiling its attractiveness, or actually reducing its usefulness. New products which lead to new and improved ways of doing the work become available every day, so the methods need continuous study and improvement.

Information in the Book

Today it is not considered necessary to record full acquisition or accession information in the book. In public libraries the price (whichever price is recorded on the shelf list) may be noted on the slip or order card left in the book for shelf-listing or penciled lightly in the book itself. The first right-hand page following the title page is a good place for all information—call number, price if needed, copy or accession number, and, if work is done for more than one agency, the symbol of the agency. Some libraries use the back of the title page, but leaning on it to write or stamp on it breaks or weakens the back of the book, and the indentations show through and mar the title page. If it is known from the order that the book is a duplicate, it saves work to have this indicated on the order card accompanying the book or by penciling in "dup" in the book where the call number is placed, or by some other device such as underlining the price. When checking books against bills, new titles should be separated from added copies or added volumes to expedite the cataloging work.

Ownership Marks

Some stamping is necessary to identify ownership in order to aid in the return of a straying book and to discourage theft, but perforations should *never* be used. The stamping also serves as advertising; people on the street seeing others carrying interesting-looking books with the name of the library showing may become inspired to seek the service. Books need not be stamped inside. It is best to stamp just once or possibly twice—across the top or bottom while book is held closed. This is both visible and difficult to remove, and it can be done quickly by tipping a stack of books toward one's body and, holding them firmly with one hand and arm, stamping down the pile. They can then be turned over on the other side and stamped. Stamps in two sizes will take care of most books, one stamp about three quarters of an inch in height, one about three eighths of an inch. It is well to do the stamping just after the books have cleared the ordering procedures in order to establish ownership. If book pockets are used, they may be stamped (or they may be acquired preprinted with the name of the library).

The rest of the preparations work will come after cataloging and after the call number has been penciled in the book and the book card and pocket have been prepared. The book card and pocket carry the accession number or copy number, price if desired, call number or class designation, author's surname, and short title. The book pocket is pasted in; simple and inexpensive pasting machines are available if there is work enough to justify filling and cleaning them. Strangely, there can be considerable disagreement over where the pocket goes —front or back of the book, on inside cover or on flyleaf; actually it can't make very much difference—the library should use whichever location is best for its circulation procedures. The location should be the same in all books to speed the procedures. If plastic jackets are applied, the pocket must go on the flyleaf since the jacket overlaps onto the inside of both front and back covers. Date-due slips, if used, are also pasted on the flyleaf at this time; printed and gummed ones are available from library supply houses, as, of course, are pockets and book cards.

Lettering on Spine

The next step is the lettering or marking. There is considerable study going on now to find better ways of lettering book spines, but most of the new ways are for large operations, involving specially equipped typewriters, irons for burning in call numbers, etc. The small library is still better off lettering by hand with either black India ink or white engrossing or artist's ink (whichever shows up best on the particular book). A pen or fine brush is used, and letters and numbers are made as square and straight up and down as possible. Most students can soon learn to do this. If the library can afford it, a small electric stylus which transfers pigment from paper onto the spine produces marking which will not chip off. And the library supply houses have papers with numbers and letters printed in transfer ink—by moving the paper about over the spine and rubbing appropriately marked areas with a pencil, quite professional-looking call numbers can be made; it is expensive and slow, but not too much so for the small operation. If white ink is hand-applied, a swipe of clear shellac over the number makes it last longer. It is difficult to get anything to stick to waterproof materials used on some books; sometimes, however, ammonia or alcohol will remove the gloss and make the material more receptive to lettering.

If plastic jackets are used, pressure labels are applied, those with "permanent" glue being preferred. Such labels are on sheets and can be lettered with pen and India ink or typewriter, then removed from the backing paper and pasted to book jackets or to paperbound books. A book to be jacketed is *not* also lettered on the spine of the book itself; by the time the jacket is gone, most books are ready for rebinding or discarding, and it is easier to mark the few needing it than to mark all, often unnecessarily. Call numbers should, so far as possible, appear in the same location on all books so that the books look tidy on the shelves and can be more easily shelved and located. A piece of cardboard can be used as a measure. If the book is too narrow to carry the number horizontally, it can be turned and lettered vertically; when this is done, the marking should always run in the same direction, preferably top to bottom, to make shelving and checking of shelves easier.

If special marking is needed to restrict circulation, as for reference books, or to locate special or separately shelved collections, such as short stories, Westerns, mysteries, and books for young adults, symbols may be made part of the call number ("R" or "Ref"), or printed discs ("spots") may be pasted to the spine. If author or biographee or other designation is needed for shelving, the name or word is underlined with ink, or, if not there, lettered on the spine.

Plastic Jackets

Transparent jackets, called plastic but made from acetate or Mylar, applied to the books over the colorful dust jackets have done much to dress up libraries and "sell" books, particularly in public libraries. Whenever used, they are extremely popular, and they also save binding expenditures since, with ordinary, decent care, a jacket will give a book twice as many circulations as it would have without it. Each of the library supply houses has its own style of jacket, and the library should choose the one which seems most appropriate and easiest to acquire, stock, and apply. Some have paper backing which makes them wear longer and makes them easier to apply; but it also means carrying more stock since they come in one-eighth-inch size variations and must be fitted exactly. Without the backing, one jacket can be adjusted to fit several sizes. They may be applied with tape, but pasting the overlap directly to the inside covers of the book is advised (particularly for children's books) to prevent removal. Mylar jackets are the strongest and the most expensive; they do not shrink or expand in temperature change and do not tear, although they can be cut, punched, gouged, or burned.

Some libraries use the jackets for all books; others exclude reference or other noncirculating books, prebound picture books, or other categories. Some libraries use them only for popular or special reading collections, but in general their use is increasing.

The final step in the preparations is revising (inspecting) the work, that is, making sure that everything needed is taken care of and that the call numbers, names, and titles match in all places where used. The revising and shellacking can be done at the same time, thus saving one handling.

Special Materials and Treatment

Materials other than books often require special treatment, as, indeed, may some books. If pages are uncut, they should be carefully cut with a bone cutter; loose plates or plates loosely attached should be glued down. Plates in a portfolio need to have each piece stamped with ownership and lettered in pencil with the call number. Supplements laid in a book, such as folded maps or illustrative material, answer books, etc., should have a pocket provided to hold them or else be removed, marked with call number or author, and separately shelved, possibly in a vertical file; the book from which such material was taken must be marked to indicate where the missing material is located.

Audio-visual and other non-book materials all require special preparation; see Chapter 14 for details.

Some of the work can be done in the library, some requires the binder's assistance. Products available to help with much of it include such items as pamphlet boxes, pamphlet binders, plastic sleeves or special holders for recordings, etc. The binders and the library supply houses have worked on many of the problems and can give advice.

Mending

Nothing detracts more from a library's appeal than a shabby book collection. Dirty, ragged, and smelly books repel the most ardent reader; and keeping books clean, bright, and mended is a continuing and important responsibility.

Some books, especially those bound specifically for library use, are covered with washable cloth. Shellacking or spraying the backs helps oftentimes to bring back the color, and art gum can be used to remove pencil markings.

As books are checked in from circulation, as they are shelved or used, or as those on the shelves are checked, the librarian or assistant should always look at them critically to spot torn pages, splitting backs, loose cases, and other signs of wear and tear, and to see if the plastic jackets are torn. Quick mending can be done in the library, such as mending a page or two (using transparent, flexible, paper mending tape), running paste between the spine and book cover at the joints, or tightening the book into the cover with a strip of double-stitched binding.

Unless free student or other help is available, mending beyond this point usually doesn't pay; the book should be replaced or it should be rebound. A little study will determine how much mending each library can afford. Most of the supply houses have mending materials and publish booklets of mending directions. They will also arrange mending demonstrations at library meetings. But amateurish mending with "make-do" or inappropriate materials should be avoided like the plague.

CHAPTER 14

Non-Book and Near-Book Materials

The Growing Importance of Non-Book Materials

A characteristic of library collections in the past twenty-five years is the rapid development of the use of non-book materials, and it is a development which continues at an ever-increasing pace. Not only are printed and bound books appearing at a spectacular rate, but so are other forms of communication, and a library is no longer effective if it does not make many of them available: paperbacks (or "pocket books"), pamphlets, newspapers, serials, magazines, clippings, pictures, manuscripts, typescripts, archives, documents, films, filmstrips, slides, maps, microforms, recordings (phonodiscs, tapes, and wires), as well as physical objects such as models, museum materials, globes, etc.

All must be organized for use, and, because of their variations in physical form and other complexities, a great deal of time and consideration is required merely to make decisions concerning their handling. In fact, the whole area has been moving so rapidly that most librarians find themselves making rules daily to fit the new problems, and practices have not had time to settle into accepted, uniform, and recorded patterns. It may not take more time actually to handle these materials, but it takes a disproportionate amount of time to talk about them.

Since processing and other kinds of organization of materials are dependent on use, and since in different types of libraries use varies more for these materials than for books, it may be well to consider some of the differences between them.

In Different Kinds of Libraries

The public library is in direct contact with people of all ages, of all social, economic, cultural, and educational backgrounds. While it uses some of its materials in public programs, the greatest use is in direct loans of material either to be taken from the library or to be used in reference and individual research within the building or room. The library's materials (non-book as well as book) must be made as accessible to its patrons as quickly as possible. Although librarians are available for assistance, public library borrowers like (and are encouraged) to do as much as they can for themselves. To them, the form of the material is possibly more important than the subject; therefore audio-visual materials are more likely to be grouped by form (records, music, magazines, pictures, etc.) and less likely to be classified by subject. Cards may be added to the catalog reminding the person gathering material on a subject (as for a program) of the availability of non-book materials. These are usually information cards under subjects rather than catalog cards for individual items. Or, for certain categories (as records) the catalog cards may be kept near the materials themselves rather than in the general catalog.

The school library largely serves two more or less homogeneous groups: the students attending the school and the faculty teaching those students. While it conducts programs on its own, promotes reading, loans materials, and gives reference services, its nature is fundamentally educational, and its center is the curriculum. Consequently, the subject approach to materials is more important than their form, and school libraries gain by having cards for all materials in a single ("integrated") catalog. Regardless of the debate over whether the curriculum center or instructional materials center should be a part of the library or a partner to it, the fact remains that many school libraries do have charge of the special teaching materials and must organize them. Even when the curriculum center is separate from the library, most school librarians favor the library's having cards for the materials in the card catalog. Many school libraries also have responsibility for organizing and maintaining a professional library for the teaching staff of the school or school system. The materials are prepared, then, for three broad services: to provide conventional library service to the student directly, to furnish background professional reading for the teacher, and to provide the teaching materials for the teachers to use with the students in the classrooms.

The church or parish library is urged not to become just another lending library, but to serve as an adjunct to the church's activities. It provides specialized materials to lend for reading and also provides materials for teaching and other church and Sunday school activities. It may in addition have responsibility for the official histories and papers of the church. Its audio-visual materials will seldom be loaned but will be used in classes, programs, or church services and will be located by the librarian.

General Considerations

Certain matters need to be decided in regard to non-book materials generally. First, where will they be kept? Will they be available to the public using them? Will they be assigned a subject number based on the classification scheme used by the library? Will they then be shelved, if physically possible, alongside the books in the same class? Or will they be kept in separate files or cases, special shelving, or special areas? If the last, does the subject classification really help, or is it easier and more efficient to use an accession number with the items in each category thus arranged by order of receipt? Will the materials be cataloged, that is, have catalog cards made for them? Will these cards be kept in separate files grouped by category, kept separate but interfiled with other non-book materials, or filed in the general card catalog? Will those cards in the general catalog have a different color for each type of material? In schools, is the grade level indicated; if so, how? In children's collections, is age level indicated, and, if so, how?

The decisions depend on the type of the library, the proposed use of the materials, considerations of care and preservation, and the nature of each kind of material.

In this area no particular practices can be recommended for all small libraries. What follows is very brief and, necessarily, very general. If a library has only a few items in a non-book category, it can manage with the simple procedures mentioned. If it has much material or plans to collect heavily in any field, the librarian will need to consult the specialized works: Pearson for recordings, Osborn for serials, the Music Library Association for music, the Library of Congress rules for films, etc. (See Appendix VI, pages 180-186.)

Many libraries use symbols (e.g., "F" for films, "M" for maps, etc.) which are made part of the designated number (subject classification or accession), as M940 (map of Europe), F280 (Filmstrip number 280). Colors have been used by some to designate different categories, for example, blue for filmstrips, pink for records, etc. (Many manuals—particularly older ones—specify the use of colored cards; current practice favors cards with colored edging at the top. Plastic covers with colored tops are also available. With the wider use of machine-made cards and the photocopying of cards for various uses, the time has come to consider dropping the use of colors. A stamp with the word "Map" or "Filmstrip," or other designation can be used at the upper left-hand corner of the appropriate cards. This indicates the category to every user on both the original card and photocopies.) If accession numbers are used, a simple record must be kept to indicate the last number used, and it is best to use a different sequence for each type of material. Provision must also be made for keeping statistics on additions and withdrawals. This can be done by means of a catalog card placed at the beginning of the shelf-list section devoted to the particular material. Thus a card before the listings of filmstrips would be lined off with spaces for additions and withdrawals for each year, totaled at the end of the year.

Paperbacks, Paperbound Books, Pocket Books

A book to most people is one that is hard bound. Strictly speaking, the paperback is also a book since its contents are similar to (and often the same as) those of the bound book. But, because of its small size and fragility, it demands special consideration in the library.

Many, particularly the "quality" paperbacks, which are printed on durable paper and issued and distributed by general publishers, are treated as are other books—classified, cataloged, accessioned, and prepared in the usual manner for circulation. To last long enough to justify this expensive treatment, however, most paperbacks must be given stronger backs. They can be acquired in so-called "prebound" library binding, they can be sent to a library binder, or they can be reinforced (strengthened). This is done by carefully removing the covers, pasting them to a heavier paper (such as "red-rope" or wallet), and then pasting them (with plastic adhesive) back on the book. The lettering, pasting, and other preparations are then the same as that for bound books.

Libraries (all kinds) also buy inexpensive paperbacks in quantities for lending. If processing costs can be kept down, many more people can be provided with these appealing books for curricular or extracurricular reading. The paper, binding, and margins are so inadequate and the books themselves so short-lived that they do not justify the expensive treatment recommended above for the "quality" paper books. They should be purchased in lots, as many copies at one time as possible. They should not be cataloged, shelf listed, bound, or reinforced. They should be provided with an accession number for circulation use; a symbol may be part of the accession number, such as pb 1, pb 2, etc. A book card and pocket can be prepared and inserted, the books used until worn out, then thrown away—there are no records to be corrected. The book card should give the last name of the author (as it is on the title page) and a short title of the work. Most libraries keep these books in one place, as in a display rack, although some prefer to interfile them with other books; but for nonfiction, the latter method involves checking them in the catalog and marking the class number on the spine or inside the book—and this adds to the cost.

Pamphlets

The physical difference between a pamphlet and a paperbound book is technically only the difference in size, since pamphlets usually are defined as separate publications of less than fifty (or one hundred) pages. Librarians tend to separate them on the basis of content, thinking of the pamphlet as a special treatment of a specific subject.

Most pamphlets are short-lived but valuable because they give information more up to date than books; a few have real permanent value. There are four or more different ways of treating them: (1) If of sufficient value and anticipated long life, they may be cataloged, classified, accessioned, shelf-listed, supplied with book card and pocket, bound or put in pamphlet binder, and shelved—in fact, treated as a book. (2) Some pamphlets may be treated like the paperbacks above: stamped with ownership, given simple book cards and pockets, shelved in a separate collection, or shelved in their regular place on the shelves (without cataloging or shelf-listing). Some special materials which lend themselves to this treatment include paperbacked plays, holiday materials, house plans and decorator hints, paper books of recipes, librettos, Boy or Girl Scout booklets, rules for various sports, etc. (Such material is likely to be treated this way more by public libraries than by schools.) (3) Certain pamphlets of particular value to a subject may be given a general classification number preceded by a small "p," and dropped into a pamphlet box shelved at the beginning of the books in that classification. For instance, pamphlets on France might be lettered p914.4, contained in a box marked "France" and "p914.4," and shelved before the 914.4 books. Because of possible loss, this may not be wise for shelves open to the public, but it does save the librarian's time and makes the publications more easily accessible to the patron. (4) The most common way of treating pamphlets is to put them into folders or manila envelopes to be filed in a legal-size vertical file—the "Information File," "Pamphlet File," or "Vertical File." The pamphlet is stamped with ownership and with date of receipt, lettered on its face (upper left-hand corner) with a subject selected from the library's official list of subject headings (*Sears List, Readers' Guide, Standard Catalog*, or some other single source of subjects). Each folder is on a different broad subject, and a card list of the subjects used, plus a few cross-reference cards, is kept handy to the desk. Other libraries, school libraries particularly, put cards in the catalog under the subjects used, referring the user to the Vertical File. Some libraries prepare book cards and pockets for these pamphlets, but it is an expensive and time-consuming process. Others use slips or printed forms ("form cards") to charge them out, indicating number of pamphlets under each subject.

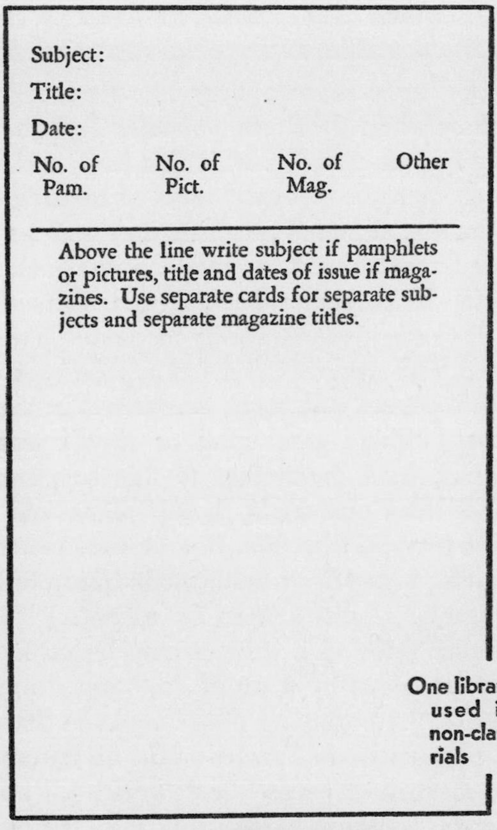

Subject:

Title:

Date:

| No. of | No. of | No. of | Other |
| Pam. | Pict. | Mag. | |

Above the line write subject if pamphlets or pictures, title and dates of issue if magazines. Use separate cards for separate subjects and separate magazine titles.

One library's form card used in circulating non-classified materials

FIGURE 17

Periodicals and Newspapers

A periodical is defined by the *A.L.A. Glossary of Library Terms* as "a publication with a distinctive title intended to appear in successive (usually unbound) numbers or parts at stated or regular intervals and, as a rule, for an indefinite time." Newspapers follow the same definition except that "their chief function is to disseminate news."

For either of these a checking card similar to the type shown in Figure 18 is used to enter each issue as it is received. These cards are available from library supply houses and may be obtained for different publication frequencies, such as daily, weekly, monthly, quarterly, etc. The record of receipt may be either a single check under the appropriate date or a notation of the number of the issue.

YEAR	Vol	Jan	Feb	Mar	Apr	May	Jun	Jul	Aug	Sept	Oct	Nov	Dec	Suppls	Ind
1964	20	4 18 11 25	1 15 8 22 29												

Weekly (entered by date) (usable also for entry by number)

YEAR	Vol	Jan	Feb	Mar	Apr	May	Jun	Jul	Aug	Sept	Oct	Nov	Dec	Suppls	Ind
1964	10	✓		✓		✓									

Bimonthly (usable also for entry by number or date received)

YEAR	Vol	Jan	Feb	Mar	Apr	May	Jun	Jul	Aug	Sept	Oct	Nov	Dec	Suppls	Ind
1962	35		#30		#31	#32				#33-34					

Irregular

YEAR	Vol	Jan	Feb	Mar	Apr	May	Jun	Jul	Aug	Sept	Oct	Nov	Dec	Suppls	Ind
1963	23	1	2	3	4	5				6	7	8	9	✓	

Monthly for part of the year

	1	2	3	4	5	6	7	8	9	10	11	12	13	14	15	16	17	18	19	20	21	22	23	24	25	26	27	28	29	30	31
Ja	✓	✓	✓	✓	✓	✓	✓	✓	✓	✓	✓	✓	✓	✓	✓	✓	✓	✓	✓	✓	✓	✓	✓	✓	✓	✓	✓	✓	✓	✓	✓
F	✓	✓	✓	✓	✓	✓	✓	✓	✓	✓	✓	✓	✓	✓	✓	✓	✓	✓	✓	✓	✓	✓	✓	✓	✓	✓	✓	✓	✓	✓	
Mr	✓	✓	✓																												
Ap																															
My																															
Je																															
Jl																															
Ag																															
S																															
O																															
N																															
D																															

Daily

Check cards used to record receipt of serials

FIGURE 18

The magazines are stamped with ownership and arranged by title in a special section of the shelving. The current issues of at least the popular general and news magazines are displayed in a magazine section of special shelves or on a table in the reading room; the older ones are kept in special drawers or section of the stacks, arranged alphabetically by title. Those most valuable for reference use are kept for some years or as a permanent file; the more ephemeral are discarded after their usefulness is past. If the individual issue is loaned out of the library, it will need strengthening; this can be done by placing it in a commercially-made plastic cover or by pasting it into heavier covers. Those to be kept for longer reference use should be bound by a commercial library binding company, or they may be bound in the library by gluing issues of a completed volume together with plastic adhesive. (Library supply houses have materials for this work, and their salesmen will demonstrate the methods.)

After magazines are bound or made into volumes, a record should be made on catalog cards arranged alphabetically in a special "Periodicals" section of the shelf list. Those which are bound and preserved may be cataloged and the cards interfiled in the card catalog, but it is more satisfactory to prepare a listing on sheets in a pamphlet binder or on tabs in a simple visible file (available from the Library Bureau Division of Remington Rand or Acme Visible Records). Such listings can show the names of all periodicals and serials received, whether bound or not, and may also include non-periodical serials (see pages 102-103). The listing shows what volumes the library holds. For example:

> Time, v.20-   1945-   (Indicates the library has a file from 1945 and is still receiving it.)
> Vanity Fair, v.5-10. 1925-30; ceased publication. (Indicates the library has a file for six years but is no longer receiving it.)
> Jack and Jill (current issues) (Indicates that it is being received but not kept beyond the current year.)
> The Instructor, v.₍65-73. 1954-62.₎ (Indicates that the library has a broken file of scattered numbers for the years shown.)

Magazines are not classified by subject number; if the library is large enough or if there is a special use requiring it, they may be arranged by a broad subject and kept near the books on related subjects, or in a special department. Thus, in a school, the magazines on educational methods, psychology, etc., may be kept in the teachers' professional collection. And a public library will keep magazines for children's use in the children's section.

Microforms

Microforms (microfilms, microcards, microprint, and microfiche) have not yet been adopted in small libraries, but public libraries large enough to keep files of newspapers and magazines are finding microfilms worth while even though they require the use of a reader. The film saves binding and shelving cost, and it solves the mutilation problem. Cheaper and better readers are becoming available, and films no longer have to be kept in special humidity-controlled cases. The boxes are marked with the name of the library, and the film marked at the beginning with the title of the publication, the dates covered, and the name of the library. (Special white marking pens are available.) Records for microfilms of serials, magazines, and newspapers are entered on the respective shelf-list cards along with records for bound volumes.

Serials

Some publications other than magazines or newspapers are also published in serial form. These may be issued in numbered series or as annual publications. They may be monographic series (each a different work by a separate author) or true serials of nondistinctive authorship. Reports, proceedings, bulletins, and circulars are examples of serials. Monographic series may be kept as a set under the inclusive title, or they may be broken, with each individual monograph cataloged separately, placed in the vertical file, or treated like any other book or pamphlet. The non-monographic serials are kept in sets. If important, such as local material in a public library, the set may be cataloged (see page 56) or arranged by title with the magazines and used until it ceases to have any value. For serials not cataloged, check cards should be made to indicate their receipt.

Clippings, Pictures, Reprints, and Similar Materials

Articles, pictures, news items, biographical sketches, charts, plans, etc., of local or curricular interest are often acquired or clipped for preservation. They must be dated and have their sources indicated on them. They are best mounted on sturdy cards, art paper, or mounting board (one to a sheet or two or three small ones on the same subject on one sheet); assigned broad subject headings; and put into the Pamphlet or Vertical File (see *Pamphlets,* above) or in a separate file or files. If many pictures are kept or if larger ones are used, a special picture file may be established employing steel cabinets for folders of pictures or special files permitting pictures and posters to be laid flat in sliding drawers. As with pamphlets, broad subjects are used, and a card index is prepared. These cards may be kept in a separate index (in public libraries) or filed in the catalog (in school libraries). If the latter, cards should show distinctive color or, better, should be stamped appropriately (for example, "Vertical File").

Manuscripts, Typescripts, Letters, Archives, and Other Papers

Handwritten or typed materials occasionally become part of even a small library. Lesson plans, scripts, etc., may be in the school library's teaching materials. A public library, because no one else is responsible, may become custodian of local history materials which include unpublished letters, speeches, reminiscences, or even official documents or records (archives) of organizations, firms, or government units. The church library could conceivably be the keeper of the church's official papers, sermons, etc.

These items may also be classified by subject and kept in pamphlet boxes or vertical files, possibly separate ones.

For this type of material the librarian must often consult with others—the school librarian with his faculty, the church librarian with his clergy and church officials, and the public librarian with officials, archivists, and historical or research librarians—to determine use and protective provisions.

Maps

Maps come in many forms: small flat ones, folders (such as travel and road maps), large flat maps, and wall maps. With all, the area covered is the important approach. They are arranged, therefore, by area, whether they are separately housed or included in pamphlet or vertical files (in a separate file for maps or in the general file). Some libraries classify maps by area as subject, using a preliminary symbol or letter, as M940 (for Europe).

The larger and more important maps should be cataloged, with the cards interfiled with others in the main catalog. The cards can have colored edges, a plastic cover with color, or the stamp "Map" above the call number. The information given on the card includes:

1. location symbol (e.g. M940, word "Map," case and drawer number, or accession number—the accession numbering being a separate series from that for books)
2. the area (in capital letters as for any subject)
3. publisher or issuing body
4. date
5. series, if part of one
6. size (in inches)
7. scale

```
MAP
M37        ALBUQUERQUE, N.M.
             Albuquerque and vicinity, New Mexico -
           Bernalillo Co.  United States Geological
           Survey, 1957.
             6x9"
             colored map
             Scale 1:24,000


           U.S. Geological Survey
```

Catalog card for map
(main entry under
area; arrangement
by map accession
number)

FIGURE 19

A second card, identical with the catalog card (as illustrated in Figure 19), is typed and filed in a separate section of the shelf list. The map is stamped, marked with appropriate location symbol (classification or "Map," or case number), and housed in a map case or cabinet drawer.

If not cataloged, the map is lettered like a pamphlet, with the area name as the subject, and is added to the vertical file folder.

Some small maps should be mounted on art paper or board; some large ones should be laminated or backed with cloth if they are to be much handled or folded. The practice of rolling and standing them upright in an open case is not recommended.

Music

All music presents special problems. Even the bound song books or other scores are difficult to catalog and require special rules.

Unbound music, including sheet music, is most easily handled by arranging it according to composer, uncataloged, in flat drawers. Brief cards are prepared under composer's name followed by the name of the composition. On each card there should appear a record of the number of copies and the parts, etc. These cards may be kept in a separate file (in a public library) or in the catalog (in a school library) and stamped "Music," if desirable. If the library has little music, records of holdings can be kept in the catalog. If, however, the library is custodian for an institution's choral, organ, orchestral and other performing music, separate records are better; the material is handled so much that its life is short and constant changing of catalog cards would be necessary.

Musical works, if bound or reinforced, must be carefully prepared so as to lie open and flat.

Bound music should be cataloged and treated in the same way as other books. The cataloging entry is under composer (under title for collections, folk music, etc.) and includes notes to account for parts, etc.

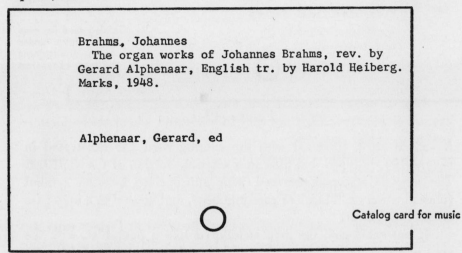

```
Brahms, Johannes
  The organ works of Johannes Brahms, rev. by
Gerard Alphenaar, English tr. by Harold Heiberg.
Marks, 1948.



Alphenaar, Gerard, ed
```

Catalog card for music

FIGURE 20

Films

Generally, small libraries do not have their own films but rely on film circuits, library centers, larger libraries, or some such source. Some libraries, however, may have their own, and the centers must organize theirs, so it is worth while to consider them briefly.

The simplest arrangement of films is by accession number, the first received being, perhaps, F1, the second F2, etc. Both the film itself and the can are marked with this number, and with the title and the name of the library. (Special pens are available now to do this marking.) They are housed in specially made shelving, with separate compartments permitting each can to stand on its side in its slot. The slots are also numbered.

The films may be fully cataloged according to Library of Congress published rules and, wherever available, with LC cards. Information includes title, producer, date, size (16 mm. or 35 mm.), color or black-and-white notation, number of reels or footage, run-

ning time, statement regarding sound track or accompanying recording, brief annotation, accompanying teaching aid, etc. (See page
151.) The cards carry the accession number and are filed in the main
catalog. Or, particularly for a public library, the catalog information may be inserted on form cards filed in a visible file separate
from the main catalog. In this case, it is advisable to have cards for
all of the subjects (which conform to the subject headings list
employed by the library) filed in the catalog. Such a card might
say, for instance:

FOLK DANCES
The Library also has films on this subject.

Filmstrips and Slides

Filmstrips are rolls of 35 mm. films, each roll consisting of several
frames or pictures. They are very important in school work, possibly
less so in public libraries.

Their treatment is similar to that outlined above for films: an
accession number (e.g., FS1, FS2, or F1, F2, etc.) is assigned and is
used on shelf marking, can, and cards. Or a subject classification
may be assigned, such as FS629.2 for automobiles. The thinking
here is that people are trained to think in terms of Dewey subjects;
but this seems a bit artificial since (1) the filmstrips require separate
housing and cannot therefore be available with other materials on the
subject, (2) the patron does not make his own selection, and (3)
arrangement of the filmstrips by subject is more complicated and
either wastes space or calls for continual shifting.

If there is considerable lending, book cards may be made and
kept in a file nearby, to be completed in pencil and used as needed.
Or printed forms to be filled out may be used to charge the material
to the borrower.

Catalog cards may be prepared for each filmstrip and filed in the
catalog. Such cards, which show a distinctive colored border or are
stamped "Filmstrip," should include location symbol, title of the
filmstrip (the main entry), and additional information which is easily
available and helpful: manufacturer, date, series, and record of
accompanying scripts, recordings, or other aids. The number of
frames and whether they are in color or black and white is included.
A note is also made regarding accompanying sound track, script, or
text. Added entries are made for subjects and significant entries;
tracings are indicated on the title card. A shelf-list card is filed in a
separate section of the shelf list and will, of course, indicate whether
more than one copy is held.

```
FILMSTRIP
FS232     The Lewis and Clark Expedition.  Enrichment
             Materials, 1955.
             44 frames
             color
             35 mm.
             Teacher's guide in V.F.


          LEWIS AND CLARK EXPEDITION
          THE WEST - DISCOVERY AND EXPLORATION
          Enrichment Materials
                                            Catalog card for film-
                                            strip (arrangement
                                            by filmstrip acces-
                 O                          sion number)
```

FIGURE 21

As with films, separate visible file records may be made, with subject references in the catalog. And, periodically, lists of available filmstrips and/or films should be prepared for distribution.

Slides are treated the same way as are films and filmstrips, except that the symbol or designation may be different (e.g., "S"). The slides are cataloged as sets, and the main entry used is the subject rather than the title, which is often nonrevealing or nondistinctive. Schools, at least, may want slides classified by broad classification. Captions may appear on the frames or on an accompanying list; such information is noted on the cards. Each slide must be marked with its location symbol and with the name of the library.

```
SLIDES
S914.6   SPAIN
             Six Spanish cities.  Roloc, 1964.
             38 col. slides
             2x2"
             Typed script in V.F.




                 O                          Catalog card for slides
                                            grouped by subject
```

FIGURE 22

Recordings

Recordings include "phonodiscs" (music or nonmusic records), tapes, and wires. Phonodiscs are made in different speeds ($16\frac{2}{3}$, $33\frac{1}{3}$, 45, and 78 rpm, i.e., revolutions per minute); they are also available for either monophonic or stereophonic record players. The early 78's were thick and easily broken or damaged; for that reason and because of the fact that they are rapidly going out of print, they are no longer in use in libraries except for historical or "listening" collections. Newer 78's are occasionally bought to secure certain recordings of sound effects, children's material, or material not otherwise available. The 45's are, for the most part, recordings of popular music and hence not acquired for library use, except, again, for some children's records. The $33\frac{1}{3}$'s (the "long-playing" records or LP's) constitute the bulk of library collections. The very slow $16\frac{2}{3}$'s for very long playing (as for the bedridden or the blind) are becoming of more interest to public libraries.

Recordings are the most complex to process of any material; and possibly public and school libraries differ most in ways of handling them, since the public library's chief concern is lending them for home use and the schools use them primarily as teaching aids.

The first decisions are concerned with location and arrangement. Location influences arrangement; both decisions depend upon who will have access to the recordings and what will be the approach. And the decisions influence the cataloging details required. Decisions are based on such questions as: Will the music and nonmusic records be divided? Will records for children's use be separate from those for adults, or students' collections separate from teachers' materials? Will recordings be divided first by speed? Will the arrangements be by manufacturers' numbers, by accession numbers, alphabetical by composer or author, or by broad or exact subject groups? If by subject, will it follow Dewey, LC, or some special scheme? Libraries have employed dozens of combinations of arrangements, but the majority of those not tied to past decisions tend to choose one of three: (1) accession number, (2) author or composer, (3) subject.

For a small collection in a public library, accession number is the simplest. The number provides identification for circulation purposes, and, it is argued, since few recordings are available at a given time and those few kept in one display case, the patron can go through all of those displayed to make his choice. From the catalog he can choose and reserve a specific work. As the collection grows, it becomes more difficult for the patron to find what he wants among the records, and he must depend more on the catalog. If the collection is not accessible to the patron, he must make all of his selections from the catalog. For these reasons, the arrangement does not matter, and recordings are shelved most easily by accession number. Author and composer arrangement is not as easily handled in closed shelves and is little more helpful on the open shelves since patrons generally tend to select by form and since so many long-playing records have no author or else have several.

A subject arrangement is perhaps best for schools since it conforms with the placement of other materials and since the classification groups the musical records by form (opera, symphony, voice, etc.). A symbol may be employed, such as Rec782. In some public libraries, children's collections are divided by age interest with color used as the code device.

Musical recordings are most often cataloged, from the label, by composer, with added entries for subject (i.e., musical form), performer, instrument, arranger, and, if distinctive, title. Separate cataloging is done for each work on a record or in an album. If the works are many or by many composers, or if there is no composer (as folk music), the main entry is under the title. Information on the card includes composer, arranger, soloist or performing group, manufacturer's name, record number, number of sides, size, speed, and the title of recording on reverse side. If there are more than two works on a record, a contents note may be added. If the recording has accompanying material (libretto, contents, historical notes, etc.) it is best kept with the records, as in a pocket pasted in the back of the album or record holder. If this is not advisable, the material is marked with the call number of the record and filed in a vertical file. A note must then be made on the catalog cards, e.g., "Miniature score in pocket" or "Libretto in Vertical File." The book card must include all pieces, e.g., "6 records, miniature score," so that, when the work is returned from circulation, the person receiving it can check at once to make sure all is accounted for. Note of any damage or missing part should be made (in ink) on the book pocket so that later borrowers will not be held responsible.

Nonmusical records are cataloged under author. If there is no author or there are many, the title is used. Thus, John Barrymore's reading of Shakespeare is under Shakespeare; Edward R. Murrow's "I Can Hear It Now" is under title. Dame Edith Sitwell reading her own poetry is under her name, but if she read from several writers, the entry would be under title. Usually the cards, appropriately stamped, will be filed in the main catalog. Some public libraries, however, prefer a small separate catalog kept handy to the record collection.

Single records are placed in protective covers or containers obtained from library supply houses; albums may be pasted to these holders, or used as they are. Records have call number and name of library lettered on the seal, and on the sleeve, album, or holder. Book cards and pockets are prepared and inserted in album or holder or pasted to the sleeve.

Recordings are shelved in special shelves which permit each to stand upright, preferably each in its own compartment. "Tubs" or display racks, such as those used in music stores, may be used for a small collection kept in the reading room. Care must be taken, of course, to prevent damage. Records should be handled only by the edges and should not be stacked. They must be protected from spilled ink and shellac and kept away from heat.

Tape recordings become even more complicated than phonodiscs since experimentation is producing more and more refinements. Already there are single-track tapes, two-track tapes, two-track monaurals (two sound tracks blended), and four-track stereos. This means that all such additional information is also included in cataloging. The assigned numbers and the library's name are lettered on the seal of the spool and on the container. Tapes are used in teaching, particularly.

Wire recordings require similar treatment if they are a part of the library's collection.

Miscellany

Other physical objects are also found in libraries. Globes, for instance, have always been used, but school libraries are now also keeping other objects, e.g., models and museum materials for classroom use. Some do not require any processing, but school libraries like to have all listed, grouped by physical form under subject, in their catalogs.

CHAPTER 15

Keeping Records Up to Date

Getting materials cataloged, organized, and into place is only part of maintaining a collection. New material comes in, and it may affect what is already there, or at least it must be fitted in with it. Books get damaged, wear out, are lost or stolen; this means records must be corrected.

Authority Records

Some libraries consider it necessary always to use the same form in the catalog for each personal and corporate name so that all cards for works by and about the person or body will file together. If the form of a name varies, references are made from unused forms to the one which is selected. (See Appendix I, pages 146-148, for examples of reference cards.)

To insure such consistent practice, an authority file of names is maintained. At one time such files were most elaborate, with cards indicating every reference work or "authority" which the cataloger consulted to "establish"—that is, find the fullest form of—the name. Such research is no longer done. It is actually necessary only to check the individual library's catalog to see if a name has been used and in what form, and to maintain a separate authority file only for those names which require cross references. This is done only to have a record of the references made so that they may be removed from the catalog when the name is no longer used. If the library has only one catalog, the cross reference may be "traced" on the main entry card of one of the author's works. This tracing would read:

x from ———

If cards are made for selected items of information (such as analytics for works in certain series, illustrator cards for selected illustrators, etc.), records must be made and kept handy to the cataloging work. Decisions are made regarding individual serials: whether they are classed and cataloged; if so, whether as sets or separately; whether analyzed, etc. These decisions may be recorded on the serials records, in a card list, or on the shelf-list card.

As was pointed out in Chapter 8, a list of classification or location symbols must be maintained to avoid duplication and to insure consistency in form. Until the library has a manual of cataloging practice, such decisions can be typed in a loose-leaf notebook or on catalog cards filed in the work area.

For cataloging work done for a library in another place, as in a centralized processing center, records must be maintained at the center showing what subjects have been used and what cross references (subject or author) have been supplied to which libraries—or else the records must be kept at the individual libraries or branches and adjustments and references made there.

In other words, although record keeping should be kept to a minimum, any information which is necessary to doing the work properly should be recorded and kept available. Such records are necessary for consistency, and each library must decide where consistency is needed and to what extent.

The printed guides or tools will also serve as authority for what has been used and what is preferred practice. In the list of subject headings, checks may be used for subjects used and for cross references made (see the introductory chapter in the Sears list). This necessitates, of course, making sure that when the last card for a subject is removed from the catalog, the list is also used to remove all the references to the subject from the catalog, and to correct "see also" references. Finally, the checkings in the list are canceled. The library's decisions or preferences in regard to classification may be written into the schedules themselves. One disadvantage of making records in the printed tools instead of making card records is that when a new edition of a tool is acquired, the checking must be transferred to the new book, unless it is decided to use both the old and the new editions simultaneously.

Duplicates, Added Copies, Replacements, Continuations

So far as cataloging treatment is concerned, duplicates, added copies, and replacements are the same thing. It might be said that duplicates are additional copies of a title acquired at the same time as the first copy, added copies are copies acquired after the first one has been cataloged, and replacements are copies acquired to take the place of withdrawn ones.

No matter what it is called, each copy of a cataloged title is given an accession or copy number. The order record should show which books are added copies, and these should be handled separately from new titles. If the classification number is on the order record (as it should be), that leads directly to the shelf list and makes it unnecessary to check the catalog. The shelf-list card is withdrawn (in actual practice a group of books would be done at one time and all shelf-list cards for them pulled); the accession information is added to the card; a book card and pocket are typed; the shelf-card is refiled immediately after work is revised; and the book is continued on its way. If there is likely to be some delay and if more than one person is going to be using the shelf list, a penciled dummy or (better) the order card, is left in place of the shelf-list card while it is out of the files. The duplicate or added-copy work can be done by a student assistant or clerk. Should a "duplicate" nonfiction book turn out to be a new edition, it requires new cataloging—a new set of cards for each edition.

For sets of books, annuals, etc., which are cataloged under an inclusive title, the added volumes (continuations) are processed in the same manner as added copies unless the new volumes cause a change in cataloging, such as changed author, editor, publisher, title, etc., in which case all of the catalog cards may have to be withdrawn and changed. Sometimes the change means complete recataloging or reclassifying.

For "open entries" or continuations, sets, etc., the catalog cards may be changed to show the new additions. For instance, the number of volumes (which is penciled in) is changed to include the new volume, and the dates are changed to include the new accession. A contents note will need to be changed to show the new title. Some libraries make these changes only on the main entry card, stamping all the other cards to read: "For full information see entry under ————." When a set is completed or a serial ceases publication, the cards are all withdrawn and changed to include final information.

Recataloging and Reclassification

A certain amount of recataloging and reclassification is always to be expected. Terms go out of usage or change in meaning; new subjects come into existence and bring about changes in older ones; so much material may accumulate under a subject in the catalog or under one class number on the shelves that subdivision becomes necessary. Organizations, institutions, and people change their names or reveal real names. All of these things create the need for recataloging or connecting old and new by means of history cards or references. New editions of the classification scheme or the subject headings list or new codes and practices change meanings, groupings, interpretations, methods. The library must keep up with as many of these changes as possible, but should not jump at every suggested change without careful consideration and the conviction that the change is definitely needed to improve the service.

Innovations, independent revisions, adaptations, or alterations of the printed tools should be scrupulously avoided. Today's improvisations too often create tomorrow's crises.

Withdrawals

A book is withdrawn from the collection when it is mutilated or too worn or soiled to be usable; no longer useful (information out of date, replaced by newer material, no longer read); lost in circulation; shown to be missing through unfilled reserves or searches; or missing in inventory. If it is a duplicate or a volume in a set and there are other copies or volumes still in use, the catalog cards are not touched, but the accession information for the missing volume is lined through on the shelf list. Some libraries use different markings or colors to indicate different types of withdrawal, e.g., ink for discarded volumes, pencil for missing ones. (The theory here is that the discarded volume is physically destroyed, but the missing one may reappear.)

If the missing volume is the only copy of the title or the last one and not to be replaced, all catalog cards are withdrawn and destroyed. The shelf-list card is also pulled but filed in a "missing" file. If the book is the last copy but is to be replaced, catalog cards are left as they are and either the shelf-list card is flagged with a colored metal clip and the date of order recorded, or else a note is added to the order record stating that it is a last copy replacement. Either process ensures the record's being cleared eventually if the replacement never comes. When the book to be withdrawn is in hand and is thus an actual discard, withdrawal procedures can be started at once; if it is missing, the records are not corrected for a year, during which time several checks for the missing book are made.

Inventory

Library inventory, as with any business, is taking stock of the property, in this case the book collection. Whether it is done once a year, twice a year, once in five years, or not at all is something to be decided according to the needs and institutional requirements. If shelves are read often to keep the collection fresh and if losses are few, the library may need inventories only infrequently or not at all. If the losses are great, if books get mixed up on the shelves, if the collection is small, or if the governing body so requires, frequent inventories may be needed.

If the charging system is one in which book cards are held by the library, inventory-taking is a simple process, and can be done for the various sections of the collection at different times. But if the charging is a photographic or transaction-card system, the process becomes more difficult, and it must be done all at one time when the library is closed to service.

The first step in taking inventory is to dismantle displays of books and to break up special collections, getting all classified books into their proper shelf-list order. The shelf-list drawer is then taken to the stacks, and the books on the shelves are checked against the cards. For each book found, a penciled notation symbol—letter or date—or a stamping is made beside its accession information on the shelf-list card. Any card with unchecked numbers is turned on end—this can be done as reading progresses, or, if time is short at this stage, the shelf-list cards can be completely scanned later. Any book incorrectly marked or not matching the record in any way is laid aside for later correction. The shelf checking is preferably done by two people, one working with the shelf list and the other reading from the shelves. As many teams can work at one time as there are shelf-list drawers, people, and space.

After a drawer is checked against the shelves, it is checked against the book cards for books in circulation. If the library uses photocharging, the checking may be done in one of two ways: (1) A group of people sit around a table, each with a shelf-list drawer, with another person reading the charge records from the film, the person concerned clearing the record in his drawer. (2) The alternative to this is to have all books which are returned after the shelf-reading, over a period equivalent to the loan period, checked against the shelf-list cards showing missing volumes. A little testing will show which method is less time consuming. After the process is completed, shelf-list cards still showing missing books are withdrawn, and a list is typed of the missing ones, giving call number, author's surname, brief title, accession or copy number. The books are searched for every three or four months; at the end of a year, those still missing are withdrawn from the records. The list of missing books is also gone over to consider replacement.

Statistics and Reports

Reports are necessary; they record history, show trends and developments, reveal accomplishments and needs, and are aids to public relations and publicity.

Statistics are needed to make reports, to show growth, work, services, and accomplishments, and to report to official statistics-gathering bodies. Statistics on cataloging may be divided into two groups—those showing the work done and those showing the holdings of the library. Both should be kept to a minimum, and compiled only if they have real use or serve a real need. Probably any public library will want to know:

number of new titles added to adult and juvenile fiction collections

number of titles withdrawn from adult and juvenile fiction collections

number of new titles added to adult and juvenile nonfiction collections

number of titles withdrawn from adult and juvenile nonfiction collections

total number of volumes added to adult and juvenile fiction

total number of volumes withdrawn from adult and juvenile fiction

total number of volumes added to adult and juvenile nonfiction

total number of volumes withdrawn from adult and juvenile nonfiction

number of titles of periodical subscriptions

number of volumes of periodicals bound

number of titles of newspapers received

number of volumes of newspapers bound

number of books mended

number of books rebound

number of books jacketed

number of rolls of microfilm added

number of recordings added and withdrawn

number of maps added and withdrawn

number of films added and withdrawn

number of slides added and withdrawn

number of filmstrips added and withdrawn

All of these figures will be added to or subtracted from the total library holdings in each category to show current holdings.

School libraries will, of course, have fewer categories to record.

Another figure sometimes kept is the number of catalog cards prepared and filed; this counting is time-consuming and has little meaning unless withdrawn cards are also counted. A fair estimate of cards prepared can be made from the number of cards taken from stock or purchased. Some libraries also break book figures down by class number; this means extra work and should be done only if real need exists.

The counts of additions can be made on a simple form slip as the work is done; or they may be taken from shelf-list cards as a group is being filed, once a week or once a month.

Appendices

Directions for Typing

Outline

A. Equipment
B. Indentions
C. A catalog card and its parts
D. General typing practices
E. Typing the author card (main entry)
F. Typing a set of cards, using unit cards
G. Typing a complete set of cards
H. Changing (adapting) printed cards
 I. Main entries other than author
J. Open entries
K. Analytics

L. Miscellaneous
 1. Conventional or form title
 2. Cross references
 3. History cards
 4. Authority cards
M. Non-book materials
 1. Vertical file materials
 2. Maps
 3. Films
 4. Filmstrips
 5. Slides
 6. Recordings
N. Shelf-list cards
O. Book cards and pockets
P. Abbreviations
Q. Some examples of shortened publishers' names

A. Equipment

1. *Typewriter* with elite or small gothic (plain, sans serif) type face

   Have keys changed on typewriter as needed, e.g., inferior brackets, accent marks (if there are books in foreign languages in the library), and script lower-case "l" (if needed) substituted for little-used keys.

   Use all-black ribbon.

   Keep keys clean so that letters won't clog.

2. *Prepared cards*

   Wilson, other printed or prepared cards

3. *Catalog cards*

   Use plain white (unlined) 3 x 5 cards from a library supply house.

4. *Erasers*

   Steel, knife-like eraser

   Typing eraser (pencil type)

   Small electric eraser if possible (cost: about $15)

5. *Heavy white thread* for tying cards together. (If more than one card is used for the same entry, cards are tied together by running the thread through the holes, tying over a pencil with square knot, and cutting thread about one third of an inch from knot.)

B. Indentions

   Set typewriter left-hand margin and tabular keys at proper indentions:

   Second space from left edge of card, for call number

   "First indention": 10 spaces from left edge of card

   "Second indention": 12 spaces from left edge of card

   "Third indention": 14 spaces from left edge of card

C. A catalog card and its parts

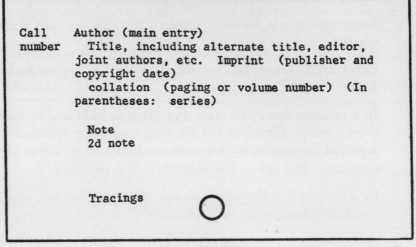

FIGURE 23

Each set of cards includes a main entry card, a shelf-list card and a card for each tracing.

D. General typing practices

1. *Strike-overs*

Never strike one letter over another.

2. *Correcting errors*

Single typing errors may be erased if this is done carefully, leaving no mark or torn surface; the correction must be in the exact spot of the letter or word removed. If several errors are made, start over with a new card.

3. *Spacing between items*

Leave one space after words or names, commas, or semi-colons.

Leave two spaces after colons or periods.

Use single hyphen (no spaces) between dates (example: 1920-1935), for inclusive paging (example: 23-46) or other numerals, and in hyphenated words (example: so-called)

Leave one space for each digit of an incomplete number or date (example: 193 -19   )

Leave two spaces between different parts of the card (title, *4 in some places; before imprint before series note* imprint, etc.)

Leave eight spaces to complete a name (example: Smith, J   Earl)

In a contents note, punctuate and space as indicated by cataloger; one preferred way is for each item to be followed by a period, one space, hyphen, one space, next item (example: *no space* Contents: The spy. - The fugitive. - The captive.)

In a subject heading, type dashes as space, hyphen, space (example: UNITED STATES - HISTORY)

4. *Spacing between lines (Figure 24)*

Lines follow one another *except:*

Leave two lines between collation line and notes, and at least three lines between end of catalog information and tracings.

```
   Price, Julia S
      The off-Broadway theater.   Scarecrow Pr., 1962.
      279p.   illus.

      Includes bibliographies.


   THEATER - NEW YORK (CITY)
   AMERICAN DRAMA - HIST & CRIT
   DRAMA - HIST & CRIT
   t
```

FIGURE 24

5. *Accent marks*

Type as written if the typewriter has accent marks; otherwise, ignore them.

6. *Capitalization*

In general, follow practices of the language, i.e., in English capitalize proper names and words derived from proper names, titles of persons, historic events, first word of a sentence, or the beginning of a title of a book or other work.

In a title main entry, if the title begins with an article, the following word is also capitalized.

(Note: Older printed cards from LC or Wilson may have less capitalization; do not change printed cards, but do not follow their style in typing.)

For capitalization of standard cataloging abbreviations, follow practice as indicated on page 159.

7. *Punctuation*

In general, follow English usage.

Type copyright dates thus: c1963. (That is, type small "c" for copyright with no period and no space before date.)

also brackets Wherever possible, avoid using double punctuation, such as period and curve (parenthesis).

Follow punctuation in subject headings exactly as given.

(Note: On Wilson cards and in the *Standard Catalog* publications, rules for Wilson publications are followed. Thus, periods are omitted after imprint, in the collation, and at the end of the annotation. Space and period are omitted after abbreviations "p" and "v" when used with a numeral, as: 150p, v4, p73. Do not change printed cards, but do not follow this practice in typing cards.)

8. *Abbreviations*

Abbreviate standard terms as listed on page 159.

Abbreviate names of states following names of places (example: Chicago, Ill.)

Abbreviate names of countries following foreign places (example: London, Eng.)

E. Typing the author card (main entry)

1. *Call number*

Type the class (classification) number on the third line from top of card, two spaces from the left-hand edge of card.

Type the initial for the author's last name directly below class number. (If books are Cuttered, full work number appears here.)

Type additional parts of call number (such as date or volume number) directly below author initial.

Use no punctuation except for decimal in class number or period after "v."

Examples:
940.54	808.3
B	On6s
1963	v.3

2. *Author's name (Figures 25 and 26)*

Type author's name at the first indention (10 spaces from left edge of card) on the third line from the top of the card.

Type last name first, followed by comma, one space, then first and middle names (if given), followed by comma, then dates (if used).

Type corporate names as written. If name runs over one line, drop to line below and begin at second indention. *third*

National Society for the Study of Secondary
 Education

FIGURE 25

If initials are used, do not follow them with periods.

Leave eight spaces after each initial.

If the main entry name is that of an editor, add "ed." after his name.

```
576     Stanley, Wendell M
S
```

```
511     Morton, John, ed.
M
```

```
623     Smith, John, 1930-        ed.
S
```

FIGURE 26

3. *The Title (Figures 27 and 28)*

Begin one line below the author's name, at second indention (12 spaces from left edge of card).

Information describing the book, such as authors, editors, edition, etc., is considered part of the title.

NOT TRUE

```
808.82  Ottemiller, John H
0           Index to plays in collections;  an author and
1963    title index to plays appearing in collections
        published between 1900 and 1962.  4th ed., rev.
        and enl.
```

```
576     Stanley, Wendell M
S           Viruses and nature of life, by Wendell M.
        Stanley and Evans G. Valens; illus. with photo-
        graphs, charts and diagrams.
```

FIGURE 27

If an alternate title is shown, the short title is followed by a semicolon, the word "or," comma, and second title.

```
Shakespeare, William
  Florizel and Perdita; or, The winter's tale
```

FIGURE 28

If title transcription takes more than one line, continue on next line at first indention.

4. *Imprint* is the publishing information such as the publisher and date of publication or of copyright. *(Figure 29)*

This information follows two spaces after the title transcription, in the same paragraph (all lines after the first start at the first indention). Small "c" precedes the copyright date.

```
576    Stanley, Wendell M
S         Viruses and nature of life, by Wendell M.
       Stanley and Evans G. Valens; illus. with photo-
       graphs, charts and diagrams.  Dutton, c1961.
```

FIGURE 29

5. *Collation* is the physical description of the book, including such information as number of pages, or number of volumes, whether illustrated, whether part of a series. *(Figure 30)*

Type this information one line below end of title paragraph, beginning at second indention.

The abbreviation "illus." follows two spaces after the paging, series (in parentheses) three spaces after paging or "illus."

No capitalization is used except for first word of series and for proper names.

Series note is in catalog entry form. (LC cards do not always do this; if using LC cards, do not change, but do not copy in typing.)

If series note runs over the line, return to first indention on next line.

If paging is not given, begin series note where paging usually appears.

```
338      Brandenburg, Frank
B           The development of Latin American private
         enterprise.  National Planning Assoc., c1964.
            136p.  illus.   (National Planning Asso-
         ciation.  Planning pamphlets, 121)
```

```
970.67    Wildschut, William
  W           Crow Indian beadwork.  Museum of the American
          Indian, Heye Foundation, 1959.
              55p.  illus.  (Museum of the American Indian,
          Heye Foundation.  Contribution, v.16)
```

```
970.67    Wildschut, William
  W           Crow Indian beadwork.  Museum of the American
          Indian, Heye Foundation, c1959.
              (Museum of the American Indian, Heye Foundation.
          Contribution, v.16)
```

FIGURE 30

6. *Notes* are sometimes added to explain history or content of the book. If used, notes follow two lines below the collation, starting at the second indention. *(Figures 31 and 32)*

They are given in paragraph form, each note beginning a new line at second indention and continuing at first indention if it runs over.

In a contents note, the items are usually followed by a period and dash (typed as space, hyphen, and space). They can, however, simply have commas or semicolons.

no space

530   Dull, Charles E
D   Modern physics, by Charles E. Dull, H.
Clark Metcalfe, and John E. Williams. Holt,
1960.

     First pub. in 1922 with title: Essentials
of modern physics.
     A textbook "designed to meet the varying
needs in the standard high-school course in
physics." Pref.

Ten poets. Seattle, 1962.

   [12] l. 32 cm.

    CONTENTS.—There is a country terrible as grace, by C. Hall.—
Ishmael, by B. Bentley.—Sand dollars, by N. Bentley.—Bouquets
from Corley, by R. F. Hugo.—From the Chinese, by C. Kizer.—
Digging out the compost, by W. H. Matchett.—Two sermons on the
psyche, by A. Stein.—The exile tells his friends, by E. Triem.—The
observer, by D. Wagoner.—Once more, the round, by T. Roethke.

    1. American poetry—Washington (State)—Seattle.   I. Hall,
Carol.

PS572.S4T4   811.082   62–4824

Library of Congress   [2]

Prize stories, 1964: The O. Henry awards; ed. and with an
    introduction by Richard Poirier. Doubleday 1964
289p

    Includes the following stories: The embarkment for Cythera, by J. Cheever; Stigmata,
by J. C. Oates; The everlasting witness, by M. Shedd; The Jewbird, by B. Malamud:
The banks of the Ohio, by S. Bingham; Night and day, day and night, by L. Ross; The
metamorphosis of Kenko, by D. Stacton; The inhabitants of Venus, by I. Shaw; The
scream on 57th Street, by H. Calisher; Something just for me, by G. Lanning; Thompson,
by G. A. Zorn; So I'm not Lady Chatterley so better I should know it now, by Sara;
Old and country tales, by S. W. Schoonover; Novotny's pain, by P. Roth; Carrion spring,
by W. Stegner

1 Short stories I Poirier, Richard, ed.   Fic

64W21,111   (W) The H. W. Wilson Company

FIGURE 31

A bibliographical note may give the title of the bibliography (in quotes) or just the word Bibliography, followed by a colon and the inclusive paging. Or it may say: Includes bibliographies (when there are several, appearing in different places).

```
Colby, Vineta, ed.
    American culture in the sixties.  Wilson,
1964.
    199p.  (The Reference shelf. v.36, no.1)

Bibliography:  p.191-199.
```

FIGURE 32

7. *Tracings* are indications of entries used on additional catalog cards, that is, added entries. *(Figure 33)*

These may be arranged in paragraph form (on printed cards) or (more usual for typed cards) in a column.

Type them at least three lines below the catalog information, at the first indention.

If there is not room on the face of the card, the card is turned and the items are typed near the bottom of the back of the card so that the card in the file can be tilted forward and easily read.

On printed cards tracings are numbered, Arabic numbers for subjects, Roman for all other.

On typed cards subjects are typed in capital letters in the form used on the cards.

A title tracing is indicated by a small "t" (no period). Series is indicated by "ser" (no period).

Tracings are typed on the main entry card and on the shelf-list card.

576   **Stanley, Wendell M**

Viruses and nature of life, by Wendell M. Stanley and Evans G. Valens; illus. with photographs, charts and diagrams. Dutton 1961

224p illus

"This book is an outgrowth of a series of eight half-hour films on the subject of viruses made by educational television station KQED in San Francisco." Publisher's note

Presents the essential facts known about viruses and about the closely related fields of genetics and cancer research. In addition to Dr Stanley, six other world authorities on virology have contributed chapters. (Publisher)

For further reading: p219

1 Viruses   ɪ Jt. auth.   ɪɪ Title   576

61W11,449   (W) The H. W. Wilson Company

---

576   Stanley, Wendell M
S

Viruses and nature of life; by Wendell M. Stanley and Evans G. Valens; illus. with photographs, charts and diagrams. Dutton, 1961. 224p. illus.

For further reading: p.219.

VIRUSES
jt auth
t

VIRUSES
jt auth
t

FIGURE 33

8. *Added cards ("run-on" or "second" cards) (Figure 34)*

If there is too much information to go on one catalog card, it is continued on a second card. Type at point of break, in parentheses: (Continued on next card)

On the second card, type the call number, the name of the author, the first two or three words of the title, followed by three dots, the date, and a period, then, in parentheses: (Card 2). Two spaces below and two spaces above the continued contents listing, type: Contents - Continued

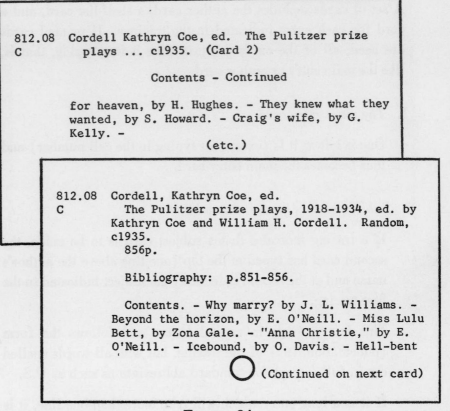

```
812.08   Cordell Kathryn Coe, ed.  The Pulitzer prize
C            plays ... c1935.  (Card 2)

                    Contents - Continued

        for heaven, by H. Hughes. - They knew what they
        wanted, by S. Howard. - Craig's wife, by G.
        Kelly. -
                         (etc.)
```

```
812.08   Cordell, Kathryn Coe, ed.
C            The Pulitzer prize plays, 1918-1934, ed. by
         Kathryn Coe and William H. Cordell.  Random,
         c1935.
            856p.

         Bibliography:  p.851-856.

         Contents. - Why marry? by J. L. Williams. -
         Beyond the horizon, by E. O'Neill. - Miss Lulu
         Bett, by Zona Gale. - "Anna Christie," by E.
         O'Neill. - Icebound, by O. Davis. - Hell-bent
                         (Continued on next card)
```

FIGURE 34

9. *Grade or age level*

Some elementary school libraries or public libraries wish to show on catalog cards for children's books the appropriate age or grade level of the material.

This, if used, is typed in the upper right-hand corner of the cards.

10. *Use of stamps*

Some information which is used again and again, such as a word showing the type of material (map, filmstrip, slides, etc.) or a notation such as "Reference book," "Ask at desk," etc., can be stamped on, either above the call number (to show special materials or special shelving) or as a note.

F. Typing a set of cards, using unit cards

A set of cards includes the author card, a shelf-list card, and a card for each entry indicated in the tracings. If printed cards are used, all of the cards are just alike before typing, that is, like the main entry or author card.

1. *The main entry card*

One is left as it is (except for typing in the call number) and thus becomes the main entry card.

2. *Subject cards (Figures 35 and 36)*

If a tracing indicates that a subject card is to be made, the second card has typed at the top (one line above the author's name and at the second indention) the subject indicated in the first tracing.

This is typed all in capital letters and follows the form (punctuation, etc.) of the tracing, but with all words spelled out in full, except for standard abbreviations such as U.S.

If it is a long entry which will take more than one line, it is started at the second line above the author's name, and the run-on line starts directly below it, also at the second in- AT 3rd dention.

Dashes are typed as follows: space, hyphen, space (example: ROME - DESCRIPTION). A subject card is made for each subject indicated in the tracings.

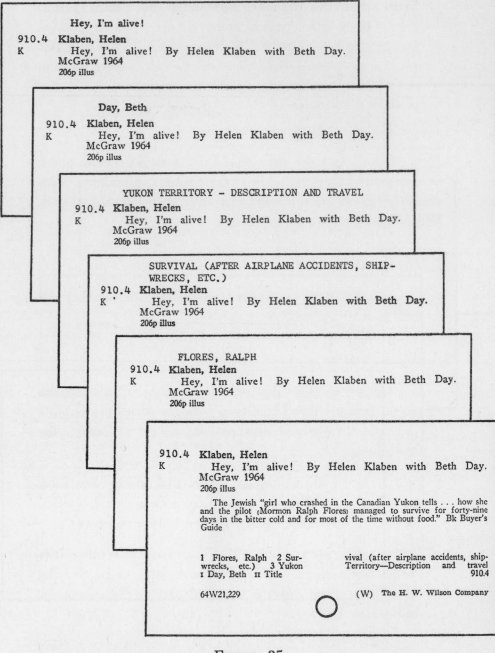

Hey, I'm alive!

910.4 Klaben, Helen
K   Hey, I'm alive! By Helen Klaben with Beth Day.
         McGraw 1964
         206p illus

Day, Beth

910.4 Klaben, Helen
K   Hey, I'm alive! By Helen Klaben with Beth Day.
         McGraw 1964
         206p illus

YUKON TERRITORY – DESCRIPTION AND TRAVEL

910.4 Klaben, Helen
K   Hey, I'm alive! By Helen Klaben with Beth Day.
         McGraw 1964
         206p illus

SURVIVAL (AFTER AIRPLANE ACCIDENTS, SHIP-
WRECKS, ETC.)

910.4 Klaben, Helen
K   Hey, I'm alive! By Helen Klaben with Beth Day.
         McGraw 1964
         206p illus

FLORES, RALPH

910.4 Klaben, Helen
K   Hey, I'm alive! By Helen Klaben with Beth Day.
         McGraw 1964
         206p illus

910.4 Klaben, Helen
K   Hey, I'm alive! By Helen Klaben with Beth Day.
         McGraw 1964
         206p illus
         The Jewish "girl who crashed in the Canadian Yukon tells . . . how she
         and the pilot (Mormon Ralph Flores) managed to survive for forty-nine
         days in the bitter cold and for most of the time without food." Bk Buyer's
         Guide

1 Flores, Ralph 2 Sur-   vival (after airplane accidents, ship-
wrecks, etc.) 3 Yukon   Territory—Description and travel
I Day, Beth II Title   910.4

64W21,229   (W) The H. W. Wilson Company

FIGURE 35

Wilson cards are also available with the added entries printed on. *(Figure 36)*

The worlds of Shakespeare

822.3   Chute, Marchette
 The worlds of Shakespeare, by Marchette Chute and Ernestine Perrie; drawings by Frederick Franck.   Dutton 1963
128p illus

Perrie, Ernestine, jt. auth.

822.3   Chute, Marchette
 The worlds of Shakespeare, by Marchette Chute and Ernestine Perrie; drawings by Frederick Franck.   Dutton 1963
128p illus

SHAKESPEARE, WILLIAM—ADAPTATIONS

822.3   Chute, Marchette
 The worlds of Shakespeare, by Marchette Chute and Ernestine Perrie; drawings by Frederick Franck.   Dutton 1963
128p illus

822.3   Chute, Marchette
 The worlds of Shakespeare, by Marchette Chute and Ernestine Perrie; drawings by Frederick Franck.   Dutton 1963
128p illus

 The "authors have offered a distillation of all Shakespeare drama in the form of a two-act play constructed out of selections from 12 of the plays. The first act presents six love scenes and the second, the world of music. The play is adapted for two actors. The authors have . . . made slight alterations in spelling and punctuation." Library J

1 Shakespeare, William—Adaptations   ɪ Jt. auth.   ɪɪ Title   822.3

63W12,803   (W)   The H. W. Wilson Company

FIGURE 36

3. *Other added entries* *(Figure 37)*

A card is made for other names indicated.

If one entry is designated "jt ed" or "ed," etc., that designation follows right after the name of the person so designated in the title position on the card.

Domanska, Janina, illus.

Leskov, Nicholas

The steel flea; a story adapted from the Russian by Babette Deutsch and Avrahm Yarmolinsky. Rev. ed. Pictures by Janina Domanska. Harper & Row 1964

56p illus

First published 1943. The 1964 edition has a new format with new illustrations

This story "tells what happened when General Platov, a Cossack chief, took to the famous gunsmiths of Toola the dancing steel flea which the English had presented to the Czar." Huntting

1 Russia—Fiction   i Illus.   ii Title   jFic

64W21,078   (W)   The H. W. Wilson Company

FIGURE 37

4. *Title entries (Figure 38)*

The word "Title" or a "t" indicates that a title card is to be made.

On the line above the author's name, beginning at the second indention, type the title up to the first punctuation break.

If the title runs to a second line, start two lines above the author and continue on the next line at the third indention.

If a second title card is to be made the tracing will read: "Title: ————" (the part of the title to use). A title card is then made, just like the first except that only the part indicated is used.

```
            A union list of publications in opaque micro-
               forms
016.099 Tilton, Eva Maude
T           A union list of publications in opaque micro-
            forms.  Scarecrow Pr., 1959.
               346p.


            t
            t:  Opaque microforms



                        O
```

```
            Opaque microforms
016.099 Tilton, Eva Maude
T           A union list of publications in opaque
            microforms.  Scarecrow  Pr., 1959.
               346p.


            t
            t:  Opaque microforms



                        O
```

FIGURE 38

5. *Series entry (Figure 39)*

> There may be a tracing for series, indicated by the word "series" or "ser" or the word followed by a colon and the form of the series to be used.

> Unless the form is indicated, the entry is made matching that in the series note on the card.

> If it is a numbered series or includes a date, that information also is typed in the entry.

```
                 The Reference shelf.   v.36, no.1
     917.3    Colby, Vineta, ed.
     C           American culture in the sixties.  Wilson,
              1963.
                 199p.  (The Reference shelf.  v.36, no.1)

              Bibliography:  p.191-199.


              U.S. - CIVILIZATION
              t
              ser

                           O
```

FIGURE 39

G. Typing a complete set of cards *(Figure 40)*

type all in full

If all of the cards have to be typed, type only the main entry and shelf-list cards in full.

For all of the added entries, prepare a shorter card. It carries, in addition to the added entry, the call number, the author's name in full, a short title, the publisher, and the date.

A short-form *title card* has only the call number, title at top, and the author's name.

```
            Viruses and nature of life
576         Stanley, Wendell M
S
```

```
            VIRUSES
576         Stanley, Wendell M
S               Viruses and nature of life.  Dutton, 1961.
```

```
576         Stanley, Wendell M
S               Viruses and nature of life, by Wendell M.
            Stanley and Evans G. Valens; illus. with
            photographs, charts and diagrams.  Dutton, 1961.
               224p.  illus.

            For further reading:  p. 219.


            VIRUSES
            jt auth
            t
```

FIGURE 40

H. Changing (adapting) printed cards *(Figure 41)*

Check the printed cards to be sure they match exactly the book being cataloged. The date may be different, or the publisher, the paging, or other detail.

If possible, change the cards by erasing the information which is wrong and typing in the corrected information. Tracings may be corrected by lining through unused parts.

If it will take more time to make all of the changes or will result in a messy card, type a new set of cards.

Price, Julia S
    The off-Broadway theater. New York, Scarecrow Press,
c1961
    282p. illus. 22 cm.
    Includes bibliography.

    1. Theater—New York (City) 2. American drama—20th cent.—
Hist. & crit. 3. Drama—Hist. & crit.   ɪ. Title.

PN2277.N5P7   ◯   792.097471   62–19731 ‡

Library of Congress   [40–1]

FIGURE 41

Note that place of publication, preliminary paging, size, etc.,
although not indicated usually, are left on printed cards since
they don't give misinformation.

I. Main entries other than author

While most books are cataloged under the author's name, thus
making the main entry that of the author's name, main entries
can take other forms:

1. *Corporate name* *(Figure 42)*

A body or an organization may be responsible for the work;
if so, the name of the group or organization appears in the
place of the author's name. The card is otherwise the same.
If the publisher is the same as the author, the name is not
repeated in the imprint.

Arco Publishing Company, New York.
    The Arco civil service home study course.
c1959.
    75p.

FIGURE 42

2. *Title entry* *(Figure 43)*

For periodicals and other serials without an author, the title is the main entry.

When the author is not known or there are many authors, the title is used as the main entry.

For title main entry cards, the title begins at the first indention, and all other lines, down to the notes, begin at the second indention. This is called "hanging indention."

```
The Torch is passed; the Associated Press
    story of the death of a President.
Associated Press, 1964.
99p.  illus.
```

FIGURE 43

3. *Set of books* *(Figure 44)*

Sometimes a set of books is cataloged as a set. If there is no author or there are many authors, the set is cataloged by title and hanging indention is used.

```
503     McGraw-Hill Encyclopedia of science and tech-
M           nology; an international reference work in
            fifteen volumes including an index.  McGraw,
            1960.
        15v.  illus., maps.
```

FIGURE 44

Note that the first word of the distinctive title (Encyclopedia) is capitalized.

(Non-book materials have special rules for cataloging and typing; see M, Non-Book Materials, pages 150-154.)

J. Open entries *(Figure 45)*

Periodicals and other serials, certain reference books, and other works are not published all at once, but are received volume by volume.

These are cataloged when the first volume arrives, but since all of the information is not available then, the entry has to be left "open," that is, for final information to be supplied later.

Some of these are under title, hence typed with hanging indention.

Some have authors.

The date of the earliest volume is given in the usual place for date and is followed by a hyphen. (After the set is complete, the date of the last volume is filled in and closed with a period.)

In place of paging, two spaces are left and then a "v" is added.

After a set is complete, the number of volumes is inserted.

A series note may be included; this also is left open, thus: (The Genealogical Society. Papers, no.6, 8

(Note that there is no punctuation after the 8, and the parentheses are not closed.)

Guide to dance periodicals. v. 1–
1931–35—
Gainesville [etc.] University of Florida Press [etc.]

v. 25–29 cm.

Quinquennial, 1931–35—1946–50; biennial, 1951–52—
Compiler: v. 1–   S. Y. Belknap.
Vol. for 1931–35 pub. in 1959.

Clapp, Jane
Museum publications. Scarecrow Pr.,
1962–
v.

Contents. – pt.1. Anthropology, archaeology,
and art. –

FIGURE 45

The information may be "closed" with each volume by changing in pencil the details of the latest volume received, thus: v.1-(3), 1961-(1963), (3)v. (The information in parentheses would be in pencil until the set is completed.) If this is done, work can be saved by keeping these records up to date only on the main entry card and stamping all the added entry cards with a note reading: "For full information see Main Entry."

K. Analytics *(Figures 46 and 47)*

A section of a work, a part of a book, or a volume of a set is sometimes important enough to be looked for separately, in which case an extra card is made to locate it. Such entries are

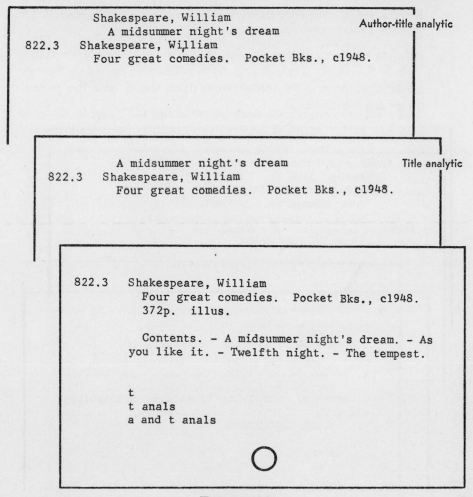

FIGURE 46

called analytics, and there are several kinds: author analytics, title analytics, subject analytics, author and title analytics, and title and author analytics.

With unit cards, these are prepared by typing the additional information above the main entry.

Single-line analytical entries are typed one line above the main entry at the second indention.

Author and title two-line entries are typed in the two lines above the main entry at the second and third indentions; title and author entries are typed at third and second indentions.

If cards are all being typed, a shortened form may be used, giving, besides the analytical entry, the call number, the author in full, a shortened title, the publisher, and the date.

Analytics are indicated in the tracings with the abbreviation "anal" followed, if necessary, by a colon and the entry for the analytic.

If the full card carries a contents note and all items in the contents are to be analyzed, one or two tracings may indicate all.

```
         ADDAMS, JANE
920.7    Nathan, Dorothy
N            Women of courage.  Random, c1964.

p.35-70.
```

```
920.7    Nathan, Dorothy
N            Women of courage.  Illus. by Carolyn Cather.
         Random, c1964.
             188p.  illus.  (U.S. landmark books, 107)

             Contents. - Susan B. Anthony. - Jane Ad-
         dams. - Mary McLeod Bethune. - Amelia Ear-
         hart. - Margaret Mead.


         WOMEN, AMERICAN
         t
         s anals              O
```

FIGURE 47

Thus, "a anals" indicates that every author listed in the contents is to have a card for his name. If the tracing says "a and t anals," two-line author and title entries are used for all works listed; "t and a anals" indicates title and author two-line entries for all works.

Subjects and subject analytics are always traced in full, such as "anal: GEOLOGY."

On occasion an analytic (particularly a subject analytic) is indicated for a section of the book and this is not made clear on the face of the card. Then the paging is given, this paging typed at the left side of the card, two spaces below the call number. The paging is indicated in the tracing: "anal: GEOLOGY. p. 180-226."

L. Miscellaneous

1. *Conventional or Form Title (Figure 48)*

If the work being cataloged is published under different titles or variations, a "form" or "conventional" title may be adopted in order to bring all of the variations together in the catalog.

Type the form title in the place where the title usually appears (second indention, one line below the author's name) and enclose within inferior brackets.

The real or title-page title follows on the line below, also starting at the second indention.

```
822.3   Shakespeare, William
          ⌐Collections⌐
          The comedies of Shakespeare.  Oxford Univ.
        Pr., 1946.
          1128p.  illus.
```

FIGURE 48

2. *Cross references (Figure 49)*

Cards are typed to refer users from terms or names not used (or in a different spelling) to those which are in the catalog.

These are cross references, called *"see" references.*

The form of the card is as follows: The term not used is at the top line (i.e., third line from the top of the card) at the second indention.

Two lines below and at the third indention appears the word "see" (not capitalized).

Two lines below this and at the first indention is the term or name which is used.

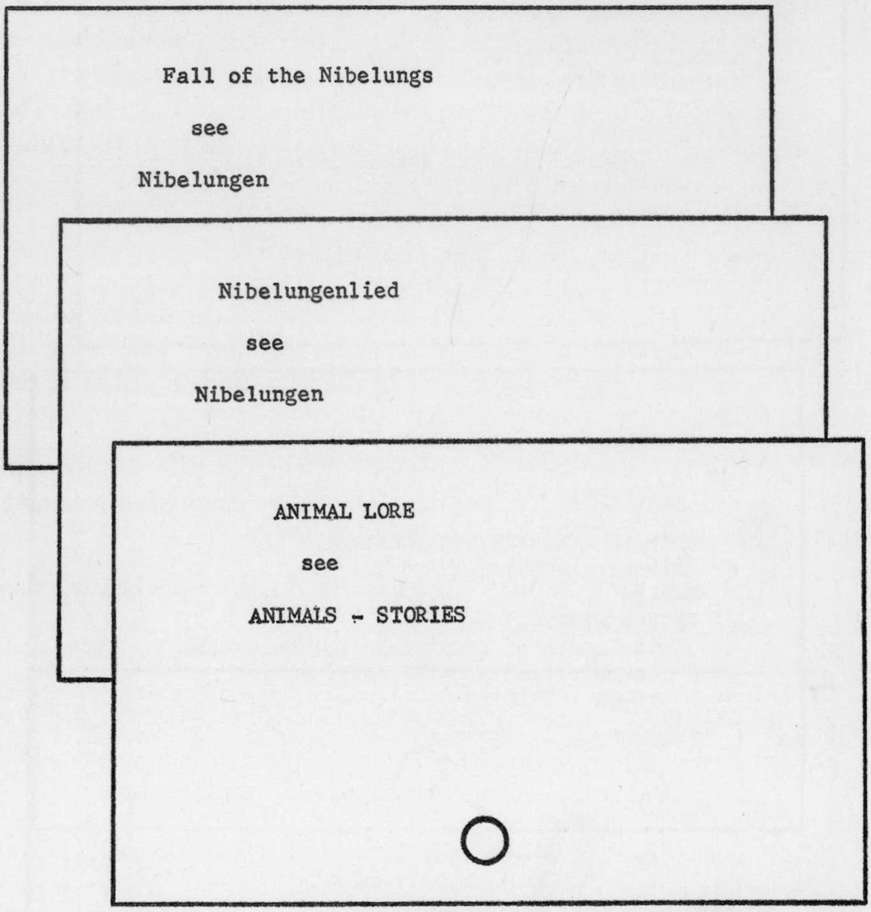

```
        Fall of the Nibelungs

            see

    Nibelungen
```

```
        Nibelungenlied

            see

    Nibelungen
```

```
        ANIMAL LORE

            see

    ANIMALS - STORIES


                        O
```

FIGURE 49

References are also made from terms which are used to other related terms which may be helpful to the reader. These are called *"see also" references*, since "see also" is used instead of "see" on reference card. They are most often used for subjects. *(Figure 50)*

They are typed in a form similar to that for "see" references.

When several terms are referred to, they are typed alphabetically, one below the other.

If subjects, the terms are all in capital letters.

Each term has a card relating it to the others.

```
    ANIMALS - STORIES

       see also

    ANIMALS -  HABITS AND BEHAVIOR
    ANIMALS IN LITERATURE
    FABLES
    NATURE STUDY
       also names of special animals with the
          subdivision STORIES, e.g.
          DOGS - STORIES

                      O
```

```
    ANIMALS IN LITERATURE

       see also

    ANIMALS - HABITS AND BEHAVIOR
    ANIMALS - STORIES
    FABLES
    NATURE STUDY
       also names of special animals with the
          subdivision STORIES, e.g.
          DOGS - STORIES

                      O
```

FIGURE 50

3. *History cards (Figure 51)*

People change their names or write under different names; organizations and other bodies may also change names.

The practice is to catalog under the name used in the book being cataloged, and to pull the various forms together by means of "history cards."

These may be in the form of a paragraph of explanatory text or in a form resembling "see also" cross references.

```
Creasey, John

   The works of this author have been published
under the following names, where they will be
found in this catalog:

Ashe, Gordon
Creasey, John
Halliday, Michael
Hunt, Kyle
Marric, J. J.
Morton, Anthony
York, Jeremy             ◯
```

```
Creasey, John

      see also

   Ashe, Gordon
   Halliday, Michael
   Hunt, Kyle
   Marric, J. J.
   Morton, Anthony
   York, Jeremy




                         ◯
```

```
        Halliday, Michael
        Cat and mouse

            see

        York, Jeremy
        Hilda, take heed


        Same work published under different titles


                         ◯
```

FIGURE 51

4. *Authority cards* *(Figure 52)*

Records must be kept to indicate what references have been made.

The information is recorded on cards, but these cards are not filed in the catalog; they are kept in a separate "authority file" in the cataloging area. All authority cards are in one file.

The authority card for a "see" reference has as entry the name or term under which cards are filed in the catalog.

Three lines below are listed the names or words under which references have been made. In front of each is a small "x," the symbol for a "see" reference.

If the library has more than one public card catalog, the authority card shows in which catalog or catalogs the reference appears. This is done by a symbol for the catalog following the term from which a cross reference is made. Thus on an authority card headed Shakespeare, William, the notation "x Shakspere a" means that a reference appears in the adult catalog referring the reader from "Shakspere" to the heading used.

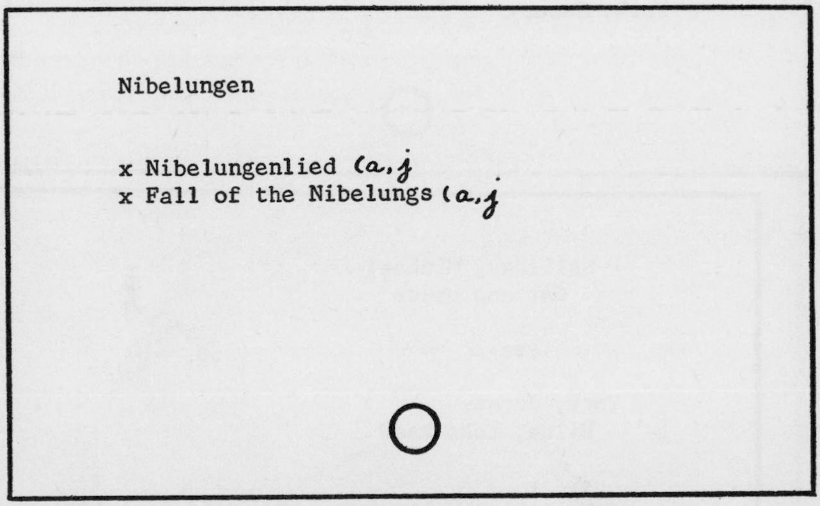

```
Nibelungen


x Nibelungenlied (a, j
x Fall of the Nibelungs (a, j
```

FIGURE 52

For every history card appearing in the catalog, a card just like it is made for the authority file; if the library has more than one catalog, the history authority card indicates in which catalog the term appears.

Whenever a *see also* card is made, a duplicate must be made for the authority file, indicating, if necessary, in which catalog it appears. Exception: authority cards need not be made for subjects taken from the subject headings list; records for these (including the catalogs in which they are used) are made in the headings list itself.

M. Non-Book Materials

1. *Vertical file materials* (pamphlets, clippings, pictures, reports, maps, etc., kept in the vertical file)

   One card is typed with the subject on it. If the index to the vertical file material is a separate one kept at the file, that is all that is done. If the card is to be filed in the catalog, either a form card or a stamp is used so that the card reads: "Material on this subject will also be found in the Vertical File."

2. *Maps (Figure 53)*

   For cataloged maps, the word "Map" is stamped or typed in the upper left-hand corner of the catalog card.

   Directly below will be the map number.

   On the same line (where the author's name appears on a book catalog card) at the first indention is typed (in capital letters) the subject (i.e., the area covered).

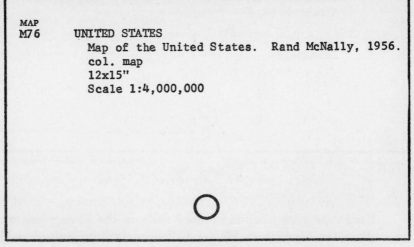

```
MAP
M76      UNITED STATES
            Map of the United States.  Rand McNally, 1956.
            col. map
            12x15"
            Scale 1:4,000,000
```

FIGURE 53

On the lines below, all at the second indention, are typed the other cataloging data: title, publisher and date, issuing body, series, scale, size, etc. (Any item running over one line carries to the first indention on the second line.)

3. *Films (Figure 54)*

The word "Film" is stamped or typed in the upper left-hand corner of the card with the accession number below it in place of the call number.

The title appears in the place of the author; this is followed by the other information in paragraph form, with hanging indention: producer, date, number of reels (if more than one), running time, indication of sound track, color or black-and-white notation, size, series note. Additional notes are added as needed, in paragraph (regular note) form. Tracings also follow same pattern as for books.

Abbreviations (see page 159) are used for this information.

Added entry cards are made as usual, with full information on each card.

```
FILM
F23      Fire, wind, and flood (Motion picture)  Vita-
            phone Corp., 1955.
            9 min., sd., b&w, 35 mm.  (Warner varieties)
            Credits:  Produced and written by Robert
         Youngson; narrator, Dwight Weist; film ed.
         Albert Helmes.



         DISASTERS
         Vitaphone Corporation


                         O
```

FIGURE 54

4. *Filmstrips (Figure 55)*

Cards are typed for individual titles in the same manner as those for films, and the word "Filmstrip" is stamped in the upper left-hand corner.

If a series is cataloged by series, the titles of the individual strips are typed, one below the other at the second indention. Shelf-list and added-entry cards follow the same pattern, with each card giving full information.

```
FILMSTRIP
FS326    LINES (Filmstrip)  Curriculum Films, 1951.
             27 fr., color, 35 mm.   (Elements of art)
             Eastman color.
             With teacher's manual.


         ART - STUDY AND TEACHING
         Curriculum Films, Inc.
         ser:  Elements of art (Filmstrip)
```

FIGURE 55

5. *Slides (Figure 56)*

Cards are made for each unit or series.

They are typed in the same form as films and filmstrips.

```
      SLIDES
 SL98-136  SPAIN
               Six Spanish cities.
               Washington, Roloc, 1964.
               38 sl.
               2x2"
               col.
               Script.


          Roloc
          t
```

FIGURE 56

If the title is not distinctive, the subject becomes the main entry; it is typed on the top line at the first indention (in capital letters) with the other information starting at the second indention, one item below the other. (The imprint data —place, producer, and date—are considered a single item.)

6. *Recordings* (phonodiscs, tapes, wires) *(Figures 57-A and 57-B)*

Appropriate stamp is used in upper left-hand corner.

A set of cards is made for each separate work on the recording, except for individual songs, sonatas, etc., which are very short.

The main entry is usually composer (for music) or author (for nonmusical recordings).

The card is typed in the same form as that for books.

```
RECORD
Rec61    Frost, Robert
            Robert Frost reading his own poems.  Library
         of Congress, Recording Laboratory album P6
         (record 26-P30) 1951.
             10 s. 12", 78 rpm.  (U.S. Library of Congress.
         Twentieth century poetry in English)
```

```
RECORD
Rec69    Doubling in brass.  RCA Victor LM 2308.  1959.
             2 s. 12", 33 1/3 rpm. stereophonic
         Symphonic band; Morton Gould, conductor.
         Contains original compositions and arrange-
         ments for band by Morton Gould and 6 marches by
         Sousa.


         BANDS (MUSIC)
         MILITARY MUSIC
         Gould, Morton
         Sousa, John Philip
```

FIGURE 57-A

```
Rec35    Hindemith, Paul
            Mathis der Maler. Angel Records.  S35949.
         1961.
            1 s. 12", 33 1/3 rpm. microgroove.
            Berlin Philharmonic Orchestra;  Herbert von
         Karajan, conductor.
            Program notes by Andrew Porter on slipcase.
            With:  Bartók, Béla.  Music, celesta, per-
         cussion and string orchestra.
```

○

○

```
SYMPHONIES
Berlin Philharmonic Orchestra
Karajan, Herbert von
t
Bartók, Béla
```

FIGURE 57-B

If the main entry is under title, performer, or subject, the hanging indention form is followed. Added entries and shelf-list cards are typed in full (unit cards).

N. Shelf-list cards *(Figures 58-A and 58-B)*

The shelf-list card is an exact copy of the main entry card in-cluding the tracings—for all types of material. (Some older Wilson cards supply shorter form; on these, add at least the tracings.)

In addition, the shelf-list card has a record of the number of volumes and number of copies of the title held by the library.

For the public library, price (whatever is charged for a lost book) is given following the accession or copy number. (Schools do not need this.)

If there is room on the front of the card, this accession information is typed there; if not, the card is flipped and the back is used. (The card is placed in the typewriter with the face of the card showing and the card right side up; when it is rolled into place, the typing on the back then runs in the opposite direction from the face and thus is easier to read when filed.)

As little punctuation as necessary is used.

```
jF        Stevenson, Robert Louis
             Treasure Island.  World



          t

cop.1  2.00 (Falls illus)
cop 2  2.25 (Doubleday. Wyeth illus)




                         O
```

```
530    Dull, Charles E
D         Modern physics [by] Charles E. Dull. H. Clark Metcalfe
       [and] John E. Williams.   Holt 1960
          662p illus (The Holt Science program)

             First published 1922 with title: Essentials of modern physics
             A textbook "designed to meet the varying needs in the standard high-
          school course in physics." Preface

   63-75  2.00
   64-16  2.25

          1 Physics I-II Jt. auths. III Title iv. t:  Essentials of
   modern physics

          61W11,312                (W)  The H. W. Wilson Company
                         O
```

FIGURE 58-A

R **Who's** who in America; a biographical dictionary of notable
920 living men and women of the United States. . . Marquis
W 1899-

  v

  "Issued biennially; first edition 1899
  "An excellent dictionary of contemporary biography containing concise biographical data, with addresses and, in case of authors, lists of
  works." Mudge

  1 U.S.—Biography—Dictionaries   920.03

          (over)
  63W12,665   (W) The H. W. Wilson Company

1958 8.00

~~1960 12.00~~
1961 15.00

1963 22.00
1961 cop 2 12.00

FIGURE 58-B

A shelf-list card for a biography is made to match the subject card rather than the author card—that is, the name of the subject of the book is put at the top, for the biography cards are arranged by subject in the shelf list.

For fiction and easy picture books, one shelf-list card is used for all editions. After the accession number the variation is shown, e.g., publisher, illustrator. (See Figure 58-A, first card.)

O. Book cards and pockets *(Figures 59-A and 59-B)*

On the book card appear the call number, the last name of the author, a short title, volume number if necessary, copy or accession number, and, sometimes for a public library, the price.

If there is no author, the form of the main entry is followed, even to hanging indention.

The book pocket carries only the call number and accession number.

For books not classified, the author's last name and a short title are added to the pocket.

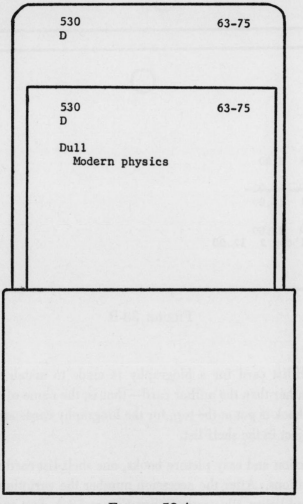

FIGURE 59-A

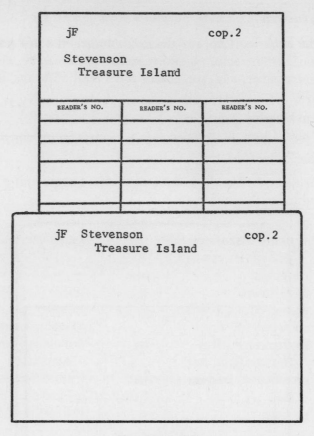

FIGURE 59-B

(The information on the card is to identify the individual volume or piece while in circulation; the information on the pocket is to check quickly the identifying information with the book card.)

Book cards are not made for noncirculating materials such as reference books, bound periodicals, microfilms, etc.

P. Abbreviations

Certain abbreviations are standard usage on catalog and book cards. (These do not include abbreviations used in tracings, which are primarily for librarians' use.) Among those used generally are:

abr.	abridged	no. (nos.)	number(s)
&	and (used in publisher's name)	p.	page, pages
		pt. (pts.)	part(s)
assoc.	association, associated	pref.	preface
bk.	book	Pr.	press (in publisher's name)
Co.	company		
cop	copy (on shelf-list card; elsewhere the period is used: cop.)	pseud.	pseudonym
		pub.	publisher, published, publication
c	copyright	rev.	revised (as edition)
dept.	department	ser.	series
ed.	edited, editor, edition	suppl.	supplement, supplemented, supplements
enl.	enlarged		
illus.	illustrations, illustrated, illustrator	tr.	translator, translation, translated
intro.	introduced, introduction	U.S.	United States
		Univ.	university (publisher)
n.d.	no date	v.	volume, volumes

Q. Some examples of shortened publishers' names

Allyn	Allyn & Bacon, Inc.
Am. Bk.	American Book Company
A.L.A.	American Library Association
Apollo Eds.	Apollo Editions
Appleton	Appleton-Century-Crofts
Arco	Arco Publishing Company, Inc.
Assoc. Pr.	Association Press
Atheneum	Atheneum Publishers
Beacon Pr.	Beacon Press, Inc.
Bowker	R. R. Bowker Company
Cambridge	Cambridge University Press
Chilton	Chilton Company
Collier	P. F. Collier & Sons
Coward	Coward-McCann
Crowell	Thomas Y. Crowell Company

Crowell-Collier	Crowell-Collier Press
Doubleday	Doubleday & Company
Dutton	E. P. Dutton & Company, Inc.
Farrar, Straus	Farrar, Straus & Company, Inc.
Grosset	Grosset & Dunlap, Inc.
Grove	Grove Press, Inc.
Harper	Harper & Row
Heath	D. C. Heath & Company
Holt	Holt, Rinehart & Winston, Inc.
Houghton	Houghton Mifflin Company
Knopf	Alfred A. Knopf, Inc.
Little	Little, Brown & Company
Little & Ives	J. J. Little & Ives Publishing Company
McGraw	McGraw-Hill Book Company, Inc.
Morrow	William Morrow & Company, Inc.
Oxford	Oxford University Press
Oxford Bk.	Oxford Book and Stationery Company
Praeger	Frederick A. Praeger, Inc.
Prentice-Hall	Prentice-Hall, Inc.
Rand McNally	Rand McNally & Company
Random	Random House, Inc.
Regnery	Henry Regnery Co.
Revell	Fleming H. Revell Company
Row	Row, Peterson & Company
Scott	Scott, Foresman & Company
Scott Pubs.	Scott Publications, Inc.
Univ. of Calif. Pr.	University of California Press
Watson-Guptill	Watson-Guptill Publications, Inc.
Watts	Franklin Watts, Inc.
Wiley	John Wiley & Sons, Inc.
Wilson	The H. W. Wilson Company
World Pub.	The World Publishing Company

Rules for Alphabetical Filing in a Small Dictionary Catalog

The following rules were compiled by the author after studying many sets of rules, published and unpublished, and after talking to many people regarding practices and preferences. A few are innovations and depart from established practice for the sake of logic and consistency. Among these are Rule 11, recommended by school librarians, reference librarians, and others as following the primary rule (file as written) and as following telephone book practice, with which library patrons are familiar; Rule 13a, according to which all entries for an author's works are arranged alphabetically, with collective titles such as *Works* included in the alphabetical sequence instead of being grouped before individual titles; and Rule 13g, which prescribes consistent chronological order even for editions of the same work.

1. Arrange the catalog cards alphabetically by the first word or name appearing at the top of the card, i.e., "the entry," disregarding a beginning article.

2. File word by word rather than letter by letter. A one-word entry comes before the word followed by succeeding words.

   Royal
   Royal personages
   Royal, Sydney
   Royalle, Guy
   Royalty

3. File all entries alphabetically, by first term, then by second, then third, etc., regardless of form of entry—names or words, main entry or added entry, author or subject or other type, forename or surname.

   The house *(title)*
   House and garden *(periodical title)*
   House, Boye *(author or added entry)*
   HOUSE CLEANING *(subject)*
   The house party *(title)*
   House, William *(name)*
   House with roots *(title)*
   Household, Geoffrey *(name)*

161

4. Disregard articles *(a, an, the)* at the beginning of an entry but take them into account elsewhere. All other words, including prepositions and pronouns, are considered in filing.

In Western deserts
Innes, Walter
Into the night

The work
Work for a man
Work for Julia
Work for the beginner
A work well done

5. File abbreviations (e.g., *Mr., Mrs., Dr., St., U.S.*) as though spelled out *(Mister, Mistress, Doctor, Saint* or *Street, United States)*. The figure & is filed as *and*.

6. A letter, single-letter word, or initial is filed at the beginning of the letter before words beginning with that letter.

ABC about collecting
ABC's of dance terminology
AB papers
ACTH
The a cappella chorus
AE's letters
A is for angel
A.L.A.
The A to Z of poodles
A-V bibliography
Aaburg, Charles
Aaron, Arthur

7. Numerals and dates in headings are filed as though spelled out and as customarily spoken in English; thus "1905" is filed as "Nineteen five"; "1,000" as "one thousand."

One
1 and 2 make 3
100
One million
1000

8. Accents and other diacritical marks and punctuation are ignored in filing. This includes an apostrophe showing possession, a plural, or an elision. Thus, "ä" is filed as "a"; "ç" as "c." Parentheses are also ignored.

Dogs follow John
The dog's following Mary
A dog's life

GEOLOGY
GEOLOGY AS A PROFESSION
Geology as a science
GEOLOGY, ECONOMIC
GEOLOGY—NEW YORK
GEOLOGY—WEST VIRGINIA

9. Hyphenated words are considered two separate words if the part preceding the hyphen can stand alone, but as one word if the part preceding the hyphen is dependent. (In case of doubt, follow the practice of a selected unabridged dictionary.)

The machine for tomorrow
Machine-made cards
Machinery

But:

The producer
Pro-European viewpoints

10. Words spelled or written two or more ways are interfiled in one place, with references from the form not used. (In deciding, follow a selected unabridged dictionary.)

Base ball	see	Baseball
Catalogue	see	Catalog
Labour	see	Labor

11. Names (including those beginning *Mac, Mc, etc.*) are always filed as written, no matter how pronounced or how close to other forms. (Allen or Allan, Smith or Smyth.)

Brown, John
Brown Mountain
Brown, Robert
Browne, Amos

Machinery
MacPherson
McBain
McMahon
M'Gregor

12. For forenames used by several people, follow the alphabetic arrangement if possible; if a descriptive phrase is needed, the phrase is employed alphabetically. For royalty, etc., the numeral is ignored unless all other designation is the same for two or more people, in which case the arrangement becomes chronological, earliest first.

Charles   *(title of work)*
Charles, A. Aldo   *(surname)*

Charles A. Coffin Foundation	*(corporate name)*
Charles and Cromwell	*(title of work)*
Charles, count of Flanders	*(forename)*
Charles County, Md.	*(place name)*
Charles d' Orleans	*(forename with title)*
Charles I, emperor of Germany	*(forename)*
Charles IV, emperor of Germany	(")
Charles V, emperor of Germany	(")
Charles IV, king of France	(")
Charles I, king of Great Britain	(")
Charles II, king of Great Britain	(")
Charles I, king of Spain	(")
Charles of Sessa	(")
Charles-Picard, Colette	*(hyphenated surname)*
Charles R. Walgreen Foundation	*(corporate name)*
Charles River, Mass.	*(place name)*
Charles the Good	*(forename and appellative)*
Charles W. Eliot and popular education	*(title of work)*

13. For entries under an author:

   a. File by the title of the work with which the person is associated whether name is main entry or secondary.

   b. If the person is a secondary entry, the card is next filed by the title of the work, disregarding main entry.

   c. If the same work appears both as title of a book and title of an analytic, file main work first.

   d. If the entry is for author and title analytic, the card is filed by author, then title, then main entry.

   e. File subject cards about an individual after all of the works *by* him. File secondly by the author of the book.

   f. File a criticism of a *work* following the entry for the work.

   g. File editions of the same work chronologically by date or number (earliest first), those with no number or date before the others.

Dickens, Charles   *(author and title of book)*
   Bleak House

Dickens, Charles   *(author and title analytic)*
   Bleak House
Dickens, Charles
   Collected works

Dickens, Charles   *(author and form title)*
   ₜA Christmas Carolₗ
   The Christmas story, a Christmas Carol

Dickens, Charles   *(author and title analytic)*
   A Christmas Carol
Leverton, Garrett
   Plays for the College theatre

DICKENS, CHARLES   *(subject criticism of a title)*
   A CHRISTMAS CAROL
Jacques, Edward
   Dickens' Christmas Carol

Dickens, Charles
   Collected works

Dickens, Charles
   The wreck of the Golden Mary

DICKENS, CHARLES   *(subject)*
Adrian, Arthur
   Georgian Hogarth

DICKENS, CHARLES   *(subject)*
Fawcett, Frank D
   Dickens the dramatist

14. If the same title appears as an entry word more than once, it is sub-arranged by author; if it is the same work, it is further sub-arranged by date of publication, earliest first. If the same title appears as a title of a periodical and another work, the periodical comes first; if the title entry for

the same work appears as both the title of an analytic and a book, the book comes first.

House beautiful; a monthly magazine *(title of periodical)*

House beautiful *(title of book)*
Jones, Adam
  House beautiful

House beautiful *(title analytic)*
Jones, Adam
  Collected stories

15. For subject entries arrange in order:
   a. Subject without subdivision, arranged by main entry
   b. Date and period subdivision, chronologically arranged, earliest first
   c. Other subdivisions alphabetically

U.S.—DESCRIPTION
U.S.—HISTORY
U.S.—HISTORY—DISCOVERY AND EXPLORATION
U.S.—HISTORY—COLONIAL PERIOD
U.S.—HISTORY—CIVIL WAR
U.S.—HISTORY—20TH CENTURY
U.S.—HISTORY—1900-1914
U.S.—HISTORY—BIBLIOGRAPHY
U.S.—HISTORY, NAVAL
U.S.—HISTORY—PERIODICALS

16. File a "see also" reference or a history card (explaining change of name, etc.) following all of the entries for the same word or phrase or name.

Library Terminology as Used in This Book

ACCESSION—A book or other library item acquired as part of a library's collections or holdings; *to accession* is to assign an identifying and sequential number to each item added to the library's collection.

ACCESSION NUMBER—A number assigned each book or other item, in order of its receipt in the library.

ADDED COPY—A copy, other than the first, of a book or other material; a duplicate.

ADDED ENTRY—A catalog entry (see *Entry*) other than the main entry; added entries may be subjects, titles, joint authors, series, etc.

ADDED VOLUME—A volume of a set of books or a serial other than the first; a continuation.

ANALYTIC—A catalog entry for a part of a book or work. There are author, title, subject, series, author and title, and title and author analytics.

ANNOTATION—A brief description of the contents of a book, subject matter of a film, etc.

ANNUAL—A work published every year, such as annual report, proceedings, yearbook.

ANONYMOUS—Applied to a work published without indication of the author.

ANONYMOUS CLASSIC—A literary work whose authorship is lost in history, such as a folk epic, folk story.

AUTHOR—The person or corporate body responsible for the creation of a book or other work.

AUTHOR ANALYTIC—A catalog entry, identifying the author of a *part* of a book or other work.

AUTHOR AND TITLE ANALYTIC—The author and title of a separate work which is part of a larger work, such as an anthology.

AUTHOR ENTRY—The name of the author of a book or other work used as the filing name in the catalog; usually the main entry.

AUTHOR NUMBER—Part of a call number—letters and numbers assigned to a book to identify the author; also called a Cutter number.

AUTHORITY FILE—A record of names or terms used as catalog entries; it is maintained in order to keep the forms uniform.

BIBLIOGRAPHIC NOTE—A note on a catalog card indicating the presence of a bibliography in the work cataloged.

BIBLIOGRAPHY—A list of books, periodical articles, or other works.

BIOGRAPHEE—The subject of a biography; the person the work is about.

BIOGRAPHER—The author of a work about another person or persons.

BIOGRAPHY—A book or work about the life of a person or persons.

BOOK CARD—A card used to charge out a book or other work; identifies the work in circulation records.

BOOK NUMBER—Part of a call number, representing the title of a work.

BOOK POCKET—A small, heavy envelope pasted in a book to hold a card.

CALL NUMBER—The number (composed of letters, numbers, and symbols) used to identify and locate a book or other library item.

CATALOGING—Indexing the contents of a library, usually on 3 x 5 cards (CATALOG CARDS) arranged in a file. The file and its contents comprise the CARD CATALOG.

CATCH or CATCHWORD TITLE—The distinctive part of the title of a book or other work, not the complete title.

CHARGING—The process of recording the loan of a book or other library item loaned for use.

CLASS, CLASSED—A subject group or grouping; a subject number assigned an item.

CLASSIFICATION—The grouping of materials by subject or form, usually according to a scheme utilizing numbers and/or letters; assigning a subject symbol to a work.

CLOSE CLASSIFICATION—Classifying material in minute subdivisions of the subject.

CLOSED ENTRY—Catalog card or other listing giving complete bibliographical information; specifically applied to completed continuations, serials which have ceased publication, etc. (See *Open Entry*.)

CLOSED SHELVES or STACKS—Library area where books are shelved, not open to the public.

CLOTHBOUND—Of a book bound in cloth pasted over stiff boards.

COLLATION—Physical description of a work, giving such information as paging, number of volumes, illustrations, size, etc.

COLLECTION—A group of books or other materials; may refer to library's entire holdings or only to a special group or part.

COLLECTIVE TITLE—The inclusive title under which a group of books or other library materials is published, each of which may also have its own individual title.

COMPILER—One who assembles a collective work, such as a book comprising articles by various individuals.

CONTENTS NOTE—A listing of separate works or pieces included within a collective work.

CONTINUATION—A title issued in parts, all pieces other than the first becoming continuations or added volumes.

CONVENTIONAL TITLE—A title chosen as the best known of a work published under many different titles or forms (also called *form title*).

COPY—One example of a book or other piece of library material; one object.

COPYRIGHT—The exclusive right granted by a government to publish a work during a specified period of years; a protection against others copying it.

COPYRIGHT DATE—The date the copyright is granted.

CORPORATE BODY—A group or body of people acting as a unit, e.g., an association, institution, government unit.

CORPORATE ENTRY—The name of a corporate body used as a filing word or phrase.

CROSS REFERENCE—A referral from words or names not used to the forms used in a catalog, bibliography, or index.

CUTTER NUMBER—Letter plus the number taken from the Cutter or Cutter-Sanborn tables, assigned to author's name to form part of call number.

DATE—Any historical date. In cataloging it refers to publication or copyright date of a work, or the birth and death dates of a person.

DATE DUE (SLIP)—Paper form pasted in a library book on which is stamped the date of the expiration of the loan period.

DESCRIPTIVE CATALOGING—Establishing the entries and providing the descriptive information given in the catalog.

DISCARD—A book or other work officially withdrawn from a library, destroyed, or otherwise disposed of.

DUMMY CARD—A card, giving brief information, left in place of an official record removed from a file.

DUPLICATE—A book or other item identical with another in content, format, etc.; in library work, the term is often used to indicate a copy of a work other than the first.

DUST JACKET—The paper covering (usually decorated) laid around a book.

EASY BOOK—A book, mostly composed of pictures, for young children.

EDITION—A distinctive text of a published work; each new edition implies additions to, or other changes in, the text.

END PAPER—The paper which lines the inside front and back covers of a book and also forms the flyleaves.

ENTRY—The word, name, or phrase under which a card is filed in the catalog; there are main entries, author entries, title entries, subject entries, series entries, etc.

FIRST INDENTION—A point ten spaces from the left edge of a catalog card; where the main entry begins on the card.

FLYLEAF—The first or last sheet in a bound book, usually blank.

FORM HEADING—A made-up or formalized phrase used as entry for certain classes of material, such as laws.

FORM TITLE—Another name for *conventional title.*

FORMAT—The physical make-up of a work: size, binding, printing, etc.

GUIDE CARD—A card slightly higher than the catalog cards, carrying letters or names or words indicating the material directly behind it in the card catalog.

HANGING INDENTION—The form of a catalog card used when the title is the main entry and is the only line on the card coming to the first indention.

HISTORY CARD—A catalog card which gives the history of successive names used by a person or an organization.

HOLDINGS—The library's collections.

IMPRINT—Publication information about a work: place, date, and publisher; usually found at the foot of the title page.

INDENTION—Distance from the left-hand side of the catalog card at which typing or printing begins.

INFORMATION FILE—Large file containing folders in which are placed pamphlets, clippings, pictures, maps, etc.; also called *vertical file.*

INVENTORY—Taking stock of the library's collections.

JOINT AUTHOR, JOINT EDITOR—A person partially responsible for the content of a publication; usually not the first named on the title page.

LC—The Library of Congress.

LC CARD—A card prepared for the Library of Congress use; printed and sold to other libraries.

LEAF, LEAVES—Pages of a publication; each leaf usually has a page of text on each side.

LIBRARY BINDING—A special durable book or magazine binding to meet specifications and requirements of heavy library usage.

LIBRARY SYSTEM—Two or more libraries affiliated for service; one may be administratively subordinate to the other, as a branch.

LIST PRICE—The price of a book or other publication listed by the publisher in catalogs and bibliographies, i.e., the retail price established by the publisher.

LOCATION SYMBOL (or MARK)—A letter, sign, or other symbol used on books or other materials in special collections, which are shelved out of classification order.

MAIN ENTRY—The primary entry for a work, usually the author entry.

MATERIAL or LIBRARY MATERIAL—Inclusive term for books, periodicals, pamphlets, maps, films, etc.—all items which are legitimate acquisitions for a library's collections.

MONOGRAPHIC SERIES—Separate nonfiction works issued, possibly at different times, under a collective title; may or may not be a numbered series.

NOTE—A phrase or sentence added to the catalog card to explain a feature of the work cataloged.

OPEN ENTRY—A catalog entry for a serial, series, set, etc., which has not yet completed publication; certain information on the card is left incomplete.

OPEN SHELVES or STACKS—Shelves of books in an area open to the public.

OUTSIZE, OVERSIZE—A book too tall to shelve in its proper order.

PAGE—(1) In a book or other publication, one side of a leaf or sheet; (2) an assistant in a public library who does book shelving and other routine work.

PAMPHLET (BOX)—A pamphlet is a publication of less than 50 (or 100) pages, usually devoted to a specific subject; a pamphlet box is a container made of cardboard in which pamphlets are filed.

PAPERBACK, PAPERBOUND BOOK, or POCKET BOOK—A book bound in paper without the rigid boards used in cloth binding. Often small in size.

PERIODICAL—"A publication with a distinctive title intended to appear in successive (usually unbound) numbers or parts at stated or regular intervals and, as a rule, for an indefinite time."—See *A.L.A. Glossary of Library Terms.*

PERIODICAL INDEX—An index to the contents of a periodical or group of periodicals.

PHONODISCS or PHONORECORDS—Phonograph records or recordings.

PICTURE BOOK—A book, mostly pictures, for small children (same as "easy" book).

PLASTIC JACKET—A transparent book jacket made of Mylar or acetate to be applied to a book over the decorated book jacket.

POCKET BOOK—See *Paperback.*

PREBIND—To bind a book in special, durable "library binding" prior to library acquisition.

PREPARATIONS—That part of library work concerned with the physical preparation of a publication for library usage; includes such tasks as marking spine, pasting in pockets, stamping ownership, applying plastic jackets, etc.

PROCESS SLIP—A slip of paper or card used by the cataloger in preparing information to be used in making catalog cards.

PROCESSING—Inclusive term for the work of acquiring, cataloging, preparing, and caring for library materials.

PSEUDONYM—Fictitious name used by an author.

PUBLICATION DATE—The year a work is published.

PUBLISHER'S CATALOG—A listing by a publisher of his current publications, publications in print, etc.

PUBLISHER'S SERIES—A series of separate works issued under a collective title, usually with some quality in common. Example: Landmark Books.

READING SHELVES—Checking the books on the shelves for accurate arrangement.

REBIND—To have a book rebound for library usage; the book which has been rebound.

REFERENCE BOOK—(1) A book, such as encyclopedia or dictionary, used to obtain specific information quickly; (2) a book restricted to use within the library.

REGIONAL CENTER or LIBRARY—Office or library which supplies work, materials, or advice to affiliated or associated libraries.

REGIONAL PROCESSING—Processing work done centrally for two or more libraries.

REPLACEMENT—A copy of a publication to take the place of one lost or discarded.

REPRINT—(1) To print a published work again usually from the original type or plates; (2) a publication which is the same as an earlier one in content; the format may be the same or different. The term is sometimes used to mean a cheaper edition of an earlier work.

REVISE—(1) To check or review work done, e.g., reading copy, checking filing, etc.; (2) to correct.

REVISED EDITION, REVISION—A publication containing new or changed material.

"SEE ALSO" REFERENCE—A referral from a name or term which has been used to others which are related to it.

"SEE" REFERENCE—A referral from a name or term not used to one which is to be found in a catalog or bibliography or index.

SEQUEL—A work, complete in itself, but following in form or content after another; in fiction, a work continuing with the same characters, locale, etc.

SEQUENTIAL—A numbering following numerical order: 1, 2, 3, etc.

SERIAL—A publication or work issued in parts which may or may not be numbered; includes periodicals, newspapers, reports, bulletins, etc.

SERIES, SERIES ENTRY, SERIES NOTE—Separate, independent works issued, usually at different times, under a collective title; a catalog entry under the name of the series; a note on the catalog card identifying the individual work with the series.

SERIES TITLE—Name of the series to which a work belongs.

SET—A work of two or more volumes.

SHELF LIST, SHELFLISTING—A file of cards, each representing a different title, arranged in the same order as are the books on the shelves; adding holdings of a library to the shelf-list card.

SHELF READING—Checking books on the shelves to ensure their proper arrangement.

SIZE—The height of a book.

SPINE—The back of a book connecting the two covers, on which is usually lettered the title of the work.

STACKS—Standing shelves for books, usually metal; the shelved collection; area in which materials are stored.

SUBJECT—A name, word, or phrase used as a catalog entry which indicates the subject content of the work cataloged.

SUBJECT ANALYTIC—A heading or catalog entry identifying the subject of a part of a work.

SUBJECT ENTRY—The catalog entry under a subject appearing at the top of the catalog card.

TITLE—The name of a work; in cataloging, the statement on the title page identifying the individual publication. "Full" title includes title, author, and additional information identifying the publication.

TITLE ANALYTIC—A catalog entry under the title of a part of a publication.

TITLE AND AUTHOR ANALYTIC—The catalog entry at the top of the card which gives the title and then the author of a part of a publication.

TITLE ENTRY—The catalog entry under the title of a publication.

TITLE PAGE—The page, usually at the beginning of a book, identifying the individual work; usually gives the author, title, publisher, date, etc.

TITLE-PAGE NAME—Author's name in the form in which it appears on the title page.

TITLE REFERENCE—A catalog card referring from a form of a title not used as an entry to the one selected; the latter is usually a conventional title.

TRACINGS—Items listed on the main entry catalog card indicating other catalog entries made for the same work, i.e., the added entries.

TRADE BIBLIOGRAPHY—A listing of the publications of one or more publishers.

UNION CATALOG—A catalog indexing the holdings of a library system, e.g., of a library and all of its branches or affiliates.

UNIT CARD—One of a set of catalog cards, all of which are alike until the added entries are added at the tops.

VERTICAL FILE—A file of large drawers in which are arranged folders containing pamphlets, pictures, clippings, maps, etc.; also called *pamphlet file* or *information file*.

VISIBLE FILE—A series of metal frames in which cards may be mounted with the headings visible one above another; used by libraries as a checking file for material received.

VISIBLE INDEX—A series of metal frames in which strips can be inserted; often used by libraries to list serial holdings.

VOLUME—The physical work complete in itself, whether a monograph which is part of a set or serial or an independent work.

Wilson Cards—Catalog cards prepared, printed, and sold by the H. W. Wilson Company.

WITHDRAWAL—A work removed from the library's collections.

YEARBOOK—A work issued annually, e.g., an almanac.

For fuller definitions and other terms see the *A.L.A. Glossary of Library Terms.*

Library Publishers and Suppliers

Some General Library Supply Houses

Acme Visible Records, Inc.
Crozet, Virginia
(visible files)

Bro-Dart Industries
56 Earl Street
Newark, New Jersey 07114
(branch offices in Los Angeles
and Toronto)

Demco Library Supplies
Box 1488
Madison, Wisconsin 53701
(branch offices in Hamden,
Connecticut and Fresno, California)

Gaylord Brothers, Inc.
155 Gifford Street
Syracuse, New York 13201
(branch office in Stockton, California)

Library Bureau
Remington Office Systems
Division
Sperry Rand Corporation
801 Park Avenue
Herkimer, New York
(branch offices in most large cities)

Library Products, Inc.
Box 130
Sturgis, Michigan 49091

John E. Sjostrom Company, Inc.
1717 North 10th Street
Philadelphia, Pennsylvania 19122
(furniture)

Cataloging Services

Alanar Book Processing Center, Inc.
P.O. Box 921
Williamsport, Pennsylvania 17702
(subsidiary of Bro-Dart Industries)

The American Library and Educational Service Company
21 Harristown Road
Glen Rock, New Jersey 07452

Crossley-VanDeusen Company, Inc.
Marcellus, New York 13108

Imperial Book Company
501 King Street
Philadelphia, Pennsylvania 19144

Lj Cards, Inc.
P.O. Box 27
Cooper Station Post Office
New York, New York 10003
    (subsidiary of R. R. Bowker Company)

The Library of Congress
Washington, D.C. 20540
    (catalog cards only)

Professional Library Service
1201 East McFadden Avenue
Santa Ana, California 92705

The H. W. Wilson Company
950 University Avenue
Bronx, New York 10452
    (catalog cards)

(For others see "Commercial Cataloging Services: A Directory," in *Library Journal*, April 1, 1964.)

Some Library Publishers

American Library Association
50 East Huron Street
Chicago, Illinois 60611

R. R. Bowker Company
1180 Avenue of the Americas
New York, New York 10036

F. W. Faxon Company, Inc.
515 Hyde Park Avenue
Boston, Massachusetts 02131

H. R. Huntting Company, Inc.
300 Burnett Road
Chicopee, Massachusetts 01020

Scarecrow Press, Inc.
257 Park Avenue
New York, New York 10010

Shoe String Press, Inc.
60 Connolly Parkway
Hamden, Connecticut 06514

The H. W. Wilson Company
950 University Avenue
Bronx, New York 10452

(For full listings and buying guide, see the "Library Buying Guide" published annually in the *Library Journal*—for 1965, the April 1, 1965, issue.)

Summary Tables of
Dewey Decimal Classification

SECOND SUMMARY: DIVISIONS *

000	GENERAL WORKS		250	Pastoral theology
			260	Christian church
010	Bibliography		270	Christian church history
020	Library science		280	Christian churches & sects
030	General encyclopedias		290	Other religions
040	General collected essays			
050	General periodicals			
060	General societies		300	SOCIAL SCIENCES
070	Newspaper journalism		310	Statistics
080	Collected works		320	Political science
090	Manuscripts & rare books		330	Economics
			340	Law
			350	Public administration
100	PHILOSOPHY		360	Social welfare
110	Metaphysics		370	Education
120	Metaphysical theories		380	Public services & utilities
130	Branches of psychology		390	Customs & folklore
140	Philosophical topics			
150	General psychology			
160	Logic		400	LANGUAGE
170	Ethics		410	Comparative linguistics
180	Ancient & medieval		420	English & Anglo-Saxon
190	Modern philosophy		430	Germanic languages
			440	French, Provençal, Catalan
200	RELIGION		450	Italian, Rumanian
210	Natural theology		460	Spanish, Portuguese
220	Bible		470	Latin & other Italic
230	Doctrinal theology		480	Classical & modern Greek
240	Devotional & practical		490	Other languages

*Reproduced from the 16th Edition of DEWEY Decimal Classification by permission of Forest Press, Inc., owners of copyright.

500	PURE SCIENCE		760	Prints & print making
510	Mathematics		770	Photography
520	Astronomy		780	Music
530	Physics		790	Recreation
540	Chemistry & allied sciences			
550	Earth sciences		800	LITERATURE
560	Paleontology		810	American literature in English
570	Anthropology & biology		820	English and Old English
580	Botanical sciences		830	Germanic literatures
590	Zoological sciences		840	French, Provençal, Catalan
			850	Italian, Rumanian
			860	Spanish, Portuguese
600	TECHNOLOGY		870	Latin & other Italic literatures
610	Medical sciences			
620	Engineering		880	Classical & modern Greek
630	Agriculture		890	Other literatures
640	Home economics			
650	Business			
660	Chemical technology		900	HISTORY
670	Manufactures			
680	Other manufactures		910	Geography, travels, description
690	Building construction		920	Biography
			930	Ancient history
			940	Europe
700	THE ARTS		950	Asia
710	Landscape & civic art		960	Africa
720	Architecture		970	North America
730	Sculpture		980	South America
740	Drawing & decorative arts		990	Other parts of world
750	Painting			

APPENDIX VI

Bibliography

Rules and Cataloging Tools

American Library Association. *A.L.A. Cataloging Rules for Author and Title Entries.* 2d ed. Chicago, American Library Association, 1949. 288p.

> This is being completely revised and rewritten. It is very detailed and elaborate; most of it is inappropriate for the small library. It is followed by the Library of Congress in preparing LC cards.

———— *A.L.A. Glossary of Library Terms; with a Selection of Terms in Related Fields.* Chicago, American Library Association, 1943. 159p.

> Definitions of terms, including those for publishing and book making. Not always the same definitions as those used in Appendix III, pages 167-175.

———— *A.L.A. Rules for Filing Catalog Cards.* Ed. by Sophie K. Hiss. Chicago, American Library Association, 1942. 120p.

> Gives various filing practices, so that each librarian may select those most appropriate for his library. It is being completely revised.

Baer, Eleanora A. *Titles in Series: A Handbook for Librarians and Students.* 2d ed. New York, Scarecrow Press, 1964. 2v.

> Includes approximately 40,000 book titles published prior to January 1963.

Code for Cataloging Music and Phono-Records. Prepared by a Joint Committee of the Music Library Association and the A.L.A. Division of Cataloging and Classification. Chicago, American Library Association, 1958. 88p.

> Includes chapters on "Simplified Rules" and "Phonorecords."

Cutter, Charles A. *Alfabetic Order Table Altered and Fitted with Three Figures by Kate E. Sanborn.* (Obtained from the H. R. Huntting Company, Chicopee Falls, Massachusetts.)

> The tables used by libraries with full call numbers including author numbers. Not recommended for small libraries. Available also with two figures, but a library large enough to use Cutter numbers is most likely large enough to want the three-figure table.

Dewey, Melvil. *Decimal Classification and Relative Index.* 16th ed. Lake Placid Club, N.Y., Forest Press, 1958. 2v.

Full classification scheme. Tables are divided and subdivided, supplying numbers for most specific subjects. Not necessary for small libraries.

———— *Decimal Classification and Relative Index.* 8th abridged ed. Lake Placid Club, N.Y., Forest Press, 1959. 495p.

Abridged edition prepared specifically for schools and small public libraries. Recommended.

Kapsner, Oliver L., O.S.B. *Catholic Subject Headings.* 5th ed. Collegeville, Minn., St. John's Abbey Press. 1963. 488p.

Used by libraries in Catholic schools and by parish libraries.

Library of Congress. *Classification. Class A-Z.* Washington, Govt. Printing Office, 1904 to date.

Classification schemes used by the Library of Congress. Not used except by large research libraries and highly specialized libraries.

———— *Decimal Classification Additions, Notes, and Decisions.* Washington, The Library, 1959 to date.

Known as "DC &," this publication, appearing at irregular intervals, gives information to supplement the DC classification between editions.

———— *Rules for Descriptive Cataloging in the Library of Congress.* Washington, The Library, 1949. 141p.

This recommends fuller cataloging than necessary for small libraries; it is being completely revised and rewritten.

———— *Cataloging Rules of the American Library Association and the Library of Congress. Additions and Changes, 1949-1958.* Washington, The Library, 1959. 76p.

———— *Rules for Descriptive Cataloging in the Library of Congress. Motion Pictures and Filmstrips.* 2d preliminary ed. Washington, The Library, 1953. 18p.

These rules are probably more complete than most small libraries will need. However, it is the only guide available, and if the library has large collections, it is worth while to follow the procedures described. It is being revised.

———— *Rules for Descriptive Cataloging in the Library of Congress. Pictures, Designs, and Other Two-Dimensional Representations.* Preliminary ed. Washington, The Library, 1959. 16p.

If the library has a large collection of these materials and plans to catalog them, it is necessary to follow these rules, since they are the only approved ones available.

————— *Subject Headings Used in the Dictionary Catalogs of the Library of Congress*. 6th ed. Washington, Govt. Printing Office, 1957. 1357p. Supplements, 1956 to date.

LC subject headings appear on LC catalog cards. Although small libraries will not follow the list in detail, those using the cards may need the list to verify usage.

Lynn, Jeanette Murphy. *An Alternative Classification for Catholic Books*. 2d ed. rev. by Gilbert C. Peterson, S.J. Washington, Catholic University of America Press, 1954. 508p.

For use with DDC and LC classification; employed, if desired or required, by Catholic schools and parish libraries.

Rue, Eloise, and LaPlante, Effie. *Subject Headings for Children's Materials*. Chicago, American Library Association, 1952. 149p.

This was designed primarily for use in school libraries. It is out of date, and there are no provisions for its revision.

Sears, Minnie E. *Sears List of Subject Headings, with Suggestions for the Beginner in Subject Heading Work*. 8th ed. Ed. by Bertha M. Frick. New York, H. W. Wilson Company, 1959. 610p.

This list is the one used by schools and small public libraries, in fact, most public libraries. The headings are also those used in tools and bibliographies prepared for these libraries. Wilson cards use Sears headings. It is fully revised about every five years. Recommended.

Smith, Elva S. *Subject Headings for Children's Books* .... Chicago, American Library Association, 1933. 235p.

Out of print and out of date, but parts still usable if combined with Sears.

Swain, Olive, comp. *Notes Used on Catalog Cards*. 2d ed. Chicago, American Library Association, 1963. 82p.

A classified collection of examples of notes used on catalog cards. Helps in phrasing notes and identifying information appropriately carried in them.

U.S. Government Printing Office. *Style Manual*. Rev. ed. Washington, Govt. Printing Office, 1959. 492p.

Every library needs a style book in its collection (either this one or the style manual published by the University of Chicago Press) for rules of punctuation, capitalization, spelling, and abbreviations, and usage in various languages.

Bibliographies and Lists of Books Which Include Cataloging Information

American Book Publishing Record (BPR) New York, R. R. Bowker Company, 1960 to date.

> A monthly periodical. Each issue contains the month's listings of books in *Publishers' Weekly*, arranged according to Dewey classification. For each title the LC cataloging information is given: author, title, publisher, dates, subjects, etc. Has annual index volumes.

Basic Book Collection for Elementary Grades. 7th ed. Chicago, American Library Association, 1960. 144p.

> Selected and annotated titles. Buying and cataloging information includes publisher, Dewey classification, Sears subject headings, LC card numbers, and indication of availability of Wilson cards. Revised every four or five years.

Basic Book Collection for High Schools. 7th ed. Chicago, American Library Association, 1963. 184p.

> Selected and annotated titles for grades 9 through 12. Buying and cataloging information includes publisher, Dewey classification, Sears subject headings, LC card numbers. Revised every few years.

Basic Book Collection for Junior High Schools. 3d ed. Chicago, American Library Association, 1960. 144p.

> Annotated list of selected titles. Includes Dewey classification, Sears subject headings, LC card numbers, and indication of availability of Wilson cards. Revised every few years.

Book Review Digest. New York, H. W. Wilson Company, 1905 to date.

> Bibliographic listing includes Dewey classification, subject headings, LC card numbers. Carries excerpts of reviews which are often helpful in determining subject and content of a book. The fiction grouping by subject in the annual and five-year indexes is particularly helpful in assigning subject headings to fiction books.

Booklist and Subscription Books Bulletin. Chicago, American Library Association, 1905 to date.

> Semimonthly listings of publications appropriate for the small or medium-sized public library. Gives brief annotations and Sears subject headings, Dewey classification numbers, LC card numbers, and notation as to availability of Wilson cards.

Children's Catalog. 10th ed. New York, H. W. Wilson Company, 1961. 915p.

> List of selected titles appropriate for elementary and junior high schools and children's collections in public libraries. Includes Dewey classification, Sears subjects, grade level. Revised every few years; kept up to date with supplements between editions.

Fiction Catalog. 7th ed. New York, H. W. Wilson Company, 1960. 650p.

Lists works of adult fiction found useful in libraries. Contains annotated author list and subject and title index.

Publishers' Weekly. New York, R. R. Bowker Company, 1872 to date.

Each issue carries a list of books published that week in the United States. For each, LC cataloging is given. Cumulated monthly by subject in *American Book Publishing Record*.

Standard Catalog for High School Libraries. 8th ed. New York, H. W. Wilson Company, 1962. 1,055p. Supplements, 1963 to date.

Selected titles. Includes Dewey classification, Sears subjects. Revised every five years. Purchase includes annual supplements through 1967.

——— *Catholic Supplement*.

Includes additional books especially selected for Catholic schools. Not available separate from the *Standard Catalog for High School Libraries*.

Standard Catalog for Public Libraries. 4th ed., 1958. New York, H. W. Wilson Company, 1959. 1,349p.

Selected titles, annotated and arranged according to Dewey classification; includes for each title classification number and Sears subject headings. Supplements issued annually and cumulated in five-year volumes. Latest: *Standard Catalog for Public Libraries: 1959-1963*. New York, 1964. 526 pages.

Manuals, Texts, and Guides

American Library Association. *Interim Standards for Small Public Libraries*. Chicago, The Association, 1962. 16p.

Brief expansion of the standards of *Public Library Service*.

——— *Church Libraries: A Guide to Their Administration and Organization*. Chicago, The Association, 1964. 7p.

Includes a bibliography of church library manuals issued by various denominations, a descriptive list of aids and services available from the national headquarters of various churches, and a list of helpful materials published by national library organizations and geographic groups of church librarians.

——— *Public Library Service: A Guide to Evaluation with Minimum Standards*. Chicago, The Association, 1956. 74p.

This is essential to any public library.

——— *Standards for School Library Programs*. Chicago, The Association, 1960. 132p.

No school library should be without this careful work.

Barden, Bertha R. *Book Numbers; a Manual for Students, with a Basic Code of Rules.* Chicago, American Library Association, 1937. 32p.

Although old, this is the simplest and clearest explanation of the use of author numbers. It also includes a brief and simple system of numbering useful for the library or the collection needing numbers simpler than those in the Cutter tables.

Chicago Public Schools. *Cataloging and Processing Procedures for Elementary School Libraries; a Manual of Practice for the Chicago Public Schools.* Chicago, Chicago Teachers College, 1959. 130p.

This is an example of a manual designed for city or state systems. Others include those for New York City, North Carolina, Georgia, etc.

Dennis, D. D. *Simplifying Work in Small Public Libraries.* Philadelphia, Drexel Institute of Technology, 1965. 80p.

A practical manual to aid in planning and organizing the work.

Drazniowsky, Roman. *Cataloging and Filing Rules for Maps and Atlases.* New York, American Geographical Society, 1964. 41p.

Helpful for a library with extensive map collections.

Haykin, David J. *Subject Headings; a Practical Guide.* Washington, Govt. Printing Office, 1951. 140p.

A discussion of subject heading practice, particularly as applied to the Library of Congress headings. Needed only by the larger libraries using those headings.

Jackson, Ellen. *A Manual for the Administration of the Federal Documents Collection in Libraries.* Chicago, American Library Association, 1955. 128p.

Includes discussion of organization and system of classification and records. For the depository library or library with sizable documents collection.

Library of Congress. *Handbook of Card Distribution.* 8th ed. Washington, 1954. 82p. (Available from Card Division, Library of Congress, Building 159, Navy Yard Annex, Washington, D.C. 20541.)

Necessary for any library which buys LC printed cards.

Mary Annette, Sister. *Manual for Cataloging School Libraries.* 4th rev. ed. The Author, Briar Cliff College, Sioux City, Iowa, 1961. 97p.

A guide for libraries in Catholic schools or parishes.

Merrill, W. S. *Code for Classifiers; Principles Governing the Consistent Placing of Books in a System of Classification.* 2d ed. Chicago, American Library Association, 1939. 177p.

Some people find this, old as it is, helpful in learning how to apply Dewey classification numbers.

Osborn, Andrew D. *Serial Publications: Their Place and Treatment in Libraries.* Chicago, American Library Association, 1955. 309p.

Most comprehensive and up-to-date work on serials. Important to any library which has much material in serial form.

Pearson, Mary D. *Recordings in the Public Library.* Chicago, American Library Association, 1963. 153p.

A comprehensive work which includes much material about recordings, including their classification, cataloging, selection, etc. Although written for the public library, there is much of value for any library collecting recordings.

Rufsvold, Margaret I. *Audio-Visual School Library Service; a Handbook for Libraries.* Chicago, American Library Association, 1949. 126p.

This work is old, but it is comprehensive and helpful in identifying areas and problems. Its recommended practices should not be followed without a study of more up-to-date material.

Straugham, Alice. *How to Organize Your Church Library.* Westwood, N.J., Fleming H. Revell Company, 1962. 64p.

This booklet gives simple and practical methods for setting up and organizing a church library. Various denominations have also prepared manuals designed to help the church or parish library become of real service to the church, not just another—and inadequate—general library.

H. W. Wilson Company. Directions and checklists for ordering Wilson printed cards.

A kit of material necessary for any library using Wilson cards.

Checklist of Individual Library Practices

The following checklist of decisions and practices, arranged in the same order as the chapters of this book, is designed to serve as a manual for the individual library. It is suggested that the cataloger, after reading through the entire book, study each chapter carefully, compare the practices recommended in it with those of his own library, then, deciding what is best or necessary for his library, check the items or note the information in the spaces indicated. By so doing, he will compile a record of the practices followed in his library. In the long run, this should save time and also make for greater consistency. Wherever pertinent, the author has indicated recommended practices with an asterisk. In some cases, however, the local situation may make different decisions necessary; different practices may be preferred for different types of libraries; and some decisions are necessarily based on the individual library's responsibilities for service.

Chapter 1. Procedures and Preliminaries

1. Type of library (public, school, church, etc.) _____

2. Present size of community served (town, school, church)

    _____

3. Potential size of community _____

4. Other library resources in the community _____

    _____

5. Number of volumes now in the library _____

6. Potential size of the library (in volumes) _____

7. The library is part of a library system ——— yes ——— no

    the system _____

    the library's relationship to the system _____

    _____

    ——— a processing center is part of the system
    ——— the library belongs to the processing center
    nature of services received _____

    _____

8. The circulation system used in this library _____
    ——— book cards are used
    ——— date due slips are used

9. Lost book policy
   —— borrowers are charged
   charges for lost books are _____

   _____

10. Business records required to be kept by the library _____

    _____

11. Readers served
    —— adults; type of service _____

    —— children; type of service _____

12. Shelving policy
    —— all books on open shelves
    —— some books in closed stacks; these include _____

    _____

    designation for books in closed stacks _____

13. Books are bought
    —— on contract
    —— by bids

14. Books are ordered
    —— daily
    —— weekly
    —— monthly
    —— semiannually
    —— annually
    —— irregularly
    Explanation _____

    _____

15. Gift books are accepted —— yes —— no

16. Different editions of nonfiction are kept —— yes —— no

17. Special collections which are specially housed _____

_____

     how cataloged and prepared _____

_____

_____

     how designated _____

Additional notes

Chapter 2. The Card Catalog

1. The library has a dictionary catalog
   *—— for adult use
   *—— for children's use
   —— for both together
   —— for other special groups, namely _____

   _____

2. Wilson cards, when available, are ordered
   *—— for adult books
   *—— for children's book
   *—— with subject headings and class number added
   —— without subject headings

3. Library of Congress cards, when available, are ordered
   —— for adult books
   —— for children's books
   *—— when Wilson cards are not available

4. Cards are obtained from a processing center —— or commercial service —— or some other source, namely _____

   _____

   —— for all books in the collection for which cards are available
   —— when Wilson cards are not available
   —— when LC cards are not available

5. For cards fully typed in the library, unit cards are used
   —— always
   *—— only for main entry (of those in the catalog)
   *—— for shelf-list card

* Recommended practice

191

6. Tracings are indicated

    *—— on face of main entry card if possible; on back if there is no room on face

    —— always on back of main entry card

    *—— on shelf-list card

7. Books cataloged and classified

    —— all books except _____

    _____

    —— all hard-cover books

    —— paperbound books

    *—— decision is made on each work according to value and use

Additional practices

* Recommended practice

Chapter 3. The Main Entry

The individual library should record here any practices which, by policy, deviate from general usage.

Chapter 4. Added Entries

1. Title entries are made
   - —— for all titles
   - —— for all titles except those beginning with common words, namely _____

     _____

   - *—— for all titles except those identical with subjects
   - *—— for catch titles
   - —— for inverted titles

2. Joint authors and joint editors
   If main entry is under the first of two authors or editors
   - *—— added entry is made for the second

   If main entry is under the first of three authors or editors
   - —— added entry is made only for the second
   - *—— added entries are made for the other two

   If main entry is under title of work by three or more authors or editors
   - *—— added entry is made only for the first author or editor
   - —— added entries are made only for the first two
   - —— added entries are made for all named on the title page

3. Entries for compiler, editor, illustrator, etc., are made
   - *—— only if their contribution is major
   - —— for all named on the title page

4. Entries are made for certain illustrators, namely _____

   _____

   _____

* Recommended practice

194

5. Title analytics are made

   *——— for all individual complete works

   ——— for works not covered by indexes

   ——— only for works listed on the title page

6. Author analytics are made

   *——— for all individual complete works

   ——— for works not covered by indexes

   ——— only for works listed on the title page

7. Subject analytics are made

   ——— for material of ——— pages or more

   *——— for separate works included in other works

   *——— for new or unusual material

8. Author and title analytics are made

   *——— for all individual complete works

   ——— for works not covered by indexes

   ——— only for works listed on the title page

9. Title and author analytics are made

   *——— for all individual complete works

   ——— for works not covered by indexes

   ——— only for works listed on the title page

10. Paging for analytics is given

   ——— for all analytics

   *——— only if the information is not shown elsewhere on the card

   ——— below the call number for all analytics

   ——— elsewhere on the card _____

* Recommended practice

11. Cards used for analytics

    *—— unit cards if available

    *—— short-form cards if cards are typed

12. Series cards are made

    —— for all series

    —— for all series except publishers' series

    —— for some publishers' series, namely _____

_____

_____

    *—— only for important series

*13. A file is kept of the names of those series for which series cards are made _____

Additional notes

* Recommended practice

Chapter 5. Form of Entry

1. For personal names
   —— birth and death dates are used
   —— dates are used in case of conflict of names
   —— one form is adopted and always used
   —— the title page form is always used
   —— the title page form is used and is then followed for other entries (for the same person)
   —— form is "established"; authorities used (in order) are _____

   _____

   _____

   —— latest form of name is used; older entries are re-cataloged, if necessary
   *—— "best-known" form is used if title pages vary
   *—— pseudonyms are used as on the title page
   —— best-known pseudonym is used for all works by an author
   —— real name is always used if information is available

2. For corporate names
   —— LC practice is followed
   *—— Wilson practice is followed
   *—— simple form is used
   —— subdivisions are used

3. Conventional titles are used
   —— generously
   *—— sparingly
   —— never

* Recommended practice

Additional notes

Chapter 6. Descriptive Cataloging

*1. The "by" phrase is used to supply needed information when the author statement on the title page differs from the name used in the main entry _____

2. Joint authors, etc., are included

    —— only if important to the work

    —— always

  *—— second author (if there are two) or second and third authors (if there are three or more named on the title page)

3. Place of publication is given

    —— except for well-known publishers

    —— except for fiction and easy books

    —— only if other than New York

  *—— never

4. Publisher is given

  *—— except for fiction and easy books

  *—— in short from

    —— never

5. Date

  *—— copyright date is preferred to imprint date

    —— imprint date is preferred to copyright date

    —— imprint date is used for all except fiction and easy books

6. Paging is used

    —— always

    —— never

  *—— never for fiction or easy books

  *—— for nonfiction

  *—— only final Arabic number

* Recommended practice

7. Illustration notation is used

    ——— never

    *——— restricted to "illus." and "map"

    ——— restricted to _____

    _____

8. Bibliography is indicated

    ——— always

    *——— if sizable or important

    ——— never

9. Series note is used

    *——— always

    ——— never

    ——— for selected series, namely _____

    _____

    _____

10. Contents notes are used

    *——— plentifully

    ——— only for _____

    _____

    _____

11. Annotations are used

    ——— always

    *——— only if available on printed cards

    ——— never

12. Periodicals

    *——— are not cataloged

* Recommended practice

*—— if cataloged, are cataJ ged under title at time of issue

—— are cataloged under latest title

13. Other serials

*—— are cataloged under title at time of issue

—— are cataloged under latest title

14. Revised works

*—— for frequently revised works, open entries are plentifully used

—— frequently revised works are not cataloged

*—— certain revised works are not cataloged, namely

_____

_____

15. Size

*—— is not given

—— is given for certain types of material, namely

_____

_____

Additional notes

Chapter 7. Subject Cataloging

1. The subject headings list used is _____

*2. "See" references are made as indicated in the headings list——

*3. Additional "see" references are made as needed ——

*4. "See also" references are made as indicated in the headings list ——

5. Additional "see also" references are made ——

*6. Subject headings for prepared cards are checked against the library's catalog to see if subjects have been used ——

7. References are revised

    *—— as each new subject is used

    —— only as conflicts occur

    —— periodically

8. General policy on subject work

* Recommended practice

Chapter 8. Classification of Books

(No practices are starred because different ones would be recommended for different types of libraries.)

1. The library classifies books according to _____

2. Dewey classification
   The class number is largely restricted to —— digits
   Class numbers which are expanded include _____

   _____

   _____

   The Abridged Dewey is followed   —— yes —— no

3. Reader interest grouping is used
   —— for all circulating books
   —— for certain categories, namely _____

   _____

   _____

   —— for changing exhibits and is shown by _____

   _____

4. Adult fiction
   —— is classified 813, 823, etc.
   —— adult fiction is not classed
   —— adult fiction in English is classed F
   —— "Fiction" is used on catalog cards

5. Juvenile fiction
   —— is classed 813, 823, etc.
   —— is not classed
   —— is classed jF

6. Picture books

—— are classed E

—— are classed ——

7. Individual biography is classed

—— 92

—— B

—— 920-929

—— other _____

8. Juvenile is indicated

—— by j

—— by other symbol(s) _____

9. Titles in both adult and juvenile collections are classed the same way   —— yes   —— no

   Exceptions _____

   _____

10. Author (Cutter) numbers are used

—— for all books

—— for all nonfiction

—— only for _____

   _____

11. Outsized books

—— are separately shelved

—— are indicated by _____

12. Materials separately shelved include _____

   _____

   _____

They are designated by _____

_____

13. Materials specially marked but not separately shelved include

_____

_____

14. A list of symbols is maintained ——— yes ——— no
It is kept _____

15. Other special practices

Chapter 9. Copy Identification

1. An accession book is maintained —— yes —— no

2. Accession record

    *—— Every cataloged volume receives an accession number, but no accession record is maintained

    —— Every cataloged volume receives an accession number taken from an accession record

3. Copy number

    —— is assigned every copy (e.g., "copy 1")

    —— is assigned every copy except the first (e.g., "copy 2")

4. Accession number

    —— is numerical, 1 to infinity

    *—— comprises date and number, e.g., _____

    —— is some other combination, e.g., _____

5. The identification is —— written *—— stamped —— typed

    *—— on the book card

    *—— on the pocket

    —— on the shelf list

    —— in the book on page ——

6. The identification is assigned

    *—— as soon as the book is cleared by the order process

    —— while the book is being shelf-listed

    —— after the book is fully prepared

    —— other practice _____

_____

* Recommended practice

Additional notes

1. Type of card used for shelf list

    *—— unit card

    —— shortened form, with the following information included _____

    _____

2. Price

    (Recommended practices are for public libraries only; price is not used in school libraries.)

    *—— price is given on shelf-list card

    —— real (discount) price is used on shelf-list card

    *—— list price is used on shelf-list card

    —— price recorded is list price raised to next even dollar

    —— price is coded, as follows: _____

    _____   _____

3. Variant editions

    *—— variant editions are shown in accession information for fiction and easy books

    —— illustrator variation for fiction and easy books is shown on shelf-list card for all illustrators

    *—— illustrator variation is shown for selected illustrators, namely _____

    _____

4. Date and source of acquisition are shown on shelf-list cards

    —— yes   *—— no

* Recommended practice

Additional notes

Chapter 11. Catalog Cards and Catalog Maintenance

Notes on library's practices

Chapter 12. Cataloging Services

Notes on library's practices

Chapter 13. *Physical Preparation of Material*

(No specific practices are recommended since libraries must meet circulation and service requirements.)

1. Price

    Information is put in book —— yes —— no

    Price is lettered in book on page ——

    Price used

    —— list

    —— real

    —— coded; code is determined by _____

    _____

    —— (coded) price is included on book card

    —— (coded) price is included on book pocket

2. Call number

    —— penciled on page ——

    —— lettered on spine, —— inches from bottom

    —— vertically lettered on spine, top to bottom

    —— vertically lettered on spine, bottom to top

3. Lettering device used _____

4. Discs are applied to spine to indicate _____

    _____

5. Lettering is shellacked —— yes —— no

6. Book is stamped with name of library on _____

7. Book pocket is pasted _____

8. Date due slip is pasted _____

9. Jackets are applied with _____

10. Plastic jackets are used on _____

_____

11. Supplements, etc., are removed from book —— yes —— no

—— filed in vertical file

—— filed elsewhere: _____

_____

—— disposition of supplement is noted on pocket

12. Other preparations

Chapter 14. Non-Book and Near-Book Materials

Material	Where housed	How arranged	Classification symbol used	If cataloged, under what entry
Paperbacks				
Pamphlets				
Periodicals				
Newspapers				
Clippings, etc.				
Pictures				
Manuscripts, Type-scripts, etc.				
Microforms				
Serials				
Maps				
Music				
Films				
Filmstrips				
Slides				
Phonodiscs, Musical				
Phonodiscs, Non-musical				
Tapes and Wire recordings				
Other physical objects				

Cards in general or separate catalog	Cards bordered or stamped	Cards in general shelf list or special file	Grade or age indicated	Physical preparation	Statistics kept

Chapter 15. Keeping Records Up to Date

1. Records for names
   —— authority record is maintained for all names used
   —— authority record is maintained only for names which require cross references
   *—— cross references are indicated as tracings on main entry cards

2. Records for subjects
   *—— printed list of subjects is checked for headings used
   —— authority card record is maintained for subjects used

3. Names and subjects are combined in one authority file ——

4. Classification decisions
   *—— are written in the printed scheme
   —— are recorded on cards
   —— are recorded in a notebook

5. Serial cataloging decisions
   —— are recorded on separate cards
   —— are recorded on shelf-list cards
   *—— are recorded in serials check file

6. Illustrator entry decisions
   —— are recorded on separate cards
   *—— are recorded in a list
   —— are recorded in name authority file

7. Other authority files maintained _____

_____

_____

* Recommended practice

8. Order cards used in cataloging work

    *—— call number for added copies or volumes is given on order card

    *—— order card is left in book for cataloging use

9. "Dummy"

    —— is left in shelf list for cards withdrawn for use

    —— order card is used as dummy

10. Open-entry cards

    —— all cards for open entry are changed to show additions

    *—— only main entries for open-entry cards are changed to show additions

11. Recataloging and reclassification policy

    *—— kept to a minimum

    —— never done

    —— always done for any change

    *—— subject changes for new terminology

    *—— subject changes for new concepts or meanings

    *—— reclassification to break up too much material within a class

    —— reclassification to conform to new edition of the scheme

    *—— reclassification to show new concepts or meanings

    *—— reclassification to avoid conflict

    —— recataloging to show all name changes

    *—— recataloging only to avoid conflict

    —— other policies on change _____

_____

_____

_____

* Recommended practice

12. Withdrawal of cards from catalog

*—— cards for discarded books are withdrawn immediately

—— cards for discarded books are withdrawn _____

_____

—— cards for missing items are withdrawn immediately

*—— cards for missing items are withdrawn after one year

—— cards for missing items are withdrawn after six months

13. Records for books ordered for replacement are shown by

*—— flagging the shelf-list card

—— flagging the order card

—— other practice _____

_____

14. Inventory is taken

—— annually

—— every three years

—— every five years

—— at other intervals _____

15. Statistics kept (see pages 116-117 and also checklist for Chapter 14, page 215)

_____

_____

_____

_____

* Recommended practice

Additional notes

Index